Mary A. Bulkley
Rye
Feb 1, 1875

THE

LIFE OF CHRIST.

HOLMAN HUNT, *Del.*

NABLOUS—THE ANCIENT SHECHEM.

THE

LIFE OF CHRIST.

BY

FREDERIC W. FARRAR, D.D., F.R.S.;

LATE FELLOW OF TRINITY COLLEGE, CAMBRIDGE;
MASTER OF MARLBOROUGH COLLEGE; AND CHAPLAIN IN ORDINARY
TO THE QUEEN.

MANET IMMOTA FIDES.

IN TWO VOLUMES.

VOL. II.

NEW YORK:
E. P. DUTTON & COMPANY,
713, BROADWAY.

CONTENTS.

CHAPTER XLIII.

INCIDENTS OF THE JOURNEY.

CHAPTER XLIV.

TEACHINGS OF THE JOURNEY.

CHAPTER XLV.

THE FEAST OF DEDICATION.

CHAPTER XLVI.

THE LAST STAY IN PERÆA.

CHAPTER XLVII.

THE RAISING OF LAZARUS.

CHAPTER LII.

The Great Denunciation.

CHAPTER LIII.

Farewell to the Temple.

CHAPTER LIV.

The Beginning of the End.

CHAPTER LV.

The Last Supper.

CHAPTER LVI.

The Last Discourse.

CHAPTER LVII.

GETHSEMANE.—THE AGONY AND THE ARREST.

CHAPTER LVIII.

JESUS BEFORE THE PRIESTS AND THE SANHEDRIN.

CHAPTER LIX.

THE INTERVAL BETWEEN THE TRIALS.

CHAPTER LX.

JESUS BEFORE PILATE.

CHAPTER LXI.

The Crucifixion.

CHAPTER LXII.

The Resurrection.

APPENDIX.

THE

LIFE OF CHRIST.

CHAPTER XXXV.

THE GREAT CONFESSION.

"These have known that Thou hast sent me."—JOHN xvii. 25.

VERY different was the reception which awaited Jesus on the farther shore. The poor heathens of Decapolis had welcomed Him with reverent enthusiasm: the haughty Pharisees of Jerusalem met Him with sneering hate. It may be that, after this period of absence, His human soul yearned for the only resting-place which He could call a home. Entering into His little vessel, He sailed across the lake to Magdala.[1] It is probable that He purposely avoided sailing to Bethsaida or Capernaum, which are a little north of Magdala, and

[1] St. Mark says (viii. 10), "the parts of Dalmanutha." Nothing is known about Dalmanutha, though uncertain identifications of it have been attempted; nor is anything known of Magadan, which is found in Matt. xv. 39, according to א, B, D, but does not seem a probable reading. If Magadan is a confused form of Megiddo, that must be an error, for Megiddo is in the middle of the plain of Esdraelon. Yet even in Mark the Codex Bezae reads "Magadan." Eusebius and Jerome (*Onomast.* s. v.) make Magadan a region about Gerasa, and therefore east of the Lake; but that is impossible. The "Melegada" of D looks like a case of transposition, and indeed this transposition is probably the source of the confusion, and may even account for the form Dalmanutha.

which had become the head-quarters of the hostile Pharisees. But it seems that these personages had kept a look-out for His arrival. As though they had been watching from the tower of Magdala for the sail of His returning vessel, barely had He set foot on shore than they came forth to meet Him. Nor were they alone: this time they were accompanied—ill-omened conjunction!—with their rivals and enemies the Sadducees, that sceptical sect, half-religious, half-political, to which at this time belonged the two High Priests, as well as the members of the reigning family.[1] Every section of the ruling classes—the Pharisees, formidable from their religious weight among the people; the Sadducees, few in number, but powerful from wealth and position; the Herodians, representing the influence of the Romans, and of their nominees the tetrarchs; the scribes and lawyers, bringing to bear the authority of their orthodoxy and their learning—were all united against Him in one firm phalanx of conspiracy and opposition, and were determined above all things to hinder His preaching, and to alienate from Him, as far as was practicable, the affections of the people among whom most of His mighty works were done.[2]

They had already found by experience that the one most effectual weapon to discredit His mission and undermine His influence was the demand of a sign—above all, a sign from heaven. If He were indeed the Messiah, why should He not give them bread from heaven as

[1] Acts iv. 1, 5; Jos. *Antt.* xv. 8, § 1.

[2] Sepp, whose learning is strangely deformed by constant extravagances, compares the eight sects of the Jews to modern schools of thought, as follows:—Pharisees = pietists; Essenes = mystics; Sadducees = rationalists; Herodians = political clubs, &c.; Zealots = radicals; Samaritans = schismatics!

Moses, they said, had done? where were Samuel's thunder and Elijah's flame? why should not the sun be darkened, and the moon turned into blood, and the stars of heaven be shaken? why should not some fiery pillar glide before them to victory, or the burst of some stormy *Bath Kol* ratify His words?

They knew that no such sign would be granted them, and they knew that He had vouchsafed to them the strongest reasons for His thrice-repeated refusal to gratify their presumptuous and unspiritual demand.[1] Had they known or understood the fact of His temptation in the wilderness, they would have known that His earliest answers to the tempter were uttered in this very spirit of utter self-abnegation. Had He granted their request, what purpose would have been furthered? It is not the influence of external forces, but it is the germinal principle of life within, which makes the good seed to grow; nor can the hard heart be converted, or the stubborn unbelief removed, by portents and prodigies, but by inward humility, and the grace of God stealing downward like the dew of heaven, in silence and unseen. What would have ensued had the sign been vouchsafed? By its actual eye-witnesses it would have been attributed to demoniac agency; by those to whom it was reported it would have been explained away; by those of the next generation it would have been denied as an invention, or evaporated into a myth.

But in spite of all this, the Pharisees and Sadducees felt that for the present this refusal to gratify their demand gave them a handle against Jesus, and was an effectual engine for weakening the admiration of the people. Yet not for one moment did He hesitate in

[1] John ii. 18; vi. 30; Matt. xii. 38.

rejecting this their temptation. He would not work any epideictic miracle at *their* bidding, any more than at the bidding of the tempter. He at once told them, as He had told them before, that "no sign should be given them but the sign of the prophet Jonah." Pointing to the western sky, now crimson with the deepening hues of sunset, He said, "When it is evening, ye say, 'Fair weather! for the sky is red;' and in the morning, 'Storm to-day, for the sky is red and frowning.' Hypocrites! ye know how to discern the face of the sky: can ye not learn the signs of the times?"[1]

As He spoke He heaved a deep inward sigh.[2] For some time He had been absent from home. He had been sought out with trustful faith in the regions of Tyre and Sidon. He had been welcomed with ready gratitude in heathen Decapolis; here, at home, He was met with the flaunt of triumphant opposition, under the guise of hypocritic zeal. He steps ashore on the lovely plain, where He had done so many noble and tender deeds, and spoken for all time such transcendent and immortal words. He came back, haply to work once more in the little district where His steps had once been followed by rejoicing thousands, hanging in deep silence on every word He spoke. As He approaches Magdala, the little village destined for all time to lend its name to a word expressive of His most divine compassion—as He wishes to enter once more the little cities and villages which offered to His homelessness the only shadow of a home—here, barely has He stepped upon the pebbly strand, barely passed through the fringe of flowering shrubs which embroider the water's

[1] Matt. xvi. 1—4; Mark viii. 10—13.
[2] Mark viii. 12, ἀναστενάξας τῷ πνεύματι αὐτοῦ.

edge, barely listened to the twittering of the innumerable birds which welcome Him back with their familiar sounds—when He finds all the self-satisfied hypocrisies of a decadent religion drawn up in array to stop His path!

He did not press His mercies on those who rejected them. As in after days His nation were suffered to prefer their robber and their murderer to the Lord of Life, so now the Galilæans were suffered to keep their Pharisees and lose their Christ. He left them as He had left the Gadarenes—rejected, not suffered to rest even in His home; with heavy heart, solemnly and sadly He left them—left them then and there—left them, to revisit, indeed, once more their neighbourhood, but never again to return publicly—never again to work miracles, to teach or preach.[1]

It must have been late in that autumn evening when He stepped once more into the little ship, and bade His disciples steer their course towards Bethsaida Julias, at the northern end of the lake. On their way they must have sailed by the bright sands of the western Bethsaida, on which Peter and the sons of Zebedee had played in their infancy, and must have seen the white marble synagogue of Capernaum flinging its shadow across the waters, which blushed with the reflected colours of the sunset. Was it at such a moment, when He was leaving Galilee with the full knowledge that His work there was at an end, and that He was sailing away from it under the ban of partial excommunication and certain death—was it at that supreme moment of sorrow that He uttered the rhythmic woe in which He upbraided the

[1] There is something emphatic both in the καταλιπὼν αὐτοὺς of Matt. xvi. 4, and in the ἀφεὶς αὐτοὺς of Mark viii. 13.

unrepentant cities wherein most of His mighty works were done?—

"Woe unto thee, Chorazin! woe unto thee, Bethsaida! for if the mighty works which have been done in you had been done in Tyre and Sidon, they would have repented long ago in sackcloth and ashes.

"But I say unto you, That it shall be more tolerable for Tyre and Sidon at the day of judgment than for you.

"And thou, Capernaum, which art exalted unto heaven, shalt be brought down to hell: for if the mighty works which have been done in thee had been done in Sodom, it would have remained until this day.

"But I say unto you, That it shall be more tolerable for the land of Sodom in the day of judgment than for thee!"

Whether these touching words were uttered on this occasion as a stern and sad farewell to His public ministry in the land He loved, we cannot tell;[1] but certainly His soul was still filled with sorrow for the unbelief and hardness of heart, the darkened intellects and corrupted consciences of those who were thus leaving for Him no power to set foot in His native land. It has been said

[1] This woe—evidently complete and isolated in character—is recorded in Matt. xi. 20—24; Luke x. 12—15. St. Matthew seems to group it with the utterances at the feast of Simon the Pharisee; St. Luke with the Mission of the Seventy. It is, perhaps, hazardous to conjecture that words so solemnly beautiful and full of warning were uttered more than once; and since the order of St. Matthew is in many places professedly unchronological, we can find no more appropriate occasion for the words than this. They have evidently the character of a farewell, and the recent visit of Jesus to the coasts of Tyre and Sidon would give them special significance here. The mention of the otherwise unknown Chorazin is an additional proof, if any were needed, of the fragmentary character of the Gospels. It is an inland town, three miles from Tell Hûm, of which the deserted ruins, discovered by Dr. Robinson, are still called Khersah.

by a great forensic orator that "no form of self-deceit is more hateful and detestable . . . than that which veils spite and falsehood under the guise of frankness, and behind the profession of religion." Repugnance to this hideous vice must have been prominent in the stricken heart of Jesus, when, as the ship sailed along the pleasant shore upon its northward way, He said to His disciples, "Take heed, and beware of the leaven of the Pharisees and Sadducees."[1]

He added nothing more; and this remark the strange simplicity of the disciples foolishly misinterpreted. They were constantly taking His figurative expressions literally, and His literal expressions metaphorically. When He called Himself the "bread from heaven," they thought the saying hard; when He said, "I have meat to eat that ye know not of," they could only remark, "Hath any man brought Him aught to eat?" when He said, "Our friend Lazarus sleepeth," they answered, "Lord, if he sleep, he shall do well." And so now, although leaven was one of the very commonest types of sin, and especially of insidious and subterranean sin, the only interpretation which, after a discussion among themselves, they could attach to His remark was, that He was warning them not to buy leaven of the Pharisees and Sadducees, or, perhaps, indirectly reproaching them because, in the sorrow and hurry of their unexpected re-embarkation, they had only brought with them one single loaf! Jesus was grieved at this utter non-comprehension, this almost stupid literalism. Did they suppose that He, at whose words the loaves and fishes had been so miraculously multiplied—that they, who

[1] Or "of Herod" (Mark viii. 15). The Herodians appear to have been mainly Sadducees.

after feeding the five thousand had gathered twelve hand-baskets, and after feeding the four thousand had gathered seven large baskets-full of the fragments that remained—did they suppose, after *that*, that there was danger lest He or they should suffer from starvation? There was something almost of indignation in the rapid questions in which, without correcting, He indicated their error. "Why reason ye because ye have no bread? Perceive ye not yet, neither understand? Have ye your heart yet hardened? Having eyes, see ye not? and having ears, hear ye not? and do ye not remember?" And then once more, after He had reminded them of those miracles, "How is it that ye do not understand?" They had not ventured to ask Him for any explanation; there was something about Him—something so awe-inspiring and exalted in His personality—that their love for Him, intense though it was, was tempered by an overwhelming reverence: but now it began to dawn upon them that something else was meant, and that He was bidding them beware, not of the leaven of bread, but of the doctrine of the Pharisees and Sadducees.

At Bethsaida Julias, probably on the following morning, a blind man was brought to Him for healing. The cure was wrought in a manner very similar to that of the deaf and dumb man in Decapolis. It has none of the ready freedom, the radiant spontaneity of the earlier and happier miracles. In one respect it differs from every other recorded miracle, for it was, as it were, tentative. Jesus took the man by the hand, led him out of the village, spat upon his eyes, and then, laying His hands upon them, asked if he saw. The man looked at the figures in the distance, and, but imperfectly cured as yet, said, "I see men as trees walking." Not until

Jesus had laid His hands a second time upon his eyes did he see clearly. And then Jesus bade him go to his house, which was not at Bethsaida; for, with an emphatic repetition of the word, he is forbidden either to *enter* into the town, or to tell it to any one *in* the town. We cannot explain the causes of the method which Christ here adopted. The impossibility of understanding what guided His actions arises from the brevity of the narrative, in which the Evangelist—as is so often the case with writers conversant with their subject—passes over many particulars, which, because they were so familiar to himself, will, he supposes, be self-explaining to those who read his words. All that we can dimly see is Christ's dislike and avoidance of these heathenish Herodian towns, with their borrowed Hellenic architecture, their careless customs, and even their very names commemorating, as was the case with Bethsaida Julias, some of the most contemptible of the human race.[1] We see from the Gospels themselves that the richness and power displayed in the miracles was correlative to the faith of the recipients: in places where faith was scanty it was but too natural that miracles should be gradual and few.[2]

Leaving Bethsaida Julias, Jesus made his way towards Cæsarea Philippi. Here, again, it seems to be distinctly intimated that He did not enter into the town itself, but only visited the "coasts" of it, or wandered about the neighbouring villages.[3] Why He bent His footsteps in that direction we are not told. It was a

[1] Herod Philip had named his renovated capital in honour of Julia, the abandoned daughter of the Emperor Augustus.

[2] No one who has rightly considered the Gospel miracles will regard this as "a damaging concession." At any rate, if so, it is a fresh proof of the entire truthfulness of the Gospels. (Matt. xiii. 58; Mark vi. 5, 6; ix. 23, &c.)

[3] Matt. xvi. 13, μέρη, "parts," or "regions; Mark viii. 27, κώμας.

town that had seen many vicissitudes. As "Laish," it had been the possession of the careless Sidonians. As "Dan," it had been the chief refuge of a warlike tribe of Israel, the northern limit of the Israelitish kingdom, and the seat of the idolatry of the golden calf. Colonised by Greeks, its name had been changed into Paneas, in honour of the cave under its towering hill, which had been artificially fashioned into a grotto of Pan, and adorned with niches, which once contained statues of his sylvan nymphs. As the capital of Herod Philip, it had been re-named in honour of himself and his patron Tiberius.[1] The Lord might gaze with interest on the noble ranges of Libanus and Anti-Libanus; He might watch the splendid and snowy mass of Hermon glittering under the dawn, or flushed with its evening glow; He might wander round Lake Phiala, and see where, according to popular belief, the Jordan, after his subterranean course, bursts rejoicing into the light: but He could only have gazed with sorrow on the city itself, with its dark memories of Israelitish apostacy, its poor mimicry of Roman imperialism, and the broken statues of its unhallowed and Hellenic cave.

But it was on His way to the northern region that there occurred an incident which may well be regarded as the culminating point of His earthly ministry.[2] He was alone. The crowd that surged so tumultuously about Him in more frequented districts, here only followed Him at a distance. Only His disciples were near Him as He stood apart in solitary prayer. And when the prayer was over, He beckoned them about

[1] On Cæsarea Philippi see Jos. *Antt.* xv. 10, § 3; *B. J.* i. 21, § 3; and for a description of its present state, Thomson, *Land and Book*, II., ch. xvi.

[2] Matt. xvi. 13—28; Mark viii. 27—ix. 1; Luke ix. 18—27.

Him as they continued their journey, and asked them those two momentous questions on the answers to which depended the whole outcome of His work on earth.

First He asked them—

"Whom do men say that I the Son of Man am?"

The answer was a sad one. The Apostles dared not and would not speak aught but the words of soberness and truth, and they made the disheartening admission that the Messiah had not been recognised by the world which He came to save. They could only repeat the idle guesses of the people. Some, echoing the verdict of the guilty conscience of Antipas, said that He was John the Baptist; some, who may have heard the sterner denunciations of His impassioned grief, caught in that mighty utterance the thunder-tones of a new Elijah; others, who had listened to His accents of tenderness and words of universal love, saw in Him the plaintive soul of Jeremiah, and thought that He had come, perhaps, to restore them the lost Urim and the vanished Ark: many looked on Him as a prophet and a precursor. None—in spite of an occasional Messianic cry wrung from the admiration of the multitude, amazed by some unwonted display of power—none dreamt of who He was. The light had shone in the darkness, and the darkness comprehended it not.

"But whom say ye that I am?"

Had that great question been answered otherwise—*could* it have been answered otherwise—the world's whole destinies might have been changed. Had it been answered otherwise, then, humanly speaking, so far the mission of the Saviour would have wholly failed, and Christianity and Christendom have never been. For the work of Christ on earth lay mainly with His disciples.

He sowed the seed, they reaped the harvest; He converted them, and they the world. He had never openly spoken of His Messiahship. John indeed had borne witness to Him, and to those who could receive it He had indirectly intimated, both in word and deed, that He was the Son of God. But it was His will that the light of revelation should dawn gradually on the minds of His children; that it should spring more from the truths He spake, and the life He lived, than from the wonders which He wrought; that it should be conveyed not in sudden thunder-crashes of supernatural majesty or visions of unutterable glory, but through the quiet medium of a sinless and self-sacrificing course. It was in the Son of Man that they were to recognise the Son of God.

But the answer came, as from everlasting it had been written in the book of destiny that it should come; and Peter, the ever warm-hearted, the *coryphaeus* of the Apostolic choir,[1] had the immortal honour of giving it utterance for them all—

"THOU ART THE CHRIST, THE SON OF THE LIVING GOD!"

Such an answer from the chief of the Apostles atoned by its fulness of insight and certitude of conviction for the defective appreciation of the multitudes.[2] It showed that at last the great mystery was revealed which had been hidden from the ages and the generations. The

[1] *ὁ πανταχοῦ θερμὸς, ὁ τοῦ χοροῦ τῶν ἀποστόλων κορυφαῖος* (Chrys. *Hom.* liv.).

[2] He says, not "we say," but "THOU ART" (Alford, *ad loc.*). St. Peter was "primus inter pares"—a leader, but among equals. Had he been more than this—had Christ's words been intended to bestow on him the least shadow of supremacy—how could James and John have asked to sit on the right hand and on the left of Christ in His kingdom? and how could the Apostles on at least two subsequent occasions have disputed who among them should be the greatest?

Apostles at least had not only recognised in Jesus of Nazareth the promised Messiah of their nation, but it had been revealed to them by the special grace of God that that Messiah was not only what the Jews expected, a Prince, and a Ruler, and a Son of David, but was *more* than this, even the Son of the living God.

With awful solemnity did the Saviour ratify that great confession. "Jesus answered and said unto him, Blessed art thou, Simon, son of Jonas:[1] for flesh and blood hath not revealed it unto thee, but my Father which is in heaven.[2] And I say unto thee, that thou art Peter (*Petros*), and on this rock (*petra*) I will build my Church, and the gates of hell shall not prevail against it.[3] And I will give unto thee the keys of the kingdom of heaven; and whatsoever thou shalt bind on earth shall be bound in heaven, and whatsoever thou shalt loose on earth shall be loosed in heaven."

Never did even the lips of Jesus utter more memor-

[1] So, too, Jesus addressed him on other solemn occasions (John xxi. 15—17).

[2] Not the common Jewish *abînu*, "our Father," but "my Father" (ὁ πατήρ μου).

[3] Similar plays on words, founded on very deep principles, are common among deep thinkers in all tongues. Our Lord was probably speaking in Aramaic, in which language the phrase "gates of hell" (שַׁעֲרֵי שְׁאוֹל, *shaare sheol*) presents a pleasing assonance. If so, He probably said, "Thou art Kephas, and on this Kepha I will," &c. Many commentators, from the earliest ages downwards, have understood "this rock" to be either the confession of Peter, or Christ himself (see abundant authorities for these opinions in the elaborate note of Bishop Wordsworth); it is difficult, however, in either of these cases to see any force in the "Thou art Peter." On the other hand, to speak of a man as "the rock" is unlike the ordinary language of Scripture. "Who is a rock save our God?" (2 Sam. xxii. 32; Ps. xviii. 31; lxii. 2; Isa. xxviii. 16; and see especially 1 Cor. iii. 11; x.). The key was a common Jewish metaphor for authority (Isa. xxii. 22; Luke xi. 52). (Gfrörer, i. 155, 283; Schöttg., *Hor. Hebr.* ii. 894.) I shall speak further on the passage in a subsequent note, but do not profess to have fully solved its difficulties.

able words. It was His own testimony of Himself. It was the promise that they who can acknowledge it are blessed. It was the revealed fact that they only *can* acknowledge it who are led thereto by the Spirit of God. It told mankind for ever that not by earthly criticisms, but only by heavenly grace, can the full knowledge of that truth be obtained. It was the laying of the corner-stone of the Church of Christ, and the earliest occasion on which was uttered that memorable word, thereafter to be so intimately blended with the history of the world.[1] It was the promise that that Church founded on the rock of inspired confession should remain unconquered by all the powers of hell. It was the conferring upon that Church, in the person of its typical representative, the power to open and shut, to bind and loose, and the promise that the power faithfully exercised on earth should be finally ratified in heaven.

"Tute haec omnia dicuntur," says the great Bengel, "nam quid ad Romam?" "all these statements are made with safety; for what have they to do with Rome?"[2] Let him who will wade through all the controversy necessitated by the memorable perversions of this memorable text, which runs as an inscription round the interior of the great dome of St. Peter's. But little force is needed to overthrow the strange inverted pyramids of argument which have been built upon it. Were it not a matter of history, it would have been deemed incredible that on so baseless a foundation should have been rested the fan-

[1] It is a remarkable fact that the word ἐκκλησία occurs but once again in the Gospels (Matt. xviii. 17).

[2] The following texts are alone sufficient to prove finally that St. Peter in no way exercised among the Apostles any paramount or supreme authority:—Matt. xviii. 1; Eph. ii. 20; Rev. xxi. 14; 2 Cor. xi. 5 xii. 11; Gal. ii. 9, 11; Luke xxii. 24, 26; John xxi. 19—23, &c.

tastic claim that abnormal power should be conceded to the bishops of a Church which almost certainly St. Peter did not found, and in a city in which there is no indisputable proof that he ever set his foot. The immense arrogancies of sacerdotalism; the disgraceful abuses of the confessional; the imaginary power of absolving from oaths; the ambitious assumption of a right to crush and control the civil power; the extravagant usurpation of infallibility in wielding the dangerous weapons of anathema and excommunication; the colossal tyrannies of the Popedom, and the detestable cruelties of the Inquisition—all these abominations are, we may hope, henceforth and for ever, things of the past. But the Church of Christ remains, of which Peter was a chief foundation, a living stone. The powers of hell have *not* prevailed against it; it still has a commission to fling wide open the gates of the kingdom of heaven; it still may loose us from idle traditional burdens and meaningless ceremonial observances; it still may bind upon our hearts and consciences the truths of revealed religion and the eternal obligations of the Moral Law.

To Peter himself the great promise was remarkably fulfilled. It was he who converted on the day of Pentecost the first great body of Jews who adopted the Christian faith; it was he who admitted the earliest Gentile into the full privileges of Christian fellowship.[1] His confession made him as a rock, on which the faith of many was founded, which the powers of Hades might shake, but over which they never could prevail. But, as has been well added by one of the deepest most venerable, and most learned Fathers of the ancient

[1] Peter himself points to this fact as a fulfilment of Christ's promise (Acts xv. 7).

Church, "If *any one* thus confess, when flesh and blood have not revealed it unto him, but our Father in heaven, *he*, too, shall obtain the promised blessings; as the letter of the Gospel saith indeed to the great St. Peter, but as its spirit teacheth to every man who hath become like what that great Peter was."[1]

It may be said that, from that time forth, the Saviour might regard one great portion of His work on earth as having been accomplished. His Apostles were now convinced of the mystery of His being; the foundations were laid on which, with Himself as the chief corner-stone, the whole vast edifice was to be hereafter built.

But He forbade them to reveal this truth as yet. The time or such preaching had not yet come. They were yet wholly ignorant of the true method of His manifestation. They were yet too unconfirmed in faith even to

[1] Origen. A full consideration of this great utterance to St. Peter must be sought for in works professedly theological, but I may here call special attention to a calm and admirable sermon, "Confession and Absolution," by my friend Professor Plumptre (Isbister, 1874), in which he points out the distinction which must be carefully drawn between three separate things too often confounded—viz., the "Power of the Keys," the power to bind and loose, and the power to remit or retain. 1. The first (since the delivery of a key formed the ordination of a Scribe) meant the "power to open the treasury of the Divine oracles, and bring them out to Christ's disciples (cf. Matt. xiii. 52; Luke xi. 52; Matt. xxiii. 4). To those who heard, it must have implied the *teaching* power of the Church. 2. The power to bind and loose, afterwards conferred on all the disciples (Matt. xviii. 18), gave them a power like that exercised by the Rabbis (*e.g.*, the school of Shammai, which, according to the Jewish proverb, *bound*, and the school of Hillel which *loosed*)—the power, namely, to declare what precepts are, and what are not, binding (cf. Matt. xxiii. 4; Acts x. 28). It implied, therefore, the *legislative* action of the Church. 3. The power to forgive and retain sins (John xx. 22, 23) far transcended these, and was distinctly *rejected* by the Scribes. It belongs to the *prophetic* office of the Church, and had direct reference to the gift of the Holy Spirit, and "was possible only so far as the prophetic gift, in greater or less measure, was bestowed on those who exercise it" (Plumptre, *ubi supra*, pp. 45—48). For wise views of this subject, see also Hooker, *Eccl. Pol.*, VI. iv. 1, 2.

remain true to Him in His hour of utmost need. As yet He would be known as the Christ to those only whose spiritual insight could see Him immediately in His life and in His works. As yet He would neither strive nor cry, nor should His voice be heard in the streets.[1] When their own faith was confirmed beyond all wavering by the mighty fact of His resurrection, when their hearts had been filled with the new Shechînah of God's Holy Spirit, and their brows, with final consecration, had been mitred with Pentecostal flame, then, but not till then, would the hour have come for them to go forth and teach all nations that Jesus was indeed the Christ, the Son of the Living God.

But although they now knew Him, they knew nothing as yet of the way in which it was His will to carry out His divine purposes. It was time that they should yet further be prepared; it was time that they should learn that, King though He was, His kingdom was not of this world; it was time that all idle earthly hopes of splendour and advancement in the Messianic kingdom should be quenched in them for ever, and that they should know that the kingdom of God is not meat and drink, but righteousness, and peace, and joy in believing.

Therefore He began, calmly and deliberately, to reveal to them His intended journey to Jerusalem, His rejection by the leaders of His nation, the anguish and insult that awaited Him, His violent death, His resurrection on the third day. He had, indeed, on previous occasions given them divers and distant intimations[2] of

[1] Matt. xii. 19; Isa. xlii. 1.

[2] Matt. x. 38; John iii. 14. But now ἤρξατο δεικνύειν (Matt. xvi. 21). A still further gradation, a still clearer prophecy, may be observed from time to time as the day approached (Matt. xvi. 21; xvii. 22; xx. 18; xxvi. 2.

these approaching sufferings, but now for the first time He dwelt on them distinctly, and that with full freedom of speech.[1] Yet even now He did not reveal in its entire awfulness the *manner* of His approaching death. He made known unto them, indeed, that He should be rejected by the elders and chief priests and scribes—by all the authorities, and dignities, and sanctities of the nation—but not that He should be delivered to the Gentiles. He warned them that He should be killed, but He reserved till the time of His last journey to Jerusalem the horrible fact that He should be crucified.[2] He thus revealed to them the future only as they were best able to bear it, and even then, to console their anguish and to support their faith, He told them quite distinctly, that on the third day He should rise again.

But the human mind has a singular capacity for rejecting that which it cannot comprehend—for ignoring and forgetting all that does not fall within the range of its previous conceptions. The Apostles, ever faithful and ever simple in their testimony, never conceal from us their dulness of spiritual insight, nor the dominance of Judaic preconceptions over their minds. They themselves confess to us how sometimes they took the literal for the figurative,[3] and sometimes the figurative for the

[1] Mark viii. 32, *καὶ παῤῥησίᾳ τὸν λόγον ἐλάλει.* Earlier and dimmer intimations were John ii. 19 ("Destroy this Temple"); iii. 14 ("shall the Son of Man be lifted up"); Matt. ix. 15 ("the Bridegroom shall be taken away from them"); John vi. 51 ("my flesh will I give for the life of the world"); Matt. xvi. 4 ("the sign of the prophet Jonas").

[2] Matt. xvi. 21, *ἀποκτανθῆναι*, but in xx. 19, *σταυρῶσαι.* The manner of His death was, however, distinctly intimated in the metaphor of "taking up the cross," immediately afterwards (xvi. 24).

[3] *Ex. gr.*, the leaven of the Pharisees (Matt. xvi. 7); the meat they know not of (John iv. 32); the sleep of death (John xi. 12).

literal.[1] They heard the announcement, but they did not realise it. "They understood not this saying, and it was hid from them, that they perceived it not."[2] Now as on so many other occasions a supernatural awe was upon them, "and they feared to ask Him."[3] The prediction of His end was so completely alien from their whole habit of thought, that they would only put it aside as irrelevant and unintelligible—some mystery which they could not fathom; and as regards the resurrection, when it was again prophesied to the most spiritual among them all, they could only question among one another what the rising from the dead should mean.[4]

But Peter, in his impetuosity, thought that he understood, and thought that he could prevent; and so he interrupted those solemn utterances by his ignorant and presumptuous zeal. The sense that it had been given to him to perceive and utter a new and mighty truth, together with the splendid eulogium and promise which he had just received, combined to inflate his intellect and misguide his heart; and taking Jesus by the hand or by the robe,[5] he led Him a step or two aside from the disciples, and began to advise, to instruct, to rebuke his Lord. "God forbid,"[6] he said; "this shall certainly *not*

[1] What defileth a man (Matt. xv. 17). See too John xi. 11, 16. (Lange, iii. 241.)

[2] Luke ix. 45.

[3] Mark ix. 32; Luke ii. 50; xviii. 34.

[4] Mark ix. 10.

[5] Matt. xvi. 22, προσλαβόμενος αὐτὸν. There is, as Stier points out (ii. 328), a happy instinctive irony in the ἤρξατο ἐπιτιμᾶν of Mark viii. 32, compared to the ἤρξατο διδάσκειν of verse 31.

[6] Such seems to be the meaning of ἵλεώς σοι, Κύριε (Matt. xvi. 22). It is literally "[May God be] merciful to thee," rather than, as in the margin of the E. V., "pity thyself." The phrase is a kind of expletive, like *Di meliora! praefiscini! Di averruncent!* in Latin; and *Gott bewahre!* in German. The Hebrew expression to which it corresponds is sometimes

happen to thee." With a flash of sudden indignation our Lord rebuked his worldliness and presumption. Turning away from him, fixing His eyes on the other disciples, and speaking in the hearing of them all—for it was fit that they who had heard the words of vast promise should hear also the crushing rebuke—He exclaimed, "Get thee behind me, Satan! thou art a stumbling-block unto me; for thy thoughts are not the thoughts of God, but of men." This thy mere carnal and human view—this attempt to dissuade me from my "baptism of death"—is a sin against the purposes of God.[1] Peter was to learn—would that the Church which professes to have inherited from him its exclusive and superhuman claims had also learnt in time!—that he was far indeed from being infallible—that he was capable of falling, aye, and with scarcely a moment's intermission, from heights of divine insight into depths of most earthly folly.

"*Get thee behind me, Satan!*"—the very words which He had used to the tempter in the wilderness. The rebuke was strong, yet to our ears it probably conveys a meaning far more violent than it would have done to the ears that heard it. The word Satan means no more than "adversary," and, as in many passages of the Old Testament, is so far from meaning the great Adversary of mankind, that it is even applied to opposing angels. The word, in fact, was among the Jews, as in the East

rendered in the LXX. by μὴ γένοιτο and μηδαμῶς (Josh. xxii. 29; 1 Sam. xii. 23; xx. 2). (See Schleusner, *Lex. in N. T.*, s. v.)

[1] "Those whose intentions towards us are the best," says Stier, "are the most dangerous to us when their intentions are merely human" (ii. 332). How often, alas! are a man's real foes they of his own household; his friends, who love him best, become in their worldliness his worst enemies. They drag him down from heights of self-sacrifice to the vulgar, the conventional, the comfortable.

generally, and to this day, a very common one for anything bold, powerful, dangerous—for every secret opponent or open enemy.[1] But its special applicability in this instance rose from the fact that Peter was in truth adopting the very line of argument which the Tempter himself had adopted in the wilderness. And in calling Peter an offence (*σκάνδαλον*), Jesus probably again alluded to his name, and compared him to a stone in the path over which the wayfarer stumbles. The comparison must have sunk deeply into the Apostle's mind, for he too in his Epistle warns his readers against some to whom, because they believe not, the Headstone of the Corner became "a stone of stumbling and a *rock of offence*" (*πέτρα σκανδάλου*, 1 Pet. ii. 8).

But having thus warned and rebuked the ignorant affection of unspiritual effeminacy in His presumptuous Apostle, the Lord graciously made the incident an occasion for some of His deepest teaching, which He not only addressed to His disciples, but to all.[2] We learn quite incidentally from St. Mark, that even in these remote regions His footsteps were sometimes followed by attendant crowds,[3] who usually walked at a little distance from

[1] For instance, in Numb. xxii. 22, 32, the same Hebrew word שָׂטָן is twice used of the angel who went to withstand Balaam; in 1 Kings xi. 14 it is used of Hadad, and in verse 23 of Rezon; in 1 Sam. xxix. 4 the Philistines use it of David. See too Ps. cix. 6, marg., &c. (*v. infr.*, Vol. I., p. 236). The same remark is true of the Koran. Among the Rabbis are to be found such expressions as, "When the bull rushes at a man, Satan leaps up between his horns." They always drag the notion in when they can, as in Targ. Jonath., Exod. xxxii. 19, &c. "If a woman's hair is uncovered," says R. Simeon, "evil spirits come and sit upon it" (Wetstein, *ad* 1 Cor. xi. 10). "'If that young Sheit . . ,' I exclaimed, '*about to use an epithet generally given in the East to such adventurous youths*,'" &c. (Layard's *Nineveh*, i. 287). Layard adds in a note that Sheitan is usually applied to a clever, cunning, daring fellow.

[2] Luke ix. 23.

[3] Cf. Mark viii. 34; vii. 24.

Him and His disciples, but were sometimes called to Him to hear the gracious words which proceeded out of His mouth. And alike they and His disciples were as yet infected with the false notions which had inspired the impetuous interference of Peter. To them, therefore, He addressed the words which have taught us for ever that the essence of all highest duty, the meaning of all truest life—alike the most acceptable service to God, and the most ennobling example to men—is involved in the law of self-sacrifice.[1] It was on this occasion that He spoke those few words which have produced so infinite an effect on the conscience of mankind. "What is a man profited, if he shall gain the whole world, and lose his own soul? or what shall a man give in exchange for his soul?" And then, after warning them that He should Himself be judged, He consoled them under this shock of unexpected revelation by the assurance that there were some standing there who should not taste of death till they had seen the Son of Man coming in His kingdom. If, as all Scripture shows, "the kingdom of the Son of Man" be understood in a sense primarily spiritual, then there can be no difficulty in understanding this prophecy in the sense that, ere all of them passed away, the foundations of that kingdom should have been established for ever in the abolition of the old and the establishment of the new dispensation. Three of them were immediately to see Him transfigured;[2] all but one were to be witnesses of His resur-

[1] The metaphorical sense of "taking up the cross" is well illustrated by Plato, *De Rep.* ii. 362 A., ἀνασχινδυλευθήσεται. 2 Cor. iii. 18; Rom. xii. 2 could lead to no mistake.

[2] The translators of our Bible seem to have understood the Transfiguration as the first fulfilment of the prophecy, by separating it from the verses which precede it in St. Mark (ix. 1), and making it introduce the

rection; one at least—the beloved disciple—was to survive that capture of Jerusalem and destruction of the Temple which were to render impossible any literal fulfilment of the Mosaic law. And the prophecy may have deeper meanings yet than these—meanings still more real because they are still more wholly spiritual. "If we wish not to fear death," says St. Ambrose, "let us stand where Christ is; Christ is your Life; He is the very Life which cannot die."

following narrative. Cf. 2 Pet. i. 16: "eye-witnesses (ἐπόπται) of His majesty" is there referred expressly to the Transfiguration, and appealed to as the confirmation of the preaching which had proclaimed "the power and coming" of Christ. See, too, 1 John i. 1; iv. 14.

CHAPTER XXXVI.

THE TRANSFIGURATION.

"And this voice which came from heaven we heard, when we were with Him in the holy mount."—2 PETER i. 18.

NONE of the Evangelists tell us about the week which followed this memorable event. They tell us only that "after six days" He took with Him the three dearest and most enlightened of His disciples,[1] and went with them—the expression implies a certain solemnity of expectation[2]—up a lofty mountain, or, as St. Luke calls it, simply "*the* mountain."

The supposition that the mountain intended was Mount Tabor has been engrained for centuries in the tradition of the Christian Church; and three churches and a monastery erected before the close of the sixth century attest the unhesitating acceptance of this belief. Yet it is almost certain that Tabor was not the scene of that great epiphany. The rounded summit of that picturesque and wood-crowned hill, which forms so fine a feature in the landscape, as the traveller approaches the

[1] Matt. xvii. 1—13; Mark ix. 2—13; Luke ix. 28—36. The "about eight days after" of St. Luke (ix. 28) is merely an inclusive reckoning, but is one of the touches which are valuable as showing the independence of his narrative, which gives us several new particulars.

[2] ἀναφέρει. Comp. Luke xxiv. 51.

northern limit of the plain of Esdraelon, had probably from time immemorial been a fortified and inhabited spot,[1] and less than thirty years after this time, Josephus, on this very mountain, strengthened the existing fortress of Itaburion. This, therefore, was not a spot to which Jesus could have taken the three Apostles "apart by themselves." Nor, again, is there the slightest intimation that the six intervening days had been spent in travelling southwards from Cæsarea Philippi, the place last mentioned; on the contrary, it is distinctly intimated by St. Mark (ix. 30), that Jesus did not "pass through Galilee" (in which Mount Tabor is situated) till after the events here narrated. Nor again does the comparatively insignificant hill Paneum, which is close by Cæsarea Philippi, fulfil the requirements of the narrative.[2] It is, therefore, much more natural to suppose that our Lord, anxious to traverse the Holy Land of His birth to its northern limit, journeyed slowly forward till He reached the lower slopes of that splendid snow-clad mountain, whose glittering mass, visible even as far southward as the Dead Sea, magnificently closes the northern frontier of Palestine—the Mount Hermon of Jewish poetry. Its very name means "the mountain," and the scene which it witnessed would well suffice to procure for it the distinction of being the only mountain to which in Scripture is attached the epithet "holy."[3] On those dewy pasturages, cool and fresh with the breath of the snow-clad heights above them, and offering that noble solitude, among the grandest scenes of Nature, which He desired as the refreshment of His soul for the

[1] Chisloth-tabor (Josh. xix. 12; Judg. iv. 6).

[2] Πανεῖον. The town is called on coins Καισάρεια ὑπὸ Πανείῳ.

[3] 2 Peter i. 18.

mighty struggle which was now so soon to come, Jesus would find many a spot where He could kneel with His disciples absorbed in silent prayer.

And the coolness and solitude would be still more delicious to the weariness of the Man of Sorrows after the burning heat of the Eastern day and the incessant publicity which, even in these remoter regions, thronged his steps. It was the evening hour when He ascended,[1] and as He climbed the hill-slope with those three chosen witnesses—"the Sons of Thunder and the Man of Rock"—doubtless a solemn gladness dilated His whole soul; a sense not only of the heavenly calm which that solitary communion with His Heavenly Father would breathe upon the spirit, but still more than this, a sense that He would be supported for the coming hour by ministrations not of earth, and illuminated with a light which needed no aid from sun or moon or stars. He went up to be prepared for death, and He took His three Apostles with Him that, haply, having seen His glory—the glory of the only Begotten of the Father, full of grace and truth—their hearts might be fortified, their faith strengthened, to gaze unshaken on the shameful insults and unspeakable humiliation of the cross.

There, then, He knelt and prayed, and as He prayed He was elevated far above the toil and misery of the world which had rejected Him. He was transfigured before them, and His countenance shone as the sun, and His garments became white as the dazzling snow-fields above them. He was enwrapped in such an aureole of glistering brilliance—His whole presence breathed so

[1] This is evident from Luke ix. 32, 37, especially when compared with Luke vi. 12.

divine a radiance—that the light, the snow, the lightning[1] are the only things to which the Evangelist can compare that celestial lustre. And, lo! two figures were by His side.[2] "When, in the desert, He was girding Himself for the work of life, angels of life came and ministered unto Him; now, in the fair world, when He is girding Himself for the work of death, the ministrants come to Him from the grave—but from the grave conquered—one from that tomb under Abarim, which His own hand had sealed long ago; the other from the rest into which He had entered without seeing corruption. There stood by Him Moses and Elias, and spake of His decease. And when the prayer is ended, the task accepted, then first since the star paused over Him at Bethlehem, the full glory falls upon Him from heaven, and the testimony is borne to His everlasting sonship and power—'Hear ye Him.'"[3]

It is clear, from the fuller narrative of St. Luke, that the three Apostles did not witness the beginning of this marvellous transfiguration. An Oriental, when his

[1] λευκὰ ὡς τὸ φῶς (Matt. xvii. 2); λευκὰ λίαν ὡς χιὼν (Mark ix. 3); λευκὸς . . . ἐξαστράπτων (Luke ix. 29). It is interesting to observe that St. Luke, writing for Greeks and Romans, avoids the word μετεμορφώθη used by the other Evangelists, because his readers would associate that word with the conceptions with which they were familiar in Nicander, Antoninus Liberalis, and Ovid. (See Valcknaer, quoted by Bishop Wordsworth, *ad loc.*)

[2] The καὶ ἰδοὺ of Matt. xvii. 3 shows how intense was the impression which the scene had made on the imagination of those who witnessed it. "The two who appeared to Him were the representatives of the Law and the Prophets: both had been removed from this world in a mysterious manner; . . . . both, like the greater One with whom they spoke, had endured that supernatural fast of forty days and nights; both had been on the holy mount in the visions of God. And now they came, solemnly, to consign into His hands, once and for all, in a symbolical and glorious representation, their delegated and expiring power." (Alford.)

[3] Ruskin, *Mod. Painters*, iii. 392.

prayers are over, wraps himself in his *abba*,[1] and, lying down on the grass in the open air, sinks in a moment into profound sleep. And the Apostles, as afterwards they slept at Gethsemane, so now they slept on Hermon. They were heavy, "weighed down" with sleep, when suddenly starting into full wakefulness of spirit, they saw and heard.[2]

In the darkness of the night, shedding an intense gleam over the mountain herbage, shone the glorified form of their Lord. Beside Him, in the same flood of golden glory,[3] were two awful shapes, which they knew or heard to be Moses and Elijah. And the Three spake together, in the stillness, of that coming decease at Jerusalem, about which they had just been forewarned by Christ.

And as the splendid vision[4] began to fade—as the majestic visitants were about to be separated from their Lord, as their Lord Himself passed with them into the overshadowing brightness—Peter, anxious to delay their presence, amazed, startled, transported, not knowing what he said[5]—not knowing that Calvary would be a

[1] Hence the merciful provision of the Mosaic law, that the outer robe was to be restored at night if taken as a pledge for debt. (See Exod. xxii. 26.)

[2] So I would render διαγρηγορήσαντες in Luke ix. 32. It is a non-classical word, and has this meaning in Byzantine writers. Or perhaps the δια may imply "waking after an interval"—"in the middle of it all." Both the context and the grammar sufficiently show that (though it occurs here only in the N. T.) it cannot mean "having kept awake," as Alford and Archbishop Trench (following Rost and Palm) render it.

[3] ὀφθέντες ἐν δόξῃ (Luke ix. 31).

[4] τὸ ὅραμα (Matt. xvii. 9). The word, which occurs eleven times in the Acts, but not elsewhere in the N. T., is applied to dreams (Acts xvi. 10; xviii. 9) and ecstacies (Acts xi. 5), but also to any impression on the *spirit* which is as clear as an impression on the senses (Acts vii. 31). Hence Phavorinus says, ὁράματά εἰσι προφητῶν, ὅσα ἐγρηγορότες βλέπουσι οἱ προφῆται.

[5] This touch in all probability comes to us from St. Peter himself (Mark ix. 6).

spectacle infinitely more transcendent than Hermon—not knowing that the Law and the Prophets were now fulfilled—not fully knowing that his Lord was unspeakably greater than the Prophet of Sinai and the Avenger of Carmel—exclaimed, "Rabbi, it is best for us to be here;[1] and let us make three tabernacles, one for thee, and one for Moses, and one for Elias." Jesus might have smiled at the naïve proposal of the eager Apostle, that they six should dwell for ever in little *succôth* of wattled boughs on the slopes of Hermon. But it was not for Peter to construct the universe for his personal satisfaction. He had to learn the meaning of Calvary no less than that of Hermon. Not in cloud of glory or chariot of fire was Jesus to pass away from them, but with arms outstretched in agony upon the accursed tree; not between Moses and Elias, but between two thieves, who "were crucified with Him, on either side one."

No answer was vouchsafed to his wild and dreamy words; but, even as he spake, a cloud—not a cloud of thick darkness as at Sinai, but a cloud of light, a Shechînah of radiance—overshadowed them, and a voice from out of it uttered, "This is my beloved Son; hear Him." They fell prostrate, and hid their faces on the grass.[2] And as—awaking from the overwhelming shock of that awful voice, of that enfolding Light—they raised their eyes and gazed suddenly all around them,[3] they

[1] καλὸν in the New Testament seems sometimes to have a superlative sense. Cf. Matt. xviii. 8; xxvi. 24, &c., and Gen. xxxviii. 26, where טוֹב means "better," as "bona," in Plaut. *Rud.* iv. 4, 70. (Schleusner, s. v.)

[2] Matt. xvii. 6.

[3] Mark ix. 8, ἐξάπινα περιβλεψάμενοι (cf. Matt. xvii. 8), one of the many inimitably graphic touches of truthfulness and simplicity—touches never yet found in any "myth" since the world began—with which in all three Evangelists this narrative abounds. We have proofs that on two of the three spectators this scene made an indelible impression. St. John most

found that all was over. The bright cloud had vanished. The lightning-like gleams of shining countenances and dazzling robes had passed away;[1] they were alone with Jesus, and only the stars rained their quiet lustre on the mountain slopes.

At first they were afraid to rise or stir, but Jesus, their Master—as they had seen Him before He knelt in prayer, came to them, touched them—said, "Arise, and be not afraid."

And so the day dawned on Hermon, and they descended the hill; and as they descended, He bade them tell no man until He had risen from the dead. The vision was for them; it was to be pondered over by them in the depths of their own hearts in self-denying reticence; to announce it to their fellow-disciples might only awake *their* jealousy and their own self-satisfaction; until the resurrection it would add nothing to the faith of

clearly alludes to it in John i. 14; 1 John i. 1. St. Peter (if, as I believe, the Second Epistle is genuine) is dwelling on it in 2 Peter i. in a manner all the more striking because it is partly unconscious. Thus, he not only appeals to it in confirmation of his preaching, but he uses just before the unusual word ἔξοδος for "death" [2 Peter i. 15 (cf. Luke ix. 31): it is, however, possible that δόξαν *may* here be the reading, as it seems to have been read by St. Chrysostom], and σκήνωμα (ver. 13; cf. Matt. xvii. 4) for "tabernacle;" and immediately after speaks (ver. 19) of "a light shining in a dark place," and immediately preceding the dawn—which is another, and, so far as I am aware, hitherto unnoticed trace of the fact that the Transfiguration (of which the writer's mind is here so full) took place by night. On the word ἔξοδος Bengel finely remarks, "Vocabulum valde grave, quo continetur passio, crux, mors, resurrectio, adscensio." Archbishop Trench aptly compares "Post obitum, vel potius *excessum*, Romuli" (Cic. *Rep.* ii. 30), and says that St. Peter by the word ἐπόπτης (2 Peter i. 16) seems to imply a sort of *initiation* into holy mysteries (*Studies in the Gospels*, p. 206). Many have resolved the narrative of the Transfiguration into a myth; it is remarkable that, in this verse, St. Peter *is expressly repudiating the very kind of myths* (μῦθοι σεσοφισμένοι) under which this would be classed.

[1] "Finis legis Christus; Lex et Prophetia ex Verbo; quae autem ex Verbo coeperunt, in Verbo desinunt" (St. Ambrose). (Wordsworth, in Matt. xvii. 8.)

others, and might only confuse their conceptions of what was to be His work on earth. They kept Christ's command, but they could not attach any meaning to this allusion. They could only ask each other, or muse in silence, what this resurrection from the dead could mean. And *another* serious question weighed upon their spirits. They had seen Elias. They now knew more fully than ever that their Lord was indeed the Christ. Yet "how say the Scribes"—and had not the Scribes the prophecy of Malachi in their favour?[1]—"that Elias must first come and restore all things?" And then our Lord gently led them to see that Elias indeed had come, and had not been recognised, and had received at the hand of his nation the same fate which was soon to happen to Him whom he announced. Then understood they that He spake to them of John the Baptist.[2]

[1] Mal. iv. 5. The LXX., without any authority from the Hebrew, read here Ἠλίαν τὸν Θεσβίτην.

[2] Luke i. 17, "in the spirit and power of Elias;" cf. Matt. xi. 10. The Jewish expectation of Elias is well known. A thing of unknown ownership may be kept by the finder "till the coming of Elias." He was to restore to the Jews the pot of manna, the rod of Aaron, &c., and his coming generally was to be a *χρόνος ἀποκαταστάσεως* (cf. Acts iii. 21). See Lightfoot, *Hor. Hebr.* in Matt. xvii. 10, 11.

CHAPTER XXXVII.

THE DEMONIAC BOY.

Τινὲς δέ φασιν ὅτι ἡ ὄψις αὐτοῦ ὡραιοτέρα γινομένη ἀπὸ τοῦ φωτὸς . . . . ἐφείλκετο τούς ὄχλους.—THEOPHYL.

THE imagination of all readers of the Gospels has been struck by the contrast—a contrast seized and immortalised for ever in the great picture of Raphael—between the peace, the glory, the heavenly communion on the mountain heights, and the confusion, the rage, the unbelief, the agony which marked the first scene that met the eyes of Jesus and His Apostles on their descent to the low levels of human life.[1]

For in their absence an event had occurred which filled the other disciples with agitation and alarm. They saw a crowd assembled and Scribes among them, who with disputes and victorious inuendoes were pressing hard upon the diminished band of Christ's chosen friends.[2]

Suddenly at this crisis the multitude caught sight of Jesus. Something about His appearance, some unusual majesty, some lingering radiance, filled them with amazement, and they ran up to Him with saluta-

[1] Matt. xvii. 14—21; Mark ix. 14—29; Luke ix. 37—45.

[2] There were, of course, many Jews, and therefore naturally there would be Scribes, in the kingdom of Philip.

tions.[1] "What is your dispute with them?" He sternly asked of the Scribes. But the Scribes were too much abashed, the disciples were too self-conscious of their faithlessness and failure, to venture on any reply. Then out of the crowd struggled a man, who, kneeling before Jesus, cried out, in a loud voice,[2] that he was the father of an only son whose demoniac possession was shown by epilepsy, in its most raging symptoms, accompanied by dumbness, atrophy, and a suicidal mania. He had brought the miserable sufferer to the disciples to cast out the evil spirit, but their failure had occasioned the taunts of the Scribes.

The whole scene grieved Jesus to the heart. "O faithless and perverse generation," He exclaimed, "how long shall I be with you? how long shall I suffer you?" This cry of His indignation seemed meant for all—for the merely curious multitude, for the malicious Scribes, for the half-believing and faltering disciples. "Bring him hither to me."

The poor boy was brought, and no sooner had his eye fallen on Jesus, than he was seized with another paroxysm of his malady. He fell on the ground in violent convulsions, and rolled there with foaming lips. It was the most deadly and intense form of epileptic lunacy on which our Lord had ever been called to take compassion.[3]

He paused before He acted. He would impress the

[1] Mark ix. 14. We here follow mainly the full and vivid narrative of St. Mark.

[2] Matt. xvii. 14; Luke ix. 38.

[3] Matt. xvii. 15, σεληνιάζεται καὶ κακῶς πάσχει. This describes, at any rate, the natural side of his malady; but there is, in truth, to such maladies *no* purely *natural* side. They belong to some mystery of iniquity which we can never understand. They are due, not to the στάσις but to the ἀπόστασις of human nature.

d *

scene in all its horror on the thronging multitude, that they might understand that the failure was not of Him. He would at the same time invoke, educe, confirm the wavering faith of the agonised suppliant.

"How long has this happened to him?"

"From childhood: and often hath it flung him both into fire and into water to destroy him; but *if at all thou canst*, take pity on us and help us."

"*If thou canst?*"[1] answered Jesus—giving him back his own word—"all things are possible to him that believeth."

And then the poor hapless father broke out into that cry, uttered by so many millions since, and so deeply applicable to an age which, like our own, has been described as "destitute of faith, yet terrified at scepticism"—"*Lord, I believe; help thou mine unbelief.*"

Meanwhile, during this short colloquy, the crowd had been gathering more and more, and Jesus, turning to the sufferer, said, "Dumb and deaf spirit, I charge thee, come out of him, and enter no more into him." A yet wilder cry, a yet more fearful convulsion followed His words, and then the boy lay on the ground, no longer wallowing and foaming, but still as death. Some said, "He is dead." But Jesus took him by the hand, and, amid the amazed exclamations of the multitude, restored him to his father, calm and cured.

Jesus had previously given to His disciples the power of casting out devils, and this power was even exercised in His name by some who were not among His

[1] This seems to be the force of Mark ix. 23, *εἶπεν αὐτῷ τὸ εἰ δύνασαι πιστεῦσαι, παντα δυνατὰ τῷ πιστεύοντι*, which is the best reading (א, B, C, L, and some versions). For this use of *τὸ* see Matt. xix. 18; Luke ix. 46, &c. "As for the 'if thou canst'—all things are, &c." It is taken thus by the Æthiopic version, and "proclivi lectioni praestat ardua."

professed disciples.[1] Nor had they ever failed before. It was therefore natural that they should take the first private opportunity to ask Him the cause of their discomfiture. He told them frankly that it was because of their unbelief. It may be that the sense of His absence weakened them; it may be that they felt less able to cope with difficulties while Peter and the sons of Zebedee were also away from them; it may be, too, that the sad prophecy of His rejection and death had worked with sinister effect on the minds of the weakest of them. But, at any rate, He took this opportunity to teach them two great lessons: the one, that there are forms of spiritual, physical, and moral evil so intense and so inveterate, that they can only be exorcised by prayer, united to that self-control and self-denial of which fasting is the most effectual and striking symbol;[2] the other, that to a perfect faith all things are possible. Faith, like a grain of mustard-seed, could even say to Hermon itself,[3] "Be thou removed, and cast into the waves of the Great Sea, and it should obey."

Jesus had now wandered to the utmost northern limit of the Holy Land, and He began to turn His steps homewards. We see from St. Mark that His return was designedly secret and secluded, and possibly not along the high roads, but rather through the hills and valleys of Upper Galilee to the westward of the

[1] Mark ix. 38.

[2] It must, however, be noticed that the *καὶ νηστείᾳ* (Mark ix. 29) is a more than dubious reading. It is not found in א or B, and the corresponding verse in Matt. xvii. 21 is omitted by א, B, as well as by various versions. Tischendorf omits both. See, however, Matt. vi. 16—18; ix. 15.

[3] "Removing mountains" was among the Jews a common hyperbole for the conquest of stupendous difficulties. A great teacher was called by the Rabbis עֹקֵר הָרִים (*gokêr hârîm*), or "uprooter of mountains." See many instances in Lightfoot, *Hor. Hebr.* in Matt. xxi. 21.

Jordan.[1] His object was no longer to teach the multitudes who had been seduced into rejecting Him, and among whom He could hardly appear in safety, but to continue that other and even more essential part of His work, which consisted in the training of His Apostles. And now the constant subject of His teaching[2] was His approaching betrayal, murder, and resurrection. But He spoke to dull hearts; in their deep-seated prejudice they ignored his clear warnings, in their faithless timidity they would not ask for further enlightenment. We cannot see more strikingly how vast was the change which the resurrection wrought in them than by observing with what simple truthfulness they record the extent and inveteracy of their own shortcomings, during those precious days while the Lord was yet among them.

The one thing which they *did* seem to realise was that some strange and memorable issue of Christ's life, accompanied by some great development of the Messianic kingdom, was at hand; and this unhappily produced the only effect in them which it should *not* have produced. Instead of stimulating their self-denial, it awoke their ambition; instead of confirming their love and humility, it stirred them up to jealousy and pride. On the road—remembering, perhaps, the preference which had been shown at Hermon to Peter and the sons of Zebedee—they disputed among themselves, "Which should be the greatest?"

[1] For the variety of readings on Matt. xvii. 22, ἀναστρεφομένων, συστρεφ., στρεφ., &c., see Keim, *Gesch. Jesu*, ii. 581. The παρεπορεύοντο of Mark ix. 30 is of uncertain meaning. We have already considered it in Mark ii. 23 (cf. Matt. xii. 1) [*v. supra*, Vol. I., p. 436]; and in Mark xi. 20; xv. 29, it means "passing by," as in Matt. xxvii. 39, the only other passage where it occurs. In Deut. ii. 14, it is simply used for הָלַךְ, "he walked."

[2] Mark ix. 31, ἐδίδασκεν . . . ἔλεγεν.

At the time our Lord took no notice of the dispute. He left their own consciences to work. But when they reached Capernaum and were in the house, then He asked them, "What they had been disputing about on the way?"[1] Deep shame kept them silent, and that silence was the most eloquent confession of their sinful ambitions. Then He sat down, and taught them again, as He had done so often, that he who would be first must be last of all, and servant of all, and that the road to honour is humility. And wishing to enforce this lesson by a symbol of exquisite tenderness and beauty, He called to Him a little child, and set it in the midst, and then, folding it in his arms, warned them that unless they could become as humble as that little child, they could not enter into the kingdom of heaven.[2] They were to be as children in the world; and he who should receive even one such little child in Christ's name, should be receiving Him, and the Father who sent Him.

The expression "in my name" seems to have suggested to St. John a sudden question, which broke the thread of Christ's discourse. They had seen, he said, a man who was casting out devils in Christ's name; but since the man was not one of them, they had forbidden him. Had they done right?[3]

[1] See, for what follows, Matt. xviii. 1—35; Mark ix. 33—50; Luke ix. 46—50; which three passages I assume to be one and the same continuous discourse suggested by the same incidents, but told with varying completeness by the three Evangelists.

[2] The impossible tradition—mentioned by Nicephorus—that this was the martyr St. Ignatius, perhaps arose from a mistaken interpretation of his name Θεοφόρος as though it had been Θεόφορος; but this name was derived from his celebrated interview with Trajan.

[3] Bruce (*Training of the Twelve*, p. 234) quotes an apt illustration from the life of Baxter, whose followers condemned Sir Matthew Hale as unconverted, because he did not attend their weekly prayer meetings! "I,"

"No," Jesus answered; "let the prohibition be removed." He who could do works of mercy in Christ's name could not lightly speak evil of that name. He who was not against them was with them. Sometimes indifference is opposition; sometimes neutrality is aid."[1]

And then, gently resuming His discourse—the child yet nestling in His arms, and furnishing the text for His remarks—He warned them of the awful guilt and peril of offending, of tempting, of misleading, of seducing from the paths of innocence and righteousness, of teaching any wicked thing, or suggesting any wicked thought to one of those little ones, whose angels see the face of His Father in heaven. Such wicked men and seducers, such human performers of the devil's work—addressing them in words of more bitter, crushing import than any which He ever uttered—a worse fate, He said, awaited *them*, than to be flung with the heaviest millstone round their neck into the sea.[2]

And He goes on to warn them that no sacrifice could be too great if it enabled them to escape any possible

said Baxter, ... "that have seen his love to all good men, and the blamelessness of his life, thought better of his piety than of mine own." (*Reliquiae Baxter*, iii. 47.)

[1] On another occasion Christ had said what seemed to be the reverse of this—viz., "He who is not with me is against me" (Matt. xii. 30). But it is easy to see that the two truths are but complementary to each other. "Qui n'a appris dans le cours d'une vie active, que, selon les circonstances et les personnes, celui qui s'abstient de concourir et se tient à l' écart tantôt donne appui et force, tantôt au contraire nuit et entrâve" (Guizot, *Medit.* i. 279). Contrast the quiet insight and wisdom of this remark with Renan's "deux règles de prosélytisme tout à fait opposées et une contradiction amenée par une lutte passionnée." Cf. Sueton, *Jul. Caes.* 75: "Denuntiante Pompeio, pro hostibus se habiturum qui reipublicae defuissent, ipse medios et neutrius partis suorum sibi numero futuros pronuntiavit." (I owe this remarkably apposite reference to Mr. Garnett.)

[2] Μύλος ὀνικὸς (Matt. xviii. 6; Luke xvii. 2). The *rechem*, or runner-stone, *i.e.* the upper millstone, so heavy as to be turned by an ass.

temptations to put such stumbling-blocks in the way of their own souls, or the souls of others. Better cut off the right hand, and enter heaven maimed—better hew off the right foot, and enter heaven halt—better tear out the right eye, and enter heaven blind—than suffer hand or foot or eye to be the ministers of sins which should feed the undying worm or kindle the quenchless flame. Better be drowned in this world with a millstone round the neck, than carry that moral and spiritual millstone of unresisted temptation which can drown the guilty soul in the fiery lake of alienation and despair. For just as salt is sprinkled over every sacrifice for its purification, so must every soul be purged by fire; by the fire, if need be, of the severest and most terrible self-sacrifice. Let this refining, purging, purifying fire of searching self-judgment and self-severity be theirs. Let not this salt lose its savour, nor this fire its purifying power. "Have salt in yourselves, and be at peace with one another."[1]

And thus, at once to confirm the duty of this mutual peace which they had violated, and to show them that, however deeply rooted be God's anger against those who lead others astray, *they* must never cherish hatred even against those who had most deeply injured them, He taught them how, first by private expostulation, then if necessary by public appeal, at once most gently and most effectually to deal with an offending brother. Peter, in the true spirit of Judaic formalism, wanted a specific limit to the number of times when forgiveness should be

[1] Isa. xxxiii. 14, 15: "Who among us shall dwell with devouring fire? who among us shall dwell with everlasting burnings? He that walketh righteously, and speaketh uprightly, . . . he shall dwell on high." We are again reminded of that fine ἄγραφον δόγμα already quoted, "He who is near me, is near the fire."

granted; but Jesus taught that the times of forgiveness should be practically unlimited.[1] He illustrated that teaching by the beautiful parable of the servant, who, having been forgiven by his king a debt of ten thousand talents, immediately afterwards seized his fellow-servant by the throat, and would not forgive him a miserable little debt of one hundred pence, a sum 1,250,000 times as small as that which he himself had been forgiven. The child whom Jesus had held in His arms might have understood that moral; yet how infinitely more deep must its meaning be to us—who have been trained from childhood in the knowledge of His atoning love—than it could have been, at the time when it was spoken, to even a Peter or a John.

[1] The Rabbinic rule only admitted a triple forgiveness, referring to Amos i. 3; Job xxxiii. 29 (marg., "twice" and "thrice").

CHAPTER XXXVIII.

A BRIEF REST IN CAPERNAUM.

"Vade et scito nos esse in alio regno reges et filios regis."—LUTHER, *in* Matt. xiii.

ONE more incident, related by St. Matthew only, marked his brief stay on this occasion in Capernaum.

From time immemorial there was a precedent for collecting, at least occasionally, on the recurrence of every census, a tax of "half a shekel, after the shekel of the sanctuary," of every Jew who had reached the age of twenty years, as a "ransom for his soul," unto the Lord.[1] This money was devoted to the service of the Temple, and was expended on the purchase of the sacrifices, scapegoats, red heifers, incense, shewbread, and other expenses of the Temple service. After the return from the captivity, this *be ah*, or half-shekel, became a voluntary annual tax of a third of a shekel;[2] but at some subsequent period it had again returned to its original amount. This tax was paid by every Jew in every part of the world, whether rich or poor; and, as on the first occasion of its payment, to show that the souls of all alike are equal before God, "the rich paid

[1] Exod. xxx. 11—16. The English "tribute-money" is vague and incorrect; for the tribute was a *denarius* paid to the Roman emperor.

[2] Neh. x. 32.

no more, and the poor no less." It produced vast sums of money, which were conveyed to Jerusalem by honourable messengers.[1]

This tax was only so far compulsory that when first demanded, on the 1st of Adar, the demand was made quietly and civilly; if, however, it had not been paid by the 25th, then it seems that the collectors of the contribution (*tobhîn shekalîm*) might take a security for it from the defaulter.

Accordingly, almost immediately upon our Lord's return to Capernaum, these *tobhîn shekalîm* came to St. Peter, and asked him, quite civilly, as the Rabbis had directed, "Does not your master pay the didrachmas?"[2]

The question suggests two difficulties—viz., Why had our Lord not been asked for this contribution in previous years? and why was it now demanded in autumn, at the approach of the Feast of Tabernacles, instead of in the month Adar, some six months earlier? The answers seem to be that priests and eminent rabbis were regarded as exempt from the tax;[3] that our Lord's

[1] Philo (*De Monarch.* ii. 3) calls them ἱεροπομποί. These collections are alluded to in Cic. *Pro Flacco*, 28; Dio Cass. lxvi. 7; Jos. *B. J.* vii. 6, §6; *Antt.* xviii. 9, §1; and other passages collected by Wetstein, Lightfoot, &c. Taking the shekel roughly at 1s. 6d., the collection would produce £75,000 for every million contributors.

[2] The *didrachmum* was a Greek coin exactly equivalent to half a shekel; the stater or silver *tetradrachmum* was a shekel. The stater and the Roman denarius (which was rather more than a fourth of its value) were the two common coins at this time: the actual *didrachm* had fallen into disuse. It is true that the LXX. translate *shekel* by δίδραχμον and half-shekel by ἥμισυ τοῦ διδράχμου, but it is now generally agreed that this is because they adopt the Alexandrian, not the Attic scale. The value of a *didrachm* was about eighteen-pence. (See Madden, *Hist. of Jewish Coinage*, p. 235; Leake, *Numism. Hellen.*, Append. 2, 3; Akerman, *Numism. Illustr. to the N. Test.*, p. 14.)

[3] So the *Pirke Abhôth*, iv. 5, quoted by Stier, ii. 362.

frequent absence from Capernaum had caused some irregularity; and that it was permitted to pay arrears some time afterwards.[1]

The fact that the collectors inquired of St. Peter instead of asking Jesus Himself, is another of the very numerous indications of the awe which He inspired even into the heart of His bitterest enemies; as in all probability the fact of the demand being made at all shows a growing desire to vex His life, and to ignore His dignity. But Peter, with his usual impetuous readiness, without waiting, as he should have done, to consult His Master, replied, "Yes."[2]

If he had thought a moment longer—if he had known a little more—if he had even recalled his own great confession so recently given—his answer might not have come so glibly. This money was, at any rate, in its original significance, a redemption-money for the soul of each man;[3] and how could the Redeemer, who redeemed all souls by the ransom of His life, pay this money-ransom for his own? And it was a tax for the Temple services. How, then, could it be due from Him whose own mortal body was the new spiritual Temple of the Living God? He was to enter the vail of the

[1] There even seems to be some evidence (adduced by Greswell, *Dissert.* ii. 377) to show that it might be paid at either of the yearly feasts.

[2] It appears (Jost, *Gesch. des Judenth.* i. 218) that there had been a great dispute between the Pharisees and Sadducees as to whether this tax should be voluntary or compulsory, and that, after long debate, the Pharisees had carried the day. Perhaps, therefore, the demand was made of our Lord by way of testing which side he would take, and if so we may understand His words to St. Peter as sanctioning the universal principle that all gifts to God should be given "not grudgingly or of necessity." See a very interesting article by Professor Plumptre, in Smith's *Bibl. Dict.*, on "Tribute."

[3] Exod. xxx. 11, 12, *eesh kopher naphshô*, λύτρα τῆς ψυχῆς. (Philo, *ubi supr.*)

Holiest with the ransom of His own blood. But He paid what He did not owe, to save us from that which we owed, but could never pay.[1]

Accordingly, when Peter entered the house, conscious, perhaps, by this time, that his answer had been premature—perhaps also conscious that at that moment there were no means of meeting even this small demand upon their scanty store—Jesus, without waiting for any expression of his embarrassment, at once said to him, "What thinkest thou, Simon? the kings of the earth, from whom do they take tolls and taxes? from their own sons, or from those who are not their children?"

There could be but one answer—"From those who are not their children."

"Then," said Jesus, "the sons are free." I, the Son of the Great King, and even thou, who art also His son, though in a different way, are not bound to pay this tax. If we pay it, the payment must be a matter, not of positive obligation, as the Pharisees have lately decided, but of free and cheerful giving.

There is something beautiful and even playful in this gentle way of showing to the impetuous Apostle the dilemma in which his hasty answer had placed his Lord. We see in it, as Luther says, the fine, friendly, loving intercourse which must have existed between Christ and His disciples. It seems, at the same time, to establish the eternal principle that religious services should be maintained by spontaneous generosity and an innate sense of duty rather than in consequence of external compulsion. But yet, what is lawful is not always expedient, nor is there anything more thoroughly unchristian than the violent maintenance of the strict letter of

[1] Cf. Ps. lxix. 5; Aug. *Serm.* 155.

our rights. The Christian will always love rather to recede from something of his privilege—to take less than is his due. And so He, in whose steps all ought to walk, calmly added, "Nevertheless, lest we should offend them" (put a difficulty or stumbling-block in their way), "go thou to the sea and cast a hook, and take the first fish that cometh up; and opening its mouth thou shalt find a stater:[1] that take and give unto them for Me and for thee."[2] In the very act of submission, as Bengel finely says, "His majesty gleams forth." He would pay the contribution to avoid hurting the feelings of any, and especially because His Apostle had promised it in His behalf: but He could not pay it in an ordinary way, because that would be to compromise a principle. In obeying the law of charity, and of self-surrender, He would also obey the laws of dignity and truth. "He pays the tribute, therefore," says Clarius, "but taken from a fish's mouth, that His majesty may be recognised."[3]

When Paulus, with somewhat vulgar jocosity, calls this "a miracle for half-a-crown," he only shows his own entire misconception of the fine ethical lessons which are involved in the narrative, and which in this, as in every other instance, separate our Lord's miracles from those

[1] A stater equals four drachmas; it was a little more than three shillings, and was exactly the sum required for two people. The tax was not demanded of the other Apostles, perhaps because Capernaum was not their native town. The *shulchanîm*, or bankers to whom it was ordinarily paid, sat in each city to receive it on Adar 15. (Our information on the subject is mainly derived from the Mishna tract *Shekalîn*.)

[2] ἀντὶ, "instead of"—because the money was redemption money; "for me and for thee"—not "for us," because the money was paid differently for each. Cf. John xx. 17. (Alford.)—An interesting parallel of a king paying his own tax is adduced by Wetstein.

[3] Trench, *On the Miracles*, p. 406. His entire treatment of this miracle is suggestive and beautiful.

of the Apocrypha. Yet I agree with the learned and thoughtful Olshausen in regarding this as the most difficult to comprehend of all the Gospel miracles—as being in many respects, *sui generis*—as not falling under the same category as the other miracles of Christ. "It is remarkable," says Archbishop Trench, "*and is a solitary instance of the kind*, that the issue of this bidding is not told us." He goes on, indeed, to say that the narrative is evidently *intended* to be miraculous, and this is the impression which it has almost universally left on the minds of those who read it. Yet the literal translation of our Lord's words may most certainly be, "on opening its mouth, thou shalt get, or obtain,[1] a stater;" and although there is no difficulty whatever in supposing that a fish may have swallowed the glittering coin as it was accidentally dropped into the water,[2] nor should I feel the slightest difficulty in believing—as I hope that this book, from its first page to its last, will show—that a miracle might have been wrought, yet the peculiarities both of the miracle itself and of the manner in which it is narrated, leave in my mind a doubt as to whether, in this instance, some essential particular may not have been either omitted or left unexplained.

[1] This is a thoroughly classical and largely substantiated use of εὑρίσκω. See Liddell and Scott, *s. v.*; and for New Testament instances, see Heb. ix. 12; Luke i. 30; xi. 9; John xii. 14; Acts vii. 46.

[2] Of this there are abundant instances. There is no need to refer to the story of Polycrates (Herod. iii. 42), or to Augustine, *De Civ. Dei*, xxii. 8. Mackerel are to this day constantly caught by their swallowing a glittering piece of tin.

CHAPTER XXXIX.

JESUS AT THE FEAST OF TABERNACLES.

"Ecce Innocens inter peccatores; justus inter reprobos; pius inter improbos."—LUDOLPHUS, *Vita Christi*, p. 118.

IT was not likely that Jesus should have been able to live at Capernaum without the fact of His visit being known to some of the inhabitants. But it is clear that His stay in the town was very brief, and that it was of a strictly private character. The discourse and the incident mentioned in the last chapter are the only records of it which are left.

But it was now autumn, and all Galilee was in the stir of preparation which preceded the starting of the annual caravan of pilgrims to one of the three great yearly feasts—the Feast of Tabernacles. That feast—the Feast of Ingathering—was intended to commemorate the passage of the Israelites through the wilderness, and was celebrated with such universal joy, that both Josephus and Philo call it "the holiest and greatest feast," and it was known among the Jews as "*the* Feast" pre-eminently.[1] It was kept for seven consecutive

[1] חָגָ. Jos. *Antt.* viii. 4, § 1; xi. 5, § 5. See on the details of this Feast, Numb. xxix. 12—38; Neh. viii. 15; 2 Macc. x. 6, 7; Exod. xxiii. 16; Lev. xxiii. 34, seqq.; Deut. xvi. 13—15.

days, from the 15th to the 21st of Tisri, and the eighth day was celebrated by a holy convocation. During the seven days the Jews, to recall their desert wanderings, lived in little *succóth*, or booths made of the thickly-foliaged boughs of olive, and palm, and pine, and myrtle, and each person carried in his hands a *lulab*, consisting of palm-branches, or willows of the brook, or fruits of peach and citron.[1] During the week of festivities all the courses of priests were employed in turn; seventy bullocks were offered in sacrifice for the seventy nations of the world;[2] the Law was daily read,[3] and on each day the Temple trumpets sounded twenty-one times an inspiring and triumphant blast. The joy of the occasion was doubtless deepened by the fact that the feast followed but four days after the awful and comforting ceremonies of the Great Day of Atonement, in which a solemn expiation was made for the sins of all the people.

On the eve of their departure for this feast the family and relations of our Lord—those who in the Gospels are invariably called His "brethren," and some of whose descendants were known to early tradition as the Desposyni—came to Him for the last time with a well-meant but painful and presumptuous interference. They—like the Pharisees, and like the multitude, and like Peter—fancied that they knew better than Jesus Himself that line of conduct which would best accomplish His work and hasten the universal recognition of His

[1] Lev. xxiii. 40, marg. (*perî etz hadar* almost certainly means "citron-tree;" see Dr. Royle s. v. *Tappuach* in Kitto's *Bibl. Cycl.*); Jos. *Antt.* iii. 10, § 4, τοῦ μήλου τοῦ τῆς Περσέας προσόντος; xiii. 13, § 5, κίτρια.

[2] Thirteen bullocks the first day, twelve the second, eleven the third, and so on.

[3] Neh. viii. 18. Cf. John vii. 19.

claims. They came to Him with the language of criticism, of discontent, almost of reproaches and complaints. "Why this unreasonable and incomprehensible secrecy? it contradicts thy claims; it discourages thy followers. Thou hast disciples in Judæa: go thither, and let them too see Thy works which Thou doest? If Thou doest these things, manifest Thyself to the world." If they could use such language to their Lord and Master—if they could, as it were, thus challenge His power to the proof—it is but too plain that their knowledge of Him was so narrow and inadequate as to justify the sad parenthesis of the beloved Evangelist—"for not even His brethren believed on Him." He was a stranger unto His brethren, even an alien unto His mother's children.[1]

Such dictation on their part—the bitter fruit of impatient vanity and unspiritual ignorance—showed indeed a most blameable presumption;[2] yet our Lord only answered them with calm and gentle dignity. "No; my time to manifest myself to the world—which is *your* world also, and which therefore cannot hate you as it hates me—is not yet come. Go ye up to this feast. I choose not to go up to this feast, for not yet has my time been fulfilled."[3] So he answered them, and stayed in Galilee.

"I go not up yet unto this feast" is the rendering of the English version, adopting the reading οὔπω, "*not yet;*" but even if οὐκ, "not," be the true reading, the meaning

[1] Ps. lxix. 8; John vii. 1—9.

[2] As Stier remarks, the μετάβηθι ἐντεῦθεν, "depart hence," of John vii. 3, is a style of bold imperative which those only could have adopted who presumed on their close earthly relationship; and they seem almost ostentatiously to exclude *themselves* from the number of His disciples.

[3] The ἀναβαίνω has the sense so frequently found in the present: "I am not for going up;" "I do not choose to go up."

e *

is substantially the same.[1] The οὔπω in the next clause, "my time has *not yet* been fulfilled," distinctly intimated that such a time *would* come, and that it was not His object to intimate to His brethren—whose utter want of sympathy and reverence had just been so unhappily displayed—*when* that time would be. And there was a reason for this. It was essential for the safety of His life, which was not to end for six months more—it was essential for the carrying out of His Divine purposes, which were closely enwoven with the events of the next few days—that His brethren should *not* know about His plans. And therefore He let them depart in the completest uncertainty as to whether or not He intended to follow them.[2] Certain as they were to be asked by multitudes whether He was coming to the feast, it was necessary that they should be able to answer, with perfect truthfulness, that He was at any rate not coming with *them*, and that whether He would come before the feast was over or not they could not tell. And that this must have occurred, and that this must have been their

[1] Tischendorf reads οὐκ with א, D, K, the Cureton Syriac, &c.; on the other hand, οὔπω is the reading of B, E, F, G, H, &c. What seems decisive in favour of οὐκ is that it was more likely to be altered than the other; "proclivi lectioni praestat ardua."

[2] As early as the third century after Christ, the philosopher Porphyry, one of the bitterest and ablest of those who assaulted Christianity, charged our blessed Lord with deception in this incident; and it is therefore clear that in *his* time the reading was οὐκ (*ap.* Jer. *Adv. Pelag.* iv. 21). And even an eminent Christian commentator like Meyer has supposed that, in this instance, Jesus subsequently changed His purpose. The latter supposition is precarious, perhaps wholly irreverent; the former is utterly senseless. For even if Porphyry supposed that it could have happened, he must have seen how preposterous was the notion of St. John's holding such a view. It therefore seems to me a matter of no consequence whatever whether οὐκ or οὔπω be read; for it is quite clear that the Evangelist saw nothing in the language of our Lord but the desire to exclude His brethren from any certain knowledge of His plans.

answer, is evident from the fact that the one question buzzed about from ear to ear in those gay and busy streets was, "Where is He? is He here already? is He coming?"[1] And as He did not appear, His whole character, His whole mission, were discussed. The words of approval were vague and timid, "He is a good man;" the words of condemnation were bitter and emphatic, "Nay, but He is a *mesíth*—He deceiveth the people." But no one dared to speak openly his full thought about Him; each seemed to distrust his neighbour; and all feared to commit themselves too far while the opinion of the "Jews," and of the leading Priests and Pharisees, had not been finally or decisively declared.

And suddenly, in the midst of all these murmurs and discussions, in the middle of the feast, Jesus, unaccompanied apparently by His followers, unheralded by His friends, appeared suddenly in the Temple, and taught. By what route He had reached the Holy City—how he had passed through the bright thronged streets unnoticed—whether He joined in the innocent mirth of the festival—whether He too lived in a little *succah* of palm-leaves during the remainder of the week, and wandered among the brightly-dressed crowds of an Oriental gala day with the *lulab* and citron in His hands—whether His voice was heard in the Hallel, or the Great Hosanna—we do not know. All that is told us is that, throwing himself, as it were, in full confidence on the protection of His disciples from Galilee and those in Jerusalem, He was suddenly found seated in one of the large halls which opened out of the Temple courts, and there He taught.

For a time they listened to Him in awe-struck silence;

[1] John vii. 11, ἐζήτουν αὐτὸν καὶ ἔλεγον, κ. τ. λ.; "they kept looking for Him, and saying," &c.

but soon the old scruples recurred to them. "He is no authorised Rabbi; He belongs to no recognised school; neither the followers of Hillel nor those of Shammai claim Him; He is a Nazarene; He was trained in the shop of the Galilæan carpenter; how knoweth this man letters, having never learned?" As though the few who are taught of God—whose learning is the learning of a pure heart and an enlightened eye and a blameless life—did not unspeakably transcend in wisdom, and therefore also in the best and truest knowledge, those whose learning has but come from other men! It is not the voice of erudition, but it is, as the old Greek thinker says, the voice of Inspiration—the voice of the divine Sibyl—which, uttering things simple and unperfumed and unadorned, reacheth through myriads of years.

Jesus understood their looks. He interpreted their murmurs. He told them that His learning came immediately from His Heavenly Father, and that they, too, if they did God's will, might learn, and might understand, the same high lessons. In all ages there is a tendency to mistake erudition for learning, knowledge for wisdom; in all ages there has been a slowness to comprehend that true learning of the deepest and noblest character may co-exist with complete and utter ignorance of everything which absorbs and constitutes the learning of the schools. In *one* sense—Jesus told His hearers—they knew the law which Moses had given them; in another they were pitiably ignorant of it. They could not understand its principles, because they were not "faithful to its precepts."[1] And then He asked them openly, "Why go ye about to kill me?"

[1] Cf. Ecclus. xxi. 11, "*He that keepeth the law of the Lord getteth the understanding thereof.*" (John xiv. 15—17, 20, 21; see too Job xxviii. 28.)

That determination to kill Him was known indeed to Him, and known to some of those who heard Him, but was a guilty secret which had been concealed from the majority of the multitude. *These* answered the question, while the others kept their guilty silence. "Thou hast a devil," the people answered;[1] "who goeth about to kill Thee?" Why did they speak with such superfluous and brutal bluntness? Do not we repudiate, with far less flaming indignation, a charge which we know to be not only false, but wholly preposterous and foundationless? Was there not in the minds even of this not yet wholly alienated multitude an uneasy sense of their distance from the Speaker—of that unutterable superiority to themselves which pained and shamed and irritated them? Were they not conscious, in their carnal and vulgar aspirations, that *this* Prophet came, not to condescend to such views as theirs, but to raise them to a region where they felt that they could not breathe? Was there not even then in their hearts something of the half-unconscious hatred of vice to virtue, the repulsion of darkness against light? Would they have said, "Thou hast a devil," when they heard Him say that some of them were plotting against His life, if they had not felt that they were themselves capable at almost any moment of joining in—aye, with their own hands of executing—so base a plot?

Jesus did not notice their coarse insolence. He referred them to that one work of healing on the Sabbath day,[2] at which they were all still marvelling, with an empty wonder, that He who had the power to perform such a deed should, in performing it, have risen above

[1] John vii. 20, ὁ ὄχλος, not οἱ Ἰουδαῖοι.
[2] John v. 5.

their empty, ceremonial, fetish-worshipping notions of Sabbath sanctity. And Jesus, who ever loved to teach the lesson that love and not literalism is the fulfilling of the Law, showed them, even on their own purely ritual and Levitical principle, that His word of healing had in no respect violated the Sabbath at all. For instance, Moses had established, or rather re-established, the ordinance of circumcision on the eighth day, and if that eighth day happened to be a Sabbath, they without scruple sacrificed the one ordinance to the other, and in spite of the labour which it involved, performed the rite of circumcision on the Sabbath day. If the law of circumcision superseded that of the Sabbath, did not the law of Mercy? If it was right by a series of actions to inflict that wound, was it wrong by a single word to effect a total cure?[1] If that, which was at the best but a *sign* of deliverance, could not even on account of the Sabbath be postponed for a single day, why was it criminal not to have postponed for the sake of the Sabbath a deliverance actual and entire? And then He summed His self-defence in the one calm word, "Do not be ever judging by the mere appearance, but judge a righteous judgment;"[2] instead of being permanently content with a superficial mode of criticism, come once for all to some principle of righteous decision.

His hearers were perplexed and amazed, "Is this He against whose life some are plotting? Can He be the Messiah? Nay, He cannot be; for we know whence this speaker comes, whereas they say that none shall

[1] Stier quotes from the Rabbis a remark to this very effect, "Circumcision, which is one of the 248 members of the body, supersedes the Sabbath; how much more the whole body of a man?"

[2] John vii. 24, μὴ κρίνετε . . . ἀλλὰ . . . κρίνατε.

know whence the Messiah shall have come when he appears."

There was a certain irony in the answer of Jesus. They knew whence He came and all about Him, and yet, in very truth, He came not of Himself, but from one of whom they knew nothing. This word maddened still more some of His hearers. They longed but did not dare to seize Him, and all the more because there were some whom these words convinced, and who appealed to His many miracles as irresistible proof of His sacred claims.[1] The Sanhedrin, seated in frequent session in their stone hall of meeting within the immediate precincts of the Temple, were, by means of their emissaries, kept informed of all that He did and said, and, without seeming to do so, watched His every movement with malignant and jealous eyes. These whispered arguments in His favour, this deepened awe of Him and belief in Him, which, despite their authority, was growing up under their very eyes, seemed to them at once humiliating and dangerous. They determined on a bolder course of action. They sent out emissaries to seize Him suddenly and stealthily, at the first opportunity which should occur. But Jesus showed no fear. He was to be with them a little longer, and then, and not till then, should He return to Him that sent Him.[2] Then, indeed, they would seek Him—seek Him, not as now with hostile

[1] It is a remarkable fact that the Jews have never attempted to deny the reality of the miracles which Jesus wrought. All that the *Toldôth Jeshu*, and similar books, can say is that He performed them by means of the *Shemhammephorash*, the "Tetragrammaton," or sacred name. For the preposterous legend by which they account for "that man" (as in their hatred they always call Him) having learnt the pronunciation of the name, see the translation of the *Toldôth* by Huldric (1705), or Wagenseil, *Tela Ignea Satanae*, 1681.

[2] Cf. John viii. 21.

intentions, but in all the crushing agony of remorse and shame; but their search would be in vain. His enemies wholly failed to understand the allusion. In the troubled and terrible days which were to come they would understand it only too bitterly and well. Now they could only jeeringly conjecture that possibly He had some wild intention of going to teach among the Gentiles.[1]

So passed this memorable day; and again, on the last day of the feast,[2] Jesus was standing in the Temple. On each day of the seven, and, possibly, even on the eighth, there was a significant and joyous ceremony. At early morning the people repaired to the Temple, and when the morning sacrifice had been laid on the altar, one of the priests went down with a golden ewer to the Pool of Siloam, not far from the foot of Mount Sion.

[1] διασπορὰ τῶν Ἑλλήνων (John vii. 35) means here, in all probability, "Gentile countries among which Jews are dispersed." And such a notion would seem to those bigoted Jews only too ridiculous. A modern Rabbi at Jerusalem did not know in what quarter of the globe he was living, had never heard the name Europe, and called all other parts of the world, except Palestine, *Chutselorets* (חוצה לארץ), *i.e.* "outside the Holy Land!" (Frankl, *Jews in the East*, ii. 34, E. Tr.)

[2] The feast lasted seven days, but it is uncertain whether by "the last day, that great day of the feast," the seventh day is intended, which was the proper conclusion of the feast, or the eighth, on which the booths were taken down, but on which there were special offerings and a holy convocation (Numb. xxix. 36—38). It is said that the seventh, not being distinguished from the other days, cannot be called "the great day;" but on the other hand, the *last* day of a feast is always likely to be conspicuous for the zest of its ceremonies, and there seems to be at least some indication that such was actually the case (Buxtorf, *Syn. Jud.* xxi.; see "Feast of Tabernacles" in Smith's *Dict. of the Bible*). One Rabbi (R. Juda Hakkôdesh), in the tract *Succah*, which is our chief authority on this subject, says that the water was poured out on the eighth as well as on the previous days (*Succah*, iv. 9), but the others deny this (Surenhusius, *Mischna*, ii. 276). The eighth day of the Passover, and of Tabernacles, is in Deut. xvi. 8; Lev. xxiii. 34, called *atsereth* (E. V. "solemn assembly," marg. "day of restraint").

There, with great solemnity, he drew three *logs* of water, which were then carried in triumphant procession through the water-gate into the Temple. As he entered the Temple courts the sacred trumpets breathed out a joyous blast, which continued till he reached the top of the altar slope, and there poured the water into a silver basin on the western side, while wine was poured into another silver basin on the eastern side. Then the great Hallel was sung,[1] and when they came to the verse "Oh give thanks unto the Lord, for He is good: for His mercy endureth for ever," each of the gaily-clad worshippers as he stood beside the altars, shook his *lulab* in triumph. In the evening they abandoned themselves to such rejoicing, that the Rabbis say that the man who has not seen this "joy of the drawing water" does not know what joy means.[2]

In evident allusion to this glad custom—perhaps in sympathy with that sense of something missing which succeeded the disuse of it on the eighth day of the feast —Jesus pointed the yearnings of the festal crowd in the Temple, as He had done those of the Samaritan woman by the lonely well, to a new truth, and to one which

[1] Ps. cxiii.—cxviii. Jahn, *Archaeol. Bibl.* § 355. Even Plutarch (*Sympos.* iv. 5) alludes to the κρατηροφορία.

[2] *Succah*, v. 2. The feast was called *Shimcath beth hashoabah.* The day was called the *Hosannah Rabbah*, or "Great Hosannah," because on the seventh day the Hallel was seven times sung. The origin of the ceremony is quite obscure, but it is at least possible that the extra joy of it—the processions, illuminations, dances—commemorated the joy of the Pharisees in having got the better of Alexander Jannæus, who, instead of pouring the water on the altar, disdainfully poured it on the ground. The Pharisees in their fury hurled at his head the citron-fruits which they were carrying in their hands (Lev. xxiii. 40), and on his calling his mercenaries to his aid, a massacre of nearly six thousand ensued (Derenbourg, *Hist. Pal.* 98; Jos. *Antt.* xiii. 13, § 5, κιτρίοις αὐτὸν ἔβαλλον). This unauthorised use of the fruits as convenient missiles seems not to have been rare (*Succah*, iv. 9).

more than fulfilled alike the spiritual (Isa. xii. 3) and the historical meaning (1 Cor. x. 4) of the scenes which they had witnessed. He "stood and cried, If any man thirst, let him come unto me and drink. He that believeth on me, as the Scripture hath said, out of his belly shall flow rivers of living water."[1] And the best of them felt in their inmost soul—and this is the strongest of all the evidences of Christianity for those who believe heart and soul in a God of love who cares for His children in the family of man—that they had deep need of a comfort and salvation, of the outpouring of a Holy Spirit, which He who spake to them could alone bestow. But the very fact that some were beginning openly to speak of Him as the Prophet and the Christ, only exasperated the others. They had a small difficulty of their own creating, founded on pure ignorance of fact, but which yet to their own narrow dogmatic fancy was irresistible—"Shall Christ come out of Galilee? must He not come from Bethlehem? of David's seed?"[2]

It was during this division of opinion that the officers whom the Pharisees had dispatched to seize Jesus, returned to them without having even attempted to carry out their design. As they hovered among the Temple courts, as they stood half sheltered behind the Temple pillars, not unobserved, it may be, by Him

[1] Cf. Isa. xliii. 20; lviii. 11; lv. 1; xii. 3; and John iv. 14; vi. 35; Rev. xxii. 17. These are the *nearest* passages to "as the Scripture hath said," which must therefore be interpreted as a *general* allusion. St. Chrysostom asks, καὶ ποῦ εἶπεν ἡ γραφὴ ὅτι ποταμοὶ, κ. τ. λ.; οὐδαμοῦ. No metaphor, however, could be more intense than that offered by the longing for water in a dry and thirsty land. To see the eagerness with which men and beasts alike rush to the fountain-side after journeys in Palestine is a striking sight. The Arabs begin to sing and shout, constantly repeating the words "Snow in the sun! snow in the sun!"

[2] Micah v. 2; Isa. xi. 1; Jer. xxiii. 5, &c.

for whom they were lying in wait, they too could not fail to hear some of the divine words which flowed out of His mouth. And, hearing them, they could not fulfil their mission. A sacred spell was upon them, which they were unable to resist; a force infinitely more powerful than their own, unnerved their strength and paralysed their will. To listen to Him was not only to be disarmed in every attempt against Him, it was even to be half-converted from bitter enemies to awe-struck disciples. "Never man spake like this man," was all that they could say. That bold disobedience to positive orders must have made them afraid of the possible consequences to themselves, but obedience would have required a courage even greater, to say nothing of that rankling wound wherewith an awakened conscience ever pierces the breast of crime.

The Pharisees could only meet them with angry taunts. "What, ye too intend to accept this Prophet of the ignorant, this favourite of the accursed and miserable mob!"[1] Then Nicodemus ventured on a timid word, "Ought you not to *try*, before you condemn Him?" They had no reply to the justice of that principle: they could only fall back again on taunts—"Are you then a Galilæan?" and then the old ignorant dogmatism, "Search, and look: for out of Galilee ariseth no prophet."

Where then, as we have asked already, was Gath-hepher, whence Jonah came? where Thisbe, whence Elijah came? where Elkosh, whence Nahum came? where the northern town whence Hosea came? The more recent Jews, with better knowledge of Scripture,

[1] The ecclesiastical contempt of the Pharisees surpassed, in its habitual spirit of scorn, the worst insolence of Paganism against "the many."

declare that the Messiah *is* to come from Galilee;[1] and they settle at Tiberias, because they believe that He will rise from the waters of the Lake; and at Safed, "the city set on a hill," because they believe that He will there first fix His throne.[2] But there is no ignorance so deep as the ignorance that will not know; no blindness so incurable as the blindness which will not see. And the dogmatism of a narrow and stolid prejudice which believes itself to be theological learning is, of all others, the most ignorant and the most blind. Such was the spirit in which, ignoring the mild justice of Nicodemus, and the marvellous impression made by Jesus even on their own hostile apparitors, the majority of the Sanhedrin broke up, and went each to his own home.

[1] See Isa. ix. 1, 2, and this is asserted in the *Zohar*. See *supra*, Vol. I., p. 65.

[2] So I was assured on the shores of the Sea of Galilee.

CHAPTER XL.

THE WOMAN TAKEN IN ADULTERY.

"Thus conscience doth make cowards of us all."—SHAKESPEARE.

IN the difficulties which beset the celebrated incident which follows, it is impossible for us to arrive at any certainty as to its true position in the narrative.[1] As there must, however, be some *à priori* probability that its place was assigned with due reference to the order of events, and as there appear to be some obvious though indirect references to it in the discourses which immediately follow,[2] I shall proceed to speak of it here, feeling no shadow of a doubt that the incident really happened, even if the form in which it is preserved to us is by no means indisputably genuine.[3]

[1] John viii. 1—11. In some MSS. it is placed at the end of St. John's Gospel; in some, after Luke xxi., mainly, no doubt, because it fits on well to the verses 37, 38 in that chapter. Hitzig (*Ueber Joh. Marc.* 205) conjectured, very plausibly, that the fact which it records really belongs to Mark xii., falling in naturally between the conspiracy of the Pharisees and Herodians, and that of the Sadducees to tempt Christ—*i.e.*, between the 17th and 18th verses. In that case its order of sequence would be on the Tuesday in Passion week. On the other hand, if it has no connection with the Feast of Tabernacles, and no tinge of Johannean authorship, why should so many MSS. (including even such important ones as D, F, G) place it here?

[2] *Ex. gr.*, John viii. 15, 17, 24, 46.

[3] The whole mass of critical evidence may be seen fully treated in

At the close of the day recorded in the last chapter, Jesus withdrew to the Mount of Olives. Whether He went to the garden of Gethsemane, and to the house of

Lücke's Commentary (third edition), ii. 243—256. We may briefly summarise the grounds of its dubious genuineness by observing that (1) it is not found in some of the best and oldest MSS. (*e.g.*, ℵ, A, B, C, L); (2) nor in most of the Fathers (*e.g.*, Origen, Cyril, Chrysostom, Theophylact, Tertullian, Cyprian); (3) nor in many ancient versions (*e.g.*, Sahidic, Coptic, and Gothic); (4) in other MSS. it is marked with *obeli* and asterisks, or a space is left for it, or it is inserted elsewhere; (5) it contains an extraordinary number of various readings ("variant singula fere verba in codicibus plerisque"—Tischendorf); (6) it contains several expressions not elsewhere found in St. John; and (7) it differs widely in some respects—particularly in the *constant* use of the connecting δὲ—from the *style* of St. John throughout the rest of the Gospel. Several of these arguments are weakened—(i.) by the fact that the diversities of readings may be reduced to three main recensions; (ii.) that the rejection of the passage may have been due to a false dogmatical bias; (iii.) that the silence of some of the Fathers may be accidental, and of others prudential. The arguments in its favour are—1. It is found in some old and important uncials (D, F, G, H, K, U) and in more than 300 cursive MSS., in some of the Itala, and in the Vulgate. 2. The tendencies which led to its deliberate rejection would have rendered all but impossible its invention or interpolation. 3. It is quoted by Augustine, Ambrose, and Jerome, and treated as genuine in the Apostolic constitutions. St. Jerome's testimony (*Adv. Pelag.* ii. 6) is particularly important, because he says that in his time it was found "in multis et Graecis et Latinis codicibus"—and it must be remembered that nearly all of these must have been considerably older than any which we now possess. The main facts to be observed are, that though the dogmatic bias against the passage might be sufficient to account for its rejection, it gives us no help in explaining its want of resemblance to the style of St. John. A very simple hypothesis will account for all difficulties. If we suppose that the story of the woman accused before our Lord of many sins—to which Eusebius alludes (*H. E.* iii. 39) as existing in the Gospel of the Hebrews—is identical with this, we may suppose, without any improbability, either (i.) that St. John (as Alford hesitatingly suggests) may here have adopted a portion of current synoptic tradition, or (ii.) that the story may have been derived originally from Papias, the pupil of St. John, and having found its way into the Gospel of the Hebrews, may have been adopted gradually into some MSS. of St. John's Gospel (see Euseb. *ubi supr.*). Many recent writers adopt the suggestion of Holtzmann, that it belongs to the "Ur-marcus," or ground document of the Synoptists. Whoever embodied into the Gospels this traditionally-remembered story deserved well of the world.

its unknown but friendly owner, or whether—not having where to lay His head—He simply slept, Eastern fashion, on the green turf under those ancient olive-trees, we cannot tell; but it is interesting to trace in Him once more that dislike of crowded cities, that love for the pure, sweet, fresh air, and for the quiet of the lonely hill, which we see in all parts of His career on earth. There was, indeed, in Him nothing of that supercilious sentimentality and morbid egotism which makes men shrink from all contact with their brother-men; nor can they who would be His true servants belong to those merely fantastic philanthropists

> "Who sigh for wretchedness, yet shun the wretched,
> Nursing in some delicious solitude
> Their dainty loves and slothful sympathies."
>
> COLERIDGE, *Religious Musings.*

On the contrary, day after day, while His day-time of work continued, we find Him sacrificing all that was dearest and most elevating to His soul, and in spite of heat, and pressure, and conflict, and weariness, calmly pursuing His labours of love amid "the madding crowd's ignoble strife." But in the night-time, when men cannot work, no call of duty required His presence within the walls of Jerusalem; and those who are familiar with the oppressive foulness of ancient cities can best imagine the relief which His spirit must have felt when he could escape from the close streets and thronged bazaars, to cross the ravine, and climb the green slope beyond it, and be alone with His Heavenly Father under the starry night.

But when the day dawned His duties lay once more within the city walls, and in that part of the city where, almost alone, we hear of His presence—in the courts of His Father's house. And with the very dawn His enemies contrived a fresh plot against Him, the circumstances of which made their malice even more actually painful than it was intentionally perilous.

It is probable that the hilarity and abandonment of the Feast of Tabernacles, which had grown to be a kind of vintage festival, would often degenerate into acts of licence and immorality, and these would find more numerous opportunities in the general disturbance of ordinary life caused by the dwelling of the whole people in their little leafy booths. One such act had been detected during the previous night, and the guilty woman had been handed over to the Scribes[1] and Pharisees.

Even had the morals of the nation at that time been as clean as in the days when Moses ordained the fearful ordeal of the "water of jealousy"[2]—even had these rulers and teachers of the nation been elevated as far above their contemporaries in the real, as in the professed, sanctity of their lives—the discovery, and the threatened punishment, of this miserable adulteress could hardly have failed to move every pure and noble mind to a compassion which would have mingled largely with the horror which her sin inspired. They might, indeed, even on those suppositions, have inflicted the established penalty with a sternness as inflexible as that of the Pilgrim Fathers in the early days of Salem or Providence; but the sternness of a severe and pure-hearted judge is not a sternness which precludes all pity; it is a sternness which would not willingly inflict one

[1] It is observable that in no other passage of St. John's Gospel (though frequently in the Synoptists) are the Scribes mentioned among the enemies of Christ; but here a few MSS. read *οἱ ἀρχιερεῖς*, "the chief priests."

[2] See Numb. v. 14—29.

unnecessary pang—it is a sternness *not* incompatible with a righteous tenderness, but *wholly* incompatible with a mixture of meaner and slighter motives, *wholly* incompatible with a spirit of malignant levity and hideous sport.

But the spirit which actuated these Scribes and Pharisees was not by any means the spirit of a sincere and outraged purity. In the decadence of national life, in the daily familiarity with heathen degradations, in the gradual substitution of a Levitical scrupulosity for a heartfelt religion, the morals of the nation had grown utterly corrupt. The ordeal of the "water of jealousy" had long been abolished, and the death by stoning as a punishment for adultery had long been suffered to fall into desuetude. Not even the Scribes and Pharisees—for all their external religiosity—had any genuine horror of an impurity with which their own lives were often stained.[1] They saw in the accident which had put this guilty woman into their power nothing but a chance of annoying, entrapping, possibly even endangering this Prophet of Galilee, whom they already regarded as their deadliest enemy.

It was a curious custom among the Jews to consult distinguished Rabbis in cases of doubt and difficulty;[2] but there was no doubt or difficulty here. It was long since the Mosaic law of death to the adulteress had been demanded or enforced; and even if this had not been the case, the Roman law would, in all probability, have

[1] As is distinctly proved by the admissions of the Talmud, and by the express testimony of Josephus. In the tract *Sotah* it is clear that the Mosaic ordeal of the "water of jealousy" had fallen into practical desuetude from the commonness of the crime. We are there told that R. Johanan Ben Zakkai abolished the use of it (see Surenhusius, *Mischna*, ii. 290, 293).

[2] Sepp, *Leben Jesu*, iv. 2, 17.

prevented such a sentence from being put in execution. On the other hand, the civil and religious penalties of divorce were open to the injured husband; nor did the case of this woman differ from that of any other who had similarly transgressed. Nor, again, even if they had honestly and sincerely desired the opinion of Jesus, could there have been the slightest excuse for haling the woman herself into His presence, and thus subjecting her to a moral torture which would be rendered all the more insupportable from the close seclusion of women in the East.

And, therefore, to subject her to the superfluous horror of this odious publicity—to drag her, fresh from the agony of detection, into the sacred precincts of the Temple[1]—to subject this unveiled, dishevelled, terror-stricken woman to the cold and sensual curiosity of a malignant mob—to make her, with total disregard to her own sufferings, the mere passive instrument of their hatred against Jesus; and to do all this—not under the pressure of moral indignation, but in order to gratify a calculating malice—showed on their parts a cold, hard cynicism, a graceless, pitiless, barbarous brutality of heart and conscience, which could not but prove, in every particular, revolting and hateful to One who alone was infinitely tender, because He alone was infinitely pure.

And so they dragged her to Him, and set her in the midst—flagrant guilt subjected to the gaze of stainless Innocence, degraded misery set before the bar of perfect

[1] It is indeed said in the Talmud (*Sotah*, 1, 5) that adulteresses were to be judged at the gate of Nikanor, between the Court of the Gentiles and that of the women (Surenhusius, *Mischna*, iii. 189); but this does not apply to the mere loose asking of an opinion, such as this was.

Mercy. And then, just as though their hearts were not full of outrage, they glibly begin, with ironical deference, to set before Him their case. "Master, this woman was seized in the very act of adultery. Now, *Moses* in the Law commanded us to stone[1] *such;* but what sayest *Thou* about her?"

They thought that now they had caught Him in a dilemma. They knew the divine trembling pity which had loved where others hated, and praised where others scorned, and encouraged where others crushed; and they knew how that pity had won for Him the admiration of many, the passionate devotion of not a few. They knew that a publican was among His chosen, that sinners had sat with Him at the banquet, and harlots unreproved had bathed His feet, and listened to His words. Would He then acquit this woman, and so make Himself liable to an accusation of heresy, by placing Himself in open disaccord with the sacred and fiery Law? or, on the other hand, would He belie His own compassion, and be ruthless, and condemn? And, if He did, would He not at once shock the multitude, who were touched by His tenderness, and offend the civil magistrates by making Himself liable to a charge of sedition? How could He possibly get out of the difficulty? Either alternative—heresy or treason, accusation before the Sanhedrin or delation to the Procurator,

[1] The τὰς τοιαύτας is contemptuous; but where was the partner of her crime? The Law commanded that he too should be put to death (Lev. xx. 10). As to stoning being the proper punishment of adultery, a needless difficulty seems to have been raised (see Deut. xxii. 22—24). There is no ground whatever for concluding with Lightfoot (*Hor. Hebr.* ad loc.) that she was merely betrothed. (See Ewald, *Gesch. Christus*, 480; *Alterthümsk*, 254—268; Hitzig, *Joh. Marc.* 209.) The Rabbis say that "death," where no form of it is specified, is meant to be strangulation; but this is not the case (compare Exod. xxxi. 14 with Numb. xv. 32—35).

opposition to the orthodox or alienation from the many —would serve equally well their unscrupulous intentions. And one of these, they thought, *must* follow. What a happy chance this weak, guilty woman had given them!

Not yet. A sense of all their baseness, their hardness, their malice, their cynical parade of every feeling which pity would temper and delicacy repress, rushed over the mind of Jesus. He blushed for His nation, for His race; He blushed, not for the degradation of the miserable accused, but for the deeper guilt of her unblushing accusers.[1] Glowing with uncontrollable disgust that modes of opposition so irredeemable in their meanness should be put in play against Him, and that He should be made the involuntary centre of such a shameful scene—indignant (for it cannot be irreverent to imagine in Him an intensified degree of emotions which even the humblest of His true followers would have shared) that the sacredness of His personal reserve should thus be shamelessly violated, and that those things which belong to the sphere of a noble reticence should be thus cynically obtruded on His notice—He bent His face forwards from His seat, and as though He did not, or would not, hear them, stooped and wrote with His finger on the ground.

For any others but such as these it would have been enough. Even if they failed to see in the action a symbol of forgiveness—a symbol that the memory of things thus written in the dust might be obliterated and forgotten[2]—still any but these could hardly have failed

[1] In the Rabbinical treatise *Berachôth*, R. Papa and others are reported to have said that it is better for a man to throw himself into a furnace than to make any one blush in public, which they deduced from Gen. xxxviii. 25. (Schwab, *Berachôth*, p. 404.)

[2] Comp. Jer. xvii. 13.

to interpret the gesture into a distinct indication that in such a matter Jesus would not mix Himself.[1] But they saw nothing and understood nothing, and stood there unabashed, still pressing their brutal question, still holding, pointing to, jeering at the woman, with no compunction in their cunning glances, and no relenting in their steeled hearts.

The scene could not last any longer; and, therefore, raising Himself from His stooping attitude, He, who could read their hearts, calmly passed upon them that sad judgment involved in the memorable words—

"Let him that is without sin[2] among you, first cast the stone at her."[3]

It was not any abrogation of the Mosaic law; it was, on the contrary, an admission of its justice, and doubtless it must have sunk heavily as a death-warrant upon the woman's heart. But it acted in a manner wholly unexpected. The terrible law stood written; it was not the time, it was not His will, to rescind it. But, on the other hand, they themselves, by not acting on the law, by referring the whole question to Him as though it needed a new solution, had practically confessed that the law was at present valid in theory alone, that it had fallen into desuetude, and that even with His authority they had no intention of carrying it into action. Since, therefore, the whole proceeding was on their part illegal and irregular, He transfers it by these words from the forum of law to that of conscience. The judge may sometimes be obliged to condemn the criminal brought before

[1] It seems to have been well understood. See Wetstein *ad loc.*

[2] *i.e.* free from the taint of this class of sins. Cf. Luke vii. 37.

[3] πρῶτος τὸν λίθον (E, G, H, K, &c.). Cf. Deut. xvii. 7. (Surenhusius, *Mischna*, iv. 235.)

him for sins of which he has himself been guilty, but the position of the self-constituted accuser who eagerly demands a needless condemnation is very different. Herein to condemn her would have been in God's sight most fatally to have condemned themselves; to have been the first to cast the stone at her would have been to crush themselves.

He had but glanced at them for a moment, but that glance had read their inmost souls. He had but calmly spoken a few simple words, but those words, like the still small voice to Elijah at Horeb, had been more terrible than wind or earthquake. They had fallen like a spark of fire upon slumbering souls, and lay burning there till "the blushing, shame-faced spirit" mutinied within them. The Scribes and Pharisees stood silent and fearful; they loosed their hold upon the woman; their insolent glances, so full of guile and malice, fell guiltily to the ground. They who had unjustly inflicted, now justly felt the overwhelming anguish of an intolerable shame, while over their guilty consciences there rolled, in crash on crash of thunder, such thoughts as these:— "Therefore thou art inexcusable, O man, whosoever thou art that judgest: for wherein thou judgest another, thou condemnest thyself: for thou that judgest doest the same things. But we are sure that the judgment of God is according to truth against them which commit such things. And thinkest thou this, O man, that judgest them which do such things and doest the same, that thou shalt escape the judgment of God? or despisest thou the riches of His goodness, and forbearance, and long-suffering; not knowing that the goodness of God leadeth thee to repentance? but after thy hardness and impenitent heart treasurest up to thyself wrath against the day of wrath and revelation of the righteous judgment of God, who will render to every man according to his deeds." They were "*such*" as the woman they had condemned, and they dared not stay.

And so, with burning cheeks and cowed hearts, from the eldest to the youngest, one by one gradually, silently they slunk away. He would not add to their shame and confusion of face by watching them: He had no wish further to reveal His knowledge of the impure secrets of their hearts; He would not tempt them to brazen it out before Him, and to lie against the testimony of their own memories; He had stooped down once more, and was writing on the ground.[1]

And when He once more raised His head, all the accusers had melted away: only the woman still cowered before Him on the Temple-floor. She, too, *might* have gone: none hindered her, and it might have seemed but natural that she should fly anywhere to escape her danger, and to hide her guilt and shame. But remorse, and, it may be, an awful trembling gratitude, in which hope struggled with despair, fixed her there before her Judge. His look, the most terrible of all to meet, because it was the only look that fell on her from a soul robed in the unapproachable majesty of a stainless innocence, was at the same time the most gentle, and the most forgiving. Her stay was a sign of her penitence; her penitence, let us trust, a certain pledge of her future forgiveness. "Two things," as St. Augustine finely says, "were here left alone together—Misery and Mercy."

[1] The MS. U (the Cod. Nanianus in St. Mark's at Venice) has here the curious reading ἔγραψεν εἰς τὴν γῆν ἑνὸς ἑκάστου αὐτῶν τὰς ἁμαρτίας—"He wrote on the ground the sins of each one of them;" which shows how early began the impossible and irrelevant surmises as to *what* He wrote. This is the only passage where Christ is said to have written anything.

"Woman," He asked, "where are those thine accusers? did no one convict thee?"

"No man, Lord." It was the only answer which her lips could find power to frame; and then she received the gracious yet heart-searching permission to depart—

"Neither do I convict thee. Go; henceforth sin no more."[1]

Were the critical evidence against the genuineness of this passage far more overwhelming than it is, it would yet bear upon its surface the strongest possible proof of its own authentic truthfulness. It is hardly too much to say that the mixture which it displays of tragedy and of tenderness—the contrast which it involves between low, cruel cunning, and exalted nobility of intellect and emotion—transcends all power of human imagination to have invented it; while the picture of a divine insight reading the inmost secrets of the heart, and a yet diviner love, which sees those inmost secrets with larger eyes than ours, furnish us with a conception of Christ's power and person at once too lofty and too original to have been founded on anything but fact. No one could have invented, for few could even appreciate, the sovereign purity and ineffable charm—the serene authority of condemnation, and of pardon—by which the story is so deeply characterised. The repeated instances in which, without a moment's hesitation, He foiled the crafty designs of His enemies, and in foiling them taught for ever some eternal principle of thought and action, are among the most unique and decisive

[1] "Convict" is perhaps better than "condemn" (which means "convict and sentence") here. Perhaps ἡ γυνὴ, the less direct address, is better than γύναι. After μηκέτι I read ἀπὸ τοῦ νῦν with D, omitting καὶ. But every variation of reading is uncertain in this paragraph.

proofs of His more than human wisdom; and yet not one of those gleams of sacred light which were struck from Him by collision with the malice or hate of man was brighter or more beautiful than this. The very fact that the narrative found so little favour in the early centuries of Church history[1]—the fact that whole Churches regarded the narrative as dangerous in its tendency[2]—the fact that eminent Fathers of the Church either ignore it, or speak of it in a semi-apologetic tone—in these facts we see the most decisive proof that its real moral and meaning are too transcendent to admit of its having been originally invented, or interpolated without adequate authority into the sacred text. Yet it is strange that any should have failed to see that in the ray of mercy which thus streamed from heaven upon the wretched sinner, the sin assumed an aspect tenfold more heinous, tenfold more repulsive to the conscience of mankind—to every conscience which accepts it as a law of life that it should strive to be holy as God is holy, and pure as He is pure.

However painful this scene must have been to the holy and loving heart of the Saviour, it was at least alleviated by the sense of that compassionate deliverance—deliverance, we may trust, for Eternity, no less than Time—which it had wrought for one guilty soul. But the scenes that followed were a climax of perpetual

[1] St. Augustine (*De Conjug. Adult.* ii. 6) says that some people of weak faith removed the paragraph from their MSS., "quasi permissionem peccandi tribuerit Qui dixit Deinceps noli peccare."—St. Ambrose too says that "non mediocrem scrupulum movere potuit imperitis." (*Apol. David*, ii. 1.)

[2] The Patriarch Nikon (in the tenth century) distinctly says that the passage had been expunged from the Armenian Version because it was thought pernicious for the majority (βλαβερὰν τοῖς πολλοῖς). Bishop Wordsworth thinks that the extreme severity of the Eastern Church against adultery facilitated the rejection of the passage by them.

misunderstandings, fluctuating impressions, and bitter taunts, which caused the great and joyous festival to end with a sudden burst of rage, and an attempt of the Jewish leaders to make an end of Him—not by public accusation, but by furious violence.

For, on the same day—the *eighth* day of the feast if the last narrative has got displaced, the day *after* the feast if it belongs to the true sequence of events—Jesus continued those interrupted discourses which were intended almost for the last time to set clearly before the Jewish nation His divine claims.

He was seated at that moment in the Treasury—either some special building[1] in the Temple so called, or that part of the court of the women which contained the thirteen chests with trumpet-shaped openings—called *shopheróth*—into which the people, and especially the Pharisees, used to cast their gifts. In this court, and therefore close beside Him, were two gigantic candelabra, fifty cubits high and sumptuously gilded,[2] on the summit of which, nightly, during the Feast of Tabernacles, lamps were lit which shed their soft light over all the city. Round these lamps the people, in their joyful enthusiasm, and even the stateliest Priests and Pharisees, joined in festal dances, while, to the sound of flutes and other music, the Levites, drawn up in array on the fifteen steps which led up to the court, chanted the beautiful Psalms which early received the title of "Songs of Degrees."[3]

In allusion to these great lamps, on which some

[1] Jos. *Antt.* xix. 6, § 1. Compare Luke xxi. 1; Mark xii. 41.

[2] Pictures of these colossal lamps are given in Surenhusius's *Mischna*, ii. 260. The wicks of the four lamps which stood on each candelabrum were made of the cast-off clothes of the priests.

[3] Ps. cxx.—cxxxiv.

circumstance of the moment may have concentrated the attention of the hearers, Christ exclaimed to them, "I am the Light of the world." It was His constant plan to shape the illustrations of His discourses by those external incidents which would rouse the deepest attention, and fix the words most indelibly on the memories of His hearers. The Pharisees who heard His words charged Him with idle self-glorification; but He showed them that He had His Father's testimony, and that even were it not so, the Light can only be seen, only be known, by the evidence of its own existence; without it, neither itself nor anything else is visible.[1] They asked Him, "Where is Thy Father?" He told them that, not knowing *Him*, they *could* not know His Father; and then He once more sadly warned them that His departure was nigh, and that *then* they would be unable to come to Him. Their only reply was a taunting inquiry whether, by committing suicide, He meant to plunge Himself in the darkest regions of the grave?[2] Nay, He made them understand, it was *they*, not *He*, who were from below—*they*, not He, who were destined, if they persisted in unbelief of His eternal existence, to that dark end. "Who art thou?" they once more asked, in angry and faithless perplexity. "Altogether that which I am telling you,"[3] He calmly

[1] "Testimonium sibi perhibet lux: . . . sibi ipsa testis est, ut cognoscatur lux." (Aug.)

[2] See Jos. *B. Jud.* iii. 8, § 5, *τούτων μὲν ἅδης δέχεται τὰς ψυχὰς σκοτιώτερος.*

[3] John viii. 25, *τὴν ἀρχὴν ὅτι καὶ λαλῶ ὑμῖν.* A vast number of renderings have been proposed for this text. Some may be rejected at once—as Lücke's, "To begin with, why do I even speak to you?" and Meyer's, "Do ye ask what I say to you at the first?" That of De Wette, Stier, Alford, &c., is "*Essentially that which I speak*"—*i.e.*, My *being* is My *revelation*—*I am the Word.* The objection to the rendering in our English version is that it makes *λαλῶ*, "*I am speaking*," equivalent to *ἔλεξα*, "I said;" but, on

answered. They wanted Him to announce Himself as the Messiah, and so become their temporal deliverer; but He will only tell them the far deeper, more eternal truths, that He is the Light, and the Life, and the Living Water, and that He came from the Father—as they, too, should know when they had lifted Him up upon the cross. They were looking solely for the Messiah of the Jews: He would have them know Him as the Redeemer of the world, the Saviour of their souls.

As they heard Him speak, many, even of these fierce enemies, were won over to a belief in Him: but it was a wavering belief, a half belief, a false belief, a belief mingled with a thousand worldly and erroneous fancies, not a belief which had in it any saving power, or on which He could rely. And He put it to an immediate test, which revealed its hollowness, and changed it into mad hatred. He told them that faithfulness and obedience were the marks of true discipleship, and the requisites of true freedom. The word freedom acted as a touchstone to show the spuriousness of their incipient faith. *They* knew of no freedom but that political free-

the other hand, we never elsewhere find Christ using such an expression as "I *am* that which I *speak*." The same objection applies to the interpretation of Augustine and others, "I am, what I am saying to you, *The Beginning*" (Rev. xxi. 6; xxii. 13; 1 John ii. 13). Lange seems to me to be right in rendering it "To start with (or, 'in the first place'), that which I represent Myself as being." Mr. Monro suggests to me the view that the question of the Jews, Σὺ τίς εἶ, evidently refers to the mysterious ἐγώ εἰμι of the previous verse (ver. 24). Treating the question as virtually an interruption, Jesus tells them (ver. 28) that they should not understand the ἐγώ εἰμι till a later experience; but returning to λόγος and λαλῶ (vv. 37, 38, 40, 43) gives a hint as to the ἐγώ εἰμι in 44, 47, and a yet fuller answer in 57, 58; yet not so full or clear as in ix. 37. On this view viii. 25 might perhaps mean, "I will tell you first of all *what I say*."

dom which they falsely asserted; they resented the promise of future spiritual freedom in lieu of the achievement of present national freedom. So Jesus showed them that they were still the slaves of sin, and in name only, not in reality, the children of Abraham, or the children of God. They were absorbed with pride when they thought of the purity of their ancestral origin, and the privilege of their exclusive monotheism;[1] but He told them that in very truth they were, by spiritual affinity, the affinity of cruelty and falsehood,[2] children of him who was a liar and a murderer from the beginning—children of the devil.[3] That home-rebuke stung them to fury. They repaid it by calling Jesus a Samaritan, and a demoniac.[4] Our Lord gently put the taunt aside, and once more held out to them the gracious promise that if they will but keep His sayings, they not only shall not die in their sins, but shall not see death. Their dull, blind hearts could not even imagine a spiritual meaning in His words. They could only charge Him with demoniac arrogance and insolence in making Himself greater than Abraham and the prophets, of whom *they* could

[1] Alike the Bible and the Talmud abound in proofs of the intense national arrogance with which the Jews regarded their religion and their descent.

[2] John viii. 44. Untruthfulness seems to have been in all ages a failing of the Jewish national character. "Listen to all, but *believe no one—not even me*," said the Hebrew poet Sapir to Dr. Frankl (*Jews in the East*, E. Tr., ii. 11).

[3] I am aware that some make Jesus call the Jews not "children," but "*brethren* of the devil," translating τοῦ πατρὸς τοῦ διαβόλου (ver. 44), of "the father of the devil," and rendering the end of verse 44 "*he* is a liar, and his father too;" but I do not understand this demonology.

[4] John viii. 48, "Thou art a Samaritan" (what intense national hatred breathes in the words!), "and hast a demon." Similarly the Arabs attribute all madness to evil spirits (δαιμονᾶς = *Medjnoun enté*). (Renan, *Vie de Jésus*, 272.)

only think as dead.[1] Jesus told them that in prophetic vision, perhaps too by spiritual intuition, in that other world, Abraham, who was not dead, but living, saw and rejoiced to see His day. Such an assertion appeared to them either senseless or blasphemous. "Abraham has been dead for seventeen centuries; Thou art not even fifty[2] years old; how are we to understand such words as these?" Then very gently, but with great solemnity, and with that formula of asseveration which He only used when He announced His most solemn truths, the Saviour revealed to them His eternity, His Divine pre-existence before He had entered the tabernacle of mortal flesh:

"Verily, verily I say unto you, Before Abraham came into existence, I am."[3]

Then, with a burst of impetuous fury—one of those

[1] Luke xvi. 22; Matt. xxii. 32.

[2] In some valueless MSS. this is quite needlessly corrected into "forty." It is strange that modern writers like Gfrörer should have revived the mistaken inference of Irenæus from this verse that Jesus lived fifty years on earth. The belief that He died at the age of thirty-three may be regarded as nearly certain, and it cannot even be safely conjectured from this passage either that the sorrows of His lot had marred His visage, or that the deep seriousness of His expression made Him appear older than He was. It is obvious that the Jews are speaking generally, and in round numbers: "*Thou hast not yet reached even the full years of manhood,* and hast *Thou* seen Abraham?"

[3] John viii. 58, *πρὶν Ἀβραὰμ γενέσθαι, ἐγὼ εἰμι.* There could be no more distinct assertion of His divine nature. I have pointed out elsewhere that those who deny this must either prove that He never spoke those words, or must believe that He—the most lowly and sinless and meek-hearted of men—was guilty of a colossal and almost phrenetic intoxication of vanity and arrogance. For the Jews, more intensely than any other nation which the world has ever known, recognised the infinite transcendence of God, and therefore for a Jew, *being merely man,* to claim Divinity, would not only be inconsistent with ordinary sense and virtue, but inconsistent with anything *but sheer blasphemous insanity.* See the Author's Hulsean Lectures, *The Witness of History to Christ,* p. 85.

paroxysms of sudden, uncontrollable, frantic rage to which this people has in all ages been liable upon any collision with its religious convictions—they took up stones to stone Him.[1] But the very blindness of their rage made it more easy to elude them. His hour was not yet come. With perfect calmness He departed unhurt out of the Temple.

[1] The unfinished state of the Temple buildings would supply them with huge stones close at hand.

CHAPTER XLI.

THE MAN BORN BLIND.

"He from thick films shall purge the visual ray,
And on the sightless eyeball pour the day."—POPE.

EITHER on His way from the Temple, after this attempted assault, or on the next ensuing Sabbath,[1] Jesus, as He passed by, saw a man blind from his birth, who, perhaps, announced his miserable condition as he sat begging by the roadside, and at the Temple gate.[2]

All the Jews were trained to regard special suffering as the necessary and immediate consequence of special sin. Perhaps the disciples supposed that the words of our Lord to the paralytic whom He had healed at the Pool of Bethesda, as well as to the paralytic at Capernaum, might seem to sanction such an impression. They asked, therefore, how this man came to be born blind. Could it be in consequence of the sins of his parents? If not, was there any way of supposing that it could have been for his own? The supposition in

[1] It is impossible to decide between these alternatives. If it was on the *same* Sabbath, the extreme calmness of our Lord, immediately after circumstances of such intense excitement, would be very noticeable. In either case the narrative implies that the ebullition of homicidal fury against Him was transient.

[2] John v. 14.

the former case seemed hard; in the latter, impossible.[1] They were therefore perplexed.

Into the unprofitable regions of such barren speculation our Lord refused to follow them, and He declined, as always, the tendency to infer and to sit in judgment upon the sins of others. Neither the man's sins, He told them, nor those of his parents, had caused that lifelong affliction; but now, by means of it,[2] the works of God should be made manifest. He, the Light of the world, must for a short time longer dispel its darkness. Then He spat on the ground, made clay with the spittle, and smearing it on the blind man's eyes, bade him "go wash in the Pool of Siloam."[3] The blind man went, washed, and was healed.

[1] Exod. xx. 5. We can hardly imagine that those simple-minded Galilæans were familiar with the doctrine of metempsychosis (Jos. *Antt.* xviii. 1, § 3; *B. J.* ii. 8, § 14); or the Rabbinic dogma of ante-natal sin; or the Platonic and Alexandrian fancy of pre-existence; or the modern conception of proleptic punishment for sins anticipated by foreknowledge.

[2] The Greek idiom does not here imply, as its literal English equivalent appears to do, that the man had been born blind solely *in order* that God's glory might be manifested in his healing. The ἵνα expresses a *consequence,* not a *purpose*—it has, technically speaking, a *metabatic,* not a *telic* force. This was pointed out long ago by Chrysostom and Theophylact, and Glassius in his valuable *Philolog. Sacr.*, pp. 529, 530, gives many similar instances—*e.g.*, Rom. iii. 4; v. 20; and comp. John xi. 4; xii. 40. It would, however, carry me too far if I attempted to enter into the subject further here.

[3] "Which," adds St. John—or *possibly* a very ancient gloss—"means Sent." It is found in all MSS., but not in the Persian and Syriac versions. The remark is rather *allusive* than *etymological,* and connects the name of the fountain with the name of the Messiah; but the possible grammatical accuracy of the reference seems now to be admitted. (See Neander, *Life of Christ,* p. 199; Ebrard, *Gosp. Hist.*, p. 317; Hitzig, *Isaiah,* 97.) Justin Martyr (*Dial. c. Tryph.* 63, p. 81) refers to the Messiah as ἀπόστολος, perhaps with a view to Isa. viii. 6. The fact that "the waters of Siloah that flow softly" were supposed, like those of other intermittent springs near Jerusalem, to have a healing power, would help the man's faith. Even Mohammedans say that "Zemzem and Siloah are the two fountains of Paradise."

The saliva of one who had not recently broken his fast was believed among the ancients to have a healing efficacy in cases of weak eyes, and clay was occasionally used to repress tumours on the eyelids.[1] But that these instruments in no way detracted from the splendour of the miracle is obvious; and we have no means of deciding in this, any more than in the parallel instances, why our Lord, who sometimes healed by a word, preferred at other times to adopt slow and more elaborate methods of giving effect to His supernatural power. In this matter He never revealed the principles of action which doubtless arose from His inner knowledge of the circumstances, and from His insight into the hearts of those on whom His cures were wrought. Possibly He had acted with the express view of teaching more than one eternal lesson by the incidents which followed.

At any rate, in this instance, His mode of action led to serious results. For the man had been well known in Jerusalem as one who had been a blind beggar all his life, and his appearance with the use of his eyesight caused a tumult of excitement. Scarcely could those who had known him best believe even his own testimony, that he was indeed the blind beggar with whom they had been so familiar. They were lost in amazement, and made him repeat again and again the story of his cure. But that story infused into their astonishment a fresh element of Pharisaic indignation; for this cure also had been wrought on a Sabbath day. The Rabbis had

[1] See Suet. *Vesp.* 7; Tac. *Hist.* iv. 8; Plin. *H. N.* xxviii. 7; and other classical passages quoted by Wetstein and subsequent commentators. Such indications as that of St. John are, under these circumstances, an invaluable mark of truth; for what mythopœic imagination, intent only on glorifying its object, would invent particulars which might be regarded as depreciatory?

forbidden any man to smear even one of his eyes with spittle on the Sabbath, except in cases of mortal danger. Jesus had not only smeared *both* the man's eyes, but had actually mingled the saliva with clay! This, as an act of mercy, was in the deepest and most inward accordance with the very causes for which the Sabbath had been ordained, and the very lessons of which it was meant to be a perpetual witness. But the spirit of narrow literalism and slavish minuteness and quantitative obedience—the spirit that hoped to be saved by the algebraical sum of good and bad actions—had long degraded the Sabbath from the true idea of its institution into a pernicious superstition. The Sabbath of Rabbinism, with all its petty servility, was in no respect the Sabbath of God's loving and holy law. It had degenerated into that which St. Paul calls it, a *πτωχικὸν στοιχεῖον*, or "beggarly element."[1]

And these Jews were so imbued with this utter littleness, that a unique miracle of mercy awoke in them less of astonishment and gratitude than the horror kindled by a neglect of their Sabbatical superstition. Accordingly, in all the zeal of letter-worshipping religionism, they led off the man to the Pharisees in council. Then followed the scene which St. John has recorded in a manner so inimitably graphic in his ninth chapter. First came the repeated inquiry, "how the thing had been done?" followed by the repeated assertion of some of them that Jesus could not be from God, because He had not observed the Sabbath; and the reply of others that to press the Sabbath-breaking was to admit the miracle, and to admit the miracle was to establish the fact that He who performed it could not be the criminal

[1] Gal. iv. 9.

whom the others described. Then, being completely at a standstill, they asked the blind man *his* opinion of his deliverer; and he—not being involved in their vicious circle of reasoning—replied with fearless promptitude, "He is a Prophet."[1]

By this time they saw the kind of nature with which they had to deal, and anxious for any loophole by which they could deny or set aside the miracle, they sent for the man's parents. "Was this their son? If they asserted that he had been born blind, how was it that he now saw?" Perhaps they hoped to browbeat or to bribe these parents into a denial of their relationship, or an admission of imposture; but the parents also clung to the plain truth, while, with a certain Judaic servility and cunning, they refused to draw any inferences which would lay them open to unpleasant consequences. "This is certainly our son, and he was certainly born blind; as to the rest, we know nothing. Ask him. He is quite capable of answering for himself."

Then—one almost pities their sheer perplexity—they turned to the blind man again. He, as well as his parents, knew that the Jewish authorities had agreed to pronounce the *cherem*, or ban of exclusion from the synagogue, on any one who should venture to acknowledge Jesus as the Messiah; and the Pharisees probably hoped that he would be content to follow their advice, to give glory to God,[2] *i.e.*, deny or ignore the

[1] And the Jews themselves went so far as to say that "if a prophet of undoubted credentials should command all persons to light fires on the Sabbath day, arm themselves for war, kill the inhabitants, &c., it would behove all to rise up without delay and execute all that he should direct without scruple or hesitation." (Maimonides, *Porta Mosis*, p. 29 [Pocock]; Allen's *Mod. Judaism*, p. 26.)

[2] "As if they would bind him to the strictest truthfulness" (Lange, iii.

miracle, and to accept their dictum that Jesus was a sinner.

But the man was made of sturdier stuff than his parents. He was not to be overawed by their authority, or knocked down by their assertions. He breathed quite freely in the halo-atmosphere of their superior sanctity. "*We know*," the Pharisees had said, "that this man is a sinner." "Whether He is a sinner," the man replied, "*I* do *not* know; *one thing I do know*, that, being blind, now I see." Then they began again their weary and futile cross-examination. "What did He do to thee? *how* did He open thine eyes?" But the man had had enough of this. "I told you once, and ye did not attend. Why do ye wish to hear again? Is it possible that ye too wish to be His disciples?" Bold irony this—to ask these stately, ruffled, scrupulous Sanhedrists, whether he was really to regard them as anxious and sincere inquirers about the claims of the Nazarene Prophet! Clearly here was a man whose presumptuous honesty would neither be bullied into suppression nor corrupted into a lie. He was quite impracticable. So, since authority, threats, blandishments had all failed, they broke into abuse. "*Thou* art His disciple: *we* are the disciples of Moses; of *this* man we know nothing." "Strange," he replied, "that *you* should know nothing of a man who yet has wrought a miracle such as not even Moses ever wrought; and we know that neither He nor any one else could have done

335). "The words are an adjuration to tell the truth (comp. Josh. vii. 19)," says Dean Alford; but he seems to confuse it with a phrase like *Al-hamdu lillâh*, "to God be the praise" (of your care), which is a different thing, and would require τὴν δόξαν. A friend refers me to 2 Cor. xi. 31 for a similar adjuration; cf. Rom. ix. 1, 5.

it, unless He were from God."[1] What! shades of Hillel and of Shammai! was a mere blind beggar, a natural ignorant heretic, altogether born in sins, to be teaching *them!* Unable to control any longer their transport of indignation, they flung him out of the hall, and out of the synagogue.

But Jesus did not neglect His first confessor. He, too, in all probability had, either at this or some previous time, been placed under the ban of lesser excommunication, or exclusion from the synagogue;[2] for we scarcely ever again read of His re-entering any of those synagogues which, during the earlier years of His ministry, had been His favourite places of teaching and resort. He sought out and found the man, and asked him, "Dost *thou* believe on the Son of God?" "Why,[3] who is He, Lord," answered the man, "that I should believe on Him?"

"Thou hast both seen Him, and it is He who talketh with thee."[4]

[1] There is no healing of the blind in the Old Testament, or in the Acts.

[2] It is true that this mildest form of excommunication (*nezîphah*) was only temporary, for thirty days; and that it applied to only one synagogue. But if it were once pronounced, the time could easily be extended, so as to make it a *niddouî* (נִדּוּי) for ninety days, and the decree be adopted by other synagogues (Gfrörer, *Jahrh. d. Heils*, i. 183). Exclusion from the synagogue did not, however, involve exclusion from the Temple, where *a separate door* was provided for the excommunicate. The last stage of excommunication was the *cherem* or *shammatta*, which was as bad as the Roman *interdictio ignis et aquae.* The Jews declare that Joshua Ben Perachiah had been the teacher of Jesus, and excommunicated Him to the blast of 400 rams'-horns. (Wagenseil, *Sota*, p. 1057.) But this Joshuah Ben Perachiah lived in the reign of Alexander Jannæus, who died B.C. 79!

[3] καὶ τίς ἐστι (John ix. 36). The καὶ as often indicates a question full of surprise and emotion. See Jelf's *Greek Syntax*, § 759. Cf. Mark x. 26 (καί τις δύναται σωθῆναι; "Who *then* can be saved?"); Luke x. 29; 2 Cor. ii. 2.)

[4] Professor Westcott points out the striking fact that this spontaneous

"Lord, I believe," he answered; and he did Him reverence.

It must have been shortly after this time that our Lord pointed the contrast between the different effects of His teaching—they who saw not, made to see; and those who saw, made blind. The Pharisees, ever restlessly and discontentedly hovering about Him, and in their morbid egotism always on the look-out for some reflection on themselves, asked "if they too were blind." The answer of Jesus was, that in natural blindness there would have been no guilt, but to those who only stumbled in the blindness of wilful error a claim to the possession of sight was a self-condemnation.

And when the leaders, the teachers, the guides were blind, how could the people see?

The thought naturally led Him to the nature of true and false teachers, which He expanded and illustrated in the beautiful apologue—half parable, half allegory—of the True and the False Shepherds. He told them that He was the Good Shepherd,[1] who laid down His life for the sheep; while the hireling shepherds, flying from danger, betrayed their flocks. He, too, was that door of the sheepfold, by which all His true predecessors alone had entered, while all the false—from the first thief who had climbed into God's fold—had broken in some other way. And then He told them that of His own

revelation to the outcast from the synagogue *finds its only parallel* in the similar revelation (John iv. 26) to the outcast from the nation" (*Characteristics of the Gosp. Miracles*, p. 61).

[1] Speaking of this allegory, Mr. Sanday points out the circumstance that the only other allegory in the Gospels is in John xv. "The Synoptists have no allegories as distinct from parables. The fourth Evangelist no parables as a special form of allegory" (*Fourth Gospel*, p. 167). As the phrase is ὁ ποιμὴν ὁ καλὸς, not ἀγαθὸς, perhaps it had better be rendered "*true* shepherd," rather than "good." But καλὸς is untranslateable.

free will He would lay down His life for the sheep, both of this and of His other flocks,[1] and that of His own power He would take it again. But all these divine mysteries were more than they could understand; and while some declared that they were the nonsense of one who had a devil and was mad, others could only plead that they were not like the words of one who had a devil, and that a devil could not have opened the eyes of the blind.

Thus, with but little fruit for them, save the bitter fruit of anger and hatred, ended the visit of Jesus to the Feast of Tabernacles. And since His very life was now in danger, He withdrew once more from Jerusalem to Galilee, for one brief visit before He bade to His old home His last farewell.

[1] In John x. 16, there is an unfortunate obliteration of the distinction between the αὐλή, "fold," and ποίμνη, "flock," of the original.

CHAPTER XLII.

FAREWELL TO GALILEE.

"I see that all things come to an end: but thy commandment is exceeding broad."—Ps. cxix. 96.

IMMEDIATELY after the events just recorded, St. John narrates another incident which took place two months subsequently, at the winter Feast of Dedication.[1] In accordance with the main purpose of his Gospel, which was to narrate that work of the Christ in Judæa, and especially in Jerusalem, which the Synoptists had omitted, he says nothing of an intermediate and final visit to Galilee, or of those last journeys to Jerusalem respecting parts of which the other Evangelists supply us with so many details. And yet that Jesus must have returned to Galilee is clear, not only from the other Evangelists, but also from the nature of the case and from certain incidental facts in the narrative of St. John himself.[2]

[1] John x. 22—42. The Feast of Tabernacles was at the end of September or early in October. The Dedication was on December 20.

[2] See John x. 25 (which evidently refers to His last discourse to them two months before) and 40 ("again"). Besides, the expression of John x. 22, "And it was the Dedication at Jerusalem," would have little meaning if a new visit were not implied; and those words are perhaps added for the very reason that the Dedication might be kept anywhere else.

It is well known that the whole of one great section in St. Luke—from ix. 51 to xviii. 15—forms an episode in the Gospel narrative of which many incidents are narrated by this Evangelist alone, and in which the few identifications of time and place all point to one slow and solemn progress from Galilee to Jerusalem (ix. 51; xiii. 22; xvii. 11; x. 38). Now *after* the Feast of Dedication our Lord retired into Peræa, until He was summoned thence by the death of Lazarus (John x. 40—42; xi. 1—46); after the resurrection of Lazarus, He fled to Ephraim (xi. 54); and He did not leave His retirement at Ephraim until He went to Bethany, six days before His final Passover (xii. 1).

This great journey, therefore, from Galilee to Jerusalem, so rich in occasions which called forth some of His most memorable utterances, must have been either a journey to the Feast of Tabernacles or to the Feast of Dedication. That it *could* not have been the former may be regarded as settled, not only on other grounds, but decisively because that was a *rapid* and a *secret* journey, this an eminently public and leisurely one.

Almost every inquirer seems to differ to a greater or less degree as to the exact sequence and chronology of the events which follow. Without entering into minute and tedious disquisitions where absolute certainty is impossible, I will narrate this period of our Lord's life in the order which, after repeated study of the Gospels, appears to me to be the most probable, and in the separate details of which I have found myself again and again confirmed by the conclusions of other independent inquirers. And here I will only premise my conviction—

1. That the episode of St. Luke up to xviii. 30,

mainly refers to a single journey, although unity of subject, or other causes, may have led the sacred writer to weave into his narrative some events or utterances which belong to an earlier or later epoch.[1]

2. That the order of the facts narrated even by St. Luke alone is not,[2] and does not in any way claim to be,[3] strictly chronological; so that the place of any event in the narrative by no means necessarily indicates its true position in the order of time.

3. That this journey is identical with that which is partially recorded in Matt. xviii. 1—xx. 16; Mark x. 1—31.

4. That (as seems obvious from internal evidence[4]) the events narrated in Matt. xx. 17—28; Mark x. 32—45; Luke xviii. 31—34, belong not to this journey, but to the *last* which Jesus ever took—the journey from *Ephraim* to Bethany and Jerusalem.

Assuming these conclusions to be justified—and I

[1] *E.g.*, ix. 57—62 (cf. Matt. viii. 19—22); xi. 1—13 (cf. Matt. vi. 9—15; vii. 7—12); xi. 14—26 (cf. Matt. ix. 32—35); xi. 29—xii. 59 (compared with parts of the Sermon on the Mount, &c.). Of course the dull and recklessly adopted hypothesis of a constant repetition of *incidents* may here come in to support the preconceived notions of some harmonists; but it is an hypothesis mainly founded on a false and unscriptural view of inspiration, and one which must not be adopted without the strongest justification. The occasional repetition of *discourses* is a much more natural supposition, and one inherently probable from the circumstances of the case.

[2] *E.g.*, x. 38—42; xiii. 31—35; xvii. 11—19.

[3] The notes of time and place throughout are of the vaguest possible character, evidently because the form of the narrative is here determined by other considerations (see x. 1, 25, 38; xi. 1, 14; xii. 1, 22; xiii. 6, 22; xiv. 1; xvii. 12, &c.). There seems to be *no ground whatever* for supposing that St. Luke meant to claim absolute chronological *accuracy* by the expression, *παρηκολουθηκότι ἀκριβῶς*, in i. 3; and indeed it seems clear from a study of his Gospel that, though he followed the historical sequence as far as he was able to do so, he often groups events and discourses by spiritual and subjective considerations.

[4] See, among other passages, Mark x. 17; Matt. xix. 16.

believe that they will commend themselves as at least probable to any who really study the data of the problem—we naturally look to see if there are any incidents which can only be referred to this last residence of Jesus in Galilee after the Feast of Tabernacles. The sojourn must have been a very brief one, and seems to have had no other object than that of preparing for the Mission of the Seventy, and inaugurating the final proclamation of Christ's kingdom throughout all that part of the Holy Land which had as yet been least familiar with His word and works. His instructions to the Seventy involved His last farewell to Galilee, and the delivery of those instructions synchronised, in all probability, with His actual departure. But there are two other incidents recorded in the 13th chapter, which probably belong to the same brief sojourn—namely, the news of a Galilæan massacre, and the warning which He received of Herod's designs against His life.

The home of Jesus during these few last days would naturally be at Capernaum, His own city; and while He was there organising a solemn departure to which there would be no return, there were some who came and announced to Him a recent instance of those numerous disturbances which marked the Procuratorship of Pontius Pilate. Of the particular event to which they alluded nothing further is known; and that a few turbulent zealots should have been cut down at Jerusalem by the Roman garrison was too common-place an event in these troublous times to excite more than a transient notice. There were probably hundreds of such outbreaks of which Josephus has preserved no record. The inflammable fanaticism of the Jews at this epoch—the restless hopes which were constantly kindling them to fury against the Roman Governor,[1] and which made them the ready dupes of every false Messiah—had necessitated the construction of the Tower of Antonia, which flung its threatening shadow over the Temple itself. This Tower communicated with the Temple by a flight of steps, so that the Roman legionaries could rush down at once, and suppress any of the disturbances which then, as now, endangered the security of Jerusalem at the recurrence of every religious feast.[2] And of all the Jews, the Galilæans, being the most passionately turbulent and excitable, were the most likely to suffer in such collisions. Indeed, the main fact which seems in this instance to have struck the narrators, was not so much the actual massacre as the horrible incident that the blood of these murdered rioters had been actually mingled with the red streams that flowed from the victims they had been offering in sacrifice.[3] And those who brought the news to Christ did so, less with any desire to complain of the sanguinary boldness of the Roman Governor, than with a curiosity

[1] Acts xxi. 34. Three thousand Jews had been massacred by Archelaus in one single Paschal disturbance thirty years before this time; and on one occasion Pilate had actually disguised his soldiers as peasants, and sent them to use their daggers freely among the mob. (See Jos. *Antt.* xvii. 9, § 3; 10, § 2; xviii. 3, § 1; *B. J.* ii. 9, § 4.)

[2] The Turkish Government have, with considerable astuteness, fixed the annual pilgrimage of Mohammedans to the *Tomb* of the Prophet Moses (!) at the very time when the return of Easter inundates Jerusalem with Christian pilgrims. I met hundreds of these servants of the Prophet in the environs of the Sacred City during the Easter of 1870, and they would be a powerful assistance to the Turks in case of any Christian outbreak in the Church of the Holy Sepulchre.

[3] The same fact recurs more than once in the details of the siege of Jerusalem. It is clear, however, that some links are missing to our comprehension of this story; for one would have expected that Galilæans butchered in the Temple by a Roman Governor would have been looked upon as martyrs rather than as criminals.

about the supposed crimes which must have brought upon these slaughtered worshippers so hideous and tragical a fate.

The Book of Job stood in Hebrew literature as an eternal witness against these sweeping deductions of a confident uncharity; but the spirit of Eliphaz, and Zophar, and Bildad still survived,[1] and our Lord on every occasion seized the opportunity of checking and reproving it. "Do ye imagine," He said, "that these Galilæans were sinners above all the Galilæans, because they suffered such things? I tell you, Nay: but, except ye repent, ye shall all likewise perish." And then He reminded them of another recent instance of sudden death, in which "the Tower in Siloam" had fallen, and crushed eighteen people who happened to be under it;[2] and He told them that so far from these poor sufferers having been specially criminal, they should all, if they did not repent, be involved in a similar destruction. No doubt, the main lesson which Christ desired to teach, was that every circumstance of life, and every violence of man, was not the result either of idle accident or direct retribution, but formed part of one great scheme of Providence in which man is permitted to recognise the one prevailing law—viz., that the so-called accidents of life happen alike to all, but that all should in due time receive according to their works.[3] But His words had also a more literal fulfilment; and, doubtless, there may have been some among His hearers who lived to call them to mind when the Jewish race was being miserably decimated by

[1] Job iv. 7; viii. 20; xxii. 5.

[2] Ewald supposes that these men had been engaged in constructing the aqueduct which the Jews regarded as impious, because Pilate had sequestrated the corban money for this secular purpose (Jos. *B. J.* ii. 9, § 4).

[3] See Amos. iii. 6; ix. 1.

the sword of Titus, and the last defenders of Jerusalem, after deluging its streets with blood, fell crushed among the flaming ruins of the Temple, which not even their lives could save.

The words were very stern: but Christ did not speak to them in the language of warning only; He held out to them a gracious hope. Once, and again, and yet again; the fig-tree might be found a barren cumberer of the ground,[1] but there was ONE to intercede for it still; and even yet—though now the axe was uplifted, nay, though it was at its backmost poise—even yet, if at the last the tree, so carefully tended, should bring forth fruit, that axe should be stayed, and its threatened stroke should not rush through the parted air.

Short as His stay at His old home was meant to be, His enemies would gladly have shortened it still further. They were afraid of, they were weary of, the Lord of Life. Yet they did not dare openly to confess their sentiments. The Pharisees came to Him in sham solicitude for His safety, and said, "Get thee out, and depart hence; for Herod is wanting to kill thee."[2]

Had Jesus yielded to fear—had He hastened His departure in consequence of a danger, which even if it had any existence, except in their own imaginations, had at any rate no immediate urgency—doubtless, they would have enjoyed a secret triumph at His expense. But His answer was supremely calm: "Go," He said, "and tell this fox,[3] Behold, I am casting out devils, and working

[1] Luke xiii. 7, *ἱνατί καὶ τὴν γῆν καταργεῖ;* "Why does it even render the ground barren?" There seems to be a natural reference to the three years of our Lord's own ministry.

[2] The assertion was probably quite untrue. It is inconsistent with Luke xxiii. 8.

[3] Luke xiii. 32, *τῇ ἀλώπεκι ταύτῃ*, as though Herod were with them in

cures to-day and to-morrow, and on the third my work is done."[1] And then He adds, with the perfect confidence of security mingled with the bitter irony of sorrow, "But I must go[2] on my course to-day, and to-morrow, and the day following; for it cannot be that a prophet perish out of Jerusalem." And, perhaps, at this sorrowful crisis His oppressed feelings may have found vent in some pathetic cry over the fallen sinful city, so red with the blood of her murdered messengers, like that which He also uttered when He wept over it on the summit of Olivet.[3]

The little plot of these Pharisees had entirely failed. Whether Herod had really entertained any vague intention of seeing Jesus and putting Him to death as he

person, as he was like them in cunning. "Non quod haec verba de Herode non dixerit, sed quod in personâ Herodis, quam illi sibi induebant . . . eos notaverit atque refellerit" (Maldon).

[1] Vulg. "consummor;" or, perhaps, "I shall reach my goal:" such seems to be at least an admissible rendering of the difficult word τελειοῦμαι (cf. Phil. iii. 12; Acts xx. 24). I have given it the sense which it has in John xix. 28. The word was afterwards used of a martyr's death, as in the inscription ὁ ἅγιος Θῶμας λόγχῃ . . τελειοῦται (Routh, *Rel. Sacr.* i. 376, *ap.* Wordsworth, *ad loc.*); and even of natural death (Euseb. *Vit. Const.* 47). Cf. "Sic Tiberius *finivit*" (Tac. *Ann.* vi. 50). (Schleusner.)

[2] πορεύεσθαι used in a different sense from their previous πορεύου. The πλὴν seems to mean, "Yet, though my remaining time is short, I shall not further shorten it, for," &c. Of course the "to-day," &c., means a time indefinite, yet brief.

[3] Marvellously has that woe been fulfilled. Every Jewish pilgrim who enters Jerusalem to this day has a rent made in his dress, and says, "Zion is turned into a desert, it lies in ruins!" (Dr. Frankl, *Jews in the East*, E. Tr. ii. 2.) Sapir, the Jewish poet of Wilna, addressed Dr. Frankl thus—"Here all is dust. After the destruction of the city, the whole earth blossoms from its ruins; but here there is no verdure, no blossom, only a bitter fruit—sorrow. Look for no joy here, either from men or from mountains" (*id.* p. 9). A wealthy and pious Jew came to settle at Jerusalem: after two years' stay he left it with the words, "Let him that wishes to have neither *aulom haze* ('the pleasures of this life') nor *aulom habo* ('those of the life to come') live at Jerusalem" (*id.* p. 120).—The translation is Dr. Frankl's, not mine.

had put to death His kinsman John, or whether the whole rumour was a pure invention, Jesus regarded it with consummate indifference. Whatever Herod might be designing, His own intention was to finish His brief stay in Galilee in His own due time, and not before. A day or two yet remained to Him in which He would continue to perform His works of mercy on all who sought Him; after that brief interval the time would have come when He should be received up,[1] and He would turn His back for the last time on the home of His youth, and "set His face steadfastly to go to Jerusalem." Till then—so they must tell their crafty patron, whom they themselves resembled—He was under an inviolable protection, into which neither their malice nor his cruelty could intrude.

And He deservedly bestowed on Herod Antipas the sole word of pure unmitigated contempt which is ever recorded to have passed His lips. Words of burning anger He sometimes spoke—words of scathing indignation—words of searching irony—words of playful humour; but some are startled to find Him using words of sheer contempt. Yet why not? there can be no noble soul which is wholly destitute of scorn. The "scorn of scorn" must exist side by side with the "love of love." Like anger, like the power of moral indignation, scorn

[1] Luke ix. 51, ἐν τῷ συμπληροῦσθαι τὰς ἡμέρας τῆς ἀναλήψεως αὐτοῦ—*i.e.*, as Euthymius adds, ἀπὸ γῆς εἰς οὐρανόν. The word is, in the New Testament, a ἅπαξ λεγόμενον, but it is mere sophistry to make it fall in with any harmonistic scheme by giving it the meaning of "His reception by men," as Wieseler does (*Synops.*, pp. 295—297). Even Lange has now abandoned it as untenable. It can only mean what the verb ἀνελήφθη means in Acts i. 2, 22 (cf. Mark xvi. 19), and in the LXX. (2 Kings ii. 9—11). The word occurs in the title of an Apocryphal book, the 'Ανάληψις Μώσεως, or Assumption of Moses, and Irenæus speaks of τὴν ἔνσαρκον εἰς τους οὐρανοὺς ἀνάληψιν. Sophocles gives several instances of its use in the *Apost. Constitutions*, and later writers.

has its due place as a righteous function in the economy of human emotions, and as long as there are things of which we rightly judge as contemptible, so long must contempt remain. And if ever there was a man who richly deserved contempt, it was the paltry, perjured princeling—false to his religion, false to his nation, false to his friends, false to his brethren, false to his wife—to whom Jesus gave the name of "this fox." The inhuman vices which the Cæsars displayed on the vast theatre of their absolutism—the lust, the cruelty, the autocratic insolence, the ruinous extravagance—all these were seen in pale reflex in these little Neros and Caligulas of the provinces—these local tyrants, half Idumæan, half Samaritan, who aped the worst degradations of the Imperialism to which they owed their very existence. Judæa might well groan under the odious and petty despotism of these hybrid Herodians—jackals who fawned about the feet of the Cæsarean lions.[1] Respect for "the powers that be" can hardly, as has well been said, involve respect for all the impotences and imbecilities.

Whether "this fox" ever heard the manner in which our Lord had characterised him and his dominion we do not know; in lifetime they never met, until, on the morning of the crucifixion, Antipas vented upon Jesus his empty insults. But now Jesus calmly concluded His last task in Galilee. He summoned His followers together, and out of them chose seventy to prepare His

[1] What has been said of Agrippa is equally true of Antipas, viz., that "he had been the meanest thing the world had ever seen—a courtier of the early empire . . He had been corrupted by the influence of the Roman court, and had flattered the worst vices of the worst men in the worst age of the world's history." (*Paul of Tarsus*, p. 205.)

way. Their number was probably symbolic,[1] and the mission of so large a number to go before Him two and two, and prepare for His arrival in every place which He intended to visit, implies for this last journey of proclamation an immense publicity. The instructions which He gave them closely resemble those which He had issued to the Twelve; and, indeed, differ from them only in being more brief, because they refer to a more transitory office; in omitting the now needless restriction about not visiting the Gentiles and Samaritans; and perhaps in bestowing upon them less ample miraculous power.[2] They also breathe a sadder tone, inspired by the experience of incessant rejection.

And now the time has come for Him to set forth, and it must be in sorrow. He left, indeed, some faithful hearts behind Him; but how few! Galilee had rejected Him, as Judæa had rejected Him. On one side of the lake which He loved, a whole populace in unanimous deputation had besought Him to depart out of their coasts; on the other, they had vainly tried to vex His last days among them by a miserable conspiracy to frighten Him into flight. At Nazareth, the sweet mountain village of His childish days—at Nazareth, with all

[1] Some MSS. alter it into "seventy-two" to connect their number with the number of the Sanhedrin, and the elders appointed by Moses [about which, however, there is the same variation] (Exod. xxiv. 1). Others, with no authority but fancy, connect it with the ideal seventy nations of the world. (Lightfoot, *Hor. Hebr.*, in John vii. 37). These seventy nations are supposed to have been separated at Babel (see Targ. Ps. Jonath. in Gen. xi. 7, 8).

[2] Compare Matt. x. 5—42 with Luke x. 1—12. We must not press the fact that ἄρνας, "lambs," is in Luke x. 3 substituted for πρόβατα in Matt. x. 16. The prohibition to greet any one by the way is proverbial of any hasty mission (2 Kings iv. 29), and arose from the fact that Oriental greetings are much longer and more elaborate than ours. (Thomson, *Land and Book*, II. ch. xxiv.)

its happy memories of His boyhood and His mother's home—they had treated Him with such violence and outrage, that He could not visit it again. And even at Chorazin, and Capernaum, and Bethsaida—on those Eden-shores of the silver lake—in the green delicious plain, whose every field He had traversed with His apostles, performing deeds of mercy, and uttering words of love—even there they loved the whited sepulchres of a Pharisaic sanctity, and the shallow traditions of a Levitical ceremonial better than the light and the life which had been offered them by the Son of God. They were feeding on ashes; a deceived heart had turned them aside. On many a great city of antiquity, on Nineveh and Babylon, on Tyre and Sidon, on Sodom and Gomorrah, had fallen the wrath of God; yet even Nineveh and Babylon would have humbled their gorgeous idolatries, even Tyre and Sidon have turned from their greedy vanities, yea, even Sodom and Gomorrah would have repented from their filthy lusts, had they seen the mighty works which had been done in these little cities and villages of the Galilæan sea. And, therefore, "Woe unto thee, Chorazin! woe unto thee, Bethsaida!" and unto thee, Capernaum, "His own city," a yet deeper woe!

With such thoughts in His heart, and such words on His lips, he started forth from the scene of His rejected ministry; and on all this land, and most of all on that region of it, the woe has fallen. Exquisite still in its loveliness, it is now desolate and dangerous. The birds still sing in countless myriads; the water-fowl still play on the crystal mere; the brooks flow into it from the neighbouring hill, "filling their bosoms with pearl, and scattering their path with emeralds;" the aromatic herbs are still fragrant when the foot crushes them, and the tall oleanders fill the air with their delicate perfume as of old; but the vineyards and fruit-gardens have disappeared; the fleets and fishing-boats cease to traverse the lake; the hum of men is silent; the stream of prosperous commerce has ceased to flow. The very names and sites of the towns and cities are forgotten; and where they once shone bright and populous, flinging their shadows across the sunlit waters, there are now grey mounds where even the ruins are too ruinous to be distinguishable. One solitary palm-tree by one squalid street of huts, degraded and frightful beyond any, even in Palestine, still marks the site, and recalls the name of the one little town where lived that sinful penitent woman who once washed Christ's feet with her tears and wiped them with the hairs of her head.[1]

And the very generation which rejected Him was doomed to recall in bitter and fruitless agony these peaceful happy days of the Son of Man. Thirty years had barely elapsed when the storm of Roman invasion burst furiously over that smiling land. He who will, may read in the Jewish War of Josephus the hideous details of the slaughter which decimated the cities of Galilee, and wrung from the historian the repeated confession that "it was certainly God who brought the Romans to punish the Galilæans," and exposed the people of city after city "to be destroyed by their bloody enemies."[2] Immediately after the celebrated passage in which he describes the lake and plain of Genesareth as "the ambition of nature,"[3] follows a description of that

[1] The "Woe unto thee, Chorazin," and the "And thou, Capernaum," receive a very striking illustration from the photographs of the two sites by the Palestine Exploration Fund.

[2] Jos. *B. J.* iii. 7, § 31.

[3] Jos. *B. J.* iii. 10, § 8; *v. supr.*, Vol. I., p. 177. I here quote the translation of Whiston.

terrible sea-fight on these bright waters, in which the number of the slain, including those killed in the city, was six thousand five hundred. Hundreds were stabbed by the Romans or run through with poles; others tried to save their lives by diving, but if once they raised their heads were slain by darts; or if they swam to the Roman vessels had their heads or hands lopped off; while others were chased to the land and there massacred. "One might then," the historian continues, "see the lake all bloody, and full of dead bodies, for not one of them escaped. *And a terrible stink, and a very sad sight there was, on the following days over that country; for, as for the shores, they were full of shipwrecks and of dead bodies all swelled;* and as the dead bodies were inflamed by the sun, and putrified, they corrupted the air, *insomuch that the misery was not only an object of commiseration to the Jews, but even to those that hated them, and had been the authors of that misery.*" Of those that died amid this butchery; of those whom Vespasian immediately afterwards abandoned to brutal and treacherous massacre between Taricheæ and Tiberias; of those twelve hundred "old and useless" whom he afterwards caused to be slain in the stadium; of the six thousand whom he sent to aid Nero in his attempt to dig through the Isthmus of Athos; of the thirty thousand four hundred whom he sold as slaves—may there not have been many who in their agony and exile, in their hour of death and day of judgment,[1] recalled Him whom they had repudiated, and remembered that the sequel of all those gracious words which had proceeded out of His lips had been the "woe" which their obduracy called forth!

[1] Since writing the above I have read the powerful descriptions of the

There could not but be sorrow in such a parting from such a scene. And yet the divine spirit of Jesus could not long be a prey to consuming sadness. Out of the tenebrous influences cast about it from the incessant opposition of unbelief and sin, it was ever struggling into the purity and peace of heaven, from the things seen and temporal to the things unseen and eternal, from the shadows of human degradation into the sunlight of God's peace. "In that hour Jesus rejoiced in spirit," and what a joy! what a boundless, absorbing exultation,[1] as He thought no longer of judgment but of compassion; as He turned not with faint trust but perfect knowledge to "the larger hope;" as He remembered how *that* which was hidden from the wise and prudent had been revealed unto babes; as he dwelt upon the thought that He was sent not to the rich and learned few, but to the ignorant and suffering many; as He told His disciples, that into *His*, yea, into His own loving hands, had His Father committed all power, and that in Him they would see and know the spirit of His Father, and thereby might see and know that revelation for which many kings and prophets had sighed in vain. And then, that even in the hour of denunciation not one of them might doubt His own or His Father's love, He uttered in that same hour of

same facts in Renan's *L'Antechrist*, p. 277. He says, "Il y a dans l'histoire peu d'exemples d'une race entière ainsi broyée."

[1] ἠγαλλιάσατο. It seems clear that Luke x. 21 belongs closely to the address which closes in verse 16, though St. Luke pauses to record in the intermediate verses the return of the Seventy. This must be evident to any one who compares the passage with Matt. xi. 20—27; and unless we adopt the unlikely hypothesis that *both series* of words were uttered twice in different connections, it is clear that St. Luke's context here suits them best; and, moreover, this mark of time here given by St. Luke is slightly the more definite of the two.

rapt and exalted ecstacy, those tenderest words ever uttered in human language as God's message and invitation to His children in the suffering family of man, "Come unto me all ye that labour and are heavy laden, and I will give you rest. Take my yoke upon you, and learn of me; for I am meek and lowly in heart; and ye shall find rest unto your souls."

So, over a temporary sorrow there triumphed an infinite and eternal joy. There are some who have dwelt too exclusively on Jesus as the Man of Sorrows; have thought of His life as of one unmitigated suffering, one almost unbroken gloom. But in the Bible—though there alone—we find the perfect compatibility, nay, the close union of joy with sorrow; and myriads of Christians who have been "troubled on every side, yet not distressed; perplexed, but not in despair; persecuted, but not forsaken; cast down, but not destroyed," can understand how the Man of Sorrows, even in the days of His manhood, may have lived a life happier, in the true sense of happiness—happier, because purer, more sinless, more faithful, more absorbed in the joy of obedience to His Heavenly Father—than has been ever granted to the sons of men. The deep pure stream flows on its way rejoicing, even though the forests overshadow it, and no transient sunshine flickers on its waves.

And if, indeed, true joy — the highest joy — be "severe, and chaste, and solitary, and incompatible," then how constant, how inexpressible, what a joy of God, must have been the joy of the Man Christ Jesus, who came to give to all who love Him, henceforth and for ever, a joy which no man taketh from them—a joy which the world can neither give nor take away.

CHAPTER XLIII.

INCIDENTS OF THE JOURNEY.

"Religionis non est religionem cogere."—TERT. *Ad Scap.* 2.

WE are not told the exact route taken by Jesus as He left Gennesareth; but as He probably avoided Nazareth, with its deeply happy and deeply painful memories, He may have crossed the bridge at the southern extremity of the Lake, and so got round into the plain of Esdraelon either by the valley of Bethshean,[1] or over Mount Tabor and round Little Hermon,[2] passing Endor and Nain and Shunem on His way.

Crossing the plain, and passing Taanach and Megiddo, He would reach the range of hills which form the northern limit of Samaria; and at the foot of their first ascent lies the little town of En-gannim, or the "Fountain of Gardens."[3] This would be the first Samaritan village at which He would arrive, and hither, apparently, He had sent two messengers "to make ready for Him." Although the incident is mentioned by St. Luke before the Mission of the Seventy, yet that is probably due to his subjective choice of order, and we may suppose that

[1] Now the *Wady Mujeidah.*

[2] Along part of the *Wady Bireh.*

[3] Luke ix. 51—56. En-gannim is still a very pleasant spot, deserving its poetic name, which is now corrupted into Jenîn.

there were two of the seventy who were dispatched to prepare the way for Him spiritually as well as in the more ordinary sense; unless, indeed, we adopt the conjecture that the messengers may have been James and John, who would thus be likely to feel with special vividness the insult of His rejection. At any rate the inhabitants—who to this day are not remarkable for their civility to strangers[1]—absolutely declined to receive or admit Him. Previously indeed, when He was passing through Samaria on His journey northwards, He had found Samaritans not only willing to receive, but anxious to detain His presence among them, and eager to listen to His words. But now in two respects the circumstances were different; for now He was professedly travelling to the city which they hated and the Temple which they despised, and now He was attended, not by a few Apostles, but by a great multitude, who were accompanying Him as their acknowledged Prophet and Messiah. Had Gerizim and not Jerusalem been the goal of His journey, all might have been different; but now His destination and His associates inflamed their national animosity too much to admit of their supplying to the weary pilgrims the ordinary civilities of life. And if the feelings of this little frontier village of En-gannim were so unmistakably hostile, it became clear that any attempt to journey through the whole breadth of Samaria, and even to pass under the shadow of their rival sanctuary, would be a dangerous if not a hopeless task.[2] Jesus therefore altered the course of His journey,

[1] So we were told on the spot, though we experienced no personal rudeness there. "They are," says Dr. Thomson, "fanatical, rude, and rebellious" (*Land and Book*, II., ch. xxx.).

[2] The exacerbation between Jews and Samaritans was always at its worst during the anniversaries of the national feasts; and it often broke

and turned once more towards the Jordan valley. Rejected by Galilee, refused by Samaria, without a word He bent His steps towards Peræa.

But the deep discouragement of this refusal to receive Him was mingled in the minds of James and John with hot indignation. There is nothing so trying, so absolutely exasperating, as a failure to find food and shelter, and common civility, after the fatigue of travel, and especially for a large multitude to begin a fresh journey when they expected rest. Full, therefore, of the Messianic kingdom, which now at last they thought was on the eve of being mightily proclaimed, the two brothers wanted to usher it in with a blaze of Sinaitic vengeance, and so to astonish and restore the flagging spirits of followers who would naturally be discouraged by so immediate and decided a repulse. "Lord, wilt Thou that we command fire to come down from heaven, and *consume them*, even as Elias did?" "What wonder," says St. Ambrose, "that the Sons of Thunder wished to flash lightning?" And this their fiery impetuosity seemed to find its justification not only in the precedent of Elijah's conduct,[1] but in the fact that it had been

out into acts of open hostility. In consequence of this, the caravans of Galilæan pilgrims seem in many instances [though by no means always (Jos. *Antt.* xx. 6, § 1; *Vit.* 52)] to have chosen the route on the east of Jordan. The Jews accused the Samaritans of wilfully molesting their harmless travellers, even of the horrible crime of having lit false fire-signals to show the time of new moon, and of having polluted their Temple by scattering in it the bones of the dead (see Jos. *Antt.* xviii. 2, § 2; *B. J.* ii. 12, §§ 3, seqq.). (*Vid. supra,* Vol. I., p. 209.)

[1] 2 Kings i. 10—12. The ὡς καὶ Ἠλίας ἐποίησε (Luke ix. 54) is omitted (perhaps on dogmatic grounds) in א, B, L. But as Bishop Andrewes says, "The times require sometimes one spirit, sometimes another. Elias' time, Elias' spirit." The notion, however, that the brothers received the name "Boanerges" (בְּנֵי רֶגֶשׁ) from this circumstance is quite groundless. (See Vol. I., p. 256.)

displayed in this very country of Samaria. Was it more necessary in personal defence of a single prophet than to vindicate the honour of the Messiah and His attendants? But Jesus turned and rebuked them. God's heaven has other uses than for thunder. "They did not know," He told them, "what spirit they were of."[1] They had not realised the difference which separated Sinai and Carmel from Calvary and Hermon. He had come to save, not to destroy; and if any heard His words and believed not, He judged them not.[2] And so, without a word of anger, He went to a different village;[3] and doubtless St. John, who by that time *did* know of what spirit he was, remembered these words of Christ when he went with Peter into Samaria to confirm the recent converts, and to bestow upon them the gift of the Holy Ghost.

Perhaps it may have been on this occasion—for certainly no occasion would have been more suitable than that furnished by this early and rude repulse—that Jesus, turning to the great multitudes that accompanied Him,[4] delivered to them that memorable dis-

[1] The words are omitted in many MSS. (א, A, B, C, E, L, &c.). Alford, however, supposes that they "have been unsparingly tampered with" because they stood in the way of ecclesiastical censures. They occur in D, and in some good versions.

[2] John iii. 17; xii. 47.

[3] The ἑτέραν (Luke ix. 56) probably implies that it was *not* a Samaritan village.

[4] Luke xiv. 25—33. We must ask the reader to bear in mind throughout this and the following chapter that the exact sequence of events is not here given by the Evangelists, and therefore that the certain order in which they occurred is not ascertainable. In a thoughtful but quite inconclusive pamphlet by the Rev. W. Stewart (Maclehose, Glasgow, 1873) called *The Plan of St. Luke's Gospel*, he supposes that the Evangelist arranged these unchronological incidents alphabetically by the leading conceptions of the paragraph—*e.g.*, ἀγαπᾶν, Luke x. 25—28, 29—37, 38—42; αἰτεῖν, xi. 1—4, 5—8, 9—13; ἀντιλέγιν, xi. 14—32, &c. Thus under κ (κρίνειν) would fall

course in which He warned them that all who would be His disciples must come to Him, not expecting earthly love or acceptance, but expecting alienation and opposition, and *counting the cost.* They must abandon, if need be, every earthly tie; they must sit absolutely loose to the interests of the world;[1] they must take up the cross and follow Him. Strange language, of which it was only afterwards that they learnt the full significance! For a man to begin a tower which he could not finish—for a king to enter on a war in which nothing was possible save disaster and defeat—involved disgrace and indicated folly; better not to follow Him at all, unless they followed Him prepared to forsake all that they had on earth; prepared to sacrifice the interests of time, and to live solely for those of eternity. One who believed not, would indeed suffer loss and harm, yet his lot was less pitiable than that of him who became a disciple only to be a backslider—who, facing both ways, cast like Lot's

xii. 35—38, 39—46, 47, 48, 51—53, 54—56, 57, 58, 59; xiii. 1—5, 6—9. Under χ (χαίνειν) xvi. 14, 15, 16, 17, 18, 19—31, &c. The theory, which is worked out with as much ingenuity as it admits, will at least serve to show how little chronological sequence is traceable in the great division of St. Luke x.—xviii. 31. Professor Westcott (*Introd. to Gosp.*, p. 365, 3rd ed.) arranges the contents of the section (omitting the minor divisions) as follows:—The Universal Church; The Rejection of the Jews foreshown; Preparation (ix. 43—xi. 13); Lessons of warning (xi. 14—xiii. 9); Lessons of progress (xiii. 10—xiv. 24); Lessons of discipleship (xiv. 25—xvii. 10); The coming end (xvii. 11—xviii. 30). It is obviously more probable that St. Luke was guided by some such subjective sequence, than that he should have adopted the poor expedient of an alphabetical arrangement of unclassified fragments.

[1] The "hate" of Luke xiv. 26 is adopted in strict accordance with our Lord's habit of stating the great truths which He uttered in the extremest form of what, to His hearers, must even sound like paradox, in order that their inmost essential truth—their truth without any subterfuge or qualification—might be recognised, and so fixed eternally in their memory. (See *suprà*, Vol. I., p. 268.) It was *necessary* that they should be uttered in such a way as to seize, and dominate over, the imagination of mankind for ever.

wife a longing glance on all that he ought to flee—who made the attempt, at once impotent and disastrous, to serve both God and Mammon.

As both Galilee and Samaria were now closed to Him, He could only journey on His way to Peræa, down the valley of Bethshean, between the borders of both provinces. There a very touching incident occurred.[1] On the outskirts of one of the villages a dull, harsh, plaintive cry smote His ears, and looking up He saw "ten men who were lepers," united in a community of deadly misery. They were afar off, for they dared not approach, since their approach was pollution, and they were obliged to warn away all who would have come near them by the heart-rending cry, "*Tamê! tamê!*"—"Unclean! unclean!" There was something in that living death of leprosy—recalling as it did the most frightful images of suffering and degradation, corrupting as it did the very fountains of the life-blood of man, distorting his countenance, rendering loathsome his touch, slowly encrusting and infecting him with a plague-spot of disease far more horrible than death itself—which always seems to have thrilled the Lord's heart with a keen and instantaneous compassion. And never more so than at this moment. Scarcely had He heard their piteous cry of "Jesus, Master, have mercy on us," than instantly, without sufficient pause even to approach them more nearly, He called aloud to them, "Go, show yourselves unto the priests." They knew the significance of that command: they knew that it bade them hurry off to claim from the priest the recognition of their cure, the certificate of their restitution to every rite and privilege

[1] Luke xvii. 11—19.

of human life.[1] Already, at the sound of that potent voice, they felt a stream of wholesome life, of recovered energy, of purer blood, pulsing through their veins; and as they went they were cleansed.

He who has not seen the hideous, degraded spectacle of the lepers clamorously revealing their mutilations, and almost demanding alms, by the roadside of some Eastern city,[2] can hardly conceive how transcendent and immeasurable was the boon which they had thus received at the hands of Jesus. One would have thought that they would have suffered no obstacle to hinder the passionate gratitude which should have prompted them to hasten back at once—to struggle, if need be, even through fire and water, if thereby they could fling themselves with tears of heartfelt acknowledgment at their Saviour's feet, to thank Him for a gift of something more precious than life itself. What absorbing selfishness, what Jewish infatuation, what sacerdotal interference, what new and worse leprosy of shameful thanklessness and superstitious ignorance, prevented it? We do not know. We only know that of ten who were healed but *one* returned, and he was a Samaritan. On the frontiers of the two countries had been gathered, like froth at the margin of wave and sand, the misery of both;[3] but while the nine Jews were infamously thankless, the one Samaritan

[1] Lev. xiii. 2; xiv. 2. *V. supra*, Vol. I., p. 276.

[2] See the dreadful yet not exaggerated picture drawn by Dr. Thomson, *Land and Book*, IV., ch. xliii.; Delitzsch, *Durch Krankheit zur Genesung*, § v. I had not, however, read either that little tale, or his *Ein Tag in Capernaum*, till the whole of this book was written. I mention this because there are some accidental resemblances between my language and that of Dr. Delitzsch.

[3] So it is only in the *Biut el Masakin* ("abodes of the unfortunate"), or lepers' quarter in Jerusalem, that Jews and Mohammedans will live together.

"turned back, and with a loud voice glorified God, and fell down on his face at His feet, giving Him thanks." The heart of Jesus, familiar as He was with all ingratitude, was yet moved by an instance of it so flagrant, so all but unanimous, and so abnormal. "Were not the ten cleansed?" He asked in sorrowful surprise; "but the nine—where are they?[1] There are not found that returned to give glory to God save this alien."[2] "It is," says Lange, "as if all these benefits were falling into a deep silent grave." The voice of their misery had awaked the instant echo of His mercy; but the miraculous utterance of His mercy, though it thrilled through their whole physical being, woke no echo of gratitude in their earthy and still leprous hearts.

But, nevertheless, this alien shall not have returned in vain, nor shall the rare virtue—alas, *how* rare a virtue![3]—of his gratitude go unrewarded. Not his body alone, but the soul—whose value was so infinitely more precious, just as its diseases are so infinitely more profound—should be healed by His Saviour's word.

"Arise and go," said Jesus; "thy faith hath saved thee."

[1] Luke xvii. 17, οὐχὶ οἱ δέκα ἐκαθαρίσθησαν; οἱ δε ἐννέα, ποῦ;

[2] ἀλλογενής.

[3] Wordsworth's lines—

"I've heard of hearts unkind, kind deeds
With coldness still returning,
Alas! the gratitude of men
Hath oftener left me mourning,"

have been often quoted; but if he found gratitude a common virtue, his experience must have been exceptional.

CHAPTER XLIV.

TEACHINGS OF THE JOURNEY.

ועשו סיג לתו, "And make a fence for the Law."—*Pirke Abhôth*, i. 1.

EVEN during this last journey our Lord did not escape the taunts, the opposition, the depreciating remarks—in one word, the Pharisaism—of the Pharisees and those who resembled them. The circumstances which irritated them against Him were exactly the same as they had been throughout His whole career—exactly those in which His example was most lofty, and His teaching most beneficial—namely, the performance on the Sabbath of works of mercy, and the association with publicans and sinners.

One of these sabbatical disputes occurred in a synagogue.[1] Jesus, as we have already remarked, whether because of the lesser excommunication (the *cherem*), or for any other reason, seems, during this latter period of His ministry, to have entered the synagogues but rarely. The exclusion, however, from one synagogue or more did not include a prohibition to enter *any* synagogue; and the subsequent conduct of this *rôsh hakkenéseth* seems to show that he had a certain awe of Jesus, mingled with his jealousy and suspicion. On this day there sat

[1] Luke xiii. 10—17.

among the worshippers a poor woman who, for eighteen long years, had been bent double by "a spirit of infirmity," and could not lift herself up. The compassionate heart of Jesus could not brook the mute appeal of her presence. He called her to Him, and saying to her, "Woman, thou art loosed from thine infirmity,"[1] laid His hands on her. Instantly she experienced the miraculous strengthening which enabled her to lift up the long-bowed and crooked frame, and instantly she broke into utterances of gratitude to God. But her strain of thanksgiving was interrupted by the narrow and ignorant indignation of the ruler of the synagogue. Here, under his very eyes, and without any reference to the "little brief authority" which gave him a sense of dignity on each recurring Sabbath, a woman—a member of *his* congregation—had actually had the presumption to be healed. Armed with his favourite "texts," and in all the fussiness of official hypocrisy, he gets up and rebukes the perfectly innocent multitude, telling them it was a gross instance of Sabbath-breaking for them to be healed on that sacred day, when they might just as well be healed on any of the other six days of the week. That the offence consisted solely in the being healed is clear, for he certainly could not mean that, if they had any sickness, it was a crime for them to come to the synagogue at all on the Sabbath day. Now, as the poor woman does not seem to have spoken one word of entreaty to Jesus, or even to have called His attention to her case, the utterly senseless address of this man could only by any possibility mean either "You *sick* people must not come to the synagogue

[1] Luke xiii. 12, ἀπολέλυσαι. The perfect implies the instantaneousness and permanence of the result.

at all on the Sabbath under present circumstances, for fear you should be led into Sabbath-breaking by having a miraculous cure performed upon you;" or "If any one wants to heal you on a Sabbath, you must decline." And these remarks he has neither the courage to address to Jesus Himself, nor the candour to address to the poor healed woman, but preaches *at* them both by rebuking the multitude, who had no concern in the action at all, beyond the fact that they had been passive spectators of it!

The whole range of the Gospels does not supply any other instance of an interference so illogical, or a stupidity so hopeless; and the indirect, underhand way in which he gave vent to his outraged ignorance brought on him that expression of our Lord's indignation which he had not dared openly to brave. "*Hypocrite!*" was the one crushing word with which Jesus addressed him. This silly official had been censorious with *Him* because He had spoken a few words to the woman, and laid upon her a healing hand; and with the woman because, having been bent double, she lifted herself up and glorified God! It would be difficult to imagine such a paralysis of the moral sense, if we did not daily see the stultifying effect produced upon the intellect by the "deep slumber of a decided opinion," especially when the opinion itself rests upon nothing better than a meaningless tradition. Now Jesus constantly varied the arguments and appeals by which He endeavoured to show the Pharisees of His nation that their views about the Sabbath only degraded it from a divine benefit into a revolting bondage.[1] To the Rabbis of Jerusalem He justified Himself by an appeal to His

[1] It is a curious but instructive fact that the Jews of Palestine to this day greatly resemble their Pharisaic predecessors. "I have no heart," says

own character and authority, as supported by the triple testimony of John the Baptist, of the Scriptures, and of the Father Himself, who bore witness to Him by the authority which He had given Him.[1] To the Pharisees of Galilee He had quoted the direct precedents of Scripture,[2] or had addressed an appeal, founded on their own common sense and power of insight into the eternal principles of things.[3] But the duller and less practised intellect of these Peræans might not have understood either the essential love and liberty implied by the institution of the Sabbath, or the paramount authority of Jesus as Lord of the Sabbath. It could not rise above the cogency of the *argumentum ad hominem.* It was only capable of a conviction based on their own common practices and received limitations. There was not one

Dr. Thomson, "to dwell on their absurd superstitions, their intense fanaticism, or their social and domestic institutions and manners, comprising an incredible and grotesque *mélange* of filth and finery, Pharisaic self-righteousness and Sadducean licentiousness. The following is a specimen of the puerilities enjoined and enforced by their learned Rabbis:—*A Jew must not carry on the Sabbath even so much as a pocket-handkerchief, except within the walls of the city.* If there are no walls it follows, according to their perverse logic, that he must not carry it at all! To avoid this difficulty, here in Safed, they resort to what is called *erŭv.* Poles are set up at the ends of the streets, and *strings* stretched from the one to the other. *This string represents a wall, and a conscientious Jew may carry his handkerchief anywhere within these strings.* I was once amused by a devout Israelite who was walking with me on his Sabbath. When we came to the end of the street the string was gone, and so by another fiction he was at liberty to go on without reference to what was in his pocket, *because he had not passed the wall.* The last time I was here they had abandoned this absurdity, probably to avoid the constant ridicule it brought upon them" (Thomson, *Land and Book,* II., ch. xix.). What a commentary on the kind of Sabbatarianism which Christ combated! For abundant further instances, which descend into details not only puerile but disgusting, see Buxtorf, *Syn. Jud.,* capp. xiv.—xvi.

[1] John v. 17—47, *supra,* Vol. I., p. 379.

[2] Luke vi. 3—5, *supra,* Vol. I., p. 437.

[3] Luke vi. 9, *supra,* Vol. I., p. 440.

of them who did not consider himself justified in unloosing and leading to the water his ox or his ass on the Sabbath,[1] although that involved far more labour than either laying the hand on a sick woman, or even being healed by a miraculous word! If their Sabbath rules gave way to the needs of ox or ass, ought they not to give way to the cruel necessities of a daughter of Abraham? If *they* might do much more labour on the Sabbath to abbreviate a few hours' thirst, might not He do much less to terminate a Satanically cruel bondage which had lasted, lo! these eighteen years? At reasonings so unanswerable, no wonder that His adversaries were ashamed, and that the simpler, more unsophisticated people rejoiced at all the glorious acts of mercy which He wrought on their behalf.[2]

Again and again was our Lord thus obliged to redeem this great primeval institution of God's love from these narrow, formal, pernicious restrictions of an otiose and unintelligent tradition. But it is evident that He attached as much importance to the noble and loving freedom of the day of rest as they did to the stupefy-

[1] It might, moreover, as they were well aware, have been avoided altogether if their Oriental laziness, and want of real earnestness, had not prevented them from rendering such tasks unnecessary by procuring a supply of water overnight. But this kind of letter-worship must of its very nature be purely artificial.

[2] They might say, If she has been bound these eighteen years, surely she might wait yet one day longer! But that very circumstance He makes an argument for the contrary, for he who loves his neighbour as himself would rather say, Not one moment longer must she suffer, if help can be afforded her! Could it be *forbidden* thus to help? The "*ought not*" of verse 16 catechetically answers, with infinite condescension, the inconsiderate, proud, and unintelligent "*ought*" of verse 14. "*Men ought*" was the theme there; so now the "*ought*" is abundantly returned; "*ought not* she, according to the law of love, which specially ordains God's works for the Sabbath, as man's labour for the remaining days to be loosed from this misery?" (Stier, iv. 51.)

ing inaction to which they had reduced the normal character of its observance. Their absorbing attachment to it, the frenzy[1] which filled them when He set at naught their Sabbatarian uncharities, rose from many circumstances. They were wedded to the religious system which had long prevailed among them, because it is easy to be a slave to the letter, and difficult to enter into the spirit; easy to obey a number of outward rules, difficult to enter intelligently and self-sacrificingly into the will of God; easy to entangle the soul in a network of petty observances, difficult to yield the obedience of an enlightened heart; easy to be haughtily exclusive, difficult to be humbly spiritual; easy to be an ascetic or a formalist, difficult to be pure, and loving, and wise, and free; easy to be a Pharisee, difficult to be a disciple; very easy to embrace a self-satisfying and sanctimonious system of rabbinical observances, very difficult to love God with all the heart, and all the might, and all the soul, and all the strength. In laying His axe at the root of their proud and ignorant Sabbatarianism, He was laying His axe at the root of all that "miserable micrology" which they had been accustomed to take for their religious life. Is the spirit of the sects so free in these days from Pharisaic taint as not to need such lessons? Will not these very words which I have written—although they are but an expansion of the lessons which Jesus incessantly taught—yet give offence to some who read them?

One more such incident is recorded—the sixth embittered controversy of the kind in which they had

[1] Luke vi. 11, ἐπλήσθησαν ἀνοίας. The attachment to the Sabbath was not all religious; it was due in part to the obstinate conservatism of an exclusive nationality, and as such it even attracted heathen notice (Ovid, *Ars Amat.* i. 415; Juv. *Sat.* xiv. 98—100).

involved our Lord.[1] Nothing but Sabbatarianism which had degenerated into monomania could account for their so frequently courting a controversy which always ended in their total discomfiture. On a certain Sabbath, which was the principal day for Jewish entertainments,[2] Jesus was invited to the house of one who, as he is called a ruler of the Pharisees, must have been a man in high position, and perhaps even a member of the Sanhedrin. The invitation was one of those to which He was so often subjected, not respectful or generous, but due either to idle curiosity or downright malice. Throughout the meal He was carefully watched by hostile scrutiny. The Pharisees, as has been well said, "performed the duty of religious espionage with exemplary diligence."[3] Among the unbidden guests who, Oriental fashion, stood about the room and looked on, as they do to this day during the continuance of a meal, was a man afflicted with the dropsy. The prominent position in which he stood, combined with the keen watchfulness of the Pharisees, seems to show that he had been placed there designedly, either to test Christ's willing-

[1] Luke xiv. 1—6. The others were the healing at Bethesda (John v. 10, Vol. I., p. 375); the scene in the corn-field (Mark ii. 23, *id.*, p. 434); the healing of the withered hand (Matt. xii. 10, *id.*, p. 439), of the blind man at Siloam (John ix. 14, *supr.*, p. 82), and of the paralytic woman (Luke xiii. 14, *supr.*, p. 113).

[2] Neh. viii. 9—12. No cooking was done (Exod. xvi. 23); but, as those feasts *must* have necessitated more or less labour, the fact shows how little real earnestness there was in the Jewish Sabbatarianism; how fast and loose they could play with their own convictions; how physical self-indulgence and unintelligent routine had usurped the place of spiritual enlightenment. On the contrary, there was no inconsistency whatever in our Lord's *accepting* such invitations; there was nothing wrong in them, and nothing out of accordance with true principles; and therefore Jesus could sanction them with His presence. But had there been any true principle involved in the Jewish view, *they* ought to have *thought* them wrong.

[3] Bruce, *Training of the Twelve*, p. 27. Luke xiv. 1—6.

ness to respect their Sabbath prejudices, or to defeat His miraculous power by the failure to cure a disease more inveterate, and less amenable to curative measures, than any other. If so, this was another of those miserable cases in which these unfeeling teachers of the people were ready to make the most heart-rending shame or the deepest misery a mere tool to be used or thrown aside, as chance might serve, in their dealings with Jesus. But this time Jesus anticipated, and went to meet half way the subtle machinations of this learned and distinguished company. He asked them the very simple question—

"Is it lawful to heal on the Sabbath day?"

They *would* not say "Yes;" but, on the other hand, they dared not say "No!" Had it been unlawful, it was their positive function and duty to say so then and there, and without any subterfuge to deprive the poor sufferer, so far as in them lay, of the miraculous mercy which was prepared for him, and to brave the consequences. If they dared not say so—either for fear of the people, or for fear of instant refutation, or because the spell of Christ's awful ascendancy was upon them, or out of a mere splenetic pride, or—to imagine better motives—because in their inmost hearts, if any spot remained in them uncrusted by idle and irreligious prejudices, they felt that it *was* lawful, and more than lawful, RIGHT—then, by their own judgment, they left Jesus free to heal without the possibility of censure. Their silence, therefore, was, even on their own showing, and on their own principles, His entire justification. His mere simple question, and their inability to answer it, was an absolute decision of the controversy in His favour. He therefore took the man, healed him, and let him go.

And then He appealed, as before, to their own practice. "Which of you shall have a son,[1] or (even) an ox, fallen into a pit, and will not straightway pull him out on the Sabbath day?" They knew that they *could* only admit the fact, and then the argument *à fortiori* was irresistible; a man was more important than a beast; the extrication of a beast involved more labour by far than the healing of a man. Their base little plot only ended in the constrained and awkward silence of a complete refutation which they were too ungenerous to acknowledge.

Jesus deigned no farther to dwell on a subject which to the mind of every candid listener had been set at rest for ever, and He turned their thoughts to other lessons. The dropsy of their inflated self-satisfaction was a disease far more difficult to heal than that of the sufferer whom they had used to entrap Him. Scarcely was the feast ready, when there arose among the distinguished company one of those unseemly struggles for precedence which—common, nay, almost universal as they are—show the tendencies of human nature on its weakest and most contemptible side.[2] And nothing more clearly showed the essential hollowness of Pharisaic religion than its intense pride and self-exaltation. Let one anecdote suffice. The King Jannæus had on one occasion invited several Persian Satraps, and among

[1] It seems certain that *υἱὸς*, not *ὄνος*, is the true reading in Luke xiv. 5; an immense preponderance of the best MSS. (A, B, and ten uncials) and versions (the Syriac, Persian, Sahidic, &c.) is in its favour; the apparent strangeness of the collocation is removed by certain Rabbinic parallels—*e.g.*, *Babha Kama*, 5, 6 (quoted by Sepp). There can be no question that the Jews had always *theoretically* admitted, and acted on, the very principle which our Lord asserts; and they do so to this day—*e.g.*, the Jews of Tiberias, with all their Sabbatarianism, *bathe often* on the Sabbath.

[2] Luke xiv. 7—11.

the guests asked to meet them was the Rabbi Simeon Ben Shetach. The latter on entering seated himself at table between the King and the Queen. Being asked his reason for such a presumptuous intrusion, he replied that it was written in the Book of Jesus Ben Sirach, "Exalt wisdom and she shall exalt thee, and shall make thee sit among princes."[1]

The Jews at this period had adopted the system of *triclinia* from the Greeks and Romans, and the "chief seat" (πρωτοκλισία) was the middle seat in the central *triclinium*. Observing the anxiety of each guest to secure this place for himself,[2] our Lord laid down a wiser and better principle of social courtesy, which involved the far deeper lesson of spiritual humility. Just as in earthly society the pushing, intrusive, self-conceited man must be prepared for many a strong rebuff, and will find himself often compelled to give place to modest merit, so in the eternal world, "whosoever exalteth himself shall be abased, and he that humbleth himself shall be exalted." Pride, exclusiveness, self-glorification, have no place in the kingdom of God. Humility is the only passport which can obtain for us an entrance there.

"Humble we must be, if to heaven we go;
High is the roof there, but the gate is low."

And He proceeded to teach them another lesson, addressed to some obvious foible in the character of His host.[3] Luxury, ostentation, the hope of a return, are not true principles of hospitality. A richer recompense awaits the kindness bestowed upon the poor than the adulatory entertainment of the friendly and the rich. In

[1] Ecclus. xv. 5; xxxix. 4; cf. Prov. iv. 8. The anecdote is quoted by Sepp, *Leben Jesu*, II. iii. 6.

[2] Luke xiv. 7, ἐξελέγοντο, "They were picking out for themselves."

[3] Luke xiv. 12—14.

receiving friends and relatives, do not forget the helpless and the afflicted.[1] Interested beneficence is nothing in the world but a deceitful selfishness. It may be that thou wouldest have won a more eternal blessing if that dropsical man had been invited to remain—if those poor lookers-on were counted among the number of the guests.

At this point one of the guests, perhaps because he thought that these lessons were disagreeable and severe, interposed a remark which, under the circumstances, rose very little above the level of a vapid and misleading platitude.[2] He poured upon the troubled waters a sort of general impersonal aphorism. Instead of profiting by these Divine lessons, he seemed inclined to rest content with "an indolent remission of the matter into distant futurity," as though he were quite sure of that blessedness, of which he seems to have a very poor and material conception. But our Lord turned his idle poor remark into a fresh occasion for most memorable teaching. He told them a parable to show that "to eat bread in the kingdom of heaven" might involve conditions which

[1] Our Lord knew that the conscience of each hearer, even unaided by the ordinary idioms of Oriental speech, would rightly understand the bold and sometimes almost paradoxical form into which He purposely cast His precepts. That the "call not thy friends" means "call not only thy friends, but also," &c., has been admitted by all except a few fanatical commentators. Even sceptics have seen that our Lord's sayings are not to be attacked on methods of interpretation which would make them repulsive to natural affection no less than to common sense. See, for other passages which require similar principles of interpretation, Matt. v. 46, 47 (Luke vi. 32—34); ix. 13; Luke xiv. 26 (comp. Matt. x. 37); John vi. 27; 1 Cor. i. 17; xv. 10. This is a well-known principle of Hebrew grammar, "Comparativus saepe ita circumscribitur, ut alterum et quidem inferius ex duobus comparatis *negetur*, alterum affirmetur, cui excellentia tribuenda est" (Glass, *Phil. Sacr.*, p. 468). See Prov. viii. 10; and *supr.*, p. 109. It is of course obvious to add that the truest kindness and charity to the poor would in these days by no means consist in merely entertaining them at meals.

[2] Luke xiv. 15—24.

those who felt so very sure of doing it would not be willing to accept. He told them of a king who had sent out many invitations to a great banquet, but who, when the due time came,[1] was met by general refusals. One had his estate to manage, and was positively obliged to go and see a new addition to it. Another was deep in buying and selling, and all the business it entailed. A third was so lapped in contented domesticity that his coming was out of the question. Then the king, rejecting, in his anger, these disrespectful and dilatory guests, bade his slaves go at once to the broad and narrow streets, and bring in the poor and maimed, and lame and blind; and when that was done, and there still was room, he sent them to urge in even the houseless wanderers by the hedges and the roads. The application to all present was obvious. The worldly heart—whether absorbed in the management of property, or the acquisition of riches, or the mere sensualisms of contented comfort—was incompatible with any desire for the true banquet of the kingdom of heaven. The Gentile and the Pariah, the harlot and the publican, the labourer of the roadside and the beggar of the streets, these might be there in greater multitudes than the Scribe with his boasted learning, and the Pharisee with his broad phylactery. "For I say unto you," He added in His own person, to point the moral more immediately to their own hearts, "that none of those men who were called shall taste of my supper." It was the lesson which He so often pointed. "To be invited is one thing, to accept the invitation is another. Many are called, but few are chosen. Many—as the

[1] These customs remain unchanged. The message *Tefŭddŭlû, el'asha hâder*, "Come, for the supper is ready," may be heard to this day; and to refuse is a high insult. (Thomson, *Land and Book*, I., chap. ix.)

heathen proverb said—'Many bear the *narthex*, but few feel the inspiring god' (πολλοί τοι ναρθηκοφόροι παῦροι δέ τε βάκχοι)."

Teachings like these ran throughout this entire period of the Lord's ministry. The parable just recorded was, in its far-sided and many-reaching significance, a reproof not only to the close exclusiveness of the Pharisees, but also to their worldliness and avarice. On another occasion, when our Lord was mainly teaching His own disciples, He told them the parable of the Unjust Steward,[1] to show them the necessity of care and faithfulness, of prudence and wisdom, in so managing the affairs and interests and possessions of this life as not to lose hereafter their heritage of the eternal riches. It

[1] Luke xvi. 1—13. If such immense and needless difficulties had not been raised about this parable, it would have seemed almost superfluous to say that the point held up for imitation in the steward is not his injustice and extravagance, but the foresight (φρονίμως, "prudently," not as in the E.V., "wisely") with which he anticipated, and the skill with which he provided against, his ultimate difficulties. It really seems as if commentators were so perplexed by the parable as hardly to have got beyond Julian's foolish and unworthy criticism, that it commends and sanctions cheating! What can be clearer than the very simple deductions? This steward, having been a bad steward, showed diligence, steady purpose, and clear sagacity in his dishonest plan for extricating himself from the consequences of past dishonesty; be ye faithful stewards, and show the same diligence, purpose, sagacity, in subordinating the present and the temporal to the requirements of the eternal and the future. Just as the steward made himself friends of the tenants, who, when his income failed, received him into their houses, so do *ye* use your wealth—(and time, opportunity, knowledge, is wealth, as well as money)—for the good of your fellow-men; that when you leave earth poor and naked, these fellow-men may welcome you to treasures that *never* fail. Such seems to be the meaning of verse 9, which is somewhat difficult. The lesson is, in fact, the same as in the famous ἄγραφον δόγμα, "Show yourselves approved money-changers." The parables of the Unjust Judge and the Importunate Suitor (ἀναίδεια, Luke xi. 8) show quite as clearly as this parable that the lesson conveyed by a parable may be enforced by principles of *contrast*, and may involve no commendation of those whose conduct conveys the lesson. It is very probable that both these parables were drawn from circumstances which had recently occurred.

was impossible—such was the recurrent burden of so many discourses—to be at once worldly and spiritual; to be at once the slave of God and the slave of Mammon. With the supreme and daring paradox which impressed His divine teaching on the heart and memory of the world, He urged them to the foresight of a spiritual wisdom by an example drawn from the foresight of a criminal cleverness.

Although Christ had been speaking in the first instance to the Apostles, some of the Pharisees seem to have been present and to have heard Him; and it is a characteristic fact that this teaching, more than any other, seems to have kindled their most undisguised derision. They began to treat Him with the most open and insolent disdain. And why? Because they were Pharisees, and yet were fond of money.[1] Had not they, then, in their own persons, successfully solved the problem of "making the best of both worlds?" Who could doubt *their* perfect safety for the future? nay, the absolute certainty that they would be admitted to the "chief seats," the most distinguished and conspicuous places in the world to come? Were they not, then, standing

[1] Luke xvi. 14, *ἐξεμυκτήριζον αὐτόν.* The vice of avarice seems inherent in the Jewish race. To this day, says Dr. Thomson, speaking of the Jews in Palestine, "Everybody trades, speculates, cheats. The shepherd-boy on the mountain talks of *piastres* from morning till night; so does the muleteer on the road, the farmer in the field, the artisan in the shop, the merchant in his magazine, the pacha in his palace, the kadi in the hall of judgment, the mullah in the mosque, the monk, the priest, the bishop—money, money, money! the desire of every heart, the theme of every tongue, the end of every aim. Everything is bought and sold—each prayer has its price, each sin its tariff." (II. ch. xxvii.)—Quarrels about the money, complaints of the greed and embezzlement of the Rabbis, wrong distribution of the *chaluka*, or alms, and the *kadima*, or honorary pay, form the main history of the Jews in modern Jerusalem. It is a profoundly melancholy tale, and no one who knows the facts will deny it—least of all pious and worthy Jews. (*Vide* Frankl, *Jews in the East, passim.*)

witnesses of the absurdity of the supposition that the love of money was incompatible with the love of God?

Our Lord's answer to them is very much compressed by St. Luke,[1] but consisted, first, in showing them that respectability of life is one thing, and sincerity of heart quite another. Into the new kingdom, for which John had prepared the way, the world's lowest were pressing in, and were being accepted before them; the Gospel was being rejected by them, though it was not the destruction, but the highest fulfilment of the Law. Nay—such seems to be the meaning of the apparently disconnected verse which follows[2]—even to the Law itself, of which not one tittle[3] should fail, they were faithless, for they could connive at the violation of its most distinct provisions. In this apparently isolated remark He alluded, in all probability, to their relations to Herod Antipas, whom they were content to acknowledge and to flatter, and to whom not one of them had dared to use the brave language of reproach which had been used by John the Baptist, although, by the clearest decisions of the Law which they professed to venerate, his divorce from the daughter of Aretas was adulterous,

[1] Luke xvi. 15—18.

[2] Cf. Luke vii. 29; xv. 1; Matt. xi. 12, 13. This is Luther's interpretation, and seems to be the correct one, though Stier does not think it worthy of refutation.

[3] "Tittle," *κεραία* (Luke xvi. 17); *i.e.*, the smallest turn or stroke of a letter, like the minute points which distinguish ב from כ (Orig., ad Ps. xxxiii.). (Wetstein.)—This is one of Christ's expressions which receive interesting illustration from the Rabbis. In *Jer. Sanhedr.*, f. 20, the Book of Deuteronomy prostrates itself before God, and complains that Solomon has robbed it of the letter *jod* (in the letter *nashîm*) by taking many wives. God answers that Solomon shall perish, but not the letter *jod*. R. Honna said that the *jod* which God took from the name Sarai He divided in half, giving half to Abra*h*am, half to Sara*h* (because ה (*h*) = 5, י (*yod*) = 10), &c. (Gfrörer, i. 236.)

and his marriage with Herodias was doubly adulterous, and worse.

But to make the immediate truth which He had been explaining yet more clear to them, He told them the parable of the Rich Man and Lazarus.[1] Like all of our Lord's parables, it is full of meaning, and admits of more than one application; but at least they could not miss the one plain and obvious application, that the decision of the next world will often reverse the estimation wherein men are held in this; that God is no respecter of persons; that the heart must make its choice between the "good things" of this life and those which the externals of this life do not affect. And what may be called the epilogue of this parable contains a lesson more solemn still—namely, that the means of grace which God's mercy accords to every living soul are ample for its enlightenment and deliverance; that if these be neglected, no miracle will be wrought to startle the absorbed soul from its worldly interests; that "if they hear not Moses and the Prophets, neither will they be

[1] It is a curious, but perhaps accidental, coincidence that in this parable alone is any name given; as also Lazarus is the only recipient—with the exception of Bartimæus—of our Lord's miracles who is distinctly named. Perhaps there may be some reference intended to names written in heaven, but forgotten on earth, and blazoned on earth, but unrecorded in heaven (comp. the ἐτάφη of verse 22 with the silence about the burial of Lazarus). The name Lazarus, however [either לֹא עֵזֶר, *Lo ezer* (Chald. *La*) (?), "Not help," ἀβοήθητος (Theophyl.), or better, אֵלִי עֵזֶר, *Eli ezer*, "God my help"], is particularly appropriate. Herberger, quoted by Stier, says, "We have in this parable a veritable window opened into hell, through which we can see what passes there." But inferences of this kind must be very cautiously pressed. It is a wise and well-established rule, that "*Theologia parabolica non est demonstrativa.*" Some see in "the five brethren" a reference to the five sons of Annas (Jos. *Antt.* xx. 9, § 1)—an entirely questionable allusion (Sepp, *Leben Jesu*, II. vi. 11). Some very ingenious speculations on the subject of Lazarus may be seen in Prof. Plumptre's *Lazarus and other Poems* (note).

persuaded though one rose from the dead." *Auditu fideli salvamur*, says Bengel, *non apparitionibus*—"We are saved by faithful hearing, not by ghosts."

This constant reference to life as a time of probation, and to the Great Judgment, when the one word "Come," or "Depart," as uttered by the Judge, should decide all controversies and all questions for ever, naturally turned the thoughts of many listeners to these solemn subjects. But there is a great and constant tendency in the minds of us all to refer such questions to the case of others rather than our own—to make them questions rather of speculative curiosity than of practical import. And such tendencies, which rob moral teaching of all its wholesomeness, and turn its warnings into mere excuses for uncharity, were always checked and discouraged by our Lord. A special opportunity was given Him for this on one occasion during those days in which He was going "through the cities and villages, teaching, and journeying toward Jerusalem."[1] He had—not, perhaps, for the first time—been speaking of the small beginnings and the vast growth of the kingdom of heaven alike in the soul and in the world; and one of His listeners, in the spirit of unwise though not unnatural curiosity, asked Him, "Lord, are there few that be saved?" Whether the question was dictated by secure self-satisfaction, or by despondent pity, we cannot tell; but in either case our Lord's answer involved a disapproval of the inquiry, and a statement of the wholly different manner in which such questions should be approached. "Few" or "many" are relative terms. Waste not the precious opportunities of life in idle wonderment, but *strive*. Through that narrow gate, none—not were they

[1] Luke xiii. 22—30; Matt. xiii. 31, 32; Mark iv. 30, 31.

j *

a thousand times of the seed of Abraham—can enter without earnest effort. And since the efforts, the wilful efforts, the erring efforts of many fail—since the day will come when the door shall be shut, and it shall be for ever too late to enter there—since no impassioned appeal shall then admit, no claim of olden knowledge shall then be recognised—since some of those who in their spiritual pride thought that they best knew the Lord, shall hear the awful repudiation, "I know you not"—*strive ye* to be of those that enter in. For many *shall* enter from every quarter of the globe, and yet thou, O son of Abraham, mayest be excluded. And behold, once more—it may well sound strange to thee,[1] yet so it is—"there are last which shall be first, and there are first which shall be last."[2]

Thus each vapid interruption, each scornful criticism, each erroneous question, each sad or happy incident, was made by Jesus, throughout this journey, an opportunity for teaching to His hearers, and through them to all the world, the things that belonged unto their peace. And He did so once more, when "a certain lawyer" stood up tempting Him, and asked—not to obtain guidance, but to find subject for objection—the momentous question, "What must I do to obtain eternal life?" Jesus, seeing through the evil motive of his question, simply asked him what was the answer to that question which was

1 Such is the general significance of καὶ ἰδοὺ in the Gospels. It is used twenty-three times in St. Matthew, sixteen in St. Luke, but not in St Mark.

2 Dante, in his *Inferno*, has finely expanded this truth:—

"He in the world was one
For arrogance noted; to his memory
No virtue lent its lustre. . . . There above
How many hold themselves for mighty kings
Who here, like swine, shall wallow in the mire,
Leaving behind them horrible dispraise."

given in the Law which it was the very object of the man's life to teach and to explain. The lawyer gave the best summary which the best teaching of his nation had by this time rendered prevalent. Jesus simply confirmed his answer, and said, "This do, and thou shalt live." But wanting something more than this, and anxious to justify a question which from his own point of view was superfluous, and which had, as he well knew, been asked with an ungenerous purpose, the lawyer thought to cover his retreat by the fresh question, "And who is my neighbour?" Had Jesus asked the man's own opinion on this question, He well knew how narrow and false it would have been; He therefore answered it Himself, or rather gave to the lawyer the means for answering it, by one of His most striking parables. He told him how once a man, going down the rocky gorge which led from Jerusalem to Jericho, had fallen into the hands of the robbers, whose frequent attacks had given to that descent the ill-omened name of "the bloody way," and had been left by these Bedawîn marauders, after the fashion which they still practise, bleeding, naked, and half dead upon the road. A priest going back to his priestly city had passed that way, caught a glimpse of him, and crossed over to the other side of the road. A Levite, with still cooler indifference, had come and stared at him, and quietly done the same. But a Samaritan journeying that way—one on whom he would have looked with shuddering national antipathy, one in whose very shadow he would have seen pollution—a good Samaritan, pattern of that Divine Speaker whom men rejected and despised, but who had come to stanch those bleeding wounds of humanity, for which there was no remedy either in the ceremonial or the moral law—

came to him, pitied, tended him, mounted him on his own beast, trudged beside him on the hard, hot, dusty, dangerous road, and would not leave him till he had secured his safety, and generously provided for his future wants. Which of these three, Jesus asked the lawyer, was *neighbour* to him who fell among thieves? The man was not so dull as to refuse to see; but yet, knowing that he would have excluded alike the Samaritans and the Gentiles from his definition of "neighbours," he has not the candour to say at once, "*The Samaritan*," but uses the poor periphrasis, "He that did him the kindness." "Go," said Jesus, "and do thou likewise." I, the friend of publicans and sinners, hold up the example of this Samaritan to thee.[1]

We must not, however, suppose that these two months of mission-progress were all occupied in teaching which, however exalted, received its external shape and impulse from the errors and controversies which met the Saviour on His way. There were many circumstances during these days which must have filled His soul with joy.

Pre-eminent among these was the return of the Seventy.[2] We cannot, of course, suppose that they returned in a body, but that from time to time, two and two, as our Lord approached the various cities and villages whither He had sent them, they came to give Him an account of their success. And that success was such as to fill their simple hearts with astonishment and exultation. "Lord," they exclaimed, "even the devils are subject unto us through Thy name." Though He had given them no special commission to heal demoniacs, though in one conspicuous instance even the Apostles

[1] Luke x. 25—37. [2] Luke x. 17—20.

had failed in this attempt, yet now they could cast out devils in their Master's name. Jesus, while entering into their joy, yet checked the tone of over-exultation, and rather turned it into a nobler and holier channel. He bade them feel sure that good was eternally mightier than evil; and that the victory over Satan—his fall like lightning from heaven—had been achieved and should continue for ever. Over all evil influences He gave them authority and victory, and the word of His promise should be an amulet to protect them from every source of harm. They should go upon the lion and adder, the young lion and the dragon should they tread under feet;[1] because He had set His love upon them, therefore would He deliver them: He would set them up because they had known His name. And yet there was a subject of joy more deep and real and true—less dangerous because less seemingly personal and conspicuous than this—on which He rather fixed their thoughts: it was that their names had been written, and stood unobliterated,[2] in the Book of Life in heaven.

And besides the gladness inspired into the heart of Jesus by the happy faith and unbounded hope of His disciples, He also rejoiced in spirit that, though rejected and despised by Scribes and Pharisees, He was loved and worshipped by Publicans and Sinners. The poor to whom He preached His Gospel—the blind whose eyes He had come to open—the sick whom He had come to heal—the lost whom it was His mission to seek and save;—these all thronged with heartfelt and pathetic gratitude to the Good Shepherd, the Great Physician.

[1] Ps. xci. 13, 14. Wetstein shows that Christ here adopted a familiar metaphor, found also in the Rabbis.

[2] ἐγγέγραπται (Luke x. 20; Rev. xx. 12, 15). See Clemens, *Ep. ad Cor.* xlv., with Dr. Lightfoot's note.

The Scribes and Pharisees as usual murmured,[1] but what mattered that to the happy listeners? To the weary and heavy-laden He spoke in every varied form of hope, of blessing, of encouragement. By the parable of the Importunate Widow He taught them the duty of faith, and the certain answer to ceaseless and earnest prayer.[2] By the parable of the haughty, respectable, fasting, alms-giving, self-satisfied Pharisee—who, going to make his boast to God in the Temple, went home less justified than the poor Publican, who could only reiterate one single cry for God's mercy as he stood there beating his breast, and with downcast eyes—He taught them that God loves better a penitent humility than a merely external service, and that a broken heart and a contrite spirit were sacrifices which He would not despise.[3] Nor was this all. He made them feel that they were dear to God; that, though erring children, they were His children still. And, therefore, to the parables of the Lost Sheep and the Lost Drachma, He added that parable in which lies the whole Gospel in its richest and tenderest grace—the Parable of the Prodigal Son.

Never certainly in human language was so much—such a world of love and wisdom and tenderness—com-

[1] Luke xv. 1, 2. This is the third instance in which this self-righteous exclusiveness is rebuked. The first was at the house of Simon the Pharisee (Luke vii. 39; see Vol. I., p. 301); the second at Matthew's feast (Matt. ix. 11; Vol. I., p. 348); and the same thing occurred again in the case of Zacchæus (Luke xix. 7). In each of these instances Jesus with a deep irony "argued with His accusers on their own premises, accepting *their* estimate of *themselves* and of the class with whom they deemed it discreditable to associate, as righteous and sinful respectively." (Bruce, *Training of the Twelve*, p. 28.)

[2] Luke xviii. 1—8.

[3] Luke xviii. 9—14.

pressed into such few immortal words.[1] Every line, every touch of the picture is full of beautiful eternal significance. The poor boy's presumptuous claim for all that life could give him—the leaving of the old home—the journey to a far country—the brief spasm of "enjoyment" there—the mighty famine in that land—the premature exhaustion of all that could make life noble and endurable—the abysmal degradation and unutterable misery that followed—the coming to himself, and recollection of all that he had left behind—the return in heart-broken penitence and deep humility—the father's far-off sight of him, and the gush of compassion and tenderness over this poor returning prodigal—the ringing joy of the whole household over him who had been loved and lost, and had now come home—the unjust jealousy and mean complaint of the elder brother—and then that close of the parable in a strain of music—"*Son, thou art ever with me, and all that I have is thine. It was meet that we should make merry, and be glad: for this thy brother was dead, and is alive again; was lost, and is found*"—all this is indeed a divine epitome of the wandering of man and the love of God such as no literature has ever equalled, such as no ear of man has ever heard elsewhere. Put in the one scale all that Confucius, or Sakya Mouni, or Zoroaster, or Socrates ever wrote or said—and they wrote and said many beautiful and holy words—and put in the other the Parable of the Prodigal Son alone, with all that this single parable connotes and means, and can any candid spirit doubt which scale would outweigh the other in eternal preciousness—in divine adaptation to the wants of man?

[1] I have already touched on this parable (*supra*, Vol. I., p. 426); but a few more words on the subject will perhaps be pardoned here.

So this great journey grew gradually to a close. The awful solemnity—the shadow, as it were, of coming doom—the half-uttered "too late" which might be dimly heard in its tones of warning—characterise the single record of it which the Evangelist St. Luke has happily preserved.[1] We seem to hear throughout it an undertone of that deep yearning which Jesus had before expressed—"I have a baptism to be baptised with; and how am I straitened until it be accomplished!" It was a sorrow for all the broken peace and angry opposition which His work would cause on earth—a sense that He was prepared to plunge into the "willing agony" of the already kindled flame.[2] And this seems to have struck the minds of all who heard Him; they had an expectation, fearful or glad according to the condition of their consciences, of something great. Some new manifestation—some revelation of the thoughts of men's hearts—was near at hand. At last the Pharisees summoned up courage to ask Him "when the kingdom of God should come?"[3] There was a certain impatience, a certain materialism, possibly also a tinge of sarcasm and depreciation in the question, as though they had said, "When is all this preaching and preparation to end, and the actual time to arrive?" His answer, as usual, indi-

[1] As the main events and teaching of this episode in St. Luke (ix. 51—xviii. 14) are not recorded by the other Synoptists, and as the narratives of the three meet again at Luke xviii. 15; Matt. xix. 13; Mark x. 13, it is a natural and reasonable supposition that the things narrated beyond that point belong to a time subsequent to the journey. We can, of course, only conjecture why St. Luke is almost our sole authority for this period of two months; it is, however, possible that both St. Matthew and St. Peter (who was the informant of St. Mark) were but little with Jesus at this time, and were themselves engaged in a mission similar to that of the Seventy.

[2] Luke xii. 49—53.

[3] Luke xvii. 20—37.

cated that their *point of view* was wholly mistaken. The coming of the kingdom of God could not be ascertained by the kind of narrow and curious watching[1] to which they were addicted. False Christs and mistaken Rabbis might cry "*Lo here!*" and "*Lo there!*" but that kingdom was already in the midst of them;[2] nay, if they had the will and the wisdom to recognise and to embrace it, that kingdom was *within them.* That answer was sufficient to the Pharisees, but to His disciples He added words which implied the fuller explanation. Even *they* did not fully realise that the kingdom *had already* come. Their eyes were strained *forward* in intense and yearning eagerness to some glorious future; but in the future, glorious as it would be, they would still look *backward* with yet deeper yearning, not unmingled with regret, to this very past—to these days of the Son of Man, in which they were seeing and their hands handling the Word of Life. In those days, let them not be deceived by any "Lo there! Lo here!" nor let them waste in feverish and fruitless restlessness the calm and golden opportunities of life.[3] For that coming of the Son of Man should be bright, sudden, terrible, universal, irresistible as the lightning flash; but before that day He must suffer and be rejected. Moreover, that gleam of His second advent would flame upon the midnight of a sensual, unexpectant world, as the flood rolled over the festive sensualism in the days of Noah, and the fire and brimstone streamed from

[1] Luke xvii. 20, παρατήρησις. Cf. xiv. 1.

[2] That ἐντὸς ὑμῶν may have this meaning is proved by the passage of Xenophon (*Anab.* i. 10, 3) cited by Alford; but the other meaning is probably included. Cf. Rom. xiv. 17; John i. 26; xii. 35, &c.; and Deut. xxx. 14.

[3] See 2 Thess. *passim.*

heaven upon the glittering rottenness of the Cities of the Plain. Woe to those who should in that day be casting regretful glances on a world destined to pass away in flame! For though till then the business and companionships of life should continue, and all its various fellowships of toil or friendliness, that night would be one of fearful and of final separations!

The disciples were startled and terrified by words of such strange solemnity. "Where, Lord?" they ask in alarm. But to the "where" there could be as little answer as to the "when," and the coming of God's kingdom is as little geographical as it is chronological.[1] "Wheresoever the body is," He says, "thither will the vultures be gathered together."[2] The mystic Armageddon is no place whose situation you may fix by latitude and longitude. Wherever there is individual wickedness, wherever there is social degeneracy, wherever there is deep national corruption, thither do the eagle-avengers of the Divine vengeance wing their flight from far: thither from the ends of the earth come nations of a fierce countenance, "swift as the eagle flieth," to rend and to devour. "Her young ones also suck up blood: and where the slain are, there is she."[3]

[1] See Stier, iv. 287.

[2] The Jews, and indeed the ancients generally, classed the vulture with the eagle. I cannot believe the interpretation of Chrysostom, Theophylactus, &c., that the "body" is Christ, and the gathering eagles are His saints. All that can be said for this view may be seen in Bishop Wordsworth on Matt. xxiv. 28; but a reference to Job xxxix. 30, "Her young ones also suck up blood; *and where the slain are, there is she,*" seems alone sufficient to refute it.

[3] Deut. xxviii. 49; Job xxxix. 30. Cf. Hab. i. 8, "They shall fly as the eagle that hasteth to eat;" Hos. viii. 1, "Set the trumpet to thy mouth. He shall fly as an eagle against the house of the Lord, because they have transgressed my covenant, and trespassed against my law." In fact, the best commentary to the metaphor will be found in Rev. xix. 17—21.

Jerusalem—nay, the whole Jewish nation—was falling rapidly into the dissolution rising from internal decay; and already the flap of avenging pinions was in the air. When the world too should lie in a state of morbid infamy, then should be heard once more the rushing of those "congregated wings."

Is not all history one long vast commentary on these great prophecies? In the destinies of nations and of races has not the Christ returned again and again to deliver or to judge?

CHAPTER XLV.

THE FEAST OF DEDICATION.

Thrice blessed whose lives are faithful prayers,
Whose loves in higher love endure;
What souls possess themselves so pure,
Or is there blessedness like theirs?—TENNYSON.

NOWHERE, in all probability, did Jesus pass more restful and happy hours than in the quiet house of that little family at Bethany, which, as we are told by St. John, "He loved." The family, so far as we know, consisted only of Martha, Mary, and their brother Lazarus. That Martha was a widow—that her husband was, or had been, Simon the Leper—that Lazarus is identical with the gentle and holy Rabbi of that name mentioned in the Talmud—are conjectures that may or may not be true;[1] but we see from the Gospels that they were a family in easy circumstances, and of sufficient dignity and position to excite considerable attention not only in their own little village of Bethany, but even in Jerusalem. The lonely little hamlet, lying among its peaceful uplands, near Jerusalem, and yet completely hidden from it by the summit of Olivet, and thus

"Not wholly in the busy world, nor quite
Beyond it,"

must always have had for the soul of Jesus an especial

[1] *Peah*, f. 21, 2, quoted by Sepp, iii. 8.

charm; and the more so because of the friends whose love and reverence always placed at His disposal their holy and happy home. It is there that we find Him on the eve of the Feast of the Dedication, which marked the close of that public journey designed for the full and final proclamation of His coming kingdom.[1]

It was natural that there should be some stir in the little household at the coming of such a Guest, and Martha, the busy, eager-hearted, affectionate hostess, "on hospitable thoughts intent," hurried to and fro with excited energy to prepare for His proper entertainment. Her sister Mary, too, was anxious to receive Him fittingly,[2] but her notions of the reverence due to Him were of a different kind. Knowing that her sister was only too happy to do all that could be done for His material comfort, she, in deep humility, sat at His feet and listened to His words.

Mary was not to blame, for her sister evidently enjoyed the task which she had chosen of providing as best she could for the claims of hospitality, and was quite able, without any assistance, to do everything that was required. Nor was Martha to blame for her active service; her sole fault was that, in this outward activity, she lost the necessary equilibrium of an inward calm. As she toiled and planned to serve Him, a little touch of jealousy disturbed her peace as she saw her quiet sister sitting—"idly" she may have thought—at the feet of their great Visitor, and leaving the trouble to fall on her.

[1] St. Luke, as Stier observes, may have anticipated the true order of this anecdote in order to let it throw light on the question of the lawyer, "What must I *do?*" (See Luke x. 25, 38—42.) This, if correct, is a good illustration of the subjective considerations which seem to dominate in this episode of his Gospel.

[2] Luke x. 39, ἣ καὶ παρακαθίσασα . . ἤκουεν.

If she had taken time to think, she could not but have acknowledged that there may have been as much of consideration as of selfishness in Mary's withdrawal into the background in their domestic administration; but to be just and noble-minded is always difficult, nor is it even possible when any one meanness, such as petty jealousy, is suffered to intrude. So, in the first blush of her vexation, Martha, instead of gently asking her sister to help her, if help, indeed, were needed—an appeal which, if we judge of Mary aright, she would instantly have heard—she almost impatiently, and not quite reverently, hurries in,[1] and asks Jesus if He really did not care to see her sister sitting there with her hands before her, while *she* was left single-handed to do all the work. Would He not tell her (Martha could not have fairly added that common piece of ill-nature, "It is of no use for *me* to tell her") to go and help?

An imperfect soul, seeing what is good and great and true, but very often failing in the attempt to attain to it, is apt to be very hard in its judgments on the shortcomings of others. But a divine and sovereign soul—a soul that has more nearly attained to the measure of the stature of the perfect man—takes a calmer and gentler, because a larger-hearted view of those little weaknesses and indirectnesses which it cannot but daily see. And so the answer of Jesus, if it were a reproof, was at any rate an infinitely gentle and tender one, and one which would purify but would not pain the poor faithful heart of the busy, loving matron to whom it was addressed. "Martha, Martha," so He said—and as we hear that most natural address may we not imagine the half-sad,

[1] Such seems to be the force of ἐπιστᾶσα in St. Luke, who almost alone uses the word [xx. 1 (cf. ii. 38); Acts xxiii. 27 (cf. 1 Thess. v. 3)].

half-playful, but wholly kind and healing smile which lightened His face?—"thou art anxious and bustling about many things, whereas but one thing is needful;[1] but Mary chose for herself the good part, which shall not be taken away from her." There is none of that exaltation here of the contemplative over the active life which Roman Catholic writers have seen in the passage, and on which they are so fond of dwelling. Either may be necessary, both must be combined. Paul, as has well been said, in his most fervent activity, had yet the contemplativeness and inward calm of Mary; and John, with the most rapt spirit of contemplation, could yet practise the activity of Martha. Jesus did not mean to reprobate any amount of work undertaken in His service, but only the spirit of fret and fuss—the want of all repose and calm—the ostentation of superfluous hospitality—in doing it; and still more that tendency to reprobate and interfere with others, which is so often seen in Christians who are as anxious as Martha, but have none of Mary's holy trustfulness and perfect calm.

It is likely that Bethany was the home of Jesus during His visits to Jerusalem, and from it a short and delightful walk over the Mount of Olives would take Him to the Temple. It was now winter-time, and the

[1] The *μεριμνᾷς* alludes to her inward solicitude, the *τυρβάζῃ* to her outward fussiness; in fact, if we may adopt such colloquial terms, "fretting" and "fussing" would exactly represent the two words. The various readings, *ὀλίγων δέ ἐστι χρεία, ὀλίγων δέ ἐστι χρεία ἢ ἑνός* (א, B, L, the Coptic, &c.), might have risen from the notion that at any rate more than one thing would be required for the meal; but in point of fact an Eastern meal usually consists of one common dish. Altogether, it seems clear that the first and obvious meaning—as was so customary with our Lord—was meant to *involve* the high and spiritual meaning. Perhaps the *ὀλίγων* (supported by the consensus of א and B) may have been omitted in some MSS., from a desire to *enforce* this spiritual lesson.

Feast of the Dedication was being celebrated.[1] This feast was held on the 25th of Cisleu, and, according to Wieseler, fell this year on Dec. 20. It was founded by Judas Maccabæus in honour of the cleansing of the Temple in the year B.C. 164, six years and a half after its fearful profanation by Antiochus Epiphanes. Like the Passover and the Tabernacles, it lasted eight days, and was kept with great rejoicing.[2] Besides its Greek name of Encænia, it had the name of *τὰ φῶτα*, or the Lights, and one feature of the festivity was a general illumination to celebrate the legendary miracle of a miraculous multiplication, for eight days, of the holy oil which had been found by Judas Maccabæus in one single jar sealed with the High Priest's seal.[3] Our Lord's presence at such a festival sanctions the right of each Church to ordain its own rites and ceremonies, and shows that He looked with no disapproval on the joyous enthusiasm of national patriotism.

The eastern porch of the Temple still retained the name of Solomon's Porch, because it was at least built of the materials which had formed part of the ancient Temple.[4] Here, in this bright colonnade, decked for the feast with glittering trophies, Jesus was walking up and down, quietly, and apparently without companions,

[1] John x. 22. Called by the Jews *Chanûkkah.*

[2] Some account of these events may be seen in 1 Macc. iv. 52—59; 2 Macc. x. 1—8. "They decked the fore-front of the Temple with crowns of gold and with shields" (Jos. *Antt.* xii. 7, § 7).

[3] *Shabbath,* 21 *b*; *Rosh-hashanah,* 24 *b* (Derenbourg, *Hist. Pal.* 62; Jos. *Antt.* xii. 7, § 7). The eight days had in reality been necessary for the work to be done. Perhaps Pers. *Sat.* v. 180 seqq. are a description of the *Chanûkkah,* though called by mistake "*Herodis* dies" (Id. 165). See a good account of the Feast by Dr. Ginsburg, in Kitto's *Bibl. Cycl.* i. 653.

[4] Jos. *Antt.* xx. 9, § 7. That the actual porch, in its original state, had been left standing, is wholly improbable.

sometimes, perhaps, gazing across the valley of the Kidron at the whited sepulchres of the prophets, whom generations of Jews had slain, and enjoying the mild winter sunlight, when, as though by a preconcerted movement, the Pharisaic party and their leaders suddenly surrounded[1] and began to question Him. Perhaps the very spot where He was walking, recalling as it did the memories of their ancient glory—perhaps the memories of the glad feast which they were celebrating, as the anniversary of a splendid deliverance wrought by a handful of brave men who had overthrown a colossal tyranny—inspired their ardent appeal. "How long," they impatiently inquired, "dost thou hold our souls in painful suspense? If thou really art the Messiah, tell us with confidence. Tell us *here*, in Solomon's Porch, *now*, while the sight of these shields and golden crowns, and the melody of these citherns and cymbals, recall the glory of Judas the Asmonæan—wilt thou be a mightier Maccabæus, a more glorious Solomon? shall these citrons, and fair boughs, and palms, which we carry in honour of this day's victory, be carried some day for thee?"[2] It was a strange, impetuous, impatient appeal, and is full of significance. It forms their own strong condemnation, for it shows distinctly that He had spoken words and done deeds which would have justified and substantiated such a claim had He chosen definitely to assert it. And if He had in so many words asserted it—above all, had He asserted it in the sense and with the objects which they required—it is probable that they would

[1] John x. 24, ἐκύκλωσαν οὖν αὐτὸν (cf. Luke xxi. 20; Heb. xi. 30) καὶ ἔλεγον.

[2] 2 Macc. x. 7. These *lulabîm* assimilated the feast still more closely to the Feast of Tabernacles.

have instantly welcomed Him with tumultuous acclaim. The place where they were speaking recalled the most gorgeous dreams of their ancient monarchy; the occasion was rife with the heroic memories of one of their bravest and most successful warriors; the political conditions which surrounded them were exactly such as those from which the noble Asmonæan had delivered them. One spark of that ancient flame would have kindled their inflammable spirits into such a blaze of irresistible fanaticism as might for the time have swept away both the Romans and the Herods, but which—since the hour of their fall had already begun to strike, and the cup of their iniquity was already full—would only have antedated by many years the total destruction which fell upon them, first when they were slain by myriads at the destruction of Jerusalem by Titus, and afterwards when the false Messiah, Bar-Cochebas, and his followers were so frightfully exterminated at the capture of Bethyr.

But the day for political deliverances was past; the day for a higher, deeper, wider, more eternal deliverance had come. For the former they yearned, the latter they rejected. Passionate to claim in Jesus an exclusive temporal Messiah, they repelled Him with hatred as the Son of God, the Saviour of the world. That He was their Messiah in a sense far loftier and more spiritual than they had ever dreamed, His language had again and again implied; but the Messiah in the sense which they required He was not, and would not be. And therefore He does not mislead them by saying, "I *am* your Messiah," but He refers them to that repeated teaching, which showed how clearly such had been His claim, and to the works which bore witness to that claim.[1] Had they been sheep of His flock—and He here reminds them of that great discourse which He had delivered at the Feast of Tabernacles two months before—they would have heard His voice, and then He would have given them eternal life, and they would have been safe in His keeping; for no one would then have been able to pluck them out of His Father's hand, and he added solemnly, "I and my Father are one."

His meaning was quite unmistakable. In these words He was claiming not only to be Messiah, but to be Divine. Had the oneness with the Father which He claimed been nothing more than that subjective union of faith and obedience which exists between all holy souls and their Creator—His words could have given no more offence than many a saying of their own kings and prophets; but "*ecce Judaei intellexerunt quod non intelligunt Ariani!*"—they saw at once that the words meant infinitely more. Instantly they stooped to seize some of the scattered heavy stones[2] which the unfinished Temple buildings supplied to their fury, and, had His hour been come, He could not have escaped the tumultuary death which afterwards befell His proto-martyr. But His undisturbed majesty disarmed them with a word: "Many good deeds did I show you from my Father: for which of these do ye mean to stone me?"[3] Not for any good deed, they replied, "but for blasphemy, and because thou, being a mere man,[4] art making thyself God." The reply of Jesus is one of those broad gleams of illumination which

[1] See John v. and viii. *passim.*
[2] John x. 31, ἐβάστασαν. The word in John viii. 59 is ἦραν.
[3] John x. 32, λιθάζετε.
[4] ἄνθρωπος (ver. 33). See Lev. xxiv. 10—16.

He often sheds on the interpretation of the Scriptures: "Does it not stand written in your Law," He asked them, "'I said, Ye are gods?'[1] If he called them gods (*Elohim*) to whom the Word of God came—and such undeniably *is* the case in your own Scriptures—do ye say to Him whom the Father sanctified and sent into the world, 'Thou blasphemest,' because I said, 'I am the Son of God?'" And He appealed to His life and to His works, as undeniable proofs of His unity with the Father. If His sinlessness and His miracles were not a proof that He *could* not be the presumptuous blasphemer whom they wished to stone—what further proof could be given? They, nursed in the strictest monotheism, and accustomed only to think of God as infinitely far from man, might have learnt even from the Law and from the Prophets that God is near—is in the very mouth and in the very heart—of those who love Him, and even bestows upon them some indwelling brightness of His own eternal glory. Might not this be a sign to them, that He who came to fulfil the Law and put a loftier Law in its place—He to whom all the prophets had witnessed—He for whom John had prepared the way—He who spake as never man spake—He who did the works which none other man had ever done since the foundation of the world—He who had ratified all His words, and given significance to all His deeds, by the blameless beauty of an absolutely stainless life—was indeed speaking the truth when He said that He was one with the Father, and that He was the Son of God?

The appeal was irresistible. They dared not stone Him; but, as He was alone and defenceless in the midst of them, they tried to seize Him. But they could not.

[1] Ps. lxxxii. 6.

His presence overawed them. They could only make a passage for Him, and glare their hatred upon Him as He passed from among them. But once more, here was a clear sign that all teaching among them was impossible. He could as little descend to their notions of a Messiah, as they could rise to His. To stay among them was but daily to imperil His life in vain. Judæa, therefore, was closed to Him, as Galilee was closed to Him. There seemed to be one district only which was safe for Him in His native land, and that was Peræa, the district beyond the Jordan. He retired, therefore, to the other Bethany—the Bethany beyond Jordan, where John had once been baptising—and there He stayed.

What were the incidents of this last stay, or the exact length of its continuance, we do not know. We see, however, that it was not exactly private, for St. John tells us that many resorted to Him there,[1] and believed on Him, and bore witness that John—whom they held to be a Prophet, though he had done no miracle—had borne emphatic witness to Jesus in that very place, and that all which He had witnessed was true.

[1] John x. 41, 42. For Bethany, *v. supra*, Vol. I., p. 140.

CHAPTER XLVI.

THE LAST STAY IN PERÆA.

"At evening time it shall be light."—ZECH. xiv. 7.

WHEREVER the ministry of Jesus was in the slightest degree public, there we invariably find the Pharisees watching, lying in wait for Him, tempting Him, trying to entrap Him into some mistaken judgment or ruinous decision. But perhaps even *their* malignity never framed a question to which the answer was so beset with difficulties as when they came to "tempt" Him with the problem, "Is it lawful for a man to put away his wife for every cause?"[1]

The question was beset with difficulties on every side, and for many reasons. In the first place, the institution of Moses on the subject was ambiguously expressed. Then this had given rise to a decided opposition of opinion between the two most important and flourishing of the rabbinic schools. The difference of the schools had resulted in a difference in the customs of the nation. Lastly the theological, scholastic, ethical, and national difficulties were further complicated by political ones, for the prince in whose domain the ques-

[1] Matt. xix. 3—12; Mark x. 2—12.

tion was asked was deeply interested in the answer, and had already put to death the greatest of the prophets for his bold expression of the view which was most hostile to his own practice. Whatever the truckling Rabbis of Galilee might do, St. John the Baptist, at least, had left no shadow of a doubt as to what was his interpretation of the Law of Moses, and he had paid the penalty of his frankness with his life.

Moses had laid down the rule that when a man had married a wife, and "she find no favour in his eyes because he hath found some uncleanness (marg., 'matter of nakedness,' Heb. עֶרְוַת דָּבָר, *ervath dabhar*) in her, then let him write a bill of divorcement, and give it in her hand, and send her out of his house. And when she is departed out of his house, she may go and be another man's wife."[1] Now in the interpretation of this rule, everything depended on the meaning of the expression *ervath dabhar*, or rather on the meaning of the single word *ervath*. It meant, generally, a stain or desecration, and Hillel, with his school, explained the passage in the sense that a man might "divorce his wife for any disgust which he felt towards her;"[2] even—as the celebrated R. Akiba ventured to say—if he saw any other woman who pleased him more;[3] whereas the

[1] Deut. xxiv. 1, 2. Literally, *ervath dabhar* is "nakedness of a matter" (blösse *im irgend etwas*). (Ewald, *Hebr. Gram.*, § 286, f.)

[2] The κατὰ πᾶσαν αἰτίαν of Matt. xix. 3 is a translation of the עַל כָּל דָּבָר (*al côl dabhar*), which was Hillel's exposition of the disputed passage. (See Buxtorf, *De Syn. Jud.* 29.) Almost the identical phrase is found in Jos. *Antt.* iv. 8, § 23, καθ' ἃς δηποτοῦν αἰτίας. Cf. Ecclus. xxv. 26, "If she go not as thou wouldest have her, cut her off from thy flesh."

[3] The comments of the Rabbis were even more shameful: *e.g.*, "If she spin in public, go with her head uncovered," &c.; "Even if she have over-salted his soup" (*Gittin*, 90) (Selden, *De Ux. Heb.* iii. 17). This, however is explained away by modern commentators (Jost, *Gesch. Jud.* 264). Yet it is not surprising that it led to detestable consequences. Thus we are

school of Shammai interpreted it to mean that divorce could only take place in cases of scandalous unchastity. Hence the Jews had the proverb that in this matter, as in so many others, "Hillel loosed what Shammai bound."

Shammai was morally right and exegetically wrong; Hillel exegetically right and morally wrong. Shammai was only right in so far as he saw that the *spirit* of the Mosaic legislation made no divorce justifiable *in foro conscientiae,* except for the most flagrant immorality; Hillel only right in so far as he saw that Moses had left an opening for divorce *in foro civili* in slighter cases than these. But under such circumstances, to decide in favour of either school would not only be to give mortal offence to the other, but also either to exasperate the lax many, or to disgust the high-minded few. For in those corrupt days the vast majority acted at any rate on the principle laid down by Hillel, as the Jews in the East continue to do to this day. Such, in fact, was the universal tendency of the times. In the heathen, and especially in the Roman world, the strictness of the marriage bond had been so shamefully relaxed, that, whereas, in the Republic, centuries had passed before there had been one single instance of a frivolous divorce, under the Empire, on the contrary, divorce was the rule, and faithfulness the exception. The days of the Virginias, and Lucretias, and Cornelias had passed; this was the age of the Julias, the Poppaeas, the Messalinas, the Agrippinas—the days in which, as

told in *Bab. Jômah,* f. 18, 2, that Rabbi Nachman, whenever he went to stay at a town for a short time, openly sent round the crier for a wife during his abode there (Lightfoot, *Hor. Heb. in loc.*). See Excursus III., "Jesus and Hillel;" and Excursus IX., "Hypocrisy of the Pharisees."

Seneca says, women no longer reckoned their years by the consuls, but by the number of their repudiated husbands. The Jews had caught up the shameful precedent, and since polygamy had fallen into discredit, they made a near approach to it by the ease with which they were able to dismiss one wife and take another.[1] Even Josephus, a Pharisee of the Pharisees, who on every possible occasion prominently lays claim to the character and position of a devout and religious man, narrates, without the shadow of an apology, that his first wife had abandoned him, that he had divorced the second after she had borne him three children, and that he was then married to a third. But if Jesus decided in favour of Shammai—as all His previous teaching made the Pharisees feel sure that in this particular question He *would* decide—then He would be pronouncing the public opinion that Herod Antipas was a double-dyed adulterer, an adulterer adulterously wedded to an adulterous wife.

But Jesus was never guided in any of His answers by principles of expediency, and was decidedly indifferent alike to the anger of multitudes and to the tyrant's frown. His only object was to give, even to such inquirers as these, such answers as should elevate them to a nobler sphere. Their axiom, "*Is it lawful?*" had it been sincere, would have involved the

[1] Divorce is still very common among the Eastern Jews; in 1856 there were *sixteen cases of divorce* among the small Jewish population of Jerusalem. In fact, a Jew may divorce his wife at any time and for any cause, he being himself the sole judge; the only hindrance is that, to prevent divorces in a mere sudden fit of spleen, the bill of divorce must have the concurrence of three Rabbis, and be written on ruled vellum, containing neither more nor less than twelve lines; and it must be given in the presence of ten witnesses. (Allen's *Mod. Judaism*, p. 428.)

answer to their own question. Nothing is lawful to any man who *doubts* its lawfulness. Jesus, therefore, instead of answering them, directs them to the source where the true answer was to be found. Setting the primitive order side by side with the Mosaic institution—meeting their "*Is it lawful?*" with "*Have ye not read?*"—He reminds them that God, who at the beginning had made man male and female, had thereby signified His will that marriage should be the closest and most indissoluble of all relationships[1]—transcending and even, if necessary, superseding all the rest.

"Why, then," they ask—eager to entangle Him in an opposition to "the fiery law"—"did Moses *command* to give a writing of divorcement and put her away?" The form of their question involved one of those false turns so common among the worshippers of the letter; and on this false turn they based their inverted pyramid of yet falser inferences. And so Jesus at once corrected them: "Moses, indeed, for your hardheartedness *permitted* you to put away your wives; but from the beginning it was not so;" and then he adds as formal and fearless a condemnation of Herod Antipas—without naming him—as could have been put in language, "Whoever putteth away his wife and marrieth another, except for fornication, committeth adultery; and he who marrieth the divorced woman committeth adultery:"[2] and Herod's case was the worst conceivable instance of both forms of adultery, for he, while married to an innocent and undivorced wife, had wedded the guilty

[1] Gen. ii. 24. "They two" is in the LXX., but not in the Hebrew.

[2] It appears from St. Matthew that Jesus uttered this precept to the Pharisees, as well as confided it afterwards to His disciples. See Matt. xix. 9; Mark x. 11 (*vide supra*, p. 127).

but still undivorced wife of Herod Philip, his own brother and host; and he had done this, without the shadow of any excuse, out of mere guilty passion, when his own prime of life and that of his paramour was already past.

If the Pharisees chose to make any use of this to bring Jesus into collision with Antipas, and draw down upon Him the fate of John, they might; and if they chose to embitter still more against Him the schools of Hillel and of Shammai, *both* of which were thus shown to be mistaken—that of Hillel from deficiency of moral insight, that of Shammai from lack of exegetical acumen—they might; but meanwhile He had once more thrown a flood of light over the difficulties of the Mosaic legislation, showing that it was provisional, not final—transitory, not eternal. That which the Jews, following their famous Hillel, regarded as a Divine permission of which to be proud, was, on the contrary, a tolerated evil permitted to the outward life, though not to the enlightened conscience or the pure heart—was, in fact, a standing witness against their hard and imperfect state.[1]

The Pharisees, baffled, perplexed, ashamed as usual, found themselves again confronted by a transcendently loftier wisdom, and a transcendently diviner insight than their own, and retired to hatch fresh plots equally malicious, and destined to be equally futile. But nothing can more fully show the necessity of Christ's teaching than the fact that even the disciples were startled and depressed by it. In this bad age, when corruption was so universal—when in Rome marriage had fallen into such

[1] See Deut. x. 16; Isa. xlviii. 4; Ezek. iii. 7, &c. And yet, according to Geiger and a host of imitators, Jesus was a Rabbi of the school of Hillel, and taught nothing original! (See Excursus III.)

contempt and desuetude that a law had to be passed which rendered celibates liable to a fine—they thought the pure strictness of our Lord's precept so severe that celibacy itself seemed preferable; and this opinion they expressed when they were once more with Him in the house. What a fatal blow would have been given to the world's happiness and the world's morality, had He assented to their rash conclusion! And how marvellous a proof is it of His Divinity, that whereas every other pre-eminent moral teacher—even the very best and greatest of all—has uttered or sanctioned more than one dangerous and deadly error which has been potent to poison the life or peace of nations—*all* the words of the Lord Jesus were absolutely holy, and divinely healthy words. In His reply He gives none of that entire preference to celibacy which would have been so highly valued by the ascetic and the monk, and would have troubled the consciences of many millions whose union has been blessed by Heaven.[1] He refused to pronounce upon the condition of the celibate so absolute a sanction. All that He said was that this saying of theirs as to the undesirability of marriage had *no* such unqualified bearing; that it was impossible and undesirable for all but the rare and exceptional few. Some, indeed, there were who were unfitted for holy wedlock by the circumstances of their birth or constitution;[2] some, again, by the infamous, though then common, cruelties and

[1] Consider the pernicious influence exercised over millions of Buddhists to this day by Sakya Mouni's exaltation of ascetic celibacy!

[2] Matt. xix. 10—12. The Rabbis similarly distinguished between three sorts of εὐνοῦχοι—the *serîs chammah* ("of the sun," or "of nature"), the *serîs adam* (per homines), and the *serîs bîdî shamayîm* (of God). The passages of the Rabbis, quoted by Schöttgen *in loc.*, show that the metaphorical sense given to the third class is justified, and that the Jews applied it to any who practised moderate abstinence.

atrocities of the dominant slavery; and some who withdrew themselves from all thoughts of marriage for religious purposes, or in consequence of higher necessities. These were not better than others, but only different. It was the duty of some to marry and serve God in the wedded state; it might be the duty of others not to marry, and so to serve God in the celibate state.[1] There is not in these words of Christ all that amount of difficulty and confusion which some have seen in them. His precepts find their best comment in the 7th and 9th chapters of the First Epistle to the Corinthians, and His clear meaning is that, besides the rare instances of natural incapacity for marriage, there are a few others—and to these few alone the saying of the disciples applied—who could accept the belief that *in peculiar times*, or *owing to special circumstances*, or *at the paramount call of exceptional duties*, wedlock must by them be rightly and wisely foregone, because they had received from God the gift and grace of continence, the power of a chaste life, resulting from an imagination purified and ennobled to a particular service.

And then, like a touching and beautiful comment on these high words, and the strongest of all proofs that there was in the mind of Christ no admiration for the "voluntary service" which St. Paul condemns, and the "works of supererogation" which an erring Church upholds—as a proof of His belief that marriage is honourable in all, and the bed undefiled—He took part in a scene that

[1] It is well known that Origen, the most allegorising of commentators, unhappily took this verse literally: other passages of Christ's teaching might have shown him that such an offence against the order and constitution of Providence was no protection against sensual sin; and indeed this great and holy man lived to see and to confess that in this matter he had been nobly mistaken—nobly, because the error of the intellect was combined with the most fervid impulses of a self-sacrificing heart.

has charmed the imagination of poet and painter in every age. For as though to destroy all false and unnatural notions of the exceptional glory of religious virginity, He, among whose earliest acts it had been to bless a marriage festival, made it one of His latest acts to fondle infants in His arms. It seems to have been known in Peræa that the time of His departure was approaching; and conscious, perhaps, of the words which He had just been uttering, there were fathers and mothers and friends who brought to Him the fruits of holy wedlock—young children and even babes[1]—that He might touch them and pray over them. Ere He left them for ever, they would bid Him a solemn farewell; they would win, as it were, the legacy of His special blessing for the generation yet to come. The disciples thought their conduct forward and officious.[2] They did not wish their Master to be needlessly crowded and troubled; they did not like to be disturbed in their high colloquies. They were indignant that a number of mere women and children should come obtruding on more important persons and interests. Women were not honoured, nor children loved in antiquity as now they are; no halo of romance and tenderness encircled them; too often they were subjected to shameful cruelties and hard neglect. But He who came to be the friend of all sinners, and the helper of all the suffering and the sick, came also to elevate woman to her due honour, centuries before the Teutonic element of modern society was dreamt of,[3] and to be the protector

[1] Matt. xix. 13, *παιδία*; Luke xviii. 15, *τὰ βρέφη*, "their babes."

[2] Comp. the haughty repulsion of the Shunamite woman by Gehazi (2 Kings iv. 27).

[3] Whereas the Essenian celibacy rose distinctly out of contempt for and distrust of woman (Jos. *B. J.* ii. 8, § 2, *τὰς τῶν γυναίκων ἀσελγείας φυλασσόμενοι*). The author of Ecclesiasticus speaks in the harshest tone of women.

and friend of helpless infancy and innocent childhood. Even the unconscious little ones were to be admitted into His Church by His sacrament of baptism, to be made members of Him, and inheritors of His kingdom. He turned the rebuke of the disciples on themselves; He was as much displeased with them, as they had been with the parents and children. "Suffer the little children," He said, in words which each of the Synoptists has preserved for us in all their immortal tenderness—"Suffer the little children to come unto me, and forbid them not, for of such is the kingdom of heaven." And when He had folded them in His arms, laid His hands upon them, and blessed them, He added once more His constantly needed, and therefore constantly repeated, warning, "Whosoever shall not receive the kingdom of heaven as a little child, shall not enter therein."[1]

When this beautiful and deeply instructive scene was over, St. Matthew tells us that He started on His way, probably for that new journey to the other Bethany of which we shall hear in the next chapter; and on this road occurred another incident, which impressed itself so deeply on the minds of the spectators that it, too, has been recorded by the Evangelists in a triple narrative.

A young man of great wealth and high position seems suddenly to have been seized with a conviction that he had hitherto neglected an invaluable opportunity, and that One who could alone explain to him the true meaning and mystery of life was already on his way to depart from among them. Determined, therefore, not to be too late, he came running, breathless, eager—in a way

[1] Comp. Mark ix. 35; Luke xxii. 26; Matt. xx. 26, 27; xxiii. 11.

that surprised all who beheld it—and, prostrating himself before the feet of Jesus, exclaimed, "Good Master, what good thing shall I do that I may inherit life?"[1]

If there was something attractive in the mingled impetuosity and humility of one so young and distinguished, yet so candid and earnest, there was in his question much that was objectionable. The notion that he could gain eternal life by "doing some good thing," rested on a basis radically false. If we may combine what seems to be the true reading of St. Matthew, with the answer recorded in the other Evangelists, our Lord seems to have said to him, "Why askest thou me about the good?[2] and why callest thou me good? One is the good, even God." He would as little accept the title "Good," as He would accept the title "Messiah," when given in a false sense. He would not be regarded as that mere "good Rabbi," to which, in these days, more than ever, men would reduce Him. So far, Jesus would show the youth that when he came to Him as to one who was more than man, his entire address, as well as his entire question, was a mistake. No mere man can lay any other foundation than that which is laid, and if the ruler

[1] For similar questions put to Rabbis, see Wetstein, *ad loc.* The ἀγαθὲ in Matt. xix. 16 is omitted by ℵ, B, D, L, &c., but it is found in Mark and Luke; the ἀγαθὸν in Matthew is undoubted, and perhaps the variation of readings is partly accounted for by the use of the word twice.

[2] The reading τί με ἐρωτᾷς περὶ τοῦ ἀγαθοῦ, in Matt. xix. 17, seems undoubtedly the right reading (ℵ, B, D, L, &c., the Cureton Syriac, and some of the chief Fathers). It springs naturally from the form of the young man's question; and it has certainly not been altered from doctrinal reasons, for there is no various reading in Mark x. 18; Luke xviii. 19. It is remarkable that the title "*good* Rabbi" was utterly unknown to the Jews, and does not occur once in the Talmud (Lightfoot, *Hor. Hebr. ad loc.*). There was, therefore, an obvious impropriety in the use of it by the young ruler from *his* point of view. The emphasis of our Lord's question falls on "*good*," not on "*me*;" for in the latter case it would be ἐμὲ, not με (Meyer).

committed the error of simply admiring Jesus as a Rabbi of pre-eminent sanctity, yet no Rabbi, however saintly, was accustomed to receive the title of "good," or prescribe any amulet for the preservation of a virtuous life. And in the same spirit, He continued: "But if thou wilt enter into life, keep the commandments."

The youth had not expected a reply so obvious and so simple. He cannot believe that He is merely referred to the Ten Commandments, and so He asks, in surprise, "What sort of commandments?" Jesus, as the youth wanted to *do* something, tells him merely of those of the Second Table, for, as has been well remarked, "Christ sends the proud to the *Law*, and invites the *humble* to the *Gospel*." "Master," replied the young man in surprise, "all these have I observed from my youth."[1] Doubtless in the mere letter he may have done so, as millions have; but he evidently knew little of all that those commandments had been interpreted by the Christ to mean. And Jesus, seeing his sincerity, looking on him loved him,[1] and gave him one short crucial test of his real condition. He was not content with the common-place; he aspired after the heroical, or rather *thought* that he did; therefore Jesus gave him an heroic act to do. "One thing," He said, "thou lackest," and bade him go, sell all that he had, distribute it to the poor, and come and follow Him.

[1] When the Angel of Death came to fetch the R. Chanina, he said, "Go and fetch me the Book of the Law, and *see whether there is anything in it which I have not kept*" (Gfrörer, ii. 102; Philo, i. 400).

[2] ἠγάπησεν (Mark x. 21). The word means "esteemed," and the aorist makes it mean "*was pleased with*." Origen says, "Dilexit eum, vel *osculatus est* eum;" and it was the custom of the Rabbis to kiss the head of any pupil who had answered well; but this would require ἐφίλησε, not ἠγάπησε.

It was too much. The young ruler went away very sorrowful, grief in his heart, and a cloud upon his brow,[1] for he had great possessions. He preferred the comforts of earth to the treasures of heaven; he would not purchase the things of eternity by abandoning those of time; he made, as Dante calls it, "the great refusal." And so he vanishes from the Gospel history; nor do the Evangelists know anything of him farther. But the sad stern imagination of the poet follows him, and there, among the myriads of those who are blown about like autumn leaves on the confines of the other world, blindly following the flutter of a giddy flag, rejected by Heaven, despised even by hell, hateful alike to God and to his enemies, he sees

> "l'ombra di colui
> Che fece per viltate il gran rifiuto,"[2]

(The shade of him, who made through cowardice the great refusal.)

We may—I had almost said we must—hope and believe a fairer ending for one whom Jesus, as He looked on him, could love. But the failure of this youth to meet the test saddened Jesus, and looking round at His disciples, He said, "How hardly shall they that have riches enter into the kingdom of heaven." The words once more struck them as very severe. Could then no good man be rich, no rich man be good? But Jesus

[1] λυπούμενος (Matt. xix. 22); στυγνάσας (Mark x. 22; cf. Matt. xvi. 3); περίλυπος (Luke xviii. 23).

[2] Dante, *Inferno*, iii. 60.

> "Incontanente intesi, e certo fui
> Che quest' era la setta dei cattivi
> A Dio spiacenti ed a' nemici sui."

This application of Dante's reference seems to me more probable than that he intended Pope Celestine.

only answered—softening the sadness and sternness of the words by the affectionate title "children"—"Children, how hard it is to enter into the kingdom of God;"[1] hard for *any one*, but, He added, with an earnest look at His disciples, and specially addressing Peter, as the Gospel according to the Hebrews tells us, "It is easier for a camel to go through the eye of a needle, than for a rich man to enter into the kingdom of God."[2] They might well be amazed beyond measure. Was there then no hope for a Nicodemus, for a Joseph of Arimathæa? Assuredly there was. The teaching of Jesus about riches was as little Ebionite as His teaching about marriage was Essene. Things impossible to nature are possible to grace; things impossible to man are easy to God.

Then, with a touch—was it of complacency, or was it of despair?—Peter said, "Lo, we have forsaken all, and followed thee," and either added, or implied, In what respect, then, shall we be gainers? The answer of Jesus was at once a magnificent encouragement and a solemn warning. The encouragement was that there

[1] It will be seen that I follow the very striking and probably genuine reading of ℵ, B, D, and other MSS. in Mark x. 24. The words τοὺς πεποιθότας ἐπὶ χρήματα, which our version accepts, have all the character of a gloss; and for those who "*trust* in riches" the task would not be δύσκολον, but ἀδύνατον. It is of course true that it is the *trust* in riches, not the *possession* of them, which makes it so hard to enter into the kingdom of God; but even such a mean and miserable scoffer as Lucian could see that there is always a *danger* lest those who *have* riches should trust in them.

[2] The alteration to κάμιλον, "a rope," is shown to be wrong from the commonness of similar proverbs (*e.g.*, an elephant and the eye of a needle) in the Talmud, as adduced by Lightfoot, Schöttgen, and Wetstein. The explanation that the small side gate of a city, through which a laden camel could only crush with the utmost difficulty was called a "needle's eye" is more plausible, but seems to need confirmation.

was no instance of self-sacrifice which would not even in this world, and even in the midst of persecutions, receive its hundred-fold increase in the harvest of spiritual blessings,[1] and would in the world to come be rewarded by the infinite recompense of eternal life; the warning was that familiar one which they had heard before, that many of the first should be last, and the last first.[2] And to impress upon them still more fully and deeply that the kingdom of heaven is not a matter of mercenary calculation or exact equivalent—that there could be no bargaining with the Heavenly Householder—that before the eye of God's clearer and more penetrating judgment Gentiles might be admitted before Jews, and Publicans before Pharisees, and young converts before aged Apostles—He told them the memorable Parable of the Labourers in the Vineyard. That parable, amid its other lessons, involved the truth that, while all who serve God should not be defrauded of their just and full and rich reward, there could be in heaven no murmuring, no envyings, no jealous comparison of respective merits, no base strugglings for precedency, no miserable disputings as to who had performed the maximum of service, or who had received the minimum of grace.

[1] The metaphor of the twelve thrones harmonised with the ideal hopes of the day. (See Lightfoot, *ad loc.*) For the Palingenesia (= "restoration of all things," ἀποκατάστασις) see Isa. xlii. 9; lxv. 17; Rom. viii. 19; Rev. xxi. 1, &c. With the whole passage compare 1 Cor. iii. 22; 2 Cor. vi. 10.

[2] See 2 Esdr. v. 42.

CHAPTER XLVII.

THE RAISING OF LAZARUS.

ἔχω τὰς κλεῖς τοῦ ᾅδου καὶ τοῦ θανάτου.—APOC. i. 18.

THESE farewell interviews and teachings perhaps belong to the two days after Jesus—while still in the Peræan Bethany—had received from the other Bethany, where He had so often found a home, the solemn message that "he whom He loved was sick."[1] Lazarus was the one intimate personal friend whom Jesus possessed outside the circle of His Apostles, and the urgent message was evidently an appeal for the presence of Him in whose presence, so far as we know, there had never been a death-bed scene.

But Jesus did not come. He contented Himself—occupied as He was in important works—with sending them the message that "this sickness was not to death, but for the glory of God," and stayed two days longer where He was. And at the end of those two days He said to His disciples, "Let us go into Judæa again."

[1] John xi. 1—46, ὃν φιλεῖς (quem amas), ver. 3. The same word is only used elsewhere of the love of Jesus for the beloved disciple. Where His love for the sisters is spoken of, ἠγάπα, "diligebat" ("cared for"), is used (ver. 5). It is, however, worth noticing that three times out of four the word for even the beloved disciple is ἀγαπᾶν, and that here the φιλεῖς is not the Evangelist's own word, but put by him into the mouth of another.

The disciples reminded Him how lately the Jews had there sought to stone Him, and asked Him how He could venture to go there again; but His answer was that during the twelve hours of His day of work He could walk in safety, for the light of His duty, which was the will of His Heavenly Father, would keep Him from danger. And then He told them that Lazarus slept, and that He was going to wake him out of sleep. Three of them at least must have remembered how, on another memorable occasion, He had spoken of death as sleep; but either they were silent, and others spoke, or they were too slow of heart to remember it. As they understood Him to speak of natural sleep, He had to tell them plainly that Lazarus was dead, and that He was glad of it for their sakes, for that He would go to restore him to life. "Let us also go," said the affectionate but ever despondent Thomas, "that we may die with Him"—as though he had said, "It is all a useless and perilous scheme, but still let us go."

Starting early in the morning, Jesus could easily have accomplished the distance—some twenty miles—before sunset. But, on His arrival, he stayed outside the little village. Its vicinity to Jerusalem, from which it is not two miles distant,[1] and the evident wealth and position of the family, had attracted a large concourse of distinguished Jews to console and mourn with the sisters; and it was obviously desirable to act with caution in venturing among such determined enemies. But while Mary, true to her retiring and contemplative disposition, was sitting in the house, unconscious of her Lord's approach,[2]

[1] The "was" in John xi. 18 does not *necessarily* imply that when St. John wrote the village had been destroyed; but such was probably the case.

[2] It is an interesting incidental proof of the authenticity of the narrative

the more active Martha had received intelligence that He was near at hand, and immediately went forth to meet Him. Lazarus had died on the very day that Jesus received the message of his illness; two days had elapsed while He lingered in Peræa, a fourth had been spent on the journey. Martha could not understand this sad delay. "Lord," she said, in tones gently reproachful, "if Thou hadst been here my brother had not died," yet "even now" she seems to indulge the vague hope that some alleviation may be vouchsafed to their bereavement. The few words which follow are words of most memorable import—a declaration of Jesus which has brought comfort not to Martha only, but to millions since, and which shall do to millions more unto the world's end—

"Thy brother shall rise again."

Martha evidently had not dreamt that he would now be awaked from the sleep of death, and she could only answer, "I know that he shall rise again in the resurrection at the last day."

Jesus said unto her, "I AM THE RESURRECTION AND THE LIFE: HE THAT BELIEVETH ON ME, THOUGH HE HAVE DIED, SHALL LIVE; AND HE THAT LIVETH AND BELIEVETH ON ME SHALL NEVER DIE. Believest thou this?"

It was not for a spirit like Martha's to distinguish the interchanging thoughts of physical and spiritual death which were united in that deep utterance; but, without pausing to fathom it, her faithful love supplied

—all the more valuable from being wholly undesigned—that the characters of Martha and Mary, as described in a few touches by St. John, exactly harmonise with their character as they appear in the anecdote preserved only by St. Luke (x. 38—42). (See *supra*, p. 141.) Those who reject the genuineness of St. John's Gospel must account (as Meyer says) for this "literary miracle."

the answer, "Yea, Lord, I believe that thou art the Christ, the Son of God, which should come into the world."

Having uttered that great confession, she at once went in quest of her sister, about whom Jesus had already inquired, and whose heart and intellect, as Martha seemed instinctively to feel, were better adapted to embrace such lofty truths. She found Mary in the house, and both the secrecy with which she delivered her message, and the haste and silence with which Mary arose to go and meet her Lord, show that precaution was needed, and that the visit of Jesus had not been unaccompanied with danger. The Jews who were comforting her, and whom she had thus suddenly left, rose to follow her to the tomb, whither they thought that she had gone to weep; but they soon saw the real object of her movement. Outside the village they found Jesus surrounded by His friends, and they saw Mary hurry up to Him, and fling herself at His feet with the same agonising reproach which her sister also had used, "Lord, if Thou hadst been here my brother had not died."[1] The greater intensity of her emotion spoke in her fewer words and her greater self-abandonment of anguish, and she could add no more. It may be that her affection was too deep to permit her hope to be so sanguine as that of her sister; it may be that with humbler reverence she left all to her Lord. The sight of all that love and misery, the pitiable spectacle of human bereavement, the utter futility at such a moment

[1] Martha had said, *οὐκ ἂν ὁ ἀδελφός μου ἐτεθνήκει* (John xi. 21, but *ἀπέθανεν*, א, B, C, D, &c.), "my brother would not have been dead;" Mary says, *οὐκ ἂν μοῦ ἀπέθανεν ὁ ἀδελφὸς* (ver. 32), "*my* brother [the position of the pronoun is more emphatic] would not have died."

of human consolation, the shrill commingling of a hired and simulated lamentation with all this genuine anguish, the unspoken reproach, "Oh, why didst Thou not come at once and snatch the victim from the enemy, and spare Thy friend from the sting of death, and us from the more bitter sting of such a parting?"—all these influences touched the tender compassion of Jesus with deep emotion. A strong effort of self-repression was needed[1]—an effort which shook His whole frame with a powerful shudder[2]—before He could find words to speak, and then He could merely ask, "Where have ye laid him?" They said, "Lord, come and see." As He followed them His eyes were streaming with silent tears.[3] His tears were not unnoticed, and while some of the Jews observed with respectful sympathy this proof of His affection for the dead, others were asking dubiously, perhaps almost sneeringly,[4] whether He who had opened the eyes of the blind could not have saved His friend from death? They had not heard how, in the far-off village of Galilee, He had raised the dead; but they knew that in Jerusalem He had opened the eyes of one born blind, and that seemed to them a miracle no less

[1] Such seems to be the meaning of ἐνεβριμήσατο τῷ πνεύματι (ver. 33), literally, "He was indignant with himself in spirit." (Cf. Lam. ii. 6, LXX.) I fully admit, however, the difficulty of the expression, and am not prepared to deny that it may mean "He was indignant in spirit" (at the want of faith of those who were present).

[2] ἐτάραξεν ἑαυτόν. The philosophical fancies which see in this expression a sanction of the Stoic μετριοπάθεια, as though the meaning were that Jesus merely stirred His own emotions to the exact extent which He approved, are quite misplaced. (Comp. John xii. 27; xiii. 21.) Euthymius, an excellent ancient commentator, explains it as in the text.

[3] ἐδάκρυσεν, *flevit*, "He shed tears;" not ἔκλαυσεν, *ploravit*, "He wept aloud," as over Jerusalem (Luke xix. 41).

[4] Verse 37. Alford acutely conjectures the hostile tone of the criticism, from the use of δὲ, which St. John very frequently uses in an adversative sense, as again in verse 46.

stupendous. But Jesus knew and heard their comments, and once more the whole scene—its genuine sorrows, its hired mourners, its uncalmed hatreds, all concentrated around the ghastly work of death—came so powerfully over His spirit, that, though He knew that He was going to wake the dead, once more His whole being was swept by a storm of emotion.[1] The grave, like most of the graves belonging to the wealthier Jews, was a recess carved horizontally in the rock, with a slab or mass of stone to close the entrance.[2] Jesus bade them remove this *gôlal*, as it was called. Then Martha interposed—partly from conviction that the soul had now utterly departed from the vicinity of the mouldering body, partly afraid in her natural delicacy of the shocking spectacle which the removal of that stone would reveal. For in that hot climate it is necessary that burial should follow immediately upon death,[3] and as it was the evening of the fourth day since Lazarus had died, there was too much reason to fear that by this time decomposition had set in. Solemnly Jesus reminded her of His promise, and the stone was moved from the place where the dead was laid. He stood at the entrance, and all others shrank a little backward, with their eyes still fixed on that dark and silent cave. A hush fell upon them all as Jesus raised

[1] πάλιν ἐμβριμώμενος ἐν ἑαυτῷ (John xi. 38).

[2] The village of Bethany is to this day called El-Azariyeh, a corruption of Lazarus, and a continuous memorial of the miracle. A deep cavity is shown in the middle of it as the grave of Lazarus. I visited the spot, but with no belief in it: that El-Azariyeh is the ancient Bethany is certain, but the tomb of Lazarus could not have been in the centre of it.

[3] Frankl mentions that, a few years ago, a Jewish Rabbi dying at Jerusalem at two o'clock was buried at 4.30. The emphatic remark of Martha may also have arisen from the belief that after three days the soul ceased to flutter in the neighbourhood of the body.

His eyes and thanked God for the coming confirmation of His prayer. And then, raising to its clearest tones that voice of awful and sonorous authority, and uttering, as was usual with Him on such occasions, the briefest words, He cried, "LAZARUS, COME FORTH!"[1] Those words thrilled once more through that region of impenetrable darkness which separates us from the world to come; and scarcely were they spoken when, like a spectre, from the rocky tomb issued a figure, swathed indeed in its white and ghastly cerements—with the napkin round the head which had upheld the jaw that four days previously had dropped in death, bound hand and foot and face, but not livid, not horrible—the figure of a youth with the healthy blood of a restored life flowing through his veins; of a life restored—so tradition tells us—for thirty more long years[2] to life, and light, and love.

Let us pause here to answer the not unnatural question as to the silence of the Synoptists respecting this great miracle.[3] To treat the subject fully would indeed be to write a long disquisition on the structure of the Gospels; and after all we could assign no *final* explanation of their obvious difficulties. The Gospels are, of their very nature, confessedly and designedly fragmentary, and it may be regarded as all but certain that the first three were mainly derived from a common oral tradition, or founded on one or two original, and themselves fragmentary, documents.[4] The Synoptists almost confine themselves to the Galilæan, and St. John

[1] ἐκράυγασεν (ver. 43). Comp. Matt. xii. 19; John v. 28.

[2] Epiphan. *Haer.* 66. See Hofmann, *Leben Jesu*, 357.

[3] On this question, see especially Meyer, p. 298.

[4] Luke i. 1.

to the Judæan ministry, though the Synoptists distinctly allude to and presuppose the ministry in Jerusalem, and St. John the ministry in Galilee.[1] Not one of the four Evangelists proposes for a moment to give an exhaustive account, or even catalogue, of the parables, discourses, and miracles of Jesus; nor was it the object of either of them to write a complete narrative of His three and a-half years of public life. Each of them relates the incidents which came most immediately within his own scope, and were best known to him either by personal witness, by isolated written documents, or by oral tradition;[2] and each of them tells enough to show that He was the Christ, the Son of the Living God, the Saviour of the world. Now, since the raising of Lazarus would not seem to them a greater exercise of miraculous power than others which they had recorded (John xi. 37)—since, as has well been said, no *semeiometer* had been then invented to test the relative greatness of miracles—and since this miracle fell within the Judæan cycle—it does not seem at all *more* inexplicable that they should have omitted this, than that they should have omitted the miracle at Bethesda, or the opening of the eyes of him who had

[1] I ought, perhaps, to have explained the word *Synoptists* before. It is applied to the first three Evangelists, because their Gospels can be arranged, section by section, in a tabular form. Griesbach seems to have been the first to use the word (Holtzmann in Schenkel, *Bibel Lexicon*, s. v. "Evangelien," p. 207). But although the word, so far as I am aware, is modern, the contrasts presented by the first three and the fourth Gospels were, of course, very early observed (Clem. Alex. ap. Euseb. *Hist. Ecc.* vi. 14). Professor Westcott treats of "the origin of the Gospels" with his usual learning and candour in his *Introduction*, pp. 152—195. He there mentions that if the total contents of the Gospels be represented by 100, there are 7 peculiarities in St. Mark, 42 in St. Matthew, 59 in St. Luke, and 92 in St. John.

[2] *Vid. supra*, Vol. I., p. 279, *n.*, where I have quoted the testimony of St. Augustine to this effect.

been born blind. But further than this, we seem to trace in the Synoptists a special reticence about the family at Bethany. The house in which they take a prominent position is called "the house of Simon the leper;" Mary is called simply "a woman" by St. Matthew and St. Mark (Matt. xxvi. 6, 7; Mark xiv. 3); and St. Luke contents himself with calling Bethany "a certain village" (Luke x. 38), although he was perfectly aware of the name (Luke xix. 29). There is, therefore, a distinct argument for the conjecture that when the earliest form of the Gospel of St. Matthew appeared, and when the memorials were collected which were used by the other two Synoptists, there may have been special reasons for not recording a miracle which would have brought into dangerous prominence a man who was still living, but of whom the Jews had distinctly sought to get rid as a witness of Christ's wonder-working power (John xii. 10). Even if this danger had ceased, it would have been obviously repulsive to the quiet family of Bethany to have been made the focus of an intense and irreverent curiosity, and to be questioned about those hidden things which none have ever revealed. Something, then, seems to have "sealed the lips" of those Evangelists—an obstacle which had been long removed when St. John's Gospel first saw the light.

"If they believe not Moses and the Prophets"—so ran the answer of Abraham to Dives in the parable—"neither will they be converted though one (and this, too, a Lazarus!) rose from the dead." It was even so. There were many witnesses of this miracle who believed when they saw it, but there were others who could only carry an angry and alarmed account of it to the Sanhedrin at Jerusalem.

The Sanhedrin met in a spirit of hatred and perplexity.[1] They *could* not deny the miracle; they *would* not believe on Him who had performed it; they could only dread His growing influence, and conjecture that it would be used to make Himself a king, and so end in Roman intervention and the annihilation of their political existence. And as they vainly raged in impotent counsels, Joseph Caiaphas arose to address them. He was the civil High Priest, and held the office eleven years, from A.D. 25, when Valerius Gratus placed him in it, till A.D. 36, when Vitellius turned him out. A large share indeed of the honour which belonged to his position had been transferred to Ananus, Annas—or to give him his true Jewish name, Hanan—who had simply been deprived of the High Priesthood by Roman authority, and who (as we shall see hereafter) was perhaps the *Nasî* or *Sagan*, and was, at any rate, regarded as being the real High Priest by the stricter Jews. Caiaphas, however, was at this time nominally and ostensibly High Priest.[2] As such he was supposed to have that gift of prophecy which was still believed to linger faintly in the persons of the descendants of Aaron, after the total disappearance of dreams, Urim, omens, prophets, and *Bath Kôl*, which, in descending degrees, had been the ordinary means of ascertaining

[1] John xi. 47—54.

[2] Some have seen an open irony in the expression of St. John (xi. 49), that Caiaphas was High Priest "that same year," as though the Jews had got into this contemptuous way of speaking during the rapid succession of priests—mere phantoms set up and displaced by the Roman fiat—who had in recent years succeeded each other. There must have been at least five living High Priests, and ex-High Priests at this council—Annas, Ismael Ben Phabi, Eleazer Ben Hanan, Simon Ben Kamhith, and Caiaphas, who had gained his elevation by bribery (see Reland, *Antt. Hebr.*, p. 160, where he gives lists of the High Priests from Josephus, Nicephorus, &c.).

the will of God.[1] And thus when Caiaphas rose, and with shameless avowal of a policy most flagitiously selfish and unjust,[2] haughtily told the Sanhedrin that all their proposals were mere ignorance, and that the only thing to be done was to sacrifice one victim—innocent or guilty he did not stop to inquire or to define —one victim for the whole people—ay, and, St. John adds, not for that nation only, but for all God's children scattered throughout the world—they accepted unhesitatingly that voice of unconscious prophecy. And by accepting it they filled to the brim the cup of their iniquity, and incurred the crime which drew upon their guilty heads the very catastrophe which it was committed to avert. It was this Moloch worship of worse than human sacrifice which, as in the days of Manasseh, doomed them to a second and a more terrible, and a more enduring, destruction. There were some, indeed, who were not to be found on that Hill of Evil Counsel,[3]

[1] See Jos. *B. J.* iii. 8, § 3.

[2] Some of these conspirators must have lived to learn by the result that what is morally wrong never *can* be politically expedient. The death of the Innocent, so far from saving the nation, precipitated its ruin, and that ruin fell most heavily on those who had brought it about. When the Idumeans entered Jerusalem, "Tous les membres de la caste sacerdotale qu'on put trouver furent tués. Hanan [*son* of the Gospel 'Annas'] et Jésus fils de Gamala subirent d'affreuses insultes; leurs corps furent privés de sépulture, outrage inouï chez les Juifs. Ainsi périt le fils du principal auteur de la mort de Jésus. Ce fut . . . . la fin du parti sadducéen, parti souvent hautain, égoïste et cruel. Avec Hanan périt le vieux sacerdoce juif, inféodé aux grandes familles sadducéennes . . . Grande fut l'impression, quand on contempla jetés nus hors de la ville, livrés aux chiens et aux chacals, ces aristocrates si hautement respectés . . . C'était un monde qui disparaissait. Incapable de former un État à lui seul il devait en arriver au point où nous le voyons depuis dix-huit siècles, c'est-à-dire à vivre en guise de parasite, dans la république d'autrui." (Renan, *L'Antechrist*, p. 287, who sees in all this no hand of God.)

[3] This is the name still given to the traditional site of the house of Caiaphas, where the meeting is supposed to have been held.

or who, if present, consented not to the counsel or will of them; but from that day forth the secret fiat had been issued that Jesus must be put to death. Henceforth He was living with a price upon His head.

And that fiat, however originally secret, became instantly known. Jesus was not ignorant of it; and for the last few weeks of His earthly existence, till the due time had brought round the Passover at which He meant to lay down His life, He retired in secret to a little obscure city, near the wilderness, called Ephraim.[1] There, safe from all the tumults and machinations of His deadly enemies, He spent calmly and happily those last few weeks of rest, surrounded only by His disciples, and training them, in that peaceful seclusion, for the mighty work of thrusting their sickles into the ripening harvests of the world. None, or few beside that faithful band, knew of His hiding place; for the Pharisees, when they found themselves unable to conceal their designs, had published an order that if any man knew where He was, he was to reveal it, that they might seize Him, if necessary even by violence, and execute the decision at which they had arrived. But, as yet, the bribe had no effect.

How long this deep and much-imperilled retirement

[1] *κώμη μεγίστη*, Euseb.; "villa praegrandis," Jer.; *πολίχνιον*, Jos. (Keim, III. i. 6.)—There is much uncertainty as to the position of Ephraim; it may possibly have been on the site of the modern village of Et-Taiyibeh, which is near to the wilderness (John xi. 54), and not far from Beitîn, the ancient Bethel (2 Chron. xiii. 19; Jos. *B. J.* iv. 9, § 9), and about twenty miles to the north of Jerusalem (Jerome, *Onomast.*). (See Robinson, *Bibl. Res.* i. 444 seqq.) There is no necessity to suppose with Ebrard (*Gosp. Hist.* p. 360) that it was south-east of Jerusalem. (The *Kethibh*, in 2 Chron. xiii. 19, has "*Ephron;*" the *Keri*, "Ephraim." Wieseler (*Synops.* p. 291) elaborately argues that Eusebius is right, as against Jerome, in placing it eight miles from Jerusalem, but this would hardly be far enough for safety; and if Ephraim be Et-Taiyibeh, that is very nearly if not quite twenty miles from the Holy City.)

lasted we are not told, nor can we lift the veil of silence that has fallen over its records. If the decision at which the *Beth Dín* in the house of Caiaphas had arrived was regarded as a formal sentence of death, then it is not impossible that these scrupulous legists may have suffered forty days to elapse for the production of witnesses in favour of the accused.[1] But it is very doubtful whether the destruction intended for Jesus was not meant to be carried out in a manner more secret and more summary, bearing the aspect rather of a violent assassination than of a legal judgment.

[1] Such is the supposition of Sepp, II. iii. 31, and it derives some support from the turbid legend of the Talmud, which says that forty days before His death (the legal time for the production of witnesses) Jesus was excommunicated by Joshua Ben Perachiah, to the blast of 400 trumpets.

CHAPTER XLVIII.

JERICHO AND BETHANY.

"Those mighty voices three,—
Ἰησοῦ ἐλέησον με,
Θάρσει, ἔγειραι, φωνεῖ σε,
ἡ πίστις σου σέσωκέ σε."—LONGFELLOW.

FROM the conical hill of Ephraim Jesus could see the pilgrim bands as, at the approach of the Passover, they began to stream down the Jordan valley towards Jerusalem, to purify themselves from every ceremonial defilement before the commencement of the Great Feast.[1] The time had come for Him to leave his hiding-place, and He descended from Ephraim to the high road in order to join the great caravan of Galilæan pilgrims.[2]

And as He turned His back on the little town, and began the journey which was to end at Jerusalem, a prophetic solemnity and elevation of soul struggling with the natural anguish of the flesh, which shrank from that great sacrifice, pervaded His whole being, and gave a new and strange grandeur to every gesture and every look. It was the Transfiguration of Self-sacrifice; and, like that previous Transfiguration of Glory, it filled those who beheld it with an amazement and terror which

[1] Numb. ix. 10; 2 Chron. xxx. 17; Jos. *Antt.* xvii. 9, § 3.
[2] Matt. xx. 17—19; Mark x. 32—34; Luke xviii. 31—34.

they could not explain.[1] There are few pictures in the Gospel more striking than this of Jesus going forth to His death, and walking alone along the path into the deep valley, while behind Him, in awful reverence, and mingled anticipations of dread and hope—their eyes fixed on Him, as with bowed head He preceded them in all the majesty of sorrow—the disciples walked behind and dared not disturb His meditations. But at last He paused and beckoned them to Him, and then, once more—for the third time—with fuller, clearer, more startling, more terrible particulars than ever before, He told them that He should be betrayed to the Priests and Scribes; by them condemned; then handed over to the Gentiles; by the Gentiles mocked, scourged, and—He now for the first time revealed to them, without any ambiguity, the crowning horror—*crucified;* and that, on the third day, He should rise again. But their minds were full of Messianic hopes; they were so pre-occupied with the conviction that now the kingdom of God was to come in all its splendour, that the prophecy passed by them like the idle wind; they could not, and would not, understand.

There can be no more striking comment on their inability to realise the meaning of what Jesus had said to them, than the fact that very shortly after, and during the same journey, occurred the ill-timed and strangely unspiritual request which the Evangelists proceed to record.[2] With an air of privacy and mystery, Salome, one of the constant attendants of Jesus, with her two sons, James and John, who were among the most eminent of His Apostles, came to Him with adorations, and

[1] Mark x. 32. Tischendorf, Meyer, &c., accept the reading of ℵ, B, C, L, &c., *οἱ δὲ ἀκολουθοῦντες*, as though there were *two* sets of the Apostles, of whom some in their fear had fallen behind the rest.

[2] Matt. xx. 20—28; Mark x. 35—45; Luke xviii. 32—34.

begged Him to promise them a favour. He asked what they wished; and then the mother, speaking for her fervent-hearted ambitious sons, begged that in His kingdom they might sit, the one at His right hand, and the other at His left.[1] Jesus bore gently with their selfishness and error. They had asked in their blindness for that position which, but a few days afterwards, they were to see occupied in shame and anguish by the two crucified robbers. Their imaginations were haunted by twelve thrones; His thoughts were of three crosses. They dreamt of earthly crowns; He told them of a cup of bitterness[2] and a baptism of blood. Could they indeed drink with Him of that cup, and be baptised with that baptism? Understanding perhaps more of His meaning now, they yet boldly answered, "We can;" and then He told them that they indeed *should* do so, but that to sit on His right hand and on His left was reserved for those for whom it had been prepared by His Heavenly Father.[3] The throne, says Basil, "is the price of toils, not a grace granted to ambition; a reward of righteousness, not the concession of a request."

The ten, when they heard the incident, were naturally indignant at this secret attempt of the two brothers to secure for themselves a pre-eminence of honour; little knowing that, so far as earth was concerned—and of this alone they dreamt—that premium of honour should only

[1] In Jos. *Antt.* vi. 11, § 9, Jonathan sits at Saul's right hand, Abner at his left. In the *Midrash Tehillîn,* God is represented with the Messiah on His right and Abraham on His left (Wetstein *ad loc.*). Comp. 1 Kings ii. 19 (Bathsheba); xxii. 19.

[2] John xviii. 11; Rev. xiv. 10; Ps. lxxv. 8. "Lavacrum sanguinis" (Tert. *Scorp.* 12). (Keim, iii. 43.)

[3] The English version is here not very happy in interpolating "it shall be given" (Matt. xx. 23), for the meaning is "not Mine to give *except to those for whom* it is prepared of My Father." Comp. Matt. xxv. 34; 2 Tim. iv. 8.

be, for the one a precedence in martyrdom, for the other a prolongation of suffering.[1] This would be revealed to them in due time, but even now Jesus called them all together, and taught them, as He had so often taught them,[2] that the highest honour is won by the deepest humility. The shadowy principalities of earth[3] were characterised by the semblance of a little brief authority over their fellow-men; it was natural for them to lord it, and tyrannise it over their fellows: but in the kingdom of heaven the lord of all should be the servant of all, even as the highest Lord had spent His very life in the lowest ministrations, and was about to give it as a ransom for many.

As they advanced towards Jericho,[4] through the

[1] Acts xii. 2; Rev. i. 9.

[2] Matt. xviii. 4; xxiii. 11.

[3] Mark x. 42, *οἱ δοκοῦντες ἄρχειν*, "those who profess to govern. The *κατακυριεύουσι* and *κατεξουσιάζουσι* have a slightly unfavourable sense (1 Pet. v. 3).

[4] Matt. xx. 30—34; Mark x. 46—52; Luke xviii. 35—43. Those who have a narrow, timid, superstitious, and unscriptural view of inspiration may well be troubled by the obvious discrepancies between the Evangelists in this narrative. Not only does St. Matthew mention *two* blind men, while the others only mention one, but St. Matthew says that the miracle was performed "*as they departed from Jericho*," while St. Luke most distinctly implies that it took place *before He entered it.* But no reasonable reader will be troubled by differences which do *not* affect the truthfulness—though of course they affect the *accuracy*—of the narrative; and which, without a direct and wholly needless miraculous intervention, *must* have occurred, as they actually *do* occur, in the narratives of the Evangelists, as in those of all other truthful witnesses. Of the fourteen or fifteen proposed ways of harmonising the discrepancies, *most* involve a remedy far worse than the supposed defect; but Macknight's suggestion that the miracle may have been performed *between the two Jerichos*—the ancient site of the Canaanite city, and the new semi-Herodian city—is at least possible. So, indeed, is the supposition that one of them was healed on entering, and the other on leaving the city. I believe that if we knew the exact circumstances the discrepancy would vanish; but even if it did not—if, for instance, Matthew had spoken of Bartimæus and his guide as "two blind men," or, in the course of time, any trivial inaccuracy had found its way into the early documents on which St. Luke based his Gospel—I should see nothing distressing

scorched and treeless Ghôr, the crowd of attendant pilgrims grew more and more dense about Him. It was either the evening of Thursday, Nisan 7, or the morning of Friday, Nisan 8, when they reached the environs of that famous city—the city of fragrance, the city of roses, the city of palm-trees, the "paradise of God." It is now a miserable and degraded Arab village, but was then a prosperous and populous town, standing on a green and flowery oasis,[1] rich in honey and leaf-honey, and myrobalanum, and well watered by the Fountain of Elisha and by other abundant springs. Somewhere in the vicinity of the town sat blind Bartimæus,[2] the son of Timæus, begging with a companion of his misery; and as they heard the noise of the passing multitude, and were told that it was Jesus of Nazareth who was passing by, they raised their voices in the cry, "Jesus, Thou Son of David, have mercy on us." The multitude resented this loud clamour as unworthy of the majesty of Him who was now to enter Jerusalem as the Messiah of His nation. But Jesus heard the cry, and His compassionate heart was touched. He stood still, and ordered them to be called to Him. Then the obsequious throng alter their tone, and say to Bartimæus, who is so much the more prominent in the narrative that two of the Synoptists do not even mention his companion at all—"Be of good cheer; rise, He calleth thee." With a burst of hasty joy, flinging away his *abba*, he leaped up,[3] and was led

or derogatory in such a supposition. For my views on Inspiration, I may perhaps be allowed to refer to my papers on the subject in Vol. I., p. 190, of the *Bible Educator*. On the fertility of Jericho, see Jos. *B. J.* iv. 8, § 3. The rose of Jericho is the *Anastatica Hierochuntia* of Linnæus.

[1] Ecclus. xxiv. 14.

[2] The name seems to be derived from the Aramaic *same, samia* = "blind." So Buxtorf and Hitzig, quoted by Keim, iii. 52.

[3] Mark x. 50, ἀναπηδήσας (ℵ, B, D, L, Tisch., Lachm., &c.).

to Jesus. "What willest thou that I should do for thee?" "Rabboni," he answered (giving Jesus the most reverential title that he knew),[1] "that I may recover my sight." "Go," said Jesus, "thy faith hath saved thee." He touched the eyes both of him and of his companion, and with recovered sight they followed among the rejoicing multitudes, glorifying God.

It was necessary to rest at Jericho before entering on the dangerous, rocky, robber-haunted gorge which led from it to Jerusalem, and formed a rough, almost continuous, ascent of six hours,[2] from 600 feet below to nearly 3,000 feet above the level of the Mediterranean. The two most distinctive classes of Jericho were priests and publicans; and, as it was a priestly city, it might naturally have been expected that the king, the son of David, the successor of Moses, would be received in the house of some descendant of Aaron. But the place where Jesus chose to rest was determined by other circumstances.[3] A colony of publicans was established in the city to secure the revenues accruing from the large traffic in a kind of balsam, which grew more luxuriantly there than in any other place,[4] and to regulate the exports and imports between the Roman province and the dominions of Herod Antipas. One of the chiefs of these publicans[5] was a man named Zacchæus,[6] doubly

[1] The steps of honour were Rab, Rabbi, Rabban, Rabboni.

[2] About fifteen miles.

[3] Luke xix. 1—10.

[4] Jos. *Antt.* xiv. 4, § 1; xv. 4, § 2; Justin, *Hist.* xxxvi. 3, &c.

[5] ἀρχιτελώνης. This does not necessarily imply that he had reached the rank of an actual *publicanus*, which was usually held by Roman knights, although some Jews, as we learn from Josephus, actually did attain to this rank (*B. J.* ii. 14, § 9).

[6] A Jewish name, an abbreviation of Zachariah; זַכַּי, "pure" (Ezra ii. 9); Zakkai (Jos. *Vit.* 46). Lightfoot (*Hor. Hebr. ad loc.*) thinks that he may

odious to the people, as being a Jew and as exercising his functions so near to the Holy City. His official rank would increase his unpopularity, because the Jews would regard it as due to exceptional activity in the service of their Roman oppressors, and they would look upon his wealth as a probable indication of numerous extortions. This man had a deep desire to see with his own eyes what kind of person Jesus was; but being short of stature, he was unable, in the dense crowd, to catch a glimpse of Him. He therefore ran forward, as Jesus was passing through the town, and climbed the low branches of an Egyptian fig, which overshadowed the road.[1] Under this tree Jesus would pass, and the publican would have ample opportunity of seeing one who, alone of His nation, not only showed no concentrated and fanatical hatred for the class to which he belonged, but had found among publicans His most eager listeners, and had elevated one of them into the rank of an Apostle. Zacchæus saw Him as He approached, and how must his heart have beat with joy and gratitude, when the Great Prophet, the avowed Messiah of His nation, paused under the tree, looked up, and, calling him by his name, bade him hasten and come down, because He intended to be a guest in his house. Zacchæus should not only see Him, but He would come in and sup with him, and make His abode with him—the glorious Messiah a guest of the execrated publican. With undisguised joy Zacchæus eagerly hastened down from the boughs of

be identified with the Zakkai whom the Rabbis mention as the father of Rabbi Johanan.

[1] The sycomore, or "Egyptian fig" (Luke xix. 4)—not to be confounded with the sycamine-tree or "mulberry" of Luke xvii. 6, or with the sycamore or *pseudo-platanus*, which is sometimes erroneously spelt sycomore—is exceedingly easy to climb.

the "sycomore," and led the way to his house.[1] But the murmurs of the multitude were long, and loud, and unanimous.[2] They thought it impolitic, incongruous, reprehensible, that the King, in the very midst of His impassioned followers, should put up at the house of a man whose very profession was a symbol of the national degradation, and who even in that profession was, as they openly implied, disreputable. But the approving smile, the gracious word of Jesus were more to Zacchæus than all the murmurs and insults of the crowd. Jesus did not despise him: what mattered then the contempt of the multitude? Nay, Jesus had done him honour, therefore he would honour, he would respect himself. As all that was base in him would have been driven into defiance by contempt and hatred, so all that was noble was evoked by a considerate tenderness. He would strive to be worthy, at least *more* worthy, of his glorious guest; he would at least do his utmost to disgrace Him less. And, therefore, standing prominently forth among the throng, he uttered—not to *them*, for they despised him, and for them he cared not, but to his Lord—the vow which, by one high act of magnanimity, at once attested his penitence and sealed his forgiveness. "Behold the half of my goods, Lord, I hereby give to the poor; and whatever fraudulent gain I ever made from any one, I now restore fourfold."[3] This great sacrifice of that which

[1] The square ruin in the wretched village of Rîha, the ancient Jericho, is (of course) called the house of Zacchæus, and is a Saracenic structure of the twelfth century.

[2] Luke xix. 7, ἅπαντες διεγόγγυζον.

[3] Lange and others see in the ἔι τινός τι ἐσυκοφάντησα a sort of denial that he had ever cheated—a challenge to any one to come forward and accuse him; but the Greek idiom does not imply this. Συκοφαντεῖν means to gain in base, underhand, pettifogging ways (see Exod. xxii. 1—9). Fourfold restitution was more than Zacchæus need have paid (Numb. v. 7).

had hitherto been dearest to him, this fullest possible restitution of every gain he had ever gotten dishonestly, this public confession and public restitution, should be a pledge to his Lord that His grace had not been in vain. Thus did love unseal by a single touch those swelling fountains of penitence which contempt would have kept closed for ever! No incident of His triumphal procession could have given to our Lord a deeper and holier joy. Was it not His very mission to seek and save the lost? Looking on the publican, thus ennobled by that instant renunciation of the fruits of sin, which is the truest test of a genuine repentance, He said, "Now is salvation come to this house, since he too is"—in the true spiritual sense, not in the idle, boastful, material sense alone—"a son of Abraham."[1]

To show them how mistaken were the expectations with which they were now excited—how erroneous, for instance, were the principles on which they had just been condemning Him for using the hospitality of Zacchæus—He proceeded (either at the meal in the publican's house, or more probably when they had again started) to tell them the Parable of the Pounds.[2] Adopting incidents with which the history of the Herodian family had made them familiar, He told them of a nobleman who had travelled into a far country to receive a kingdom,[3] and had delivered to each of his servants a

and evidently, if he could redeem his pledge, the bulk of his property must have been honestly acquired.

[1] The legend that he afterwards became Bishop of Cæsarea is too late to be of any value (Clem. *Hom.* ii. 1, &c.).

[2] Luke xix. 11—27.

[3] "A nobleman going into a far country to receive a kingdom" would be utterly unintelligible, had we not fortunately known that this was done both by Archelaus and by Antipas (Jos. *Antt.* xvii. 9, § 4). And in the case of Archelaus the Jews had actually sent to Augustus a deputation of fifty,

mina to be profitably employed till his return; the citizens hated him, and sent an embassy after him to procure his rejection. But in spite of this his kingdom was confirmed, and he came back to punish his enemies, and to reward his servants in proportion to their fidelity. One faithless servant, instead of using the sum entrusted to him, had hidden it in a napkin, and returned it with an unjust and insolent complaint of his master's severity. This man was deprived of his pound, which was given to the most deserving of the good and faithful servants;[1] these were magnificently rewarded, while the rebellious citizens were brought forth and slain. The parable was one of many-sided application; it indicated His near departure from the world; the hatred which should reject Him; the duty of faithfulness in the use of all that He entrusted to them; the uncertainty of His return; the certainty that, when He did return, there would be a solemn account; the condemnation of the slothful; the splendid reward of all who should serve Him well; the utter destruction of those who endeavoured to reject His power. Probably while He delivered this parable the caravan had paused, and the pilgrims had crowded round Him. Leaving them

to recount his cruelties and oppose his claims, which, though it failed at the time, was subsequently successful (Id. xvii. 13, § 2). Philippus defended the property of Archelaus during his absence from the encroachments of the Proconsul Sabinus. The magnificent palace which Archelaus had built at Jericho (Jos. *Antt.* xvii. 13, § 1) would naturally recall these circumstances to the mind of Jesus, and the parable is another striking example of the manner in which He utilised the most ordinary circumstances around Him, and made them the bases of His highest teachings. It is also another unsuspected indication of the authenticity and truthfulness of the Gospels.

[1] The surprised interpellation of the people, "Lord, he *hath* ten pounds," is an interesting proof of the intense and absorbing interest with which they listened to these parables.

to meditate on its significance, He once more moved forward alone at the head of the long and marvelling procession. They fell reverently back, and followed Him with many a look of awe as He slowly climbed the long, sultry, barren gorge which led up to Jerusalem from Jericho.[1]

He did not mean to make the city of Jerusalem His actual resting-place, but preferred as usual to stay in the loved home at Bethany. Thither He arrived on the evening of Friday, Nisan 8, A.U.C. 780 (March 31, A.D. 30), six days before the Passover, and before the sunset had commenced the Sabbath hours. Here He would part from His train of pilgrims, some of whom would go to enjoy the hospitality of their friends in the city, and others, as they do at the present day, would run up for themselves rude tents and booths in the valley of the Kedron, and about the western slopes of the Mount of Olives.

The Sabbath day was spent in quiet, and on the evening they made Him a supper.[2] St. Matthew and St. Mark say, a little mysteriously, that this feast was given in the house of Simon the leper. St. John makes no mention whatever of Simon the leper, a name which does not occur elsewhere; and it is clear from his narrative that the family of Bethany were in all respects the central figures at this entertainment. Martha seems

[1] Luke xix. 28.

[2] Matt. xxvi. 6—13; Mark xiv. 3—9; John xii. 1—9. This Sabbath preceding the Passover was called by the Jews *Shabbath Haggadôl,* or the "Great Sabbath." It is only in appearance that the Synoptists seem to place this feast two days before the Passover. They narrate it there to account for the treachery of Judas, which was consummated by his *final* arrangements with the Sanhedrin on the *Wednesday* of Holy week; but we see from St. John that this latter must have been his *second* interview with them: at the first interview all details had been left indefinite.

to have had the entire supervision of the feast, and the risen Lazarus was almost as much an object of curiosity as Jesus himself. In short, so many thronged to see Lazarus—for the family was one of good position, and its members were widely known and beloved—that the notorious and indisputable miracle which had been performed on his behalf caused many to believe on Jesus. This so exasperated the ruling party at Jerusalem that, in their wicked desperation, they actually held a consultation how they might get rid of this living witness to the supernatural powers of the Messiah whom they rejected. Now since the raising of Lazarus was so intimately connected with the entire cycle of events which the earlier Evangelists so minutely record, we are again driven to the conclusion that there must have been some good reason, a reason which we can but uncertainly conjecture, for their marked reticence on this subject; and we find another trace of this reticence in their calling Mary "a certain woman," in their omission of all allusion to Martha and Lazarus, and in their telling us that this memorable banquet was served in the house of "Simon the leper." Who then was this Simon the leper? That he was no longer a leper is of course certain, for otherwise he could not have been living in his own house, or mingling in general society. Had he then been cleansed by Jesus? and, if so, was this one cause of the profound belief in Him which prevailed in that little household, and of the tender affection with which they always welcomed Him? or, again, was Simon now dead? We cannot answer these questions, nor are there sufficient data to enable us to decide whether he was the father of Martha and Mary and Lazarus,[1] or

[1] So Ewald, *Gesch. Christ.*, 401.

as some have conjectured, whether Martha was his widow, and the inheritress of his house.

Be this as it may, the feast was chiefly memorable, not for the number of Jews who thronged to witness it, and so to gaze at once on the Prophet of Nazareth and on the man whom He had raised from the dead, but from one memorable incident which occurred in the course of it, and which was the immediate beginning of the dark and dreadful end.

For as she sat there in the presence of her beloved and rescued brother, and her yet more deeply worshipped Lord, the feelings of Mary could no longer be restrained. She was not occupied like her sister in the active ministrations of the feast, but she sat and thought and gazed until the fire burned, and she felt impelled to some outward sign of her love, her gratitude, her adoration. So she arose and fetched an alabaster vase of Indian spikenard, and came softly behind Jesus where He sat, and broke the alabaster in her hands, and poured the genuine[1] precious perfume first over His head, then over His feet, and then—unconscious of every presence save His alone—she wiped those feet with the long tresses of her hair, while the atmosphere of the whole house was filled with the delicious fragrance. It was an act of devoted sacrifice, of exquisite self-abandonment;

[1] ἀλάβαστρον μύρου νάρδου πιστικῆς πολυτελοῦς (Mark xiv. 3). Cf. "*Nardi* parvus *onyx*" (Hor. *Od.* iv. 12). The possession of so expensive an unguent shows that the family was rich. It would have been under any circumstances a princely gift (Herod. iii. 120). The word πιστικῆς, if it mean "genuine," is opposed to the *pseudo-nardus* (Plin. xii. 26); but this interpretation of the word is by no means free from difficulty, and I have no better to offer. It "was so great an ecstacy of love, sorrow, and adoration, that to anoint the feet even of the greatest monarch was long unknown; and in all the pomps and greatnesses of the Roman prodigality, it was not used till Otho taught it to Nero" (Pliny, *N. H.* xiii. 35; Jer. Taylor, III. xiii.).

and the poor Galilæans who followed Jesus, so little accustomed to any luxury, so fully alive to the costly nature of the gift, might well have been amazed that it should have all been lavished on the rich luxury of one brief moment. None but the most spiritual-hearted there could feel that the delicate odour which breathed through the perfumed house might be to God a sweet-smelling savour; that even this was infinitely too little to satisfy the love of her who gave, or the dignity of Him to whom the gift was given.

But there was one present to whom on every ground the act was odious and repulsive. There is no vice at once so absorbing, so unreasonable, and so degrading as the vice of avarice, and avarice was the besetting sin in the dark soul of the traitor Judas. The failure to struggle with his own temptations; the disappointment of every expectation which had first drawn him to Jesus; the intolerable rebuke conveyed to his whole being by the daily communion with a sinless purity; the darker shadow which he could not but feel that his guilt flung athwart his footsteps because of the burning sunlight in which for many months he now had walked; the sense too that the eye of his Master, possibly even the eyes of some of his fellow-apostles, had read or were beginning to read the hidden secrets of his heart;—all these things had gradually deepened from an incipient alienation into an insatiable repugnancy and hate. And the sight of Mary's lavish sacrifice, the consciousness that it was now too late to save that large sum for the bag[1]—the mere possession of which, apart from the sums which he could pilfer out of it, gratified his greed for gold—filled him with disgust and madness. He had a

[1] γλωσσόκομον (John xii. 6). *Vid. supr.*, Vol. I., p. 315.

devil. He felt as if he had been personally cheated; as if the money were by right *his*, and he had been, in a senseless manner, defrauded of it. "To what purpose is this waste?" he indignantly said; and, alas! how often have his words been echoed, for wherever there is an act of splendid self-forgetfulness there is always a Judas to sneer and murmur at it. "This ointment might have been sold for three hundred pence and given to the poor!" *Three hundred pence*—ten pounds or more! There was perfect frenzy in the thought of such utter perdition of good money;[1] why, for barely a third of such a sum, this son of perdition was ready to sell his Lord. Mary thought it not good enough to anele Christ's sacred feet: Judas thought a third part of it sufficient reward for selling His very life.

That little touch about its "being given to the poor" is a very instructive one. It was probably the veil used by Judas to half conceal even from himself the grossness of his own motives—the fact that he was a petty thief, and really wished the charge of this money because it would have enabled him to add to his own private store. People rarely sin under the full glare of self-consciousness; they usually blind themselves with false pretexts and specious motives; and though Judas could not conceal his baseness from the clearer eye of John, he probably concealed it from himself under the notion that he really was protesting against an act of romantic wastefulness, and pleading the cause of disinterested charity.

[1] Matt. xxvi. 8, εἰς τί ἡ ἀπώλεια αὕτη; "Immo tu, Juda, *perditionis es*" (ὁ υἱὸς τῆς ἀπωλείας, John xvii. 12). (Bengel.)—"More than three hundred pence" would be at least £10, while the thirty pieces of silver for which Judas bargained to betray Jesus were not more than £3 16*s*.

But Jesus would not permit the contagion of this worldly indignation—which had already infected some of the simple disciples—to spread any farther; nor would He allow Mary, already the centre of an unfavourable observation which pained and troubled her, to suffer any more from the consequences of her noble act. "Why trouble ye the woman?" He said. "Let her alone; she wrought a good work upon Me; for ye have the poor always with you, but Me ye have not always; for in casting this ointment on My body, she did it for My burying." And He added the prophecy—a prophecy which to this day is memorably fulfilled—that wherever the Gospel should be preached that deed of hers should be recorded and honoured.

"For My burying"—clearly, therefore, His condemnation and burial were near at hand. This was another death-blow to all false Messianic hopes. No earthly wealth, no regal elevation could be looked for by the followers of One who was so soon to die. It may have been another impulse of disappointment to the thievish traitor who had thus publicly been not only thwarted, but also silenced, and implicitly rebuked. The loss of the money, which *might* by imagination have been under his own control, burnt in him with "a secret, dark, melancholic fire." He would *not* lose everything. In his hatred, and madness, and despair, he slunk away from Bethany that night, and made his way to Jerusalem, and got introduced into the council-room of the chief priests in the house of Caiaphas, and had that first fatal interview in which he bargained with them to betray his Lord. "What are you willing to give me, and I will betray Him to you?" What greedy chafferings took place we are not told, nor whether the counteravarices of these united hatreds had a struggle before they decided on the paltry blood-money. If so, the astute Jewish priests beat down the poor ignorant Jewish Apostle. For all that they offered and all they paid was thirty pieces of silver[1]—about £3 16*s.*—the ransom-money of the meanest slave. For this price he was to sell his Master, and in selling his Master to sell his own life, and to gain in return the execration of the world for all generations yet to come. And, so for the last week of his own and his Master's life, Judas moved about with the purpose of murder in his dark and desperate heart. But as yet no day had been fixed, no plan decided on—only the betrayal paid for; and there seems to have been a general conviction that it would not do to make the attempt during the actual feast, lest there should be an uproar among the multitude who accepted Him, and especially among the dense throngs of pilgrims from His native Galilee. They believed that many opportunities would occur, either at Jerusalem or elsewhere, when the great Passover was finished, and the Holy City had relapsed into its ordinary calm.

And the events of the following day would be likely to give the most emphatic confirmation to the worldly wisdom of their wicked decision.

[1] See Exod. xxi. 32; Zech. xi. 12. The ἔστησαν of Matt. xxvi. 15 seems to imply that the money was paid down. No actual *shekels* were current at this time, but Judas may have been paid in Syrian or Phœnician tetradrachms, which were of the same weight (*v.* Madden). The paltriness of the sum (if it were not mere earnest-money) undoubtedly shows that the authorities did not regard the services of Judas as *indispensable.* He only saved them trouble and possible blood-shedding.

CHAPTER XLIX.

PALM SUNDAY.

"Ride on, ride on in majesty,
In lowly pomp ride on to die!"—HYMN.

THERE seems to have been a general impression for some time beforehand that, in spite of all which had recently happened, Jesus would still be present at the Paschal Feast. The probability of this had incessantly been debated among the people, and the expected arrival of the Prophet of Galilee was looked forward to with intense curiosity and interest.[1]

Consequently, when it became known early on Sunday morning that during the day He would certainly enter the Holy City, the excitement was very great. The news would be spread by some of the numerous Jews who had visited Bethany on the previous evening, after the sunset had closed the Sabbath, and thus enabled them to exceed the limits of the Sabbath day's journey. Thus it was that a very great multitude was prepared to receive and welcome the Deliverer who had raised the dead.

He started on foot. Three roads led from Bethany over the Mount of Olives to Jerusalem. One of these

[1] Matt. xxi. 1—11 Mark xi. 1—11; Luke xix. 28—40; John xii. 12—19.

passes between its northern[1] and central summits; the other ascends the highest point of the mountain, and slopes down through the modern village of Et Tur; the third, which is, and always must have been, the main road, sweeps round the southern shoulder of the central mass, between it and the "Hill of Evil Counsel." The others are rather mountain paths than roads, and as Jesus was attended by so many disciples, it is clear that He took the third and easiest route.

Passing from under the palm-trees of Bethany,[2] they approached the fig-gardens of Bethphage, the "House of Figs," a small suburb or hamlet of undiscovered site, which lay probably a little to the south of Bethany, and in sight of it. To this village, or some other hamlet which lay near it, Jesus dispatched two of His disciples. The minute description of the spot given by St. Mark makes us suppose that Peter was one of them, and if so he was probably accompanied by John. Jesus told them that when they got to the village they should find an ass tied, and a colt with her; these they were to loose and bring to Him, and if any objection arose on the part of the owner, it would at once be silenced by telling him that "the Lord had

[1] Traditionally called the "Hill of Offence," and by Milton, "that opprobrious hill;" the supposed site of Solomon's idolatrous temples. It is now known as the Viri Galilæi, in reference to Acts i. 11. The "Hill of Evil Counsel" is the one on which stands the ruin of the so-called "House of Caiaphas." Williams (*Holy City*, ii. 496) notices it as a curious fact that the tomb of Annas is not far from this spot.

[2] On the derivation of Bethany, *v. supr.*, p. 202, *n.* There are no palms there now, but there may have been at that period. Throughout Palestine the palm and vine and fig-tree are *far* rarer than they were. Some identify Bethphage with Abu Dis. Lightfoot, apparently with Talmudical authority, makes it a *suburb* of Jerusalem. From the fact that in a journey towards Jerusalem it is always mentioned before Bethany, we might assume that it was *east* of that village.

need of them." Everything happened as He had said. In the passage round the house—*i.e.*, tied up at the back of the house[1]—they found the ass and the foal, which was adapted for its sacred purpose because it had never yet been used.[2] The owners, on hearing their object, at once permitted them to take the animals, and they led them to Jesus, putting their garments over them to do Him regal honour.[3] Then they lifted Him upon the colt, and the triumphal procession set forth. It was no seditious movement to stir up political enthusiasm, no "insulting vanity" to commemorate ambitious triumph. Nay, it was a mere outburst of provincial joy, the simple exultation of poor Galilæans and despised disciples. He rides, not upon a war-horse, but on an animal which was the symbol of peace. The haughty Gentiles, had they witnessed the humble procession, would have utterly derided it, as indeed they did deride the record of it;[4] but the Apostles recalled in after days

[1] Mark xi. 4, *δεδεμένον πρὸς τὴν θύραν ἔξω ἐπὶ τοῦ ἀμφόδου*, not "where two ways met," as the English version translates it, following the Vulgate *bivium;* but the Hebr. חוץ (Prov. i. 20), *ἄμφοδα, αἱ ῥύμαι, ἀγυιαὶ* (Hesych.).

[2] Numb. xix. 2; Deut. xxi. 3; 1 Sam. vi. 7. Comp. Ov. *Met.* iii. 12; Hor. *Epod.* ix. 22 (Wetstein).

[3] Comp. 2 Kings ix. 13.

[4] For instance, Julian and Sapor. In fact, the Romans had all kinds of sneers against the Jews in connection with the ass (Jos. *C. Ap.* ii. 10; Tac. *Hist.* v. 3, 4). The Christians came in for a share of this stupid jest, and were called *asinarii cultores* (Minuc. Fel. *Oct.* 9; Tert. *Apol.* 16; see Keim, iii. 82). Sapor offered the Jews a horse to serve the purpose of carrying their expected Messiah, and a Jew haughtily answered him that all his horses were far below the ass which should carry the Messiah, which was to be descended from that used by Abraham when he went to offer Isaac, and that used by Moses (Sepp, sect. vi., ch. 6). If, however, He came riding on an ass, and not on the clouds, it was to be a sign of their faithlessness (Lightfoot, *ad loc.*). The ass is not in the East by any means a despised or a despicable animal (Gen. xlix. 14; xxii. 3; 2 Sam. xiii. 29; Judg. v. 10); it is curious, however, to see that, because it was despised by Europeans and Gentiles, Josephus is fond of substituting for it *κτῆνος* and

that it fulfilled the prophecy of Zechariah: "Rejoice greatly, O daughter of Sion; shout, O daughter of Jerusalem; behold, thy King cometh unto thee; He is meek, and having salvation; lowly, and riding upon an ass, and upon a colt the foal of an ass."[1] Yes, it was a procession of very lowly pomp, and yet beside it how do the grandest triumphs of aggressive war and unjust conquest sink into utter insignificance and disgrace!

Jesus mounted the unused foal, while probably some of His disciples led it by the bridle. And no sooner had He started than the multitude spread out[2] their upper garments to tapestry His path, and kept tearing or cutting down the boughs of olive, and fig, and walnut, to scatter them before Him. Then, in a burst of enthusiasm, the disciples broke into the shout, "Hosanna to the Son of David! Blessed is the King of Israel that cometh in the name of the Lord! Hosanna in the highest!"[3] and the multitude caught up the joyous strain, and told each other how He had raised Lazarus from the dead.[4]

ἵππος, and the LXX., with dishonest discretion, soften it down to *ὑποζύγιον* and *πῶλος* in Zech. ix. 9. It is clear that Jesus rode upon the foal, which by its mother's side could be led quietly along. With the *ἐπάνω αὐτῶν* = "on one of them," comp. Acts xxiii. 24. Only inferior MSS. read *αὐτοῦ*, and to understand *αὐτῶν* of the garments is harsh. After all, however, it is doubtful whether there *were* two animals or only one (*ὀνάριον*, John xii. 14; *πῶλον δεδεμένον*, Mark xi. 2; Luke xix. 30). It is in St. Matthew alone (xxi. 2, 7) that two animals are mentioned, and it is just conceivable that the *καὶ* here may be epexegetic, and simply due to parallelism.

[1] The quotation referred to is a mixture (see Glass, *Philolog. Sacr.*, p. 969) of Isa. lxii. 11; Zech. ix. 9; and the Hebrew means literally "poor (עָנִי) and riding upon an ass, *even* upon a colt, son of she-asses." (See Turpie, *Old Test. in New*, p. 222.)

[2] Matt. xxi. 8, *ἔστρωσαν . . . . ἐστρώννυον.*

[3] Hosanna = הוֹשִׁיעָה נָּא rendered by the LXX. *σῶσον δή*, "Oh save!" These various cries are all from the Psalms which formed the great Hallel, (Ps. cxiii.—cxviii.) sung at the Feast of Tabernacles (Ps. cxviii. 25).

[4] In John xii. 17, the true reading (D, E, K, L, &c.) probably is *ὅτι*, "that" or "because," *not ὅτε*, "when."

The road slopes by a gradual ascent up the Mount of Olives, through green fields and under shady trees, till it suddenly sweeps round to the northward. It is at this angle of the road that Jerusalem, which hitherto has been hidden by the shoulder of the hill, bursts full upon the view. There, through the clear atmosphere, rising out of the deep umbrageous valleys which surrounded it, the city of ten thousand memories stood clear before Him, and the morning sunlight, as it blazed on the marble pinnacles and gilded roofs of the Temple buildings, was reflected in a very fiery splendour which forced the spectator to avert his glance.[1] Such a glimpse of such a city is at all times affecting, and many a Jewish and Gentile traveller has reined his horse at this spot, and gazed upon the scene in emotion too deep for speech. But the Jerusalem of that day, with "its imperial mantle of proud towers," was regarded as one of the wonders of the world,[2] and was a spectacle incomparably more magnificent than the decayed and crumbling city of to-day. And who can interpret, who can enter into the mighty rush of divine compassion which, at that spectacle, shook the Saviour's soul? As He gazed on that "mass of gold and snow," was there no pride, no exultation in the heart of its true King? Far from it! He had dropped *silent* tears at the grave of Lazarus; here He wept aloud.[3] All the shame of His mockery, all

[1] So Josephus tells us (*B. J.* v. 5, § 6). It made those "who forced themselves to look upon it at the first rising of the sun, to turn their eyes away, just as they would have done at the sun's own rays." I came upon this spot in a walk from Bethany, not at sunrise, but under a full moon, on the night of Wednesday in Passion Week, April 14, 1870. I shall never forget the impression left by the sudden sight of the city, with its domes and minarets and twinkling lights, as it lay bathed in the Paschal moonlight.

[2] Tac. *Hist.* v. 8.

[3] John xi. 35, ἐδάκρυσεν; Luke xix. 41, ἔκλαυσεν.

the anguish of His torture, was powerless, five days afterwards, to extort from Him a single groan, or to wet His eyelids with one trickling tear; but here, all the pity that was within Him overmastered His human spirit, and He not only wept, but broke into a passion of lamentation, in which the choked voice seemed to struggle for its utterance. A strange Messianic triumph! a strange interruption of the festal cries! The Deliverer weeps over the city which it is now too late to save; the King prophesies the utter ruin of the nation which He came to rule! "If thou hadst known," He cried—while the wondering multitudes looked on, and knew not what to think or say—"If thou hadst known, even thou, at least in thy day, the things that belong unto thy peace!"[1]—and there sorrow interrupted the sentence, and, when He found voice to continue, He could only add, "but now they are hid from thine eyes. For the days shall come upon thee that thine enemies shall cast a trench about thee,[2] and compass thee round, and keep thee in on every side, and shall lay thee even with the ground, and thy children within thee; and they shall not leave in thee one stone upon another, because thou knewest not the time of thy visitation." It was the last invitation from "the Glory of God on the Mount of Olives," before that Shechînah vanished from their eyes for ever.[3]

[1] Perhaps with a play on the name Jerusalem, which might *recall* (though not derived from) יִרְאוּ שָׁלוֹם, "they shall see peace" (cf. Ps. cxxii. 6, 7). Such paronomasiæ are not only consistent with, but the usual concomitants of, deep emotion. See my *Chapters on Language*, pp. 269—276.

[2] Luke xix. 43, *χάραξ*, "a palisade." Cf. Isa. xxix. 3, 4; xxxvii. 33), properly only the *pali* on the *agger*, but sometimes of the entire *vallum* (cf. Isa. xxxvii. 33, LXX.).

[3] Commenting on Ezek. xi. 23, the Rabbis said that the Shechînah

Sternly, literally, terribly, within fifty years, was that prophecy fulfilled. Four years before the war began, while as yet the city was in the greatest peace and prosperity, a melancholy maniac traversed its streets with the repeated cry, "A voice from the east, a voice from the west, a voice from the four winds, a voice against Jerusalem and the holy house, a voice against the bridegrooms and the brides, and a voice against this whole people;" nor could any scourgings or tortures wring from him any other words except "Woe! woe! to Jerusalem; woe to the city; woe to the people; woe to the holy house!" until seven years afterwards, during the siege, he was killed by a stone from a catapult. His voice was but the renewed echo of the voice of prophecy.

Titus had not originally wished to encompass the city, but he was forced, by the despair and obstinacy of the Jews, to surround it, first with a palisaded mound, and then, when this *vallum* and *agger* were destroyed, with a wall of masonry. He did not wish to sacrifice the Temple—nay, he made every possible effort to save it—but he was forced to leave it in ashes. He did not intend to be cruel to the inhabitants, but the deadly fanaticism of their opposition so extinguished all desire to spare them, that he undertook the task of well-nigh exterminating the race—of crucifying them by hundreds, of exposing them in the amphitheatre by thousands, of selling them into slavery by myriads. Josephus tells us that, even immediately after the siege of Titus, no one, in the desert waste around him, would have recognised the beauty of Judæa; and that if any

retired eastward to the Mount of Olives, and there for three years called in vain to the peoples with human voice that they should repent; then withdrew for ever. (See Wetstein, p. 459; Keim, iii. 93.)

Jew had come upon the city of a sudden, however well he had known it before, he would have asked "what place it was?"[1] And he who, in modern Jerusalem, would look for relics of the ten-times-captured city of the days of Christ, must look for them twenty feet beneath the soil, and will scarcely find them. In one spot alone remain a few massive substructions, as though to show how vast is the ruin they represent; and here, on every Friday, assemble a few poverty-stricken Jews, to stand each in the shroud in which he will be buried, and wail over the shattered glories of their fallen and desecrated home.[2]

There had been a pause in the procession while Jesus shed His bitter tears and uttered His prophetic lamentation. But now the people in the valley of Kedron, and about the walls of Jerusalem, and the pilgrims whose booths and tents stood so thickly on the green slopes below, had caught sight of the approaching company, and heard the echo of the glad shouts, and knew what the commotion meant. At that time the palms were numerous in the neighbourhood of Jerusalem, though now but a few remain; and tearing down their green and graceful branches, the people streamed up the road to meet the approaching Prophet.[3] And when the

[1] *B. J.* vi. 1, § 1.

[2] "Before my mind's eye," says Dr. Frankl, describing his first glimpse of Jerusalem, "passed in review the deeds and the forms of former centuries. A voice within me said, '*Graves upon graves in graves!*' I was deeply moved, and, bowing in my saddle before the city of Jehovah, tears fell upon my horse's mane" (*Jews in the East*, i. 351).

[3] John xii. 13, *τὰ βαΐα τῶν φοινίκων*, "the branches of the palm-trees," which were familiar to St. John, and which, if the old derivation can stand, gave to Bethany its name. The reading *στοιβάδας ἐκ τῶν ἄγρων* in Mark xi. 8, though supported by א, B, C, L, Δ, perhaps arose from the notion that *στ.* meant "grass." Dean Stanley is the first writer who seems accurately to have appreciated the facts and order of the triumphal entry (*Sin. and*

two streams of people met—those who had accompanied Him from Bethany, and those who had come to meet Him from Jerusalem—they left Him riding in the midst, and some preceding, some following Him, advanced, shouting "Hosannas" and waving branches, to the gate of Jerusalem.

Mingled among the crowd were some of the Pharisees, and the joy of the multitude was to them gall and wormwood. What meant these Messianic cries and kingly titles? Were they not dangerous and unseemly? Why did He allow them? "Master, rebuke Thy disciples." But He would not do so. "If these should hold their peace," He said, "the stones would immediately cry out." The words may have recalled to them the threats which occur, amid denunciations against covetousness and cruelty, and the utter destruction by which they should be avenged, in the prophet Habakkuk—"For the stone shall cry out of the wall, and the beam out of the timber shall answer it." The Pharisees felt that they were powerless to stay the flood of enthusiasm.

And when they reached the walls the whole city was stirred with powerful excitement and alarm.[1] "Who is this?" they asked, as they leaned out of the lattices and from the roofs, and stood aside in the bazaars and

Palest., pp. 189, seqq. See, too, Targ. Esth. x. 15—the streets strewn with myrtle before Mordecai; Herod. vii. 54). The Maccabees were welcomed into Jerusalem with similar acclamations (2 Macc. x. 7). In *Kethubh.* f. 66, 2, we are told of robes outspread before Nakdîmon, son of Gorion (Keim, iii. 90). A singular illustration of the faithfulness and accuracy of the Evangelists was given by the wholly accidental and unpremeditated re-enactment of the very same scene when Mr. Farran, the English consul of Damascus, visited Jerusalem at a time of great distress, in 1834.

[1] ἐσείσθη (Matt. xxi. 10; cf. xxviii. 4). Perhaps they recalled the attempt made upon Jerusalem by "that Egyptian" (Acts xxi. 38).

streets to let them pass; and the multitude answered, with something of pride in their great countryman—but already, as it were, with a shadow of distrust falling over their high Messianic hopes, as they came in contact with the contempt and hostility of the capital—"This is Jesus, the Prophet of Nazareth."

The actual procession would not proceed farther than the foot of Mount Moriah (the *Har ha-beit,* Isa. ii. 2), beyond which they might not advance in travelling array, or with dusty feet.[1] Before they had reached the Shushan gate of the Temple they dispersed, and Jesus entered. The Lord whom they sought had come suddenly to His Temple—even the messenger of the covenant; but they neither recognised Him, nor delighted in Him, though His first act was to purify and purge it, that they might offer to the Lord an offering in righteousness.[2] As He looked round on all things[3] His heart was again moved within Him to strong indignation. Three years before, at His first Passover, He had cleansed the Temple; but, alas! in vain. Already greed had won the battle against reverence; already the tessel-

[1] *Berach.* ix. 5, quoted by Lightfoot.

[2] Mal. iii. 1—3.

[3] I follow the order of St. Matthew, in preference to that of St. Mark, in fixing the cleansing of the Temple on Palm Sunday, and immediately after the triumphal entry; and for these reasons: (1) because it is most unlikely that Jesus started late in the day; it would be very hot, even in that season of the year, and contrary to His usual habits. (2) If, then, He started early, and did not leave the Temple till late (Mark xi. 11), there is no indication of how the day was spent (for the journey to Jerusalem would not occupy more, at the very most, than two hours), unless we suppose that the incidents narrated in the text took place on the Sunday, as both St. Matthew, St. Luke, and St. John seem to imply. (3) The cleansing of the Temple would be a much more natural sequel of the triumphal entry, than of the quiet walk next day. (4) There is no adequate reason to account for the postponement of such a purification of the Temple till the following day.

lated floors and pillared colonnades of the Court of the Gentiles had been again usurped by droves of oxen and sheep, and dove-sellers, and usurers, and its whole precincts were dirty with driven cattle, and echoed to the hum of bargaining voices and the clink of gold.[1] In that desecrated place He would not teach. Once more, in mingled sorrow and anger, He drove them forth, while none dared to resist His burning zeal; nor would He even suffer the peaceful enclosure to be disturbed by people passing to and fro with vessels, and so turning it into a thoroughfare. The dense crowd of Jews —numbering, it is said, three millions—who crowded to the Holy City in the week of the feast, no doubt made the Court of the Gentiles a worse and busier scene on that day than at any other time, and the more so because on that day, according to the law, the Paschal lamb—which the visitors would be obliged to purchase —was chosen and set apart.[2] But no considerations of their business and convenience could make it tolerable that they should turn His Father's house, which was a house of prayer for all nations, into a place most like one of those foul caves which He had seen so often in the Wady Hammâm, where brigands wrangled over their ill-gotten spoils.[3]

[1] The vast throng of foreign pilgrims, and the necessity laid on them of changing their foreign coinage, with its heathen symbols, for the *shekel hak-kodesh*, "half-shekel, after the shekel of the sanctuary" (Exod. xxx. 13), would make the trade of these men at this time a very thriving one: their agio was a twelfth of each shekel. The presence of these money-makers distinctly contravened the law of Zech. xiv. 21, where Canaanite = merchant. See *supra*, Vol. I., p. 189, *n*.

[2] Exod. xii. 1—5. For the "booths" in the Temple Court, see Lightfoot on Matt. xxi. 12.

[3] σπηλαῖον λῃστῶν (Mördergrube, Luther) is much stronger than "den of thieves;" and if the "House of Prayer" reminded them of Jer. vii. 6, as well as Isa. lvi. 7, it would recall ideas of "innocent blood," as well as of

Not till He had reduced the Temple to decency and silence could He begin His customary ministrations. Doubtless the task was easier, because it had already been once performed. But when the miserable hubbub was over, then the Temple resumed what should have been its normal aspect. Sufferers came to Him, and He healed them. Listeners in hundreds thronged round Him, were astonished at His doctrine, hung upon His lips.[1] The very children of the Temple, in their innocent delight, continued the glad Hosannas which had welcomed Him. The Chief Priests, and Scribes, and Pharisees, and leading people saw, and despised, and wondered, and perished. They could but gnash their teeth in their impotence, daring to do nothing, saying to each other that they *could* do nothing, for the whole world had gone after Him, yet hoping still that their hour would come, and the power of darkness. If they ventured to say one word to Him, they had to retire abashed and frustrated by His calm reply. They angrily called His attention to the cry of the boys in the Temple courts, and said, "Hearest Thou what these say?" Perhaps they were boys employed in the musical services of the Temple, and if so the priestly

greedy gain. The Temple was destined in a few more years to become yet more emphatically a "murderer's cave," when the *sicarii* made it the scene of their atrocities. "The sanctuary," says Josephus (*B. J.* iv. 3, § 7), "was now become a refuge, and a shop of tyranny." "Certainly," says Ananus in his speech, "it had been good for me to die before I had seen the house of God full of so many abominations, or these sacred places, that ought not to be trodden upon at random, filled with the feet of these blood-shedding villains" (*id.* § 10). "When any of the Zealots were wounded, he went up into the Temple, and defiled that sacred floor with his blood" (*id.* § 12). "To say all in a word, no passion was so entirely lost among them as mercy" (*id.* iv. 6, § 3).

[1] Luke xix. 48, *ὁ λαὸς γὰρ ἅπας ἐξεκρέματο αὐτοῦ ἀκούων*: cf. Virg. *Æn.* iv. 79, "pendebat ab ore."

party would be still more enraged. But Jesus calmly protected the children from their unconcealed hatred. "Yea," He answered, "have ye never read, Out of the mouths of babes and sucklings Thou hast perfected praise?"[1]

So in high discourse, amid the vain attempts of His enemies to annoy and hinder Him, the hours of that memorable day passed by. And it was marked by one more deeply interesting incident. Struck by all they had seen and heard, some Greeks—probably Jewish proselytes attracted to Jerusalem by the feast—came to Philip, and asked him to procure for them a private interview with Jesus.[2] Chaldæans from the East had sought His cradle; these Greeks from the West came to His cross.[3] Who they were, and why they sought Him, we know not. An interesting tradition, but one on which unfortunately we can lay no stress, says that they were emissaries from Abgarus V., King of Edessa, who, having been made aware of the miracles of Jesus, and of the dangers to which He was now exposed, sent these emissaries to offer Him an asylum in his dominions. The legend adds that, though Jesus declined the offer, He rewarded the faith of Abgarus by writing him a letter, and healing him of a sickness.[4]

[1] Ps. viii. 2. Did they recall the sequel of the verse, "*because of Thine enemies*, that Thou mightest still the enemy and the avenger?" Similar emotional outbursts of children are adduced by Schöttgen.

[2] John xii. 20—50.

[3] Stier *ad loc.* They are called Ἕλληνες, and were therefore Gentiles, not Ἑλληνισταὶ (cf. Acts xvi. 1; John vii. 35), or Greek-speaking Jews. In the Syriac version they are called Aramæans. That they were proselytes appears from John xii. 20 (comp. Acts viii. 27).

[4] The apocryphal letter of Abgarus to Christ is given by Eusebius (*Hist. Eccl.* i. 13), who professes to derive it from Syriac documents preserved at Edessa, and quoted by Moses Chorenensis (*Hist. Arm.* ii. 28). (Herzog, *Bibl. Encykl.* s. v. "Abgar.") The letter and reply are probably as old as the

St. John mentions nothing of these circumstances he does not even tell us why these Greeks came to Philip in particular. As Bethsaida was the native town of this apostle, and as many Jews at this period had adopted Gentile appellations, especially those which were current in the family of Herod, we cannot attach much importance to the Greek form of his name.[1] It is an interesting indication of the personal awe which the Apostles felt for their Master, that Philip did not at once venture to grant their request. He went and consulted his fellow-townsman Andrew, and the two Apostles then made known the wish of the Greeks to Jesus. Whether they actually introduced the inquirers into His presence we cannot tell, but at any rate He saw in the incident a fresh sign that the hour was come when His name should be glorified. His answer was to the effect that as a grain of wheat must die before it can bring forth fruit, so the road to His glory lay through humiliation, and they who would follow Him must be prepared at all times to follow Him even to death. As He contemplated that approaching death, the human horror of it struggled with the ardour of His obedience; and conscious that to face that

third century. Abgar says that having heard of His miracles, and thence concluded His Divine nature, "I have written to ask of Thee that Thou couldest trouble Thyself to come to me, and heal this sickness which I have. For I have also heard that the Jews murmur against Thee, and wish to injure Thee. Now I have a small and beautiful city which is sufficient for both." The reply, which is almost entirely couched in Scriptural language, begins with an allusion to John xx. 29, and after declining the king's offer, adds, "When I am taken up, I will send thee one of my disciples to heal thy sickness; he shall also give salvation to thee and to them that are with thee." (B. H. Cowper, *Apocr. Gosp.*, p. 220; Hofmann, *Leben Jesu nach d. Apocr.*, p. 308.) The disease was, according to Cedrenus (*Hist.* p. 145), leprosy, and according to Procopius (*De Bell. Pers.* ii. 12) the gout.

[1] Lange (iv. 54) notices the tradition that Philip afterwards laboured in Phrygia, and Andrew in Greece.

dread hour was to conquer it, He cried, "Father, glorify Thy name!" Then for the third time in His life came a voice from heaven, which said, "I have both glorified it, and will glorify it again."[1] St. John frankly tells us that that Voice did not sound alike to all. The common multitude took it but for a passing peal of thunder; others said, "An angel spake to Him;" the Voice was articulate only to the few. But Jesus told them that the Voice was for their sakes, not for His; for the judgment of the world, its conviction of sin by the Holy Spirit, was now at hand, and the Prince of this world[2] should be cast out. He should be lifted up, like the brazen serpent in the wilderness,[3] and when so exalted He should draw all men unto Him. The people were perplexed at these dark allusions. They asked Him what could be the meaning of His saying that "the Son of Man should be lifted up?" If it meant violently taken away by a death of shame, how could this be? Was not the Son of Man a title of the Messiah? and did not the prophet imply that the reign of Messiah would be eternal?[4] The true answer to their query could only be received by spiritual hearts—they were unprepared for it, and would only have been offended and shocked by it;

[1] John xii. 28, καὶ ἐδόξασα καὶ πάλιν δοξάσω. On the previous passage see the excellent remarks of Stier. (*Vide supr.*, Vol. I., p. 115; II., p. 29.)

[2] The Jewish *Sar ha-Olam;* he whom St. Paul calls "the god of this world" (2 Cor. iv. 4). The Greek κόσμος corresponds to the Hebrew *olamîm* or "aeons." The Jews, unlike the Greeks, did not so much regard the outward beauty of Creation, as its inward significance: for them the interest of the Universe "centered rather in the moral than in the physical order" (Westcott, *Introd.* i. 25). (See Eph. ii. 2.) A Mussulman title of God is "Lord of the (three) worlds" (*Rabb al alamîn*).

[3] Comp. John iii. 14; viii. 28. Cf. "Adolescentum laudandum, ornandum, *tollendum*" (Letter of Dec. Brutus to Cicero, *Epp. ad Div.* xi. 20).

[4] "The Law" is here a general term for the Old Testament. The reference is to Ps. lxxxix. 36; comp. John x. 34.

therefore Jesus did not answer them. He only bade them walk in the light during the very little while that it should still remain with them, and so become the children of light. He was come as a light into the world, and the words which He spake should judge those who rejected Him; for those words—every brief answer, every long discourse—were from the Father; sunbeams from the Father of Lights; life-giving rays from the Life Eternal.[1]

But all these glorious and healing truths were dull to blinded eyes, and dead to hardened hearts; and even the few of higher rank and wider culture who partially understood and partially believed them, yet dared not confess Him, because to confess Him was to incur the terrible *cherem* of the Sanhedrin; and this they would not face—loving the praise of men more than the praise of God.

Thus a certain sadness and sense of rejection fell even on the evening of the Day of Triumph. It was not safe for Jesus to stay in the city, nor was it in accordance with His wishes. He retired secretly from the Temple, hid Himself from His watchful enemies, and, protected as yet outside the city walls by the enthusiasm of His Galilæan followers, "went out unto Bethany with the Twelve." But it is very probable that while He bent His steps in the direction of Bethany, He did not actually enter the village; for, on this occasion, His object seems to have been concealment, which would hardly have been secured by returning to the well-known house where so many had seen Him at the banquet on

[1] John xii. 44—50, verse 49, *δέδωκε τί εἴπω* (de sermone brevi, אָמַר) *καὶ τί λαλήσω* (de copioso, דָּבַר). (Bengel.) The *ἔκραξε* (verse 44) points to the importance of the utterance. Cf. John vii. 28, 37; xi. 43.

the previous evening. It is more likely that He sought shelter with His disciples by the olive-sprinkled slope of the hill,[1] not far from the spot where the roads meet which lead to the little village. He was not unaccustomed to nights in the open air, and He and the Apostles, wrapped in their outer garments, could sleep soundly and peacefully on the green grass under the sheltering trees. The shadow of the traitor fell on Him and on that little band. Did *he* too sleep as calmly as the rest? Perhaps: for "remorse may disturb the slumbers of a man who is dabbling with his first experiences of wrong; and when the pleasure has been tasted and is gone, and nothing is left of the crime but the ruin which it has wrought, then too the Furies take their seats upon the midnight pillow. *But the meridian of evil is, for the most part, left unvexed; and when a man has chosen his road, he is left alone to follow it to the end.*"[2]

[1] The ηὐλίσθη ἐκεῖ of Matt. xxi. 17 does not *necessarily* imply that He bivouacked in the open air. It is, however, very probable that He did so; for (1) such is the proper meaning of the word (comp. Judg. xix. 15, 20). (2) St. Luke says, ηὐλίζετο εἰς τὸ ὄρος τὸ καλούμενον Ἐλαιῶν (xxi. 37). (3) It was His custom to resort for the night to Gethsemane, where, so far as we are aware, there was no house. (4) The retiring to Bethany would hardly answer to the ἐκρύβη ἀπ' αὐτῶν of John xii. 36.

[2] Froude, *Hist. of Engl.* viii. 30.

CHAPTER L.

MONDAY IN PASSION WEEK—A DAY OF PARABLES.

"Apples of gold in PICTURES of silver."—PROV. xxv. 11.

RISING from His bivouac in the neighbourhood of Bethany while it was still early, Jesus returned at once to the city and the Temple; and on His way He felt hungry. Monday and Thursday were kept by the scrupulous religionists of the day as voluntary fasts, and to this the Pharisee alludes when he says in the Parable, "I fast twice in the week." But this fasting was a mere "work of supererogation," neither commanded nor sanctioned by the Law or the Prophets, and it was alien alike to the habits and precepts of One who came, not by external asceticisms, but with absolute self-surrender, to ennoble by Divine sinlessness the common life of men. It may be that in His compassionate eagerness to teach His people, He had neglected the common wants of life; it may be that there were no means of procuring food in the fields where He had spent the night; it may be again that the hour of prayer and morning sacrifice had not yet come, before which the Jews did not usually take a meal. But, whatever may have been the cause, Jesus hungered, so as to be driven to look for wayside fruit to sustain and refresh Him for the day's work. A few dates or figs, a piece of black bread, a draught of water, are sufficient at any time for an Oriental's simple meal.

There are trees in abundance even now throughout this region, but not the numerous palms, and figs, and walnut-trees which made the vicinity of Jerusalem like one umbrageous park, before they were cut down by Titus, in the operations of the siege. Fig-trees especially were planted by the roadside, because the dust was thought to facilitate their growth,[1] and their refreshing fruit was common property. At a distance in front of Him Jesus caught sight of a solitary fig-tree,[2] and although the ordinary season at which figs ripened had not yet arrived, yet, as it was clad with verdure, and as the fruit of a fig sets before the leaves unfold, this tree looked more than usually promising. Its rich large leaves seemed to show that it was fruitful, and their unusually early growth that it was not only fruitful but precociously vigorous. There was every chance, therefore, of finding upon it either the late violet-coloured *kermouses*, or autumn figs, that often remained hanging on the trees all through the winter, and even until the new spring leaves had come;[3] or the delicious *bakkooroth*, the first ripe on the fig-tree, of which Orientals are par-

[1] Plin. *Hist. Nat.* xv. 21, quoted by Meyer. On the right to pluck fruit, see Deut. xxiii. 24.

[2] *συκῆν μίαν* (Matt. xxi. 19), "a single fig-tree." Compare, however *μία παιδίσκη* (xxvi. 69). The *εἰ ἄρα τὶ εὑρήσει ἐν αὐτῇ* (Mark xi. 13) implies a shade of surprise at the exceptional forwardness of the tree.

[3] Plin. *H. N.* xvi. 27, "Seri fructus per hiemem in arbore manent, et aestate *inter novas frondes et folia* maturescunt" (comp. Colum. *De Arbor*, 21). Ebrard says that it is doubtful whether this applied to Palestine (*Gosp. Hist.*, p. 376, E. Tr.); but it certainly did, as is shown by the testimony of travellers and of Jewish writers. The green or unripe fig (פג, *pagh*) is only mentioned in Cant. ii. 13.

ticularly fond.[1] The difficulty raised about St. Mark's expression, that "the time of figs was not yet,"[2] is wholly needless. On the plains of Gennesareth Jesus must have been accustomed—if we may trust Josephus —to see the figs hanging ripe on the trees every month in the year excepting January and February;[3] and there is to this day, in Palestine, a kind of white or early fig which ripens in spring, and much before the ordinary or black fig.[4] On many grounds, therefore, Jesus might well have expected to find a few figs to satisfy the cravings of hunger on this fair-promising leafy tree, although the *ordinary* fig-season had not yet arrived.

But when He came up to it, He was disappointed. The sap was circulating; the leaves made a fair show; but of fruit there was none. Fit emblem of a hypocrite, whose external semblance is a delusion and sham—fit emblem of the nation in whom the ostentatious profession of religion brought forth no "fruit of good living" —the tree was barren. And it was *hopelessly* barren; for had it been fruitful the previous year, there would still have been some of the *kermouses* hidden under those broad leaves; and had it been fruitful *this* year, the *bakkooroth* would have set into green and delicious fragrance before the leaves appeared; but on this fruitless tree there was neither any promise for the future, nor any gleanings from the past.

[1] בִּכּוּרוֹת (Hos. ix. 10; Isa. xxviii. 4; Nah. iii. 12; Jer. xxiv. 2, "Very good figs, even like the figs that are first ripe").

[2] There is no need whatever to render this, "it was no favourable weather for figs," "not a good fig-year."

B. J. iii. 10, § 8.

Dr. Thomson, author of *The Land and the Book*, tells us that he has eaten these figs as early as April or May.

And therefore, since it was but deceptive and useless, a barren cumberer of the ground, He made it the eternal warning against a life of hypocrisy continued until it is too late, and, in the hearing of His disciples, uttered upon it the solemn fiat, "Never fruit grow upon thee more!" Even at the word, such infructuous life as it possessed was arrested, and it began to wither away.

The criticisms upon this miracle have been singularly idle and singularly irreverent, because they have been based for the most part on ignorance or on prejudice, By those who reject the divinity of Jesus, it has been called a penal miracle, a miracle of vengeance, a miracle of unworthy anger, a childish exhibition of impatience under disappointment, an uncultured indignation against innocent Nature. No one, I suppose, who believes that the story represents a real and miraculous fact, will daringly arraign the motives of Him who performed it; but many argue that this is an untrue and mistaken story, because it narrates what they regard as an unworthy display of anger at a slight disappointment, and as a miracle of destruction which violated the rights of the supposed owner of the tree, or of the multitude. But, as to the first objection, surely it is amply enough to say that every page of the New Testament shows the *impossibility* of imagining that the Apostles and Evangelists had so poor and false a conception of Jesus as to believe that He avenged His passing displeasure on an irresponsible object. Would He who, at the Tempter's bidding, refused to satisfy His wants by turning the stones of the wilderness into bread, be represented as having "flown into a rage"—no other expression is possible—with an unconscious tree? An absurdity so irreverent might have been found in the

Apocryphal Gospels; but had the Evangelists been capable of perpetuating it, then, most unquestionably, they could have had neither the capacity nor the desire to paint that Divine and Eternal portrait of the Lord Jesus, which their knowledge of the truth, and the aid of God's Holy Spirit, enabled them to present to the world for ever, as its most priceless possession. And as for the withering of the tree, has the householder of the parable been ever severely censured because he said of his barren fig-tree, "Cut it down, why cumbereth it the ground?" Has St. John the Baptist been ever blamed for violence and destructiveness because he cried, "And now also the axe is laid unto the root of the tree: every tree, therefore, which bringeth not forth good fruit, is hewn down and cast into the fire?" Or has the ancient Prophet been charged with misrepresenting the character of God, when he says, "*I, the Lord, have dried up the green tree,*"[1] as well as "made the dry tree to flourish?" When the hail beats down the tendrils of the vineyard—when the lightning scathes the olive, or "splits the unwedgeable and gnarlëd oak"—do any but the utterly ignorant and brutal begin at once to blaspheme against God? Is it a crime under *any* circumstances to destroy a *useless* tree? if not, is it *more* a crime to do so by miracle? Why, then, is the Saviour of the world—to whom Lebanon would be too little for a burnt-offering—to be blamed by petulant critics because He hastened the withering of one barren tree, and founded, on the destruction of its uselessness, three eternal lessons—a symbol of the destruction of impenitence, a warning of the peril of hypocrisy, an illustration of the power of faith?[2]

[1] Ezek. xvii. 24.

[2] The many-sided symbolism of the act would have been much more

They went on their way, and, as usual, entered the Temple; and scarcely had they entered it, when they were met by another indication of the intense incessant spirit of opposition which actuated the rulers of Jerusalem.[1] A formidable deputation approached them, imposing alike in its numbers and its stateliness.[2] The chief priests—heads of the twenty-four courses—the learned scribes, the leading rabbis, representatives of all the constituent classes of the Sanhedrin were there, to overawe Him—whom they despised as the poor ignorant Prophet of despicable Nazareth—with all that was venerable in age, eminent in wisdom, or imposing in authority in the great Council of the nation. The people whom He was engaged in teaching made reverent way for them, lest they should pollute those floating robes and ample fringes with a touch; and when they had arranged

vividly apparent to those more familiar than ourselves with the ancient prophets (see Hos. ix. 10; Joel i. 7; Micah vii. 1). "Even here," says Professor Westcott, "in the moment of sorrowful disappointment, as He turned to His disciples, the word of judgment became a word of promise. 'Have faith in God, and whatsoever things ye desire when ye pray, believe that ye *received* them (ἐλάβετε)'—received them already as the inspiration of the wish—'and ye shall have them'" (*Charact. of the Gosp. Miracles*, p. 25). I have dwelt at some length on this miracle, because to some able and honest thinkers it presents a real difficulty. Those who do not see in it the lessons which I have indicated (of which the first two are only *implied*, not formulated, in the Gospels), regard it as a literal construction of an illustrative metaphor—a *parable* of the power of faith (cf. Luke xxiii. 31; Rev. vi. 13; and the Koran, *Sura* 95) which has got mythically developed into a miracle. Better this, than that it should lead them to unworthy views of "Him whom the Father hath sent;" but if the above views be right, the difficulty does not seem to me by any means insuperable.

[1] It will be observed that I am following in the main the order of the eye-witness, St. Matthew, who, however, pauses to finish the story of the fig-tree, the sequel of which belongs to the next day. It is, however, clear the παραχρῆμα of St. Matthew is only used *relatively*.

[2] Mark xi. 27, περιπατοῦντος αὐτοῦ; Luke xx. 1, ἐπέστησαν (cf. Acts iv. 1; vi. 12; xxiii. 27). I have already (p. 142) noticed St. Luke's use of this word to imply something sudden or hostile.

themselves around Jesus, they sternly and abruptly asked Him, "By what authority doest thou these things, and who gave thee this authority?" They demanded of Him His warrant for thus publicly assuming the functions of Rabbi and Prophet, for riding into Jerusalem amid the hosannas of attendant crowds, for purging the Temple of the traffickers, at whose presence they connived?[1]

The answer surprised and confounded them. With that infinite presence of mind, of which the world's history furnishes no parallel, and which remained calm under the worst assaults, Jesus told them that the answer to their question depended on the answer which they were prepared to give to *His* question. "The baptism of John, was it from heaven, or of men?" A sudden pause followed. "Answer me," said Jesus, interrupting their whispered colloquy. And surely they, who had sent a commission to inquire publicly into the claims of John, were in a position to answer. But no answer came. They knew full well the import of the question. They could not for a moment put it aside as irrelevant. John had openly and emphatically testified to Jesus, had acknowledged Him, before their own deputies, not only as *a* Prophet, but as a Prophet far greater than himself—nay, more, as *the* Prophet, the Messiah. Would they recognise that authority, or would they not? Clearly Jesus had a right to demand their reply to *that* question before He could reply to theirs. But they *could* not, or rather they *would* not answer that question. It reduced them in fact

[1] Mark xi. 27—33; Matt. xxi. 23—27; Luke xx. 1—8. The Sanhedrin had sent a similar deputation to John the Baptist, but in a less hostile spirit (*v. supra*, Vol. I., p. 113).

to a complete dilemma. They *would* not say "*from heaven*," because they had in heart rejected it; they dared not say "*of men*," because the belief in John (as we see even in Josephus) was so vehement and so unanimous that openly to reject him would have been to endanger their personal safety.[1] They were reduced, therefore—they, the masters of Israel—to the ignominious necessity of saying, "We cannot tell."

There is an admirable Hebrew proverb which says, "Teach thy tongue to say, 'I do not know.'"[2] But to say "We do not know," in this instance, was a thing utterly alien to their habits, disgraceful to their discernment, a death-blow to their pretensions. It was ignorance in a sphere wherein ignorance was for them inexcusable. They, the appointed explainers of the Law—they, the accepted teachers of the people—they, the acknowledged monopolisers of Scriptural learning and oral tradition—and yet to be compelled, against their real convictions, to say, and that before the multitude, that they *could not tell* whether a man of immense and sacred influence—a man who acknowledged the Scriptures which they explained, and carried into practice the customs which they reverenced—was a divinely inspired messenger or a deluding impostor! Were the lines of demarcation, then, between the inspired Prophet (*nabî*) and the wicked seducer (*mesîth*) so dubious and indistinct? It was indeed a fearful humiliation, and one which they

[1] Jos. *Antt.* xviii. 5, § 2; Luke xx. 6. The πεπεισμένος shows the permanence of the conviction; the κατα ιθάσει (which is used here only) the violent tumult which would have been caused by a denial of John's position as a prophet. Wetstein quotes from Donat. ad Ter. *Eun.* v. 5, 11, a most apposite parallel, where Parmenio, unable to deny, and unwilling to admit, protects himself by a "*nescio.*"

[2] לַמֵּד לְשׁוֹנְךָ לֵאמֹר אֵינֶנִּי יוֹדֵעַ.

never either forgot or forgave! And yet how just was the retribution which they had thus brought on their own heads. The curses which they had intended for another had recoiled upon themselves; the pompous question which was to be an engine wherewith another should be crushed, had sprung back with sudden rebound, to their own confusion and shame.

Jesus did not press upon their discomfiture, though He well knew—as the form of his answer showed—that their "*do not know*," was a "*do not choose to say.*" Since, however, their failure to answer clearly absolved Him from any necessity to tell them further of an authority about which, by their own confession, they were totally incompetent to decide, He ended the scene by simply saying, "Neither tell I you by what authority I do these things."

So they retired a little into the background. He continued the instruction of the people which they had interrupted, and began once more to speak to them in parables, which both the multitude and the members of the Sanhedrin who were present could hardly fail to understand. And He expressly called their attention to what He was about to say. "*What think ye?*" He asked, for now it is their turn to submit to be questioned; and then, telling them of the two sons, of whom the one first flatly refused his father's bidding, but afterwards repented and did it, the other blandly promised an obedience which he never performed, He asked, "Which of these two did his father's will?" They could but answer, "the first;" and He then pointed out to them the plain and solemn meaning of their own answer. It was, that the very publicans and harlots, despite the apparent open shamelessness of their disobedience, were yet showing *them*—

them, the scrupulous and highly reputed legalists of the holy nation—the way into the kingdom of heaven. Yes, these sinners, whom they despised and hated, were streaming before them through the door which was not yet shut. For John had come to these Jews on their own principles and in their own practices,[1] and they had pretended to receive him, but had not; but the publicans and the harlots had repented at his bidding. For all their broad fringes and conspicuous phylacteries, they—the priests, the separatists, the Rabbis of these people—were *worse* in the sight of God than sinners whom they would have scorned to touch with one of their fingers.

Then He bade them "hear another parable," the parable of the rebellious husbandmen in the vineyard, whose fruits they would not yield. That vineyard of the Lord of Hosts was the house of Israel, and the men of Judah were his pleasant plants;[2] and they, the leaders and teachers, were those to whom the Lord of the vineyard would naturally look for the rendering of the produce. But in spite of all that He had done for His vineyard, there were no grapes, or only wild grapes. "He looked for judgment, but behold oppression; for righteousness, but behold a cry." And since they *could* not render any produce, and *dared* not own the barren fruitlessness for which they, the husbandmen, were responsible, they insulted, and beat, and wounded, and slew messenger after messenger whom the Lord of the vineyard sent to them. Last of all, He sent His Son, and that Son—

[1] Matt. xxi. 28—32, *ἐν ὁδῷ δικαιοσύνης*, minute obedience to the Law, the דֶּרֶךְ צְדָקָה of Prov. xvi. 31, &c. (Stier, iii. 113.)

[2] Matt. xxi. 33—46; Mark xii. 1—12; Luke xx. 9—19; Isa. v. 1—7; Ps. lxxx.

though they recognised Him, and could not *but* recognise Him—they beat, and flung forth, and slew. When the Lord of the vineyard came, what would He do to them? Either the people, out of honest conviction, or the listening Pharisees, to show their apparent contempt for what they could not fail to see was the point of the parable, answered that He would wretchedly destroy those wretches, and let out the vineyard to worthier and more faithful husbandmen. A second time they had been compelled to an admission, which fatally, out of their own mouths, condemned themselves; they had confessed with their own lips that it would be in accordance with God's justice to deprive them of their exclusive rights, and to give them to the Gentiles.

And to show them that their own Scriptures had prophesied of this their conduct, He asked them whether they had never read (in the 118th Psalm[1]) of the stone which the builders rejected, which nevertheless, by the marvellous purpose of God, became the headstone of the corner? How could they remain *builders* any longer, when the whole design of their workmanship was thus deliberately overruled and set aside? Did not their old Messianic prophecy clearly imply that God would call *other* builders to the work of His Temple? Woe to them who even stumbled—as they were doing—at that rejected stone; but even yet there was time for them to avoid the more crushing annihilation of those on whom

[1] Comp. Isa. xxviii. 16; Dan. ii. 44; Acts iv. 11; Eph. ii. 20; 1 Pet. ii. 6, 7. Leaders of the people are called *pinnôth* in Judg. xx. 2, &c. Stier points out that this was the Psalm from which the Hosanna of the multitude was taken (iii. 125). The "head of the corner" (ראשׁ or אֶבֶן פִּנָּה, κεφαλὴ γωνίας or λίθος ἀκρογωνιαῖος) is the chief or foundation stone, sometimes placed at the angle of a building, and so binding two walls together. The αὕτη of Matt. xxi. 42 (Ps. cxviii. 23, LXX.) means "this doing," and is a Hebraism for τοῦτο (זאת) as in 1 Sam. iv. 7, LXX.

that stone should fall. To reject Him in His humanity and humiliation involved pain and loss; but to be found still rejecting Him when He should come again in His glory, would not this be "utter destruction from the presence of the Lord?" To sit on the seat of judgment and condemn Him—*this* should be ruin to them and their nation; but to be condemned by Him, would not this be to be "ground to powder?"[1]

They saw now, more clearly than ever, the whole bent and drift of these parables, and longed for the hour of vengeance! But, as yet, fear restrained them; for, to the multitude, Christ was still a prophet.

One more warning utterance He spoke on this Day of Parables—the Parable of the Marriage of the King's Son. In its basis and framework it closely resembled the Parable of the Great Supper uttered, during His last journey, at a Pharisee's house; but in many of its details, and in its entire conclusion, it was different. Here the ungrateful subjects who receive the invitation, not only make light of it, and pursue undisturbed their worldly avocations, but some of them actually insult and murder the messenger who had invited them, and—a point at which the history merges into prophecy—are destroyed and their city burned. And the rest of the story points to yet further scenes, pregnant with still deeper meanings.[2] Others are invited; the wedding-feast is furnished with guests both bad and good; the king comes in, and notices one who had thrust himself into the company in his own rags, without providing or

[1] Dan. ii. 34—44.

[2] The servants are ordered to go to the διεξόδοι of the roads to search for fresh guests, but we are only told that they went into the ὁδοὶ (Matt. xxii. 9, 10); this delicate "reference to the imperfect work of human agents" is lost in our version. (Lightfoot, *Revision*, p. 68.)

accepting the wedding garment, which the commonest courtesy required.[1]

This rude, intruding, presumptuous guest is cast forth by attendant angels into outer darkness, where shall be weeping and gnashing of teeth; and then follows, for the last time, the warning urged in varying similitudes, with a frequency commensurate to its importance, that "many are called, but few are chosen."[2]

Teachings so obvious in their import filled the minds of the leading Priests and Pharisees with a more and more bitter rage. He had begun the day by refusing to answer their dictatorial question, and by more than justifying that refusal. His counter-question had not only shown His calm superiority to the influence which they so haughtily exercised over the people, but had reduced them to the ignominious silence of an hypocrisy, which was forced to shield itself under the excuse of incompetence. Then followed His parables. In the first of these He had convicted them of false professions, unaccompanied by action; in the second, He had depicted the trust and responsibility of their office, and had indicated a terrible retribution for its cruel and profligate abuse; in the third, He had indicated alike the punishment which would ensue upon a violent rejection of His invitations, and the impossibility of deceiving the eye of His Heavenly Father by a mere nominal and pretended acceptance. Lying lip-service, faithless rebellion, blind presumption, such were the sins which He had striven to bring home to their consciences. And this

[1] Zeph. i. 8.

[2] See Matt. vii. 13, 14; xix. 30; xx. 16. Those who cast forth the intruder are διάκονοι, "ministers," here representing angels; not the δοῦλοι. "Slaves" are human messengers of the earlier part of the parable, though rendered in our version by the same word.

was but a superficial outline of all the heart-searching power with which His words had been to them like a sword of the Spirit, piercing even to the dividing of the joints and marrow. But to bad men nothing is so maddening as the exhibition of their own self-deception. So great was the hardly-concealed fury of the Jewish hierarchy, that they would gladly have seized Him that very hour. Fear restrained them, and He was suffered to retire unmolested to His quiet resting-place. But, either that night or early on the following morning, His enemies held another council—at this time they seem to have held them almost daily—to see if they could not make one more combined, systematic, overwhelming effort "to entangle Him in His talk," to convict Him of ignorance or of error, to shake His credit with the multitude, or embroil Him in dangerous relations towards the civil authority. We shall see in the following chapter the result of their machinations.

CHAPTER LI.

THE DAY OF TEMPTATIONS—THE LAST AND GREATEST DAY OF THE PUBLIC MINISTRY OF JESUS.

And the door was shut."—MATT. xxv. 10.

ON the following morning Jesus rose with His disciples to enter for the last time the Temple Courts. On their way they passed the solitary fig-tree, no longer gay with its false leafy garniture, but shrivelled, from the root upwards, in every bough. The quick eye of Peter was the first to notice it, and he exclaimed, "Master, behold the fig-tree which thou cursedst is withered away." The disciples stopped to look at it, and to express their astonishment at the rapidity with which the denunciation had been fulfilled. What struck them most was the *power* of Jesus; the deeper meanings of His symbolic act they seem for the time to have missed; and, leaving these lessons to dawn upon them gradually, Jesus addressed the mood of their minds at the moment, and told them that if they would but have faith in God—faith which should enable them to offer up their prayers with perfect and unwavering confidence—they should not only be able to perform such a wonder as that done to the fig-tree, but even "if they bade this mountain"—and as He spoke He may have pointed either to Olivet or to Moriah—"to be removed, and cast into the sea, it should obey them." But, since in this one instance the power had been put forth to destroy, He added a very important warning. They were not to suppose that this emblematic act gave them any licence to wield the sacred powers which faith and prayer would bestow on them, for purposes of anger or vengeance; nay, *no* power was possible to the heart that knew not how to forgive, and the *unforgiving* heart could never be forgiven. The sword, and the famine, and the pestilence were to be no instruments for *them* to wield, nor were they even to dream of evoking against their enemies the fire of heaven or the "icy wind of death."[1] The secret of successful prayer was faith; the road to faith in God lay through pardon of transgression; pardon was possible to them alone who were ready to pardon others.

He was scarcely seated in the Temple when the result of the machinations of His enemies on the previous evening showed itself in a new kind of strategy, involving one of the most perilous and deeply laid of all the schemes to entrap and ruin Him. The deadly nature of the plot appeared in the fact that, to carry it out, the Pharisees were united in ill-omened conjunction with the Herodians; so that two parties, usually ranked against each other in strong opposition, were now reconciled in a conspiracy for the ruin of their common enemy.[2] Devotees and sycophants—hierarchical scrupu-

[1] Some suppose that a breath of the simoom had been the agent in withering the fig-tree.

[2] Matt. xxii. 15—22; Mark xii. 13—17; Luke xx. 19—26. "Not the first or last instance in history, in which priests have used politicians, even otherwise opposed to them, to crush a reformer whose zeal might be inimical to both" (Neander, p. 397, Bohn). Previously we only find

iosity and political indifferentism—the school of theocratic zeal and the school of crafty expediency—were thus united to dismay and perplex Him. The Herodians occur but seldom in the Gospel narrative. Their very designation—a Latinised adjective[1] applied to the Greek-speaking courtiers of an Edomite prince who, by Roman intervention, had become a Judæan king—showed at once their hybrid origin. Their existence had mainly a *political* significance, and they stood outside the current of religious life, except so far as their Hellenising tendencies and worldly interests led them to show an ostentatious disregard for the Mosaic law.[2] They were, in fact, mere provincial courtiers; men who basked in the sunshine of a petty tyranny which, for their own personal ends, they were anxious to uphold. To strengthen the family of Herod by keeping it on good terms with Roman imperialism, and to effect this good understanding by repressing every distinctively Jewish aspiration —this was their highest aim. And in order to do this

the Herodians in Mark iii. 6. They seem to be *political* descendants of the old *Antiochians* (2 Macc. iv. 9). (See Salvador, *Jésus Christ*, i. 162.) *Actually* they were perhaps the *Boethusîm* and their adherents, who had been allied to Herod the Great by marriage as well as by worldly interests. Herod the Great, when he fell in love with Mariamne, daughter of Simon, son of a certain Boethus of Alexandria, had made Simon High Priest by way of ennobling him. These Boethusîm had held the high-priesthood for thirty-five years, and shared its influence with the family of Annas. In point of fact, the priestly party of this epoch seem all to have been more or less Sadducees, and more or less Herodians. They had lost all hold on, and all care for, the people; and, though less openly shameless, were the lineal representatives of those bad pontiffs who, since the days of Jason and Menelaus, had tried to introduce "Greek fashions and heathenish manners" (2 Macc. iv. 13, 14).

[1] But *v. supr.*, Vol. 1., p. 442.

[2] Their attempt to represent Herod the Great as the Messiah (!) (Tert. *Praescr.* 45, "qui Christum Herodem esse dixerunt") was a thing of the past. The *genuine* Sanhedrin, urging the command of Deut. xvii. 15, had unanimously appealed against Herod.

they Græcised their Semitic names, adopted ethnic habits, frequented amphitheatres, familiarly accepted the symbols of heathen supremacy, even went so far as to obliterate, by such artificial means as they could, the distinctive and covenant symbol of Hebrew nationality. That the Pharisees should tolerate even the most temporary partnership with such men as these, whose very existence was a violent outrage on their most cherished prejudices, enables us to gauge more accurately the extreme virulence of hatred with which Jesus had inspired them. And that hatred was destined to become deadlier still. It was already at red-heat; the words and deeds of this day were to raise it to its whitest intensity of wrath.

The Herodians might come before Jesus without raising a suspicion of sinister motives; but the Pharisees, astutely anxious to put Him off His guard, did not come to Him in person. They sent some of their younger scholars, who (already adepts in hypocrisy) were to approach Him as though in all the guileless simplicity of an inquiring spirit.[1] They evidently designed to raise the impression that a dispute had occurred between them and the Herodians, and that they desired to settle it by referring the decision of the question at issue to the final and higher authority of the Great Prophet. They came to Him circumspectly, deferentially, courteously. "Rabbi," they said to Him with flattering earnestness, "we know that thou art true, and teachest the way of God in truth, neither carest thou for any man; for thou regardest not the person of men." It was as though they would entreat

[1] St. Luke (xx. 20) calls them ἐγκάθετοι, "*liers in ambush.*" Comp. Job xxxi. 9.

Him, without fear or favour, confidentially to give them His private opinion; and as though they really wanted His opinion for their own guidance in a moral question of practical importance, and were quite sure that He alone could resolve their distressing uncertainty. But why all this sly undulatory approach and serpentine ensalivation? The forked tongue and the envenomed fang appeared in a moment. "Tell us, *therefore*"—since you are so wise, so true, so courageous—"tell us, therefore, is it lawful to give tribute to Cæsar, or not?" This capitation tax,[1] which *we* all so much detest, but the legality of which these Herodians support, ought we, or ought we not, to pay it? Which of us is in the right?—we who loathe and resent, or the Herodians who delight in it?[2]

He *must*, they thought, answer "Yes" or "No;" there is no possible escape from a plain question so cautiously, sincerely, and respectfully put. Perhaps He will answer, "*Yes, it is lawful.*" If so, all apprehension of Him on the part of the Herodians will be removed, for then He will not be likely to endanger them or their views. For although there is something which looks dangerous in this common enthusiasm for Him, yet if one, whom they take to be the Messiah, should openly adhere to a heathen tyranny, and sanction its most galling imposition, such a decision will at once explode and evaporate any regard which the people may feel for Him. If, on the other hand, as is all but certain, He should adopt the views of His countryman Judas the Gaulonite, and answer, "*No, it is not lawful,*" then, in that case too,

[1] *ἐπικεφάλαιον* (Mark xii. 15, Cod. Bezae); *κῆνσον* (Matt. xxii. 17); *φόρον* (Luke xx. 22). Properly speaking, the *κῆνσος* was a poll-tax, the *φόρος* a payment for state purposes.

[2] Matt. xxii. 15—22; Luke xx. 19—26; Mark xii. 13—17.

we are equally rid of Him; for then He is in open rebellion against the Roman power, and these new Herodian friends of ours can at once hand Him over to the jurisdiction of the Procurator. Pontius Pilatus will deal very roughly with His pretensions, and will, if need be, without the slightest hesitation, mingle His blood, as he has done the blood of other Galilæans, with the blood of the sacrifices.

They must have awaited the answer with breathless interest; but even if they succeeded in concealing the hate which gleamed in their eyes, Jesus at once saw the sting and heard the hiss of the Pharisaic serpent. They had fawned on Him with their "Rabbi," and "true," and "impartial," and "fearless;" He "blights them with the flash" of one indignant word, "*Hypocrites!*" That word must have undeceived their hopes, and crumbled their craftiness into dust. "Why tempt ye me, ye hypocrites? Bring me the tribute-money."[1] They would not be likely to carry with them the hated Roman coinage with its heathen symbols, though they might have been at once able to produce from their girdles the Temple shekel. But they would only have to step outside the Court of the Gentiles, and borrow from the money-changers' tables a current Roman coin. While the people stood round in wondering silence they brought Him a denarius, and put it in His hand. On one side were stamped the haughty, beautiful features of the Emperor Tiberius, with all the wicked scorn upon the lip; on the obverse his title of *Pontifex Maximus!*[2] It was probably due to mere accident that the face of the cruel, dissolute tyrant

[1] Mark xii. 15, 16, φέρετε . . . οἱ δὲ ἤνεγκαν.

[2] See Madden, p. 247; Akerman, p. 11, where plates are given. The coin would not bear the full name Tiberius, but Ti. Cæsar.

was on this particular coin, for the Romans, with that half-contemptuous concession to national superstitions which characterised their rule, had allowed the Jews to have struck for their particular use a coinage which recorded the name without bearing the likeness of the reigning emperor.[1] "Whose image and superscription is this?" He asked. They say unto Him, "Cæsar's." *There*, then, was the simplest possible solution of their cunning question. "*Render, therefore, unto Cæsar the things that are Cæsar's.*" That alone might have been enough, for it implied that their national acceptance of this coinage answered their question, and revealed its emptiness. The very word which He used conveyed the lesson. They had asked, "Is it lawful to give" (δοῦναι)? He corrects them, and says, "Render"—"Give back" (ἀπόδοτε). It was not a voluntary gift, but a legal due; not a cheerful offering, but a political necessity. It was perfectly understood among the Jews, and was laid down in the distinctest language by their greatest Rabbis in later days, that to accept the coinage of any king was to acknowledge his supremacy.[2] By accepting the denarius, therefore, as a current coin they were openly declaring that Cæsar was their sovereign, and they—the very best of them—had settled the question that it *was* lawful to pay the poll-tax, by habitually doing so. It was their duty, then, to obey

[1] See Keim, *Gesch. Jes.* iii. 136. The Essenes had a special scruple against coins which seemed to them to violate the second commandment; and Jewish coins only bear the signs of palms, lilies, grapes, censers, &c. (See Ewald, *Gesch. Christ.*, p. 83; and the plates in Munk, Akerman, Madden, &c.)

[2] Maimonides, *Gezelah*, 5. "Ubicumque numisma alicujus regis obtinet, illic incolae regem istum pro domino agnoscunt." In another Rabbinic tract Abigail objects to David's assertion that he is king, because the coins of Saul are current (*Jer. Sanhedr.* 20, 2). See too the curious anecdote in *Avod. Zar.* f. 6, quoted by Keim.

the power which they had deliberately chosen, and the tax, under these circumstances, only represented an equivalent for the advantages which they received.[1] But Jesus could not leave them with this lesson only. He added the far deeper and weightier words—"*and to God the things that are God's.*" To Cæsar you owe the coin which you have admitted as the symbol of his authority, and which bears his image and superscription; to God you owe yourselves.[2] Nothing can more fully reveal the depth of hypocrisy in these Pharisaic questioners than the fact that, in spite of the Divine answer, and in spite of their own secret and cherished convictions, they yet made it a ground of clamorous accusation against Jesus, that He had "*forbidden to give tribute unto Cæsar!*"[3]

Amazed and humiliated at the sudden and total frustration of a plan which seemed irresistible—compelled, in spite of themselves, to admire the guileless wisdom which had in an instant broken loose from the meshes of their sophistical malice—they sullenly retired. There was nothing which even *they* could take hold of in His words. But now, undeterred by this striking failure, the Sadducees thought that they might have better success.[4] There was something more supercilious and offhand in the question which they proposed,

[1] Compare the command, given by Jeremiah (xxvii. 4—8), that the Jews should obey Nebuchadnezzar, to whom their apostacies had made them subject; so too of Tiberius, Caligula, Nero, &c. (Rom. xiii. 1; 1 Pet. ii. 13, 14). The early Christians boasted of their quiet obedience to the powers that be (Justin. *Apol.* i. 17).

[2] "Ut Caesari quidem pecuniam reddas, Deo temetipsum" (Tert. *De Idol.* xv.). (Wordsworth.)

[3] Luke xxiii. 2.

[4] Matt. xxii. 23—33; Mark xii. 18—27; Luke xx. 27—39. Hitzig (*Ueber Joh. Marc.* 209) ingeniously conjectures that the narrative of the Woman taken in Adultery belongs to this place, so that there would have

and they came in a spirit of less burning hatred, but of more sneering scorn. Hitherto these cold Epicureans had, for the most part, despised and ignored the Prophet of Nazareth.[1] Supported as a sect by the adhesion of some of the highest priests, as well as by some of the wealthiest citizens—on better terms than the Pharisees both with the Herodian and the Roman power—they were, up to this time, less terribly in earnest, and proposed to themselves no more important aim than to vex Jesus, by reducing Him into a confession of difficulty. So they came with an old stale piece of casuistry, conceived in the same spirit of self-complacent ignorance as are many of the objections urged by modern Sadducees against the resurrection of the body, but still sufficiently puzzling to furnish them with an argument in favour of their disbeliefs, and with a "difficulty" to throw in the way of their opponents. Addressing Jesus with mock respect, they called His attention to the Mosaic institution of levirate marriages, and then stated, as though it had actually occurred,[2] a coarse imaginary case, in which, on the death without issue of an eldest brother, the widow had been espoused in succession by the six younger brethren, all of whom had died one after another, leaving the widow still sur-

been on this day three separate temptations of Christ—the first *political*, the second *doctrinal*, the third *speculative*. But though Lange, Keim (iii. 138), Ellicott (p. 312), and others approve of this conjecture, it seems to me to have no probability. There is no shadow of external evidence in its favour; the subjective arrangement of the questions is rather specious than real; the events of life do not happen in this kind of order; and the attack of the Pharisees was in this instance *pre-arranged*, whereas the question about the adulteress rose spontaneously and accidentally.

[1] They are scarcely mentioned except in Matt. xvi. 1.

[2] Matt. xxii. 25, "There were *with us* seven brethren." On levirate marriages—so called from the Latin word *levir*, "a brother-in-law"—see Deut. xxv. 5—10.

viving. "Whose wife in the resurrection, when people shall rise," they scoffingly ask, "shall this sevenfold widow be?" The Pharisees, if we may judge from Talmudical writings, had already settled the question in a very obvious way, and quite to their own satisfaction, by saying that she should in the resurrection be the wife of the first husband. And even if Jesus had given such a poor answer as this, it is difficult to see—since the answer had been sanctioned by men most highly esteemed for their wisdom—how the Sadducees could have shaken the force of the reply, or what they would have gained by having put their inane and materialistic question. But Jesus was content with no such answer, though even Hillel and Shammai might have been. Even when the idioms and figures of His language constantly resembled that of previous or contemporary teachers of His nation, His spirit and precepts differ from theirs *toto caelo*.[1] He might, had He been like any other merely human teacher, have treated the question with that contemptuous scorn which it deserved; but the spirit of scorn is alien from the spirit of the dove, and with no contempt He gave to their conceited and eristic dilemma a most profound reply. Though the question came upon Him most unexpectedly, His answer was everlastingly memorable. It opened the gates of Paradise so widely that men might see therein more than they had ever seen before, and it furnished against one of the

[1] It must be steadily borne in mind that a vast majority, if not *all*, the Rabbinic parallels adduced by Wetstein, Schöttgen, Lightfoot, &c., to the words of Christ belong to a far subsequent period. These Rabbis had ample opportunities to light their dim candles at the fount of heavenly radiance, and "vaunt of the splendour as though it were their own." I do not assert that the Rabbis consciously borrowed from Christianity, but before half a century had elapsed after the resurrection, Christian thought was, so to speak, in the whole air.

commonest forms of disbelief an argument that neither Rabbi nor Prophet had conceived. He did not answer these Sadducees with the same concentrated sternness which marked His reply to the Pharisees and Herodians, because their purpose betrayed rather an insipid frivolity than a deeply-seated malice; but He told them that they erred from ignorance, partly of the Scriptures, and partly of the power of God. Had they not been ignorant of the power of God, they would not have imagined that the life of the children of the resurrection was a mere reflex and repetition of the life of the children of this world. In that heaven beyond the grave, though love remains, yet all the mere earthlinesses of human relationship are superseded and transfigured. "They that shall be accounted worthy to *obtain* that world, and the resurrection from the dead, neither marry nor are given in marriage; neither can they die any more; but are equal unto the angels; and are the children of God, being the children of the resurrection." Then as to their ignorance of Scripture,[1] He asked if they had never read in that section of the Book of Exodus which was called "the Bush," how God had described Himself to their great lawgiver as the God of Abraham, and the God of Isaac, and the God of Jacob. How unworthy would such a title have been, had Abraham and Isaac and Jacob then been but grey handfuls of crumbling dust, or dead bones, which should moulder in the Hittite's cave!

[1] Jesus proved to them the doctrine of the resurrection from the *Pentateuch*, not from the clearer declarations of the Prophets, because they attached a higher importance to the Law. It was an *à fortiori* argument, "Even Moses, &c." (Luke xx. 37). There is no evidence for the assertion that they *rejected* all the Old Testament except the Law. "The Bush" means the section so called (Exod. iii.), just as 2 Sam. i. was called "the Bow," Ezek. i. "the Chariot," &c. The Homeric poems are similarly named.

"He is not the God of the dead, but the God of the living: ye therefore do greatly err." Would it have been possible that He should deign to call Himself the God of dust and ashes? How new, how luminous, how profound a principle of Scriptural interpretation was this! The Sadducees had probably supposed that the words simply meant, "I am the God in whom Abraham and Isaac and Jacob trusted;" yet how shallow a designation would that have been, and how little adapted to inspire the faith and courage requisite for an heroic enterprise! "I am the God in whom Abraham and Isaac and Jacob trusted;" and to what, if there were no resurrection, had their trust come? To death, and nothingness, and an everlasting silence, and "a land of darkness, as darkness itself," after a life so full of trials that the last of these patriarchs had described it as a pilgrimage of few and evil years! But God meant more than this. He meant—and so the Son of God interpreted it—that He who helps them who trust Him here, will be their help and stay for ever and for ever, nor shall the future world become for them "a land where all things are forgotten."[1]

[1] R. Simeon Ben Eleazar refuted them by Numb. xv. 31 (*Sanhedrin*, 90, 6). It is, however, observable that the intellectual error, or ἀσοφία, of the Sadducees was not regarded by our Lord with one-tenth part of the indignation which He felt against the moral mistakes of the Pharisees. Doubt has been thrown by some modern writers on the Sadducean rejection of the resurrection, and it has been asserted that the Sadducees have been confounded with the Samaritans; in the above-quoted passage of the Talmud, unless it has been altered (Geiger, *Urschrift*, 129 *n*), the reading is צדוקים, not כותיים (Derenbourg, *Hist. de Palest.* 131). Some writers have said that the Sadducees merely maintained that the resurrection *could not be proved from the Law* (מן התורה); if so, we see why our Lord drew His argument from the Pentateuch. That some Jewish sects accounted the Prophets and the *Kethubhim* of much less importance than the Law is clear from *Midr. Tanchuma* on Deut. xi. 26. (Gfrörer, i. 263.)

CHAPTER LII.

THE GREAT DENUNCIATION.

"Prophesy against the shepherds of Israel, prophesy."—EZEK. xxxiv. 2.

ALL who heard them—even the supercilious Sadducees—must have been solemnised by these high answers. The listening multitude were both astonished and delighted; even some of the Scribes, pleased by the spiritual refutation of a scepticism which their reasonings had been unable to remove, could not refrain from the grateful acknowledgment, "Master, thou hast well said." The more than human wisdom and insight of these replies created, even among His enemies, a momentary diversion in His favour. But once more the insatiable spirit of casuistry and dissension awoke, and this time a scribe,[1] a student of the *Torah*, thought that *he* too would try to fathom the extent of Christ's learning and wisdom. He asked a question which instantly betrayed a false and unspiritual point of view, "Master, which is the great commandment in the Law?"

The Rabbinical schools, in their meddling, carnal,

[1] Matt. xxii. 34—40; Mark xii. 28—34. St. Matthew says, νομικὸς, a word more frequently used by St. Luke than γραμματεύς, as less likely to be misunderstood by his Gentile readers; similarly Josephus calls the scribes ἐξηγηταὶ νόμου (comp. Juv. *Sat.* vi. 544).

superficial spirit of word-weaving and letter-worship, had spun large accumulations of worthless subtlety all over the Mosaic law. Among other things they had wasted their idleness in fantastic attempts to count, and classify, and weigh, and measure all the separate commandments of the ceremonial and moral law. They had come to the sapient conclusion that there were 248 affirmative precepts, being as many as the members in the human body, and 365 negative precepts, being as many as the arteries and veins, or the days of the year: the total being 613, which was also the number of letters in the Decalogue. They arrived at the same result from the fact that the Jews were commanded (Numb. xv. 38) to wear fringes (*tsîtsith*) on the corners of their *tallîth*, bound with a thread of blue; and as each fringe had eight threads and five knots, and the letters of the word *tsîtsith* make 600, the total number of commandments was, as before, 613.[1] Now surely, out of such a large number of precepts and prohibitions, *all* could not be of quite the same value; some were "light" (*kal*), and some were "heavy" (*kobhed*). But which? and what was the greatest commandment of all? According to some Rabbis, the most important of all is that about the *tephillîn* and the *tsîtsith*, the fringes and phylacteries; and "he who diligently observes it is regarded in the same light as if he had kept the whole Law."[2]

[1] Other Rabbis reckoned 620, the numerical value of the word כֶּתֶר (*kether*), "a crown." This style of exegesis was called Gematria (Buxtorf, *Syn. Jud.* c. ix.; Bartolocci, *Lex. Rabb.* s. v.). The sages of the Great Synagogue had, however, reduced these to *eleven*, taken from Ps. xv., and observed that Isaiah reduced them to six (Isa. lv. 6, 7), Micah to three (vi. 8), and Habbakuk to one (ii. 4) (see *Maccoth*, f. 24). Hillel is *said* to have pointed a heathen proselyte to Lev. xix. 18, with the remark that "this is the essence of the Law, the rest is only commentary."

[2] Rashi on Numb. xv. 38—40. When R. Joseph asked R. Joseph Ben

Some thought the omission of ablutions as bad as homicide; some that the precepts of the Mishna were all "heavy;" those of the Law were some heavy and some light. Others considered the *third* to be the greatest commandment. None of them had realised the great principle, that the wilful violation of one commandment is the transgression of all (James ii. 10), because the object of the entire Law is the spirit of *obedience to God.* On the question proposed by the lawyer the Shammaites and Hillelites were in disaccord, and, as usual, both schools were wrong: the Shammaites, in thinking that mere trivial external observances were valuable, apart from the spirit in which they were performed, and the principle which they exemplified; the Hillelites, in thinking that *any* positive command could in itself be unimportant, and in not seeing that great principles are essential to the due performance of even the slightest duties.

Still the best and most enlightened of the Rabbis had already rightly seen that the greatest of all commands, because it was the *source* of all the others, was that which enjoined the love of the One True God. Jesus had already had occasion to express His approval of this judgment,[1] and He now repeats it. Pointing to

Rabba which commandment his father had told him to observe more than any other, he replied, "The law about tassels. Once when, in descending a ladder, my father trod on one of the threads, and tore it, he would not move from the place till it was repaired" (*Shabbath*, 118 *b*). These fringes must be of four threads, one being blue, which are to be passed through an eyelet-hole, doubled to make eight; seven are to be of equal length, the eighth to have enough over to twist into five knots, which represent the five books of the Law! &c. (Buxtorf, *ubi supra*, and Leo Modena, *Rites and Customs of the Jews*, I. ch. xi.). As for the *tephillîn*, the precepts about them were amazingly minute. For the other points see *Tanch.*, f. 73, 2; *Jer. Berach.*, f. 3, 2.

[1] Luke x. 27. *V. supr.*, p. 131.

the Scribes' *tephillîn,*[1] in which one of the four divisions contained the "*Shema*" (Deut. vi. 4)—recited twice a day by every pious Israelite—He told them that *that* was the greatest of all commandments, "Hear, O Israel, the Lord our God is one Lord;" and that the second was like to it, "Thou shalt love thy neighbour as thyself." Love to God issuing in love to man—love to man, our brother, resulting from love to our Father, God—on these two commandments hang all the Law and the Prophets.[2]

The question, in the sense in which the Scribe had put it, was one of the mere μάχαι νομικαὶ, one of those "strivings about the Law,[3] which, as they were handled by the schools, were "unprofitable and vain." But he could not fail to see that Jesus had not treated it in the idle disputatious spirit of jangling logomachy to which he was accustomed, and had not in His answer sanctioned any of the common errors and heresiee of exalting the ceremonial above the moral, or the Tradition over the Torah, or the decisions of Sopherîm above the utterances of Prophets. Still less had He fallen into the fatal error of the Rabbis, by making obedience in one particular atone for transgression in another. The commandments which He had mentioned as the greatest were not special but general—not selected out of many, but inclusive of all. The Scribe had the sense to observe, and the candour to acknowledge, that

[1] The passages inscribed on the parchment slips which were put into the cells of the little leather boxes called *tephillîn* were Exod. xiii. 1—10 11—16; Deut. vi. 4—9; xi. 13—21. The sect of Perushim, or modern Pharisees, to this day πλατύνουσι τὰ φυλακτήρια (Matt. xxiii. 5).

[2] The expression "hangs" is probably proverbial, but some have seen in it a special allusion to the hanging *tsîtsith,* which were meant to remind them of the Law (Numb. xv. 39). (Stier, iii. 184.)

[3] Titus iii. 9.

the answer of Jesus was wise and noble. "Well, Master," he exclaimed, "thou hast said the truth;" and then he showed that he had read the Scriptures to some advantage by summarising some of those grand free utterances of the Prophets which prove that love to God and love to man is better than all whole burnt-offerings and sacrifices.[1] Jesus approved of his sincerity, and said to him in words which involved both gracious encouragement and serious warning, "Thou art not far from the kingdom of heaven." It was, therefore, at once easier for him to enter, and more perilous to turn aside. When he had entered he would see that the very spirit of his question was an erroneous and faulty one, and that "whosoever shall keep the whole law, and yet offend in one point, is guilty of all."[2]

No other attempt was ever made to catch or entangle Jesus by the words of His lips. The Sanhedrin had now experienced, by the defeat of their cunning stratagems, and the humiliation of their vaunted wisdom, that one ray of light from the sunlit hills on which His spirit sat, was enough to dissipate, and to pierce through and through, the fogs of wordy contention and empty repetition in which they lived and moved and had their being. But it was well for them to be convinced how easily, had He desired it, He could have employed against them with overwhelming force the very engines which, with results so futile and so disastrous, they had put in play against Him. He therefore put to them one simple question, based on their own principles of

[1] 1 Sam. xv. 22; Hosea vi. 6; Micah vi. 6—8. Irenæus, *Haer.* i. 17, adds the ἄγραφον δόγμα, "I have long desired to hear such words, and have not yet found the speaker."

[2] James ii. 10.

interpretation, and drawn from a Psalm (the 110th), which they regarded as distinctly Messianic.[1] In that Psalm occurs the expression, "The Lord (*Jehovah*) said unto my Lord (*Adonai*), Sit thou on my right hand." How then could the Messiah be David's son? Could Abraham have called Isaac and Jacob and Joseph, or any of his own descendants near or remote, his *lord?* If not, how came David to do so? There could be but one answer—because that Son would be divine, not human—David's son by human birth, but David's Lord by divine subsistence. But they could not find this simple explanation, nor, indeed, any other; they could not find it, because Jesus was their Messiah, and they had rejected Him. They chose to ignore the fact that He was, in the flesh, the son of David; and when, as their Messiah, He had called Himself the Son of God, they had raised their hands in pious horror, and had taken up stones to stone Him. So here again—since they had rejected the clue of faith which would have led them to the true explanation—their wisdom was utterly at fault, and though they claimed so haughtily to be leaders of the people, yet, even on a topic so ordinary and so important as their Messianic hopes, they were convicted, for the second time on a single day, of being "blind leaders of the blind."

And they loved their blindness; they would not acknowledge their ignorance; they did not repent them of their faults; the bitter venom of their hatred to Him was not driven forth by His forbearance; the dense midnight of their perversity was not dispelled by His

[1] See *Midrash Tehillîn ad* Ps. cx. 1; *Beresh. Rab*, 83, 4, quoted by Wetstein; and the LXX. rendering of ver. 3, ἐκ γαστρὸς πρὸ 'Εωσφόρου. 'γέννητά σε (Keim, iii. 158). See Ecclus. li. 10. The Chaldee Paraphrast has for Adonai, "*Meyimra,*" *i.e.*, "the Word."

wisdom. Their purpose to destroy Him was fixed, obstinate, irreversible; and if one plot failed, they were but driven with more stubborn sullenness into another. And, therefore, since Love had played her part in vain, "Justice leaped upon the stage;" since the Light of the World shone for them with no illumination, the lightning flash should at last warn them of their danger. There could now be no hope of their becoming reconciled to Him; they were but being stereotyped in unrepentant malice against Him. Turning, therefore, to His disciples, but in the audience of all the people,[1] He rolled over their guilty heads, with crash on crash of moral anger, the thunder of His utter condemnation.[2] So far as they represented a legitimate external authority He bade His hearers to respect them,[3] but He warned them *not* to imitate their falsity, their oppression, their ostentation, their love of prominence, their fondness for titles, their insinuating avarice, their self-exalting pride. He bade them beware of the broadened phylacteries and exaggerated tassels—of the long robes that covered the murderous hearts, and the long prayers that diverted attention from the covetous designs.[4] And then,

[1] Some of the Temple courts had room for at least 6,000 people (Jos. *B. J.* ii. 17, § 3), and it is probable that even more were assembled in them at the Passover, the torch-dance at the Feast of Tabernacles, &c.

[2] Matt. xxiii. 1—39. The attempt of Lange to bring these eight woes into allusive contrast with the eight beatitudes seems to me an instance of that misplaced ingenuity which has done much harm to sound exegesis.

[3] In the language spoken by our Lord there was a paronomasia between Moses (*Mosheh*) and *moshab*. This is another of the interesting probable indications as to the language which He ordinarily used (v. *supr.*, Vol. I., p. 90). There is another most marked Hebraism in Matt. xxiv. 22 (where *οὐ πας = οὐδείς*, and *σάρξ = ἄνθρωπος*) and in verse 24 (*δώσουσι*), and xxvi. 18 (*ποιῶ τὸ πάσχα*).

[4] "Ye devour widows' houses." See Jos. *Antt.* xvii. 2, § 4, *οἷς . . . ὑπῆκτο ἡ γυναικωνῖτις.* Most rea ers will recall modern parallels to this fact. As to the proselytism, see *Pirke Abhôth*, iv. 2. Ewald, *Gesch. Christ.*, p. 44,

solemnly and terribly, He uttered His eightfold "*Woe unto you, Scribes and Pharisees, hypocrites,*" scathing them in utterance after utterance with a flame which at once revealed and scorched. Woe unto them, for the ignorant erudition which closed the gates of heaven, and the injurious jealousy which would suffer no others to enter in! Woe unto them for their oppressive hypocrisy and greedy cant! Woe for the proselytising fanaticism which did but produce a more perilous corruption! Woe for the blind hair-splitting folly which so confused the sanctity of oaths as to tempt their followers into gross profanity![1] Woe for the petty paltry sham-scrupulosity which paid tithes of potherbs, and thought

mentions that the word גִּיֵּר, "to proselytise," was coined at this period. As to their immense and pretentious self-assertion, see the numerous quotations and anecdotes from the Talmud in Gfrörer, *Jahrh. d. Heils.* pp. 144—149. One will be sufficient. They represent heaven itself as a Rabbinic school, of which God is the Head Rabbi. On one occasion God differs from all the angels on a question as to a leper being clean or unclean. They refer the decision to R. Ben Nachman, who is accordingly slain by Azrael, and brought to the heavenly Academy. He decides with God, who is much pleased. (*Babha Metzia,* f. 86 *a.*) The reader will be reminded of Pope's criticism on Milton—

"In quibbles angel and archangel join,
And God the Father turns a school divine."

There is a marked analogy between Rabbinism and Scholasticism. One might compare Hillel to Anselm, R. Jehuda Hakkôdesh to Thomas Aquinas, Gamaliel to Abelard, &c.

[1] The miserable quibbles by which, in consequence of such pernicious teaching, the Jews evaded their oaths, became notorious even in the heathen world. (See Martial, *Ep.* xi. 94.) The charges which our Lord uttered are amply supported by Jewish testimonies: *e.g.*, in Midrash Esth. i., f. 101, 4, it is said that there are ten portions of hypocrisy in the world, of which *nine* are at Jerusalem (Schöttgen). Keim quotes some curious parallels from the Psalms of Solomon, the Assumption of Moses, and the Book of Enoch. On the Proselytism of the Jews, see Juv. *Sat.* xiv. 101. It was expressly enjoined in the *Pirke Abhôth,* iv. 2. In tithing anise they made it a question whether it was enough to pay tithes of the flower only, or also of the seed and stalk

nothing of justice, mercy, and faith—which strained out animalculæ from the goblet, and swallowed camels into the heart![1] Woe for the external cleanliness of cup and platter contrasted with the gluttony and drunkenness to which they ministered! Woe to the tombs that simulated the sanctity of temples—to the glistening outward plaster of hypocrisy which did but render more ghastly by contrast the reeking pollutions of the sepulchre within! Woe for the mock repentance which condemned their fathers for the murder of the prophets, and yet reflected the murderous spirit of those fathers—nay, filled up and exceeded the measure of their guilt by a yet deadlier and more dreadful sacrifice! Aye, on that generation would come all the righteous blood shed upon the earth, from the blood of righteous Abel to the blood of Zacharias, whom they slew between the porch and the altar.[2] The purple cloud of retribution had

[1] διϋλίζοντες. Vulg. *excolantes*; cf. Amos vi. 6, πίνοντες διϋλισμένον οἶνον, LXX. They filtered their water through linen to avoid swallowing any unclean insect (Lev. xi. 41—43).

[2] A Zacharias, the son of Baruch or Barachias, one of the most eminent and pious men of his day, was slain thirty-four years *after* this time by the Zealots, on a false accusation, in the midst of the Temple (ἀνὰ μέσον τοῦ ἱεροῦ), and his body was flung from the Temple into the valley beneath (Jos. *B. J.* iv. 5, § 4). It is of course clear that *this* cannot be the Zacharias alluded to. Nor is there any authority for the belief of Origen, that the father of John the Baptist was martyred, or that he too was a son of Barachias. The *prophet* Zechariah was indeed a son of Berechiah (Zech. i. 1), but there is no reason to believe that he was put to death. We must therefore conclude that our Lord referred to Zechariah, *the son of Jehoiada* (which is the reading in the Gospel used by the Nazarenes), who was stoned by order of Joash "in the court of the house of the Lord." That he is referred to is clear, because (i.) this murder, in the order of the Jewish books, stood last in the Old Testament; (ii.) in dying, Zechariah had exclaimed, "*The Lord look upon it and require it;*" (iii.) the Jews themselves had many most remarkable legends about this murder (see Lightfoot on Matt. xxiii. 35; Stanley, *Lectures on the Jewish Church*, p. 402), which made a deep impression on them, and which they specially believed to have kindled God's wrath against them (2 Chron. xxiv. 18). Consequently I believe tha

long been gathering its elements of fury: upon their heads should it burst in flame!

And at that point the voice which had rung with just and noble indignation broke with the tenderest pity—"O Jerusalem, Jerusalem, thou that killest the prophets, and stonest them that are sent unto thee, how often would I have gathered thy children together, even as a hen gathereth her chickens under her wings, and ye would not![1] Behold, your house is left unto you desolate! For I say unto you, Ye shall not see me henceforth till ye shall say, Blessed is He that cometh in the name of the Lord."[2]

"Woe unto you, Scribes and Pharisees, *hypocrites*." Some have ventured to accuse these words of injustice, of bitterness—to attribute them to a burst of undignified disappointment and unreasonable wrath. Yet is sin never to be rebuked? is hypocrisy never to be un-

"son of Berechiah," which is not found (except in D) in Luke xi. 51, is a very early and erroneous gloss which has crept into the text. This is almost certainly the true explanation. In Matthew the words are omitted by א. The other suggestions—that Jehoiada had a second name, or that Zechariah was *grandson* of Jehoiada, and son of an unrecorded Berechiah—do not commend themselves by any probability. If it be asked why Jesus should have mentioned a murder which had taken place so many centuries ago, the answer seems to be that He intended to convey *this* meaning—"Your fathers, from beginning to end of your recorded history [a general expression, as we might say, 'The Jews from Genesis to Revelation'], rejected and slew God's prophets: you, as you share and consummate their guilt, so shall bear the brunt of the long-gathering Nemesis."

[1] This beautiful image also occurs in 2 Esdr. i. 30. This would be the closest parallel between the Apocrypha and any words of Christ, were it not that 2 Esdras i., ii. are interpolations found in the Latin and followed by our English version of the Apocrypha, but not found in the Arabic or Æthiopic. The germ of the image, under another form, is in Deut. xxxii. 11.

[2] *i.e.* At the Second Advent (Zech. xii. 10; Hos. iii. 4, 5). The ποσάκις indicates that the ministry of Jesus in Jerusalem had been much fuller than the Synoptists record.

masked? is moral indignation no necessary part of the noble soul? And does not Jewish literature itself most amply support the charge brought against the Pharisees by Jesus? "Fear not *true* Pharisees, but greatly fear *painted* Pharisees," said Alexander Jannæus to his wife on his deathbed. "The supreme tribunal," says R. Nachaman, "will duly punish hypocrites who wrap their *talliths* around them to appear, which they are not, true Pharisees." Nay, the Talmud itself, with unwonted keenness and severity of sarcasm, has pictured to us the seven classes of Pharisees, out of which *six* are characterised by a mixture of haughtiness and imposture. There is the "Shechemite" Pharisee, who obeys the law from self-interest (cf. Gen. xxxiv. 19); the *Tumbling* Pharisee (*nikfi*), who is so humble that he is always stumbling because he will not lift his feet from the ground; the *Bleeding* Pharisee (*kinai*), who is always hurting himself against walls, because he is so modest as to be unable to walk about with his eyes open lest he should see a woman; the *Mortar* Pharisee (*medorkia*), who covers his eyes as with a mortar, for the same reason; the *Tell-me-another-duty-and-I-will-do-it* Pharisee —several of whom occur in our Lord's ministry; and the *Timid* Pharisee, who is actuated by motives of fear alone. The seventh class only is the class of "Pharisees from love," who obey God because they love Him from the heart.[1]

[1] *Jer. Berachôth*, ix. 7; *Bab. Sota*, f. 22 *a*; *Abhôth de Rabbi Nathan*, xxxvii. (Otho, *Lex. Rab.*; Cohen, *Déicides*, E. Tr., p. 152.) Perhaps the "Shechemite" Pharisee may be "the humpbacked" (*schikmi*), *i.e.*, "qui marchait le dos voûté comme s'il portait sur ses épaules le fardeau entier de la loi" (Renan, *Vie de Jésus*, p. 204, *ed. pop.*). The passages are a littl obscure, and in minor particulars the explanations differ. *Nikfi* is explained by some to mean the "flagellant" Pharisee (Derenbourg, *Hist. Pal.* p. 71). On the enormous pretensions and consummate hypocrisy of the Pharisees

"Behold, your house is left unto you desolate!" And has not that denunciation been fearfully fulfilled?[1] Who does not catch an echo of it in the language of Tacitus—"Expassae repente delubri fores, et audita major humanâ vox *excedere Deos*." Speaking of the murder of the younger Hanan, and other eminent nobles and hierarchs, Josephus says, "I cannot but think that *it was because God had doomed this city to destruction as a polluted city, and was resolved to purge His sanctuary by fire*, that He cut off these their great defenders and well-wishers; while those that a little before had worn the sacred garments and presided over the public worship, and had been esteemed venerable by those that dwelt in the whole habitable earth, were cast out naked, and seen to be the food of dogs and wild beasts."[2] Never was a narrative more full of horrors, frenzies, unspeakable degradations, and overwhelming miseries than is the history of the siege of Jerusalem. Never was any prophecy more closely, more terribly, more overwhelmingly fulfilled than this of Christ. The men going about in the disguise of women with swords concealed under their gay robes; the rival outrages and infamies of John and Simon; the priests struck by darts from the upper court of the Temple, and falling slain by their own sacrifices; "the blood of all sorts of dead carcases—priests, strangers, profane—standing in lakes in the holy courts;" the corpses themselves lying in piles and

as a class, see *supr.*, Vol. I., p. 441, and Excursus IX., "Hypocrisy of the Pharisees."

[1] "One poor Jew . . . stood in humble prayer, with his *tephilla* wrapped round his body and arms, *weeping as he uttered the words spoken by every Jew when he sees the Holy Land*, "WOE IS ME! THY HOLY CITIES ARE TURNED INTO DESERTS." (Frankl, ii. 344.)

[2] *B. J.* iv. 5, § 2 (Whiston). Comp. Mic. iii. 12.

mounds on the very altar slopes; the fires feeding luxuriously on cedar-work overlaid with gold; friend and foe trampled to death on the gleaming mosaics in promiscuous carnage; priests, swollen with hunger, leaping madly into the devouring flames, till at last those flames had done their work, and what had been the Temple of Jerusalem, the beautiful and holy House of God, was a heap of ghastly ruin, where the burning embers were half-slaked in pools of gore.

And did not all the righteous blood shed upon the earth since the days of Abel come upon that generation? Did not many of that generation survive to witness and feel the unutterable horrors which Josephus tells?—to see their fellows crucified in jest, "some one way, and some another," till "room was wanting for the crosses, and crosses for the carcases?"—to experience the "deep silence" and the kind of deadly night which seized upon the city in the intervals of rage?—to see 600,000 dead bodies carried out of the gates?—to see friends fighting madly for grass and nettles, and the refuse of the drains?—to see the bloody zealots "gaping for want, and stumbling and staggering along like mad dogs?"—to hear the horrid tale of the miserable mother who, in the pangs of famine, had devoured her own child?—to be sold for slaves in such multitudes that at last none would buy them?—to see the streets running with blood, and the "fire of burning houses quenched in the blood of their defenders?"—to have their young sons sold in hundreds, or exposed in the amphitheatres to the sword of the gladiator or the fury of the lion, until at last, "since the people were now slain, the Holy House burnt down, and the city in flames, there was nothing farther left for the enemy to do?" In that awful siege it is believed that there perished 1,100,000 men, beside the 97,000 who were carried captive, and most of whom perished subsequently in the arena or the mine; and it was an awful thing to feel, as some of the survivors and eyewitnesses—and they not Christians—*did* feel, that "the city had deserved its overthrow by producing a generation of men who were the causes of its misfortunes;" and that "neither did any other city ever suffer such miseries, nor *did any age ever breed a generation more fruitful in wickedness than this was, since the beginning of the world*."[1]

[1] Every detail in these two paragraphs is taken from Jos. *B. J.* v. 6—vi. 10, *passim*. "A partir de ce moment la faim, la rage, le désespoir, la folie habitèrent Jérusalem. Ce fut une cage de fous furieux, une ville de hurlements et de cannibales, un enfer." (Renan, *L'Antechrist*, 506.)

CHAPTER LIII.

FAREWELL TO THE TEMPLE.

"Ecclesiâ Dei jam per totum orbem uberrime germinante Templum tamquam effoetum et vanum nullique usui bono commodum, arbitrio Dei auferendum fuit"—OROS. vii. 9.

IT must have been clear to all that the Great Denunciation recorded in the last chapter involved a final and hopeless rupture. After language such as this there could be no possibility of reconciliation. It was "too late." The door was shut. When Jesus left the Temple His disciples must have been aware that He was leaving it for ever.

But apparently as He was leaving it—perhaps while He was sitting with sad heart and downcast eyes in the Court of the Women to rest His soul, troubled by the unwonted intensity of moral indignation, and His mind wearied with these incessant assaults—another and less painful incident happened, which enabled Him to leave the actual precincts of the House of His Father with words, not of anger, but of approval. In this Court of the Women were thirteen chests called *shopherôth*, each shaped like a trumpet, broadening downwards from the aperture, and each adorned with various inscriptions. Into these were cast those religious and benevolent contributions which helped to furnish the Temple with its splendid wealth. While Jesus was sitting there the multitude were dropping their gifts, and the wealthier donors were conspicuous among them as they ostentatiously offered their gold and silver. Raising His eyes, perhaps from a reverie of sorrow, Jesus at a glance took in the whole significance of the scene.[1] At that moment a poor widow timidly dropped in her little contribution. The lips of the rich contributors may have curled with scorn at a presentation which was the very lowest legal minimum. She had given two *prutahs* (פרוטות), the very smallest of current coins; for it was not lawful, even for the poorest, to offer only *one*. A *lepton*, or *prutah*, was the eighth part of an *as*, and was worth a little less than half a farthing, so that her whole gift was of the value of less than a farthing; and with the shame of poverty she may well have shrunk from giving so trivial a gift when the rich men around her were lavishing their gold. But Jesus was pleased with the faithfulness and the self-sacrificing spirit of the gift. It was like the "cup of cold water" given for love's sake, which in His kingdom should not go unrewarded. He wished to teach for ever the great lesson that the essence of charity is self-denial; and the self-denial of this widow in her pauper condition was far greater than that of the wealthiest Pharisee who had contributed his gold. "For they all flung in of their abundance, but she of her penury cast in all she had, her whole means of subsistence." "One coin out of a little," says St. Ambrose, "is better than a treasure out of much; for it is not considered how much is given, but how much remains

[1] Luke xxi. 1, ἀναβλέψας. Passages like "He that giveth alms in secret is greater than Moses himself;" "It is as well not to give as to give ostentatiously and openly," are quoted from the Talmud.

behind." "If there be a willing mind," says St. Paul, "it is accepted according to that a man hath, and not according to that he hath not."

And now Jesus left the Temple for the last time; but the feelings of the Apostles still clung with the loving pride of their nationality to that sacred and memorable spot.[1] They stopped to cast upon it one last lingering gaze, and one of them was eager to call His attention to its goodly stones and splendid offerings—those nine gates overlaid with gold and silver, and the one of solid Corinthian brass yet more precious; those graceful and towering porches; those bevelled blocks of marble forty cubits long and ten cubits high, testifying to the toil and munificence of so many generations; those double cloisters and stately pillars; that lavish adornment of sculpture and arabesque; those alternate blocks of red and white marble, recalling the crest and hollow of the sea-waves; those vast clusters of golden grapes, each cluster as large as a man, which twined their splendid luxuriance over the golden doors.[2] They would have Him gaze with them on the rising terraces of courts—the Court of the Gentiles with its monolithic columns and rich mosaic; above this the flight of fourteen steps which led to the Court of the Women; then the flight of fifteen steps which led up to the Court of the Priests; then, once more, the twelve steps which led to the final platform crowned by the actual Holy, and Holy of Holies, which the Rabbis fondly compared for its shape

[1] Matt. xxiv. 1; Mark xiii. 1; Luke xxi. 5, 6.

[2] *Bab. Succa*, fol. 51 *a*. (De Saulcy, *Herode*, p. 239.) The Talmudists, however, confessedly speak sometimes *literally* (לפי הפשט) and sometimes *hyperbolically* (לשון הנאי); and perhaps the accounts of this golden vine, and the veil which it took 300 priests to raise, are *meant* to be taken in the latter sense (see Reland, *Antt. Hebr.*, p. 139).

to a couchant lion, and which, with its marble whiteness and gilded roofs, looked like a glorious mountain whose snowy summit was gilded by the sun.[1] It is as though they thought that the loveliness and splendour of this scene would intercede with Him, touching His heart with mute appeal. But the heart of Jesus was sad. To Him the sole beauty of a Temple was the sincerity of its worshippers, and no gold or marble, no brilliant vermilion or curiously-carven cedar-wood, no delicate sculpturing or votive gems, could change for Him a den of robbers into a House of Prayer. The builders were still busily at work, as they had been for nearly fifty years, but their work, unblessed of God, was destined—like the earthquake-shaken forum of guilty Pompeii—to be destroyed before it was finished. Briefly and almost sternly Jesus answered, as He turned away from the glittering spectacle, "Seest thou these great buildings? there shall not be left one stone upon another which shall not be thrown down." It was the final ἐκχωρῶμεν—the "Let us depart hence" of retiring Deity. Tacitus and Josephus tell us how at the siege of Jerusalem was heard that great utterance of departing gods;[2] but now it was uttered in reality, though no earthquake accompanied it, nor any miracle to show that this was the close of another great epoch in the world's history. It took place quietly, and God "was content to show

[1] This comparison is used by Josephus in that elaborate description of the Temple (*B. J.* v. 5) from which I have taken the above particulars. (Tac. *Hist.* v. 8, "*immensae opulentiae templum.*") The splendid votive offerings of kings continued till the last: *e.g.*, Agrippa hung up in it the golden chain presented to him by Caligula. Descriptions of the external appearance of the Temple and of Jerusalem at this time may be found in F. Delitzsch's pathetic story, *Durch Krankheit zur Genesung. Eine Jerusal. Gesch. d. Herodianer-Zeit.* (Leipz. 1873.)

[2] Jos. *B. J.* vi. 5, § 3; Tac. *Hist.* v. 13.

all things in the slow history of their ripening." Thirty-five years afterwards that Temple sank into the ashes of its destruction; neither Hadrian, nor Julian, nor any other, were able to build upon its site; and now that very site is a matter of uncertainty.[1]

Sadly and silently, with such thoughts in their hearts, the little band turned their backs on the sacred building, which stood there as an epitome of Jewish history from the days of Solomon onwards. They crossed the valley of Kidron, and climbed the steep foot-path that leads over the Mount of Olives to Bethany. At the summit of the hill they paused, and Jesus sat down to rest—perhaps under the green boughs of those two stately cedar-trees which then adorned the summit of the hill. It was a scene well adapted to inspire most solemn thoughts. Deep on the one side beneath Him lay the Holy City, which had long become a harlot, and which now, on this day—the last great day of His public ministry—had shown finally that she knew not the time of her visitation. At His feet were the slopes of Olivet and the Garden of Gethsemane. On the opposite slope rose the city walls, and the broad plateau crowned with the marble colonnades and gilded roofs of the Temple. Turning in the eastward direction He would look across the bare, desolate hills of the wilderness of Judæa to the purpling line of the mountains of Moab, which glow like a chain of jewels in the sunset light. In the deep, scorched hollows of the Ghôr, visible in patches of sullen cobalt, lay the mysterious waters of

[1] Titus himself was amazed at the massive structures of Jerusalem, and saw in his conquest of it the hand of God (Jos. *B. J.* vi. 9, § 1). On the desolation of the Temple, compare 4 Esdr. x. 28. (Gfrörer, *Jahrh. d Heils*, i. 72.)

the Sea of Lot. And thus, as He gazed from the brow of the hill, on either side of Him there were visible tokens of God's anger and man's sin. On the one side gloomed the dull lake, whose ghastly and bituminous waves are a perpetual testimony to God's vengeance upon sensual crime; at His feet was the glorious guilty city which had shed the blood of all the prophets, and was doomed to sink through yet deadlier wickedness to yet more awful retribution. And the setting sun of His earthly life flung deeper and more sombre colourings across the whole scene of His earthly pilgrimage.

It may be that the shadows of His thought gave a strange solemnity to His attitude and features as He sat there silent among the silent and saddened band of His few faithful followers. Not without a touch of awe His nearest and most favoured Apostles—Peter, and James, and John, and Andrew—came near to Him, and as they saw His eye fixed upon the Temple, asked Him privately, "When shall these things be? and what shall be the sign of Thy coming, and of the end of the world?"[1] Their "*when?*" remained for the present unanswered. It was the way of Jesus, when some ignorant or irrelevant or inadmissible question was put to Him, to rebuke it not directly, but by passing it over, and by substituting for its answer some great moral lesson which was connected with it, and could alone make it valuable.[2] Accordingly, this question of the Apostles drew from Him the great Eschatological Dis-

[1] Matt. xxiv., xxv.; Mark xiii. 3—37; Luke xxi. 7—38. In one of the unrecorded sayings of Christ, He answers the question thus: "When the two shall be one, and that which is without as that which is within; and the male with the female neither male nor female" (Clem. Rom. *Ep.* ii. 12; Clem. Alex. *Strom.* iii. 9, 63). (Westcott, *Introd.*, p. 431.)

[2] Comp. Luke xiii. 23, 24.

course, or Discourse of the Last Things, of which the four moral key-notes are "Beware!" and "Watch!" and "Endure!" and "Pray."

Immense difficulties have been found in this discourse, and long treatises have been written to remove them. And, indeed, the metaphorical language in which it is clothed, and the intentional obscurity in which the will of God has involved all those details of the future which would only minister to an idle curiosity or a paralysing dread, must ever make parts of it difficult to understand. But if we compare together the reports of the three Synoptists,[1] and see how they mutually throw light upon each other; if we remember that, in all three, the actual words of Jesus are necessarily condensed, and are only reported in their substance, and in a manner which admits of verbal divergencies; if we bear in mind that they are in all probability a rendering into Greek from the Aramaic vernacular in which they were spoken;[2] if we keep hold of the certainty that the object of Prophecy in all ages has been moral warning infinitely more than even the vaguest chronological indication, since to the voice of Prophecy as to the eye of God all Time is but one eternal Present, "one day as a thousand years, and a thousand years as one day;"[3] if, finally, we accept with quiet reverence, and without any idle theological

[1] Matt. xxiv., xxv.; Mark xiii.; Luke xxi.

[2] Schott, for instance, has conjectured that the εὐθέως of Matt. xxiv. 29 is an unsuccessful representative of the Aramaic פתאם. It may be so, but the difficulty it creates is in great measure removed if, on turning to Luke xxi. 25, we see that the condensation of St. Matthew has omitted a particular which would remove the reference contained in the εὐθέως far into the future.

[3] Ps. xc. 4; 2 Peter iii. 8. St. Augustine wisely says, "Latet ultimus dies, ut observentur omnes dies."

phraseology about the *communicatio idiomatum*, the distinct assertion of the Lord Himself, that to Him, in His human capacity, were not known the day and the hour, which belonged to "the times and the seasons which the Father hath kept in His own power;"—if, I say, we read these chapters with such principles kept steadily in view, then to every earnest and serious reader I feel sure that most of the difficulties will vanish of themselves.

It is evident, from comparing St. Luke with the other Synoptists, that Jesus turned the thoughts of the disciples to two horizons, one near and one far off, as He suffered them to see one brief glimpse of the landscape of the future. The boundary line of either horizon marked the winding up of an *æon*, the συντέλεια αἰῶνος; each was a great τέλος, or ending; of each it was true that the then existing γενέα—first in its literal sense of "generation," then in its wider sense of "race"—should not pass away until all had been fulfilled. And the one was the type of the other; the judgment upon Jerusalem, followed by the establishment of the visible Church on earth, foreshadowed the judgment of the world, and the establishment of Christ's kingdom at His second coming. And if the vague prophetic language and imagery of St. Matthew, and to a less degree that of St. Mark, might lead to the impression that these two events were continuous, or at least nearly conterminous with each other, on the other hand we see clearly from St. Luke that our Lord *expressly warned* the inquiring Apostles that, though many of the signs which He predicted would be followed by the immediate close of one great epoch in the world's history, on the other hand the great consummation, the final Palingenesia, *would not follow at once*, nor were they to be alarmed by the troubles and commotions of the world into any instant or feverish expectancy.[1] In fact, when once we have grasped the principle that Jesus was speaking partly and primarily of the fall of the Jewish polity and dispensation, partly and secondarily of the End of the World—but that, since He spoke of them with that varying interchange of thought and speech which was natural for one whose whole being moved in the sphere of Eternity and not of Time, the Evangelists have not clearly distinguished between the passages in which He is referring more prominently to the one than to the other—we shall then avoid being misled by any superficial and erroneous impressions, and shall bear in mind that before the final end Jesus placed two great events. The first of these was a long treading under foot of Jerusalem, until the times of the Gentiles (the *καιροὶ ἐθνῶν*, *i.e.*, their whole opportunities under the Christian dispensation) should be fulfilled;[2] the second was a preaching of the Gospel of the Kingdom to all nations in all the world.[3] Nor can we deny all probability to the supposition that while the inspired narrators of the Gospel history reported with perfect wisdom and faithfulness everything that was essential to the life and salvation of mankind, their abbreviations of what Jesus uttered, and the sequence which they gave to the order of His utterances, were to a certain extent tinged by their own subjectivity—possibly even by their own

[1] Luke xxi. 9, *δεῖ γὰρ γενέσθαι ταῦτα πρῶτον, ἀλλ' οὐκ εὐθέως τὸ τέλος.* The same thing is brought out, but in obscurer sequence, by Matt. xxiv. 6; Mark xiii. 7, *οὔπω τὸ τέλος.* See Bossuet, *Médit. Dern.* Serm. 76.

[2] Luke xxi. 24.

[3] Matt. xxiv. 14.

natural supposition—that the second horizon lay nearer to the first than it actually did in the designs of Heaven.

In this discourse, then, Jesus first warned them of false Messiahs and false prophets; He told them that the wild struggling of nations and those physical commotions and calamities which have so often seemed to synchronise with the great crises of History, were not to trouble them, as they would be but the throe of the Palingenesia, the first birth-pang of the coming time.[1] He prophesied of dreadful persecutions, of abounding iniquity, of decaying faith, of wide evangelisation as the signs of a coming end. And as we learn from many other passages of Scripture, these signs, as they did usher in the destruction of Jerusalem, so shall reappear on a larger scale before the end of all things is at hand.[2]

The next great paragraph of this speech dwelt mainly on the *immediate* future. He had foretold distinctly the destruction of the Holy City, and He now gives them indications which should forewarn them of its approach, and lead them to secure their safety. When they should see Jerusalem encompassed with armies—when the abomination which should cause desolation should stand in the Holy Place—then even from the fields, even from the housetops, they were to fly out of Judæa to the shelter of the Trans-Jordanic hills,

[1] Matt. xxiv. 8, ἀρχὴ ὠδίνων. חבלי המשיח, "les préludes de l'enfantement messianique" (Renan, *L'Antechrist*, p. 290). As to the fulfilment of these prophecies, see Jos. *Antt.* xix. 1, § 2; Tac. *Ann.* xvi. 13; xii. 38; xv. 22; Sen. *Ep.* 91, and many other passages quoted by the commentators on this Gospel. The "Jewish War" of Josephus alone shows how accurately our Lord's words foreshadowed the future; and Tacitus describing the same epoch (*Hist.* i. 2) calls it "opimum casibus, atrox proeliis, discors seditionibus, ipsâ etiam pace saevum," and proceeds to speak of earthquakes ("haustae et obrutae urbes"), adulteries, treacheries, violences, pollutions,

[2] See 1 Thess. v. 3; 2 Thess. ii. 2, &c.

from the unspeakable horrors that should follow. Nor even then were they to be carried away by any deceivableness of unrighteousness, caused by the yearning intensity of Messianic hopes. Many should cry, "Lo here! and lo there!" but let them pay no heed; for when He came, His presence, like lightning shining from the east even to the west, should be visible and unmistakable to all the world, and like eagles gathering to the carcase should the destined ministers of His vengeance wing their flight.[1] By such warnings the Christians were preserved. Before John of Giscala had shut the gates of Jerusalem, and Simon of Gerasa had begun to murder the fugitives, so that "he who escaped the tyrant within the wall was destroyed by the other that lay before the gates"[2] —before the Roman eagle waved her wing over the doomed city, or the infamies of lust and murder had driven every worshipper in horror from the Temple Courts[3]—the Christians had taken timely warning, and in the little Peræan town of Pella,[4] were beyond the reach of all the robbery, and murder, and famine, and

[1] On the interpretation of this symbol, see p. 138 on Luke xvii. 37. That the "eagles" are primarily the Romans, finds additional illustration from the Book of Enoch xcii., where Pagan foes are compared to ravens and eagles. Legionary eagles were the very commonest symbols on Roman colonial coins, and so many are still found in the East that they must have been very familiar to the Jews, who regarded them with special detestation. (Akerman, p. 15.) Cf. Jos. *Antt.* xvii. 6, § 3.

[2] Jos. *B. J.* iv. 9, § 10.

[3] On the outrages of the Zealots, see Jos. *B. J.* iv. 3, § 7. The terrifying usurpation of the Temple by these dreadful and murderous fanatics best corresponds with the βδέλυγμα τῆς ἐρημώσεως (comp. Dan. xii. 11; 1 Macc. i. 54), of which the first reference was to the profanation caused by Antiochus Epiphanes. On this "desolating wing of Abomination," see the note of Bishop Wordsworth.

[4] Euseb. (*Hist. Eccl.* iii. 5) says that they fled there in consequence of "a certain oracular utterance," and Epiphanius (*Haer.* i. 123) that they were warned by an angel.

cannibalism, and extermination which made the siege of Jerusalem a scene of greater tribulation than any that has been since the beginning of the world.[1]

Then Jesus passed to the darkening of the sun and moon, and the fallıng of the stars, and the shaking of the powers of heaven—signs which may have a meaning both literal and metaphorical—which should precede the appearing of the Son of Man in heaven, and the gathering of the elect from the four winds by the trumpet-blast of the angels. That day of the Lord should have its signs no less than the other, and He bade His disciples in all ages to mark those signs and interpret them aright, even as they interpreted the signs of the coming summer in the fig-tree's budding leaves. But that day should come to the world suddenly,. unexpectedly, overwhelmingly; and as it should be a day of reward to all faithful servants, so should it be a day of vengeance and destruction to the glutton and the drunkard, to the hypocrite and the oppressor. Therefore, to impress yet more indelibly upon their minds the lessons of watchfulness and faithfulness, and to warn them yet more emphatically against the peril of the drowsy life and the smouldering lamp,[2] He told them the exquisite Parables—so beautiful, so simple, yet so rich in instruction—of the Ten Virgins and of the Talents; and drew for them a picture of that Great Day of Judgment on which the King should separate all

[1] Matt. xxiv. 21. See Jos. *B. J.* v. 10, § 5, where he expressly says that there had been no generation so wicked, and no city so "plunged in misery from the beginning of the world."

[2] Matt. xxv. 8, *αἱ λαμπάδες ἡμῶν σβέννυνται*, not "our lamps *are gone out*," but "are smouldering," "are *being* quenched." The light of God's Holy Spirit is dying away in the "earthen vessels" of our life. To a train of thought similar to the Parable of the Talents belongs the ἄγραφον δόγμα, "Be good money-changers" (γίνεσθε τραπεζῖται δόκιμοι).

nations from one another as the shepherd divideth his sheep from the goats. On that day those who had shown the least kindness to the least of these His brethren should be accounted to have done it unto Him. But then, lest these grand eschatological utterances should lead them to any of their old mistaken Messianic notions, He ended them with the sad and now half-familiar refrain, that His death and anguish must precede all else. The occasion, the manner, the very day are now revealed to them with the utmost plainness and simplicity: "Ye know that after two days is the Passover, and the Son of Man is betrayed to be crucified."

So ended that great discourse upon the Mount of Olives, and the sun set, and He arose and walked with His Apostles the short remaining road to Bethany. It was the last time that He would ever walk it upon earth; and after the trials, the weariness, the awful teachings, the terrible agitations of that eventful day, how delicious to Him must have been that hour of twilight loveliness and evening calm; how refreshing the peace and affection which surrounded Him in the quiet village and the holy home. As we have already noticed, Jesus did not love cities, and scarcely ever slept within their precincts. He shrank from their congregated wickednesses, from their glaring publicity, from their feverish excitement, from their featureless monotony, with all the natural and instinctive dislike of delicate minds. An Oriental city is always dirty; the refuse is flung into the streets; there is no pavement; the pariah dog is the sole scavenger; beast and man jostle each other promiscuously in the crowded thoroughfares. And though the necessities of His work compelled him to visit Jerusalem, and to preach to the vast throngs from every climate and country who were congregated at its yearly festivals, yet He seems to have retired on every possible occasion beyond its gates, partly it may be for safety—partly from poverty—partly because He loved that sweet home at Bethany—and partly too, perhaps, because He felt the peaceful joy of treading the grass that groweth on the mountains rather than the city stones, and could hold gladder communion with His Father in heaven under the shadow of the olive-trees, where far from all disturbing sights and sounds, He could watch the splendour of the sunset and the falling of the dew.

And surely that last evening walk to Bethany on that Tuesday evening in Passion week must have breathed deep calm into His soul. The thought, indeed, of the bitter cup which He was so soon to drink was doubtless present to Him, but present only in its aspect of exalted sacrifice, and the highest purpose of love fulfilled. Not the pangs which He would suffer, but the pangs from which He would save; not the power of darkness which would seem to win a short-lived triumph, but the redeeming victory—the full, perfect, and sufficient atonement—these we may well, though reverently, believe to have been the subjects which dominated in His thoughts. The exquisite beauty of the Syrian evening, the tender colours of the spring grass and flowers, the wadys around Him paling into solemn grey, the distant hills bathed in the primrose light of sunset, the coolness and balm of the breeze after the burning glare—what must these have been to Him to whose eye the world of Nature was an open book, on every page of which He read His Father's name! And this was His native land. Bethany was almost to Him a second Nazareth; those whom He loved were around Him, and He was going to those whom He loved. Can we not imagine Him walking on in silence too deep for words—His disciples around Him or following Him—the gibbous moon beginning to rise and gild the twinkling foliage of the olive-trees with richer silver, and moonlight and twilight blending at each step insensibly with the garish hues of day, like that solemn twilight-purple of coming agony into which the noon-day of His happier ministry had long since begun to fade?

CHAPTER LIV.

THE BEGINNING OF THE END.

"So they weighed for my price thirty pieces of silver."—ZECH. xi. 12.

IT was inevitable that the burning words of indignation which Jesus had uttered on this last great day of His ministry should exasperate beyond all control the hatred and fury of the priestly party among the Jews. Not only had they been defeated and abashed in open encounter in the very scene of their highest dignity, and in the presence of their most devoted adherents; not only had they been forced to confess their ignorance of that very Scripture exegesis which was their recognised domain, and their incapacity to pronounce an opinion on a subject respecting which it was their professed duty to decide; but, after all this humiliation, He whom they despised as the young and ignorant Rabbi of Nazareth—He who neglected their customs and discountenanced their traditions—He on whose words, to them so pernicious, the people hung in rapt attention—had suddenly turned upon them, within hearing of the very Hall of Meeting, and had pronounced upon them—upon *them* in the odour of their sanctity—upon *them* who were accustomed to breathe all their lives the incense of unbounded adulation—a woe so searching, so scathing, so memorably intense, that none who heard it could forget it for evermore. It was time that this should end. Pharisees, Sadducees, Herodians, Priests, Scribes, Elders, Annas the astute and tyrannous, Caiaphas the abject and servile, were all now aroused; and, dreading they knew not what outburst of religious anarchy, which would shake the very foundations of their system, they met together probably on that very evening in the Palace of Caiaphas,[1] sinking all their own differences in a common inspiration of hatred against that long-promised Messiah in whom they only recognised a common enemy. It was an alliance, for His destruction, of fanaticism, unbelief, and worldliness; the rage of the bigoted, the contempt of the atheist, and the dislike of the utilitarian; and it seemed but too clear that from the revengeful hate of such a combination no earthly power was adequate to save.

Of the particulars of the meeting we know nothing; but the Evangelists record the two conclusions at which the high conspirators arrived—the one a yet more decisive and emphatic renewal of the vote that He must, at all hazards, be put to death without delay; the other, that it must be done by subtilty, and not by violence, for fear of the multitude; and that, for the same reason —*not* because of the sacredness of the Feast—the murder must be postponed, until the conclusion of the Passover had caused the dispersion of the countless pilgrims to their own homes.

This meeting was held, in all probability, on the evening of Tuesday, while the passions which the events of that day had kindled were still raging with volcanic energy. So that, at the very moment while they were

[1] The name Caiaphas—a surname of the High Priest Joseph—is only another form of Kephas, "a stone" (Salvador, *Vie de Jésus*, ii. 104).

deciding that during that Easter-tide our Passover should *not* be slain—at that very moment, seated on the slopes of Olivet, Jesus was foretelling to His disciples, with the calmest certainty, that He *should* be sacrificed on the very day on which, at evening, the lamb was sacrificed, and the Paschal feast began.

Accordingly, before the meeting was over, an event occurred which at once altered the conclusions of the council, and rendered possible the immediate capture of Jesus without the tumult which they dreaded. The eight days' respite from the bitter sentence of death, which their terror, not their mercy, had accorded Him, was to be withdrawn, and the secret blow was to be struck at once.

For before they separated a message reached them which shot a gleam of fierce joy into their hearts, while we may well imagine that it also filled them with something of surprise and awe. Conscious as they must have been in their inmost hearts how deep was the crime which they intended to commit, it must have almost startled them thus to find "the tempting opportunity at once meeting the guilty disposition," and the Evil Spirit making their way straight before their face. They were informed that the man who knew Jesus, who had been with Him, who had been His disciple—nay, more, one of the Twelve—was ready to put an immediate end to their perplexities, and to re-open with them the communication which he had already made.

The house of Caiaphas was probably in or near the Temple precincts. The gates both of the city and of the Temple were usually closed at sundown, but at the time of this vast yearly gathering it was natural that the rules should have been a little relaxed for the general convenience; and when Judas slank away from his brethren on that fatal evening he would rely on being admitted without difficulty within the city precincts, and into the presence of the assembled elders. He applied accordingly to the "captains" of the Temple, the members of the Levitical guard who had the care of the sacred buildings,[1] and they at once announced his message, and brought him in person before the priests and rulers of the Jews.

Some of the priests had already seen him at their previous meeting; others would doubtless recognise him. If Judas resembled the conception of him which tradition has handed down—

"That furtive mien, that scowling eye,
Of hair that red and tufted fell"—

they could have hardly failed to notice the man of Kerioth as one of those who followed Jesus—perhaps to despise and to detest Him, as almost the only Jew among the Galilæan Apostles. And now they were to be leagued with him in wickedness. The fact that one who had lived with Jesus, who had heard all He had said and seen all He had done—was yet ready to betray Him—strengthened *them* in their purpose; the fact that they, the hierarchs and nobles, were ready not only to praise, but even to reward Judas for what he proposed to do, strengthened *him* in his dark and desperate design. As in water face answereth to face, so did the heart of Judas and of the Jews become assimilated by the reflection of mutual sympathy. As iron sharpeneth iron, so did the blunt weapon of his brutal anger give fresh edge to their polished hate.

Whether the hideous demand for blood-money had

[1] See 2 Chron. xxxv. 8; Acts iv. 1; v. 24.

come from him, or had been suggested by them; whether it was paid immediately or only after the arrest; whether the wretched and paltry sum given—thirty shekels, the price of the meanest slave [1]—was the total reward, or only the earnest of a further and larger sum—these are questions which would throw a strong light on the character and motives of Judas, but to which the general language of the Evangelists enables us to give no certain answer. The details of the transaction were probably but little known. Neither Judas nor his venerable abettors had any cause to dwell on them with satisfaction. The Evangelists and the early Christians generally, when they speak of Judas, seem to be filled with a spirit of shuddering abhorrence too deep for words. Only one dark fact stood out before their imagination in all its horror, and that was that Judas was a traitor; that Judas had been one of the Twelve, and yet had sold his Lord. Probably he received the money, such as it was, at once. With the gloating eyes of that avarice which was his besetting sin, he might gaze on the silver coins, stamped (oh! strange irony of history!) on one side with an olive branch, the symbol of peace, on the other with a censer, the type of prayer, and bearing on them the superscription, "Jerusalem *the Holy*." [2] And probably if those

[1] About £3 16*s*. (Exod. xxi. 32; cf. Gen. xxxvii. 28; Zech. xi. 12, 13).

[2] In Matt. xxvi. 15, ἔστησαν αὐτῷ seems to mean "they paid," literally "weighed" (cf. LXX., Zech. xi. 12, 13). It cannot be rendered with the Vulgate, "constituerunt ei," which is used to harmonise it with Mark xiv. 11 (ἐπηγγείλαντο), and Luke xxii. 5 (συνέθεντο). In these matters, unimportant as regarded their purpose, the Evangelists do not profess a rigidly minute accuracy. I should infer, however, that Judas twice went before the priests—once to *promise* the betrayal, and another time to *arrange its details*. Perhaps the money had been promised on the first occasion, and paid on the second. St. Matthew only alludes vaguely to the words of Zechariah. The supposed relation between the two passages may be seen in Keil, *Minor Prophets*, ii. 373 (E. Tr.).

elders chaffered with him after the fashion of their race, as the narrative seems to imply, they might have represented that, after all, his agency was unessential; that he might do them a service which would be regarded as a small convenience, but that they could carry out their purpose, if they chose, without his aid. One thing, however, is certain: he left them a pledged traitor, and henceforth only sought the opportunity to betray his Master when no part of the friendly multitude was near.

What were the motives of this man? Who can attempt to fathom the unutterable abyss, to find his way amid the weltering chaos, of a heart agitated by unresisted and besetting sins? The Evangelists can say nothing but that Satan entered into him. The guilt of the man seemed to them too abnormal for any natural or human explanation. The narratives of the Synoptists point distinctly to avarice as the cause of his ruin.[1] They place his first overtures to the Sanhedrin in close and pointed connection with the qualm of disgust he felt at being unable to secure any pilferings from the "three hundred pence," of which, since they *might* have come into his possession, he regarded himself as having been robbed; and St. John, who can never speak of him without a shudder of disgust, says in so many words that he was an habitual thief.[2] How little insight can *they* have into the fatal bondage and diffusiveness of a besetting sin, into the dense spiritual blindness and awful infatuation with

[1] We conclude that the loss of the 300 pence was the cause of the betrayal, from the pointed manner in which the latter is narrated in immediate proximity to the former; just as we conjecture that Nadab and Abihu were intoxicated when they offered "strange fire," from the prohibition of strong drink to the priests immediately after the narration of their fate (Lev. x. 1—11).

[2] John xii. 6.

which it confounds the guilty, who cannot believe in so apparently inadequate a motive! Yet the commonest observance of daily facts which come before our notice in the moral world, might serve to show that the commission of crime results as frequently from a motive that seems miserably small and inadequate, as from some vast and abnormal temptation. Do we not read in the Old Testament of those that pollute God among the people "for handfuls of barley and for pieces of bread;" of those who sell "the righteous for silver and the poor for a pair of shoes?"[1] The sudden crisis of temptation might seem frightful, but its issue was decided by the entire tenor of his previous life; the sudden blaze of lurid light was but the outcome of that which had long burnt and smouldered deep within his heart.

Doubtless other motives mingled with, strengthened—perhaps to the self-deceiving and blinded soul substituted themselves for—the predominant one. "Will not this measure," he may have thought, "force Him to declare His Messianic kingdom? At the worst, can He not easily save Himself by miracle? If not, has He not told us repeatedly that He will die; and if so, why may I not reap a little advantage from that which is in any case inevitable? Or will it not, perhaps, be meritorious to do that of which all the chief priests approve?" A thousand such devilish suggestions may have formulated themselves in the traitor's heart, and mingled with them was the revulsion of feeling which he suffered from finding that his self-denial in following Jesus would, after all, be apparently in vain; that he would gain from it not rank and wealth, but only poverty and persecution. Perhaps, too, there was something of rancour at being rebuked; perhaps something

[1] Ezek. xiii. 19; Amos ii. 6; viii. 6.

of bitter jealousy at being less loved by Christ than his fellows; perhaps something of frenzied disappointment at the prospect of failure; perhaps something of despairing hatred at the consciousness that he was suspected. Alas! sins grow and multiply with fatal diffusiveness, and blend insensibly with hosts of their evil kindred. "The whole moral nature is clouded by them; the intellect darkened; the spirit stained." Probably by this time a turbid confused chaos of sins was weltering in the soul of Judas—malice, worldly ambition, theft, hatred of all that was good and pure, base ingratitude, frantic anger, all culminating in this foul and frightful act of treachery—all rushing with blind, bewildering fury through this gloomy soul.

"Satan entered into him." That, after all, whether a literal or a metaphorical expression,[1] best describes his awful state. It was a madness of disenchantment from selfish hopes. Having persuaded himself that the New Kingdom was a mere empty fraud, he is suffered to become the victim of a delusion, which led him into a terrible conviction that he had flung away the substance for a shadow. It had not been always thus with him. He had not been always bad. The day had been when he was an innocent boy—a youth sufficiently earnest to be singled out from other disciples as one of the Twelve—a herald of the New Kingdom not without high hopes. The poverty and the wanderings of the early period of the ministry may have protected him from temptation. The special temptation—trebly dangerous, because it appealed to his besetting sin—may have begun at that period when our Lord's work assumed a slightly more settled and organised character.[2] Even then it did

[1] "Satan" is sometimes, if not always, used by our Lord in senses obviously metaphorical (Matt. xvi. 23; Luke x. 18; xiii. 16, &c.).

[2] Luke x. 3.

not master him at once. He had received warnings of fearful solemnity;[1] for some time there may have been hope for him; he may have experienced relapses into dishonesty after recoveries of nobleness. But as he did not master his sin, his sin mastered him, and led him on, as a slave, to his retribution and ruin. Did he slink back to Bethany that night with the blood-money in his bag? Did he sleep among his fellow-apostles?—All that we know is that henceforth he was ever anxiously, eagerly, suspiciously upon the watch.

And the next day—the Wednesday in Passion week—must have baffled him. Each day Jesus had left Bethany in the morning and had gone to Jerusalem. Why did He not go on that day? Did He suspect treachery? That day in the Temple Courts the multitude listened for His voice in vain. Doubtless the people waited for Him with intense expectation; doubtless the priests and Pharisees looked out for Him with sinister hope; but He did not come. The day was spent by Him in deep seclusion, so far as we know, in perfect rest and silence. He prepared Himself in peace and prayer for the awfulness of His coming struggle. It may be that He wandered alone to the hilly uplands above and around the quiet village, and there, under the vernal sunshine, held high communing with His Father in heaven. But how the day was passed by Him we do not know. A veil of holy silence falls over it. He was surrounded by the few who loved Him and believed in Him. To them He may have spoken, but His work as a teacher on earth was done.

And on that night He lay down for the last time on earth. On the Thursday morning, He woke never to sleep again.

[1] John vi. 70.

CHAPTER LV.

THE LAST SUPPER.

οὐκ ἔφαγε τὸν νομικὸν ἀμνὸν . . . ἀλλ' αὐτὸς ἔπαθεν ὡς ἀληθὴς ἀμνός.—*Chron. Pasch.*, p. 12.

On the Tuesday evening in Passion week Jesus had spoken of the Passover as the season of His death. If the customs enjoined by the Law had been capable of rigid and exact fulfilment, the Paschal lamb for the use of Himself and His disciples would have been set apart on the previous Sunday evening; but although, since the days of the exile, the Passover had been observed, it is probable that the changed circumstances of the nation had introduced many natural and perfectly justifiable changes in the old regulations. It would have been a simple impossibility for the myriads of pilgrims to provide themselves beforehand with a Paschal lamb.

It was on the morning of Thursday—Green Thursday as it used to be called during the Middle Ages—that some conversation took place between Jesus and His disciples about the Paschal feast. They asked Him where He wished the preparation for it to be made. As He had now withdrawn from all public teaching, and was spending this Thursday, as He had spent the previous day, in complete seclusion, they probably expected that He would eat the Passover at Bethany, which for such purposes had been decided by rabbinical authority to be within the limits of Jerusalem. But His plans were otherwise. He, the true Paschal Lamb, was to be sacrificed once and for ever in the Holy City, where it is probable that in that very Passover, and on the very same day, some 260,000 of those lambs of which He was the antitype were destined to be slain.

Accordingly He sent Peter and John to Jerusalem, and appointing for them a sign both mysterious and secret, told them that on entering the gate they would meet a servant carrying a pitcher of water from one of the fountains for evening use; following him they would reach a house, to the owner of which they were to intimate the intention of the Master[1] to eat the Passover there with His disciples; and this householder—conjectured by some to have been Joseph of Arimathæa, by others John Mark—would at once place at their disposal a furnished upper room, ready provided with the requisite table and couches.[2] They found all as Jesus had said, and there "made ready the Passover." Full reasons will, however, be given in the Excursus for believing that this was not the ordinary Jewish Passover, but a meal eaten by our Lord and His Apostles on the previous evening, Thursday, Nisan 13, to which a quasi-Paschal character was given, but which was intended to supersede the Jewish festival by one of far deeper and diviner significance.[3]

[1] Mark xiv. 14. The expression seems to imply that the owner of the house was a disciple; and still more the message, "My time is at hand."

[2] Mark xiv. 15, *ἐστρωμένον*; cf. *στρῶσον σεαυτῷ* (Acts ix. 34). The notion that the word means "paved" is an error. See Ezek. xxiii. 41, LXX.

[3] See Excursus X., "Was the Last Supper an Actual Passover?"

It was towards the evening, probably when the gathering dusk would prevent all needless observation, that Jesus and His disciples walked from Bethany, by that old familiar road over the Mount of Olives, which His sacred feet were never again destined to traverse until after death. How far they attracted attention, or how it was that He whose person was known to so many—and who, as the great central figure of such great counter-agitations, had, four days before, been accompanied with shouts of triumph, as He would be, on the following day, with yells of insult—could now enter Jerusalem unnoticed with His followers, we cannot tell. We catch no glimpse of the little company till we find them assembled in that "large upper room" —perhaps the very room where three days afterwards the sorrow-stricken Apostles first saw their risen Saviour —perhaps the very room where, amid the sound of a rushing mighty wind, each meek brow was first mitred with Pentecostal flame.

When they arrived, the meal was ready, the table spread, the *triclinia* laid with cushions for the guests. Imagination loves to reproduce all the probable details of that deeply moving and eternally sacred scene; and if we compare the notices of ancient Jewish custom, with the immemorial fashions still existing in the changeless East, we can feel but little doubt as to the general nature of the arrangements. They were totally unlike those with which the genius of Leonardo da Vinci, and other great painters, has made us so familiar. The room probably had white walls, and was bare of all except the most necessary furniture and adornment. The couches or cushions, each large enough to hold three persons, were placed around three sides of one or more low tables of gaily painted wood, each scarcely higher than stools. The seat of honour was the central one of the central *triclinium*, or mat. This was, of course, occupied by the Lord. Each guest reclined at full length, leaning on his left elbow, that his right hand might be free.[1] At the right hand of Jesus reclined the beloved disciple, whose head therefore could, at any moment, be placed upon the breast of his friend and Lord.

It may be that the very act of taking their seats at the table had, once more, stirred up in the minds of the Apostles those disputes about precedence[2] which, on previous occasions, our Lord had so tenderly and beautifully rebuked.[3] The mere question of a place at table might seem a matter too infinitesimal and unimportant to ruffle the feelings of good and self-denying men at an hour so supreme and solemn; but that love for "the chief seats" at feasts and elsewhere, which Jesus had denounced in the Pharisees, is not only innate in the human heart, but is even so powerful that it has at times caused the most terrific tragedies.[4] But at this moment, when the soul of Jesus was full of such sublime purpose—when He was breathing the pure unmingled air of Eternity, and the Eternal was to Him, in spite of His mortal investiture, not only the present

[1] The custom of eating the Passover standing had long been abandoned. Reclining was held to be the proper attitude, because it was that of free men (Maimon. *Pesach.* 10, 1).

[2] Luke xxii. 24.

[3] Mark ix. 34; Matt. xviii. 1. See *supra*, pp. 37, 180. It is a not impossible conjecture that the dispute may have been stirred up by a claim of *Judas* as being an office-bearer in the little band.

[4] Many will recall the famous scene between Criemhilt and Brunhilt in the *Niebelungen.* In the Middle Ages blood was shed at the very altar of St. John's Lateran in a furious dispute about precedence between an abbot and a bishop.

but the seen—a strife of this kind must have been more than ever painful. It showed how little, as yet, even these His chosen followers had entered into the meaning of His life. It showed that the evil spirits of pride and selfishness were not yet exorcised from their struggling souls. It showed that, even now, they had wholly failed to understand His many and earnest warnings as to the nature of His kingdom, and the certainty of His fate. That *some* great crisis was at and—that their Master was to suffer and be slainath vehhey *must* have partially realised; but they seem to—regarded this as a mere temporary obscuration, to be followed by an immediate divulgence of His splendour, and the setting up on earth of His Messianic throne.

In pained silence Jesus had heard their murmured jealousies, while they were arranging their places at the feast.[1] Not by mere verbal reproof, but by an act more profoundly significant and touching, He determined to teach to them, and to all who love Him, a nobler lesson.

Every Eastern room, if it belongs to any but the very poorest, has the central part of the floor covered with mats, and as a person enters, he lays aside his sandals at the door of the room, mainly in order, not to defile the clean white mats with the dust and dirt of the road or streets, and also (at any rate among Mahometans) because the mat is hallowed by being knelt upon in prayer. Before they reclined at the table, the disciples had doubtless conformed to this cleanly and reasonable custom; but another customary and pleasant habit,

[1] John xiii. 2. γινομένου (א, B, L, &c.) is probably the right reading, but even γενομένου cannot mean "supper being ended," as in the E. V. (see xiii. 26), but "when it was supper-time."

which we know that Jesus appreciated, had been neglected. Their feet must have been covered with dust from their walk along the hot and much frequented road from Bethany to Jerusalem, and under such circumstances they would have been refreshed for the festival by washing their feet after putting off their sandals. But to wash the feet was the work of slaves; and since no one had offered to perform the kindly office, Jesus Himself, in His eternal humility and self-denial, rose from His place at the meal to do the menial service which none of His disciples had offered to do for Him.[1] Well may the amazement of the beloved disciple show itself in his narrative, as he dwells on every particular of that solemn scene. "Though He knew that the Father had given all things into His hands, and that He came from God and was going to God, He arose from the supper and laid aside His garments, and taking a towel, girded Himself." It is probable that in the utterness of self-abnegation, He entirely stripped His upper limbs, laying aside both the *simchah* and the *cetóneth,* as though He had been the meanest slave, and wrapping the towel round His waist. Then pouring water into the large copper basin with which an Oriental house is always provided, He began without a word to wash His disciples' feet, and wipe them dry with the towel which served Him as a girdle. Awe and shame kept them silent until He came to Peter, whose irrepressible emotions found vent in the surprised, half-indignant question, "Lord, dost *Thou* seek to wash *my* feet?" Thou, the Son of God, the King of Israel, who hast the words of eternal life—Thou, whose feet Oriental kings should anoint with their

[1] John xiii. 1—20.

costliest spikenard, and penitents bathe in precious tears—dost thou wash Peter's feet? It was the old dread and self-depreciation which, more than three years before, had prompted the cry of the rude fisherman of Galilee, "Depart from me, for I am a sinful man, O Lord;"[1] it was the old self-will which, a year before, had expressed itself in the self-confident dissuasion of the elated Man of Rock—"That be far from Thee, Lord; this shall not happen unto Thee."[2] Gently recognising what was good in His impetuous follower's ejaculation, Jesus calmly tells him that as yet he is too immature to understand the meaning of His actions, though the day should come when their significance should dawn upon him. But Peter, obstinate and rash—as though he felt, even more than his Lord, the greatness of Him that ministered, and the meanness of him to whom the service would be done—persisted in his opposition: "Never, never, till the end of time,"[3] He impetuously exclaims; "shalt thou wash my feet?" But then Jesus revealed to him the dangerous self-assertion which lurked in this false humility. "If I wash thee not, thou hast no share with me." Alike, thy self-conceit and thy self-disgust must be laid aside if thou wouldest be mine. My follower must accept my will, even when he least can comprehend it, even when it seems to violate his own conceptions of what I am. That calm word changed the whole current of thought and feeling in the warm-hearted passionate disciple. "No share with Thee? oh, forbid it, Heaven! Lord, not my feet only, but also my hands and my head!" But no: once more he must accept what Christ wills,

[1] See *supra*, Vol. I., p. 243. [2] See *supra*, p. 19.
[3] John xiii. 8, οὐ μὴ . . . εἰς τὸν αἰῶνα.

not in his own way, but in Christ's way. This total washing was not needed. The baptism of his initiation was over; in that laver of regeneration he had been already dipped. Nothing more was needed than the daily cleansing from minor and freshly-contracted stains The feet soiled with the clinging dust of daily sins, these must be washed in daily renovation; but the heart and being of the man, these were already washed, were cleansed, were sanctified. "Jesus saith to him, He that is bathed (λελουμένος) hath no need save to wash (νίψασθαι) his feet, but is clean every whit. And ye are clean;" and then He was forced to add with a deep sigh, "but not all." The last words were an allusion to His consciousness of one traitorous presence; for *He* knew, what as yet *they* knew not, that the hands of the Lord of Life had just washed the traitor's feet. Oh, strange unfathomable depth of human infatuation and ingratitude! that traitor, with all the black and accursed treachery in his false heart, had seen, had known, had suffered it; had felt the touch of those kind and gentle hands, had been refreshed by the cleansing water, had seen that sacred head bent over his feet, yet stained as they yet were with the hurried secret walk which had taken him into the throng of sanctimonious murderers over the shoulder of Olivet. But for him there had been no purification in that lustral water; neither was the devil within him exorcised by that gentle voice, nor the leprosy of his heart healed by that miracle-producing touch.

The other Apostles did not at the moment notice that grievous exception—"but not all." It may be that their consciences gave to all, even to the most faithful, too sad a cause to echo the words, with something of misgiving, to his own soul. Then Jesus, after having washed their feet, resumed His garments, and once more reclined at the meal. As He leaned there on His left elbow, John lay at His right, with his head quite close to Jesus' breast. Next to John, and at the top of the next mat or cushion, would probably be his brother James; and—as we infer from the few details of the meal—at the left of Jesus lay the Man of Kerioth, who may either have thrust himself into that position, or who, as the holder of the common purse, occupied a place of some prominence among the little band. It seems probable that Peter's place was at the top of the next mat, and at the left of Judas. And as the meal began, Jesus taught them what His act had meant. Rightly, and with proper respect, they called Him "Master" and "Lord," for so He was; yet, though the Lord is greater than the slave, the Sender greater than His Apostle, He their Lord and Master had washed their feet. It was a kind and gracious task, and such ought to be the nature of all their dealings with each other. He had done it to teach them humility, to teach them self-denial, to teach them love: blessed they if they learnt the lesson! blessed if they learnt that the struggles for precedence, the assertions of claims, the standings upon dignity, the fondness for the mere exercise of authority, marked the tyrannies and immaturities of heathendom, and that the greatest Christian is ever the humblest. He should be chief among them who, for the sake of others, gladly laid on himself the lowliest burdens, and sought for himself the humblest services. Again and again He warned them that they were not to look for earthly reward or earthly prosperity; the throne, and the table, and the kingdom, and the many mansions were not of earth.[1]

And then again the trouble of His spirit broke forth. He was speaking of those whom He had chosen; He was not speaking of them all. Among the blessed company sat one who even then was drawing on his own head a curse. It had been so with David, whose nearest friend had become his bitterest foe; it was foreordained that it should be so likewise with David's Son. Soon should they know with what full foreknowledge He had gone to all that awaited Him; soon should they be able to judge that, just as the man who receives in Christ's name His humblest servant receiveth Him, so the rejection of Him is the rejection of His Father, and that this rejection of the Living God was the crime which at this moment was being committed, and committed in their very midst.

There, next but one to Him, hearing all these words unmoved, full of spite and hatred, utterly hardening his heart, and leaning the whole weight of his demoniac possession against that door of mercy which even now and even here His Saviour would have opened to him, sat Judas, the false smile of hypocrisy on his face, but rage, and shame, and greed, and anguish, and treachery in his heart. The near presence of that black iniquity, the failure of even His pathetic lowliness to move or touch the man's hideous purpose, troubled the human heart of Jesus to its inmost depths—wrung from Him His agony of yet plainer prediction, "Verily, verily, I

[1] It is probable that to find the full scope of what Jesus taught on this occasion we must combine (as I have done) Luke xxii. 24—30 with John xiii. 1—17. In Luke xxii. 25 is illustrated, by the title Εὐεργέτης, "benefactor," common on the coins of the Syrian kings.

say unto you, that *one of you* shall betray me!" That night *all*, even the best beloved, were to forsake Him, but it was not *that;* that night even the boldest-hearted was to deny Him with oaths, but it was not *that;* nay, but one of them was to *betray* Him. Their hearts misgave them as they listened. Already a deep unspeakable sadness had fallen over the sacred meal. Like the sombre and threatening crimson that intermingles with the colours of sunset, a dark omen seemed to be overshadowing them—a shapeless presentiment of evil—an unspoken sense of dread. If all their hopes were to be thus blighted—if at this very passover, He for whom they had given up all, and who had been to them all in all, was indeed to be betrayed by one of themselves to an unpitied and ignominious end—if *this* were possible, *anything* seemed possible. Their hearts were troubled. All their want of nobility, all their failure in love, all the depth of their selfishness, all the weakness of their faith—

> "Every evil thought they ever thought,
> And every evil word they ever said,
> And every evil thing they ever did,"

all crowded upon their memories, and made their consciences afraid. *None* of them seemed safe from *anything,* and each read his own self-distrust in his brother-disciple's eye. And hence, at that moment of supreme sadness and almost despair, it was with lips that faltered and cheeks that paled, that each asked the humble question, "Lord, is it I?" Better always that question than "Is it *he?*"—better the penitent watchfulness of a self-condemning humility than the haughty Pharisaism of censorious pride. The very horror that breathed through their question, the very trustfulness which prompted it, involved their acquittal. Jesus only remained silent, in order that even then, if it were possible, there might be time for Judas to repent. But Peter was unable to restrain his sorrow and his impatience. Eager to know and to prevent the treachery—unseen by Jesus, whose back was turned to him as He reclined at the meal—he made a signal to John to ask "who it was."[1] The head of John was close to Jesus, and laying it with affectionate trustfulness on his Master's breast, he said in a whisper, "Lord, who is it?"[2] The reply, given in a tone equally low, was heard by St. John alone, and confirmed the suspicions with which it is evident that the repellent nature of Judas had already inspired him. At Eastern meals all the guests eat with their fingers out of a common dish, and it is common for one at times to dip into the dish a piece of the thin flexible cake of bread which is placed by each, and taking up with it a portion of the meat or rice in the dish, to hand it to another guest. So ordinary an incident of any daily meal would attract no notice whatever.[3] Jesus handed to the traitor Apostle a "sop" of this kind, and this, as He told St. John, was the sign which should indicate to him, and possibly through him to St. Peter, which was

[1] John xiii. 24. This is the reading of many MSS. (א, A, D, E, F, &c.), and of our version; but many good MSS. (B, C, L) read εἰπέ τίς ἐστι; as though St. Peter assumed that the beloved disciple, at any rate, *must* know the secret. Perhaps the true rendering should be, "Say" (to Jesus), "Who is it?"

[2] John xiii. 23, ἀνακείμενος ’ν τῷ κόλπῳ; ver. 25, ἐπιπεσὼν ἐπὶ τὸ στῆθος (א, A, D, &c.). The οὕτως of B, C, L makes it still more graphic. The impression made by this affectionate change of attitude may be seen from John xxi. 20 (ἀνέπεσεν), and the change from κόλπος to στῆθος marks the eye-witness.

[3] We can hardly argue from τὸ τρυβλίον that there was only *one* dish, though this is in itself probable enough; nor need τὸν ἄρτον (Matt. xxvi. 26) imply that there was but one loaf.

the guilty member of the little band. And then He added aloud, in words which can have but one significance, in words the most awful and crushing that ever passed His lips, "The Son of Man goeth indeed, as it is written of Him; but woe unto that man by whom the Son of Man is betrayed! It were good for that man if he had not been born!" "Words," it has been well said, "of immeasurable ruin, words of immeasurable woe"—and the more terrible because uttered by the lips of immeasurable Love; words capable, if any were capable, of revealing to the lost soul of the traitor all the black gulf of horror that was yawning before his feet. He must have known something of what had passed; he may well have overheard some fragment of the conversation, or at least have had a dim consciousness that in some way it referred to him. He may even have been aware that when his hand met the hand of Jesus over the dish there was some meaning in the action. When the others were questioning among themselves "which was the traitor?" he had remained silent in the defiant hardness of contempt or the sullen gloom of guilt; but now—stung, it may be, by some sense of the shuddering horror with which the mere possibility of his guilt was regarded—he nerved himself for the shameful and shameless question. After all the rest had sunk into silence, there grated upon the Saviour's ear that hoarse untimely whisper, in all the bitterness of its defiant mockery—not asking, as the rest had asked, in loving reverence, "*Lord*, is it I?" but with the cold formal title, "*Rabbi*, is it I?" Then that low unreproachful answer, "Thou hast said," sealed his guilt. The rest did not hear it; it was probably caught by Peter and John alone; and Judas ate the sop which Jesus had given him, and after the sop Satan entered into him. As all the winds, on some night of storm, riot and howl through the rent walls of some desecrated shrine, so through the ruined life of Judas envy and avarice, and hatred and ingratitude, were rushing all at once. In that bewildering chaos of a soul spotted with mortal guilt, the Satanic had triumphed over the human; in that dark heart earth and hell were thenceforth at one; in that lost soul sin had conceived and brought forth death. "What thou art doing, do more quickly," said Jesus to him aloud. He knew what the words implied, he knew that they meant, "Thy fell purpose is matured, carry it out with no more of these futile hypocrisies and meaningless delays." Judas rose from the feast. The innocent-hearted Apostles thought that Jesus had bidden him go out and make purchases for to-morrow's Passover, or give something out of the common store which should enable the poor to buy their Paschal lamb. And so from the lighted room, from the holy banquet, from the blessed company, from the presence of his Lord, he went immediately out, and—as the beloved disciple adds, with a shudder of dread significance letting the curtain of darkness fall for ever on that appalling figure—"*and it was night.*"

We cannot tell with any certainty whether this took place before or after the institution of the Lord's Supper—whether Judas partook or not of those hallowed symbols. Nor can we tell whether at all, or, if at all, to what extent, our Lord conformed the minor details of His last supper to the half-joyous, half-mournful customs of the Paschal feast; nor, again, can we tell how far the customs of the Passover in that day resembled those detailed to us in the Rabbinic writings. Nothing could

t *

have been simpler than the ancient method of their commemorating their deliverance from Egypt and from the destroying angel. The central custom of the feast was the hasty eating of the Paschal lamb, with unleavened bread and bitter herbs, in a standing attitude, with loins girt and shoes upon the feet, as they had eaten hastily on the night of their deliverance. In this way the Passover is still yearly eaten by the Samaritans at the summit of Gerizim,[1] and there to this day they will hand to the stranger the little olive-shaped morsel of unleavened bread, enclosing a green fragment of wild endive or some other bitter herb, which may perhaps resemble, except that it is not dipped in the dish, the very ψωμίον which Judas received at the hands of Christ. But even if the Last Supper was a Passover, we are told that the Jews had long ceased to eat it standing, or to observe the rule which forbade any guest to leave the house till morning. They made, in fact, many radical distinctions between the Egyptian (פסח מצרים) and the permanent Passover (פסח דורות) which was subsequently observed. The latter meal began by filling each guest a cup of wine, over which the head of the family pronounced a benediction. After this the hands were washed in a bason of water, and a table was brought in, on which were placed the bitter herbs, the unleavened bread, the *charoseth* (a dish made of dates, raisins, and vinegar), the paschal lamb, and the flesh of the *chagigah*. The father dipped a piece of herb in the *charoseth*, ate it, with a benediction, and distributed a similar morsel to all. A second cup of wine was then poured out; the youngest present inquired the meaning of the paschal night; the father

[1] I was present at this interesting celebration on Gerizim, on April 15, 1870.

replied with a full account of the observance; the first part of the Hallel (Ps. cvii.—cxiv.) was then sung, a blessing repeated, a third cup of wine was drunk, grace was said, a fourth cup poured out, the rest of the Hallel (Ps. cxv.—cxviii.) sung, and the ceremony ended by the blessing of the song.[1] Some, no doubt, of the facts mentioned at the Last Supper may be brought into comparison with parts of this ceremony. It appears, for instance, that the supper began with a benediction, and the passing of a cup of wine, which Jesus bade them divide among themselves, saying that He would not drink of the fruit of the vine until the kingdom of God should come.[2] The other cup—passed round after supper—has been identified by some with the third cup, the *Côs ha-beráchah* or "cup of blessing" of the Jewish ceremonial;[3] and the hymn which was sung before the departure of the little company to Gethsemane has, with much probability, been supposed to be the second part of the great Hallel.

The relation of these incidents of the meal to the various Paschal observances which we have detailed is, however, doubtful. What is not doubtful, and what has the deepest interest for all Christians, is the establishment at this last supper of the Sacrament of the Eucharist. Of this we have no few than four accounts—the brief description of St. Paul agreeing in almost verbal exactness with those of the Synoptists. In each account we clearly recognise the main facts which St. Paul expressly tells us that "he had received of the Lord"—viz., that the Lord Jesus, on the same night in which

[1] See the admirable article on the "Passover," by Dr. Ginsburg, in Kitto's *Cyclopædia*.

[2] Luke xxii. 17.

[3] 1 Cor. x. 16.

He was betrayed, took bread; and when He had given thanks, He brake it, and said, 'Take, eat; this is my body which is broken for you; this do in remembrance of me.' After the same manner also He took the cup when He had supped, saying, 'This cup is the New Testament in my blood; this do ye, as oft as ye drink it, in remembrance of me.'"[1] Never since that memorable evening has the Church ceased to observe the commandment of her Lord; ever since that day, from age to age, has this blessed and holy Sacrament been a memorial of the death of Christ, and a strengthening and refreshing of the soul by the body and blood, as the body is refreshed and strengthened by the bread and wine.[2]

[1] 1 Cor. xi. 23—25.

[2] The "transubstantiation" and "sacramental" controversies which have raged for centuries round the Feast of Communion and Christian love are as heart-saddening as they are strange and needless. They would never have arisen if it had been sufficiently observed that it was a characteristic of Christ's teaching to adopt the language of picture and of emotion. But to turn metaphor into fact, poetry into prose, rhetoric into logic, parable into systematic theology, is at once fatal and absurd. It was to warn us against such error that Jesus said so emphatically, "*It is the spirit that quickeneth; the flesh profiteth nothing: the words that I speak unto you, they are spirit and they are life*" (John vi. 63).

CHAPTER LVI.

THE LAST DISCOURSE.

"So the All-Great were the All-Loving too;
So, through the thunder, comes a human voice,
Saying, 'A heart I made, a heart beats here.'"

R. BROWNING, *Epistle of Karshish.*

No sooner had Judas left the room, than, as though they had been relieved of some ghastly incubus, the spirits of the little company revived. The presence of that haunted soul lay with a weight of horror on the heart of his Master, and no sooner had he departed than the sadness of the feast seems to have been sensibly relieved. The solemn exultation which dilated the soul of their Lord—that joy like the sense of a boundless sunlight behind the earth-born mists—communicated itself to the spirits of His followers. The dull clouds caught the sunset colouring. In sweet and tender communion, perhaps two hours glided away at that quiet banquet. Now it was that, conscious of the impending separation, and fixed unalterably in His sublime resolve, He opened His heart to the little band of those who loved Him, and spoke among them those farewell discourses preserved for us by St. John alone, so "rarely mixed of sadness and joys, and studded with mysteries as with emeralds." "Now," He said, as though with a sigh of relief, "now is the Son of Man glorified, and God is glorified in Him." The hour of that glorification—the glorification which was to be won through the path of humility and agony—was at hand. The time which remained for Him to be with them was short; as He had said to the Jews, so now He said to them, that whither He was going they could not come. And in telling them this, for the first and last time, He calls them "little children." In that company were Peter and John, men whose words and deeds should thenceforth influence the whole world of man until the end—men who should become the patron saints of nations—in whose honour cathedrals should be built, and from whom cities should be named; but their greatness was but a dim faint reflection from His risen glory, and a gleam caught from that spirit which He would send. Apart from Him they were nothing, and less than nothing—ignorant Galilæan fishermen, unknown and unheard of beyond their native village—having no intellect and no knowledge save that He had thus regarded them as His "little children." And though they could not follow Him whither He went, yet He did not say to them, as He had said to the Jews,[1] that they should seek Him and not find Him. Nay, more, He gave them a new commandment, by which, walking in His steps, and being known by all men as His disciples, they should find Him soon. That new commandment was that they should love one another. In one sense, indeed, it was not new.[2] Even in the law of Moses (Lev. xix. 18), not only had there been room for the precept, "Thou shalt love

[1] John vii. 34; viii. 21.

[2] And it is observable that the word used is *καινός*, *recens*, not *νεὸς*, *novus*.

thy neighbour as thyself," but that precept had even been regarded by wise Jewish teachers as cardinal and inclusive—as "the royal law according to the Scripture," as "the message from the beginning."[1] And yet, as St. John points out in his Epistle, though in one sense old, it was, in another, wholly new—new in the new prominence given to it—new in the new motives by which it was enforced—new because of the new example by which it was recommended—new from the new influence which it was henceforth destined to exercise. It was Love, as the test and condition of discipleship, Love as greater than even Faith and Hope, Love as the fulfilling of the Law.[2]

At this point St. Peter interposed a question. Before Jesus entered on a new topic, he wished for an explanation of something which he had not understood. Why was there this farewell aspect about the Lord's discourse? "Lord, whither goest thou?"

"Whither I go thou canst not follow me now, but thou shalt follow me afterwards."

Peter now understood that *death* was meant, but why could he not also die? was he not as ready as Thomas to say, "Let us also go that we may die with Him?"[3] "Lord, *why* cannot I follow thee now? I will lay down my life for thy sake."

Why? Our Lord *might* have answered, Because the

[1] James ii. 8; 1 John iii. 11.

[2] "For life, with all it yields of joy and woe,
And hope and fear—believe the aged friend—
Is just our chance o' the prize of learning love,
How love might be, hath been indeed, and is;
And that we hold henceforth to the uttermost
Such prize, despite the envy of the world,
And having gained truth, keep truth; that is all."
R. BROWNING, "*A Death in the Desert.*"

[3] John xi. 16.

heart is deceitful above all things; because thy want of deep humility deceives thee; because it is hidden, even from thyself, how much there still is of cowardice and self-seeking in thy motives. But He would not deal thus with the noble-hearted but weak and impetuous Apostle, whose love was perfectly sincere, though it did not stand the test. He spares him all reproach; only very gently He repeats the question, "Wilt thou lay down thy life for my sake? Verily, verily, I say unto thee, The cock shall not crow till thou hast denied me thrice!" Already it was night; ere the dawn of that fatal morning shuddered in the eastern sky—before the cock-crow, uttered in the deep darkness, prophesied that the dawn was near—Jesus would have begun to lay down His life for Peter and for all who sin; but already by that time Peter, unmindful even of this warning, should have thrice repudiated his Lord and Saviour, thrice have rejected as a calumny and an insult the mere imputation that he even knew Him. All that Jesus could do to save him from the agony of this moral humiliation—by admonition, by tenderness, by prayer to His Heavenly Father—He had done. He had prayed for him that his faith might not finally fail.[1] Satan indeed had obtained permission to sift them all[2] as wheat, and, in spite of all his self-confidence, in spite of all his protested devotion, in spite of all his imaginary sincerity, he should be but as the chaff. It is remarkable that in the parallel passage of St. Luke occurs the only instance recorded in the Gospel of our Lord having addressed Simon by that name of Peter which He had Himself bestowed. It is as though He meant to

[1] Luke xxii. 32, *ἐκλείπῃ*.

[2] Luke xxii. 31, *ἐξῃτήσατο ὑμᾶς*. Cf. Amos ix. 9.

remind the Man of Rock that his strength lay, not in himself, but in that good confession which he once had uttered. And yet Christ held out to him a gracious hope. He should repent and return to the Lord whom he should deny, and, when that day should come, Jesus bade him show that truest and most acceptable proof of penitence—the strengthening of others. And if his fall gave only too terrible a significance to his Saviour's warnings, yet his repentance nobly fulfilled those consolatory prophecies; and it is most interesting to find that the very word which Jesus had used to him recurs in his Epistle in a connection which shows how deeply it had sunk into his soul.[1]

But Jesus wished His Apostles to feel that the time was come when all was to be very different from the old spring-tide of their happy mission days in Galilee. Then He had sent them forth without purse or scrip or sandals, and yet they had lacked nothing. But the purse and the scrip were needful now—even the sword might become a fatal necessity—and therefore "he that hath no sword let him sell his garment and buy one."[2] The very tone of the expression showed that it was not to be taken in strict literalness. It was our Lord's custom—because His words, which were spoken for all time, were intended to be fixed as goads and as nails in a sure place—to clothe His moral teachings in the form of vivid metaphor and searching paradox. It was His object now to warn them of a changed condition, in which they must expect hatred, neglect, opposition, and in which even self-defence might become a paramount duty; but, as though

[1] Luke xxii. 32, ἐπίστρεψας στήρισον τοὺς ἀδελφούς. Cf. 1 Pet. v. 10.

[2] It is hardly worth observing that to render μάχαιραι "knives" in this passage is absurd.

to warn them clearly that He did *not* mean any immediate effort—as though beforehand to discourage any blow struck in defence of that life which He willingly resigned—He added that the end was near, and that in accordance with olden prophecy He should be numbered with the transgressors.[1] But as usual the Apostles carelessly and ignorantly mistook His words, seeing in them no spiritual lesson, but only the barest and baldest literal meaning. "Lord, behold here are two swords," was their almost childish comment on His words. Two swords!—as though that were enough to defend from physical violence His sacred life! as though that were an adequate provision for Him who, at a word, might have commanded more than twelve legions of angels! as though such feeble might, wielded by such feeble hands, could save Him from the banded hate of a nation of His enemies! "It is enough," He sadly said. It was not needful to pursue the subject; the subsequent lesson in Gethsemane would unteach them their weak misapprehensions of His words. He dropped the subject, and waiving aside their proffered swords, proceeded to that tenderer task of consolation, about which He had so many things to say.

He bade them not be troubled; they believed, and their faith should find its fruition. He was but leaving them to prepare for them a home in the many mansions of His Father's house. They knew whither He was going, and they knew the way.

"Lord, we know not whither thou goest, and how can we know the way?" is the perplexed answer of the melancholy Thomas.

[1] Luke xxii. 37. (Mark xv. 28 is spurious. It is not found in ℵ, A, B, C, D.) See Excursus XI., "Old Testament Quotations."

"I am the Way, the Truth, and the Life," answered Jesus; "no man cometh unto the Father but by me. If ye had known me, ye should have known my Father also; and from henceforth ye know Him, and have seen Him."

Again came one of those naïve interruptions—so faithfully and vividly recorded by the Evangelist—which yet reveal such a depth of incapacity to understand, so profound a spiritual ignorance after so long a course of divine training.[1] And we may well be thankful that the simplicity and ignorance of these Apostles is thus frankly and humbly recorded; for nothing can more powerfully tend to prove the utter change which must have passed over their spirits, before men so timid, so carnal, so Judaic, so unenlightened, could be transformed into the Apostles whose worth we know, and who—inspired by the facts which they had seen, and by the Holy Spirit who gave them wisdom and utterance—became, before their short lives were ended by violence, the mightiest teachers of the world.

"Lord, show us the Father," said Philip of Bethsaida, "and it sufficeth us!"

Show us the Father! what then did Philip expect? Some earth-shaking epiphany? Some blinding splendour in the heavens? Had he not yet learnt that He who is invisible cannot be seen by mortal eyes; that the finite cannot attain to the vision of the Infinite; that

[1] It is almost needless to remark how utterly inconsistent are some of the modern theories about the "tendency" origin of St. John's Gospel with the extraordinary vividness and insight into character displayed by this narrative. If this discourse, and the incidents which accompanied it, were otherwise than real, the obscure Gnostic who is supposed to have invented it must have been one of the greatest and most spiritually-minded men of genius whom the world has ever seen!

they who would see God must see no manner of similitudes; that His awful silence can only be broken to us through the medium of human voices, His being only comprehended by means of the things that He hath made? And had he wholly failed to discover that for these three years he had been walking with God? that neither he, nor any other mortal man, could ever know more of God in this world than that which should be revealed of Him by "the only-begotten Son which is in the bosom of the Father?"

Again there was no touch of anger, only a slight accent of pained surprise in the quiet answer, "Have I been so long with you, and yet hast thou not known me, Philip? He that hath seen me hath seen the Father, and how sayest thou then, Show us the Father?"

And then appealing to His words and to His works as only possible by the indwelling of His Father, He proceeded to unfold to them the coming of the Holy Ghost, and how that Comforter dwelling in them should make them one with the Father and with Him.

But at this point Judas Lebbæus had a difficulty.[1] He had not understood that the eye can only see that which it possesses the inherent power of seeing. He could not grasp the fact that God can become visible to those alone the eyes of whose understanding are open so that they can discern spiritual things. "Lord, how is it," he asked, "that thou wilt manifest thyself unto us, and not to the world?"

The difficulty was exactly of the same kind as Philip's had been—the total inability to distinguish between a physical and a spiritual manifestation; and without formally removing it, Jesus gave them all,

[1] John xiv. 22. The v. l. Ἰάκωβος is curious.

once more, the true clue to the comprehension of His words—that God lives with them that love Him, and that the proof of love is obedience. For all further teaching He referred them to the Comforter whom He was about to send, who should bring all things to their remembrance. And now He breathes upon them His blessing of peace, meaning to add but little more, because His conflict with the prince of this world should now begin.

At this point of the discourse there was a movement among the little company. "Arise," said Jesus, "let us go hence."

They rose from the table, and united their voices in a hymn which may well have been a portion of the great Hallel, and not improbably the 116th, 117th, and 118th Psalms. What an imperishable interest do these Psalms derive from such an association, and how full of meaning must many of the verses have been to some of them! With what intensity of feeling must they have joined in singing such words as these—"The sorrows of death compassed me, the pains of hell gat hold upon me; I found trouble and sorrow. Then called I upon the name of the Lord; O Lord, I beseech thee, deliver my soul;" or again, "What shall I render unto the Lord for all His benefits toward me? I will take the cup of salvation, and call upon the name of the Lord;" or once again, "Thou hast thrust sore at me that I might fall: but the Lord helped me. The Lord is my strength and my song, and is become my salvation. The stone which the builders refused is become the head-stone in the corner. This is the Lord's doing; it is marvellous in our eyes."

Before they started for their moonlight walk to the

Garden of Gethsemane, perhaps while yet they stood around their Lord when the Hallel was over, He once more spoke to them. First He told them of the need of closest union with Him, if they would bring forth fruit, and be saved from destruction. He clothed this lesson in the allegory of "the Vine and the Branches." There is no need to find any immediate circumstance which suggested the metaphor, beyond the "fruit of the vine" of which they had been partaking; but if any were required, we might suppose that, as He looked out into the night, He saw the moonlight silvering the leaves of a vine which clustered round the latticed window, or falling on the colossal golden vine which wreathed one of the Temple gates. But after impressing this truth in the vivid form of parable, He showed them how deep a source of joy it would be to them in the persecutions which awaited them from an angry world; and then in fuller, plainer, deeper language than He had ever used before, He told them, that, in spite of all the anguish with which they contemplated the coming separation from Him, it was actually *better* for them that His personal presence should be withdrawn in order that His spiritual presence might be yet nearer to them than it ever had been before. This would be effected by the coming of the Holy Ghost, when He who was now *with* them should be ever *in* them. The mission of that Comforter should be to convince[1] the world of sin, of righteousness, and of judgment; and He should guide *them* into all truth, and show them things to come. "He shall glorify me; for He shall receive of mine, and show it unto you." And now He was going to His Father; a little while, and they should

[1] John xvi. 8, ἐλέγξει. Cf. John viii. 9, 46; Jude 15, &c.

not see Him; and again a little while, and they should see Him.

The uncertainty as to what He meant carried the disciples once more to questions among themselves during one of the solemn pauses of His discourse. They would gladly have asked Him, but a deep awe was upon their spirits, and they did not dare. Already they had several times broken the current of His thoughts by questions which, though He did not reprove them, had evidently grieved Him by their emptiness, and by the misapprehension which they showed of all that He sought to impress upon them. So their whispered questioning died away into silence, but their Master kindly came to their relief. This, He told them, was to be their brief hour of anguish, but it was to be followed by a joy of which man could not rob them; and to that joy there need be no limit, for whatever might be their need they had but to ask the Father, and it should be fulfilled.[1] To that Father who Himself

[1] It is one of several minute coincidences (unavoidably obliterated in the English version) which show how uniformly our Lord claimed His divine origin, that whereas He used the word αἰτῶ, "peto," of all *other* prayers to God—being the word used of petitions to one who is superior—the word He uses to describe His own prayers is ἐρωτῶ, "rogo," which is (strictly speaking) the request of an equal from an equal. "'Ερωτᾶν notat familiarem petendi modum qualis inter colloquentes solet esse. Saepius de precibus Jesu occurrit (xvi. 26; xvii. 9, 15, 20) semel tantum de precibus fidelium" (Lampe). Again, when He bids His disciples believe on Him (John xiv. 1), the phrase used is πιστεύω εἰς, which never occurs elsewhere except of God, whereas the ordinary belief and trust in man is expressed by πιστεύω, with the dative (John i. 12; ii. 23; Matt. xviii. 6). Again, when He speaks of God as His Father the phrase always is ὁ πατὴρ, or ὁ πατήρ μου; but when He speaks of God as *our* Father, the word has no article. This is most strikingly seen in John xx. 17, ἀναβαίνω πρὸς τὸν πατέρα μου καὶ πατέρα ὑμῶν; where, as St. Augustine truly remarks, "Non ait Patrem *nostrum*; aliter ergo meum, aliter vestrum; naturâ meum, gratiâ vestrum" (Tract. cxxi.). "Nos per illum," says Bengel, "ille singularissime et primo."

loved them, for their belief in Him—to that Father, from whom He came, He was now about to return.

The disciples were deeply grateful for these plain and most consoling words. Once more they were unanimous in expressing their belief that He came forth from God. But Jesus sadly checked their enthusiasm. His words had been meant to give them peace in the present, and courage and hope for the future; yet He knew and told them that, in spite of all that they said, the hour was now close at hand when they should all be scattered in selfish terror, and leave Him alone—yet not alone, because the Father was with Him.

And after these words He lifted up His eyes to heaven, and uttered His great High-Priestly prayer: first, that His Father would invest His voluntary humanity with the eternal glory of which He had emptied Himself when He took the form of a servant; next, that He would keep through His own name these His loved ones who had walked with Him in the world;[1] and then that He would sanctify and make perfect not these alone, but all the myriads, all the long generations, which should hereafter believe through their word.

And when the tones of this divine prayer were hushed, they left the guest-chamber and stepped into the moonlit silence of the Oriental night.

[1] The E. V. misses the difference of tense and meaning in John xvii. 12, ἐτήρουν, *conservabam*; ἐφύλαξα, *custodivi*.

CHAPTER LVII.

GETHSEMANE—THE AGONY AND THE ARREST.

"Non mortem horruit simpliciter . . . peccata vero nostra, quorum onus illi erat impositum, suâ ingente mole eum premebant."—CALVIN (*ad* Matt. xxvi. 37).

THEIR way led them through one of the city gates—probably that which then corresponded to the present gate of St. Stephen—down the steep sides of the ravine, across the wady of the Kidron,[1] which lay a hundred feet below, and up the green and quiet slope beyond it. To one who has visited the scene at that very season of the

[1] The reading of St. John, πέραν τοῦ χειμάῤῥου τῶν κέδρων (xviii. 1; ℵ, D, τοῦ κέδρου), is probably no more than a curious instance of the Grecising of a Hebrew name, just as the brook Kishon is in 1 Kings xviii. 40 called χείμαῤῥος κισσῶν (of the Ivies): cf. LXX., 2 Sam. xv. 23; Jos. *Antt.* ix. 7, § 3. We do not hear of any cedars there, but even if τῶν Κέδρων be the true reading, the word may have been *surfrappé* by the Evangelist himself; τοῦ κεδρών is, however, the most probable reading. The Kidron is a ravine rather than a brook. No water runs in it except occasionally, after unusually heavy rains. Nor can we see any special significance—any "pathetic fallacy"—in the name Kidron, as though it meant (Stier vii. 220) "the dark brook in the deep valley," with allusion to David's humiliation (1 Kings xv. 13), and idolatrous abominations (2 Kings xxiii. 4, &c.), and the fact that it was a kind of sewer for the Temple refuse. "There," says Stier, "surrounded by such memorials and typical allusions, the Lord descends into the dust of humiliation and anguish, as His glorification had taken place upon the top of the mountain." This attempt to see more in the words of the Gospel than they can fairly be supposed to convey would soon lead to all the elaborate mysticism and trifling of Rabbinic exegesis.

year and at that very hour of the night—who has felt the solemn hush of the silence even at this short distance from the city wall—who has seen the deep shadows flung by the great boles of the ancient olive-trees, and the chequering of light that falls on the sward through their moonlight-silvered leaves, it is more easy to realise the awe which crept over those few Galilæans, as in almost unbroken silence, with something perhaps of secrecy, and with a weight of mysterious dread brooding over their spirits, they followed Him, who with bowed head and sorrowing heart walked before them to His willing doom.[1]

We are told but of one incident in that last and memorable walk through the midnight to the familiar Garden of Gethsemane.[2] It was a last warning to the disciples in general, to St. Peter in particular. It may be that the dimness, the silence, the desertion of their position, the dull echo of their footsteps, the stealthy aspect which their movements wore, the agonising sense that treachery was even now at work, was beginning already to produce an icy chill of cowardice in their hearts; sadly did Jesus turn and say to them that on that very night they should all be offended in Him—all find their connection with Him a stumbling-block in their path—and the old prophecy should be fulfilled, "I will smite the shepherd, and the sheep shall be scattered abroad." And yet, in spite of all, as a shepherd would He go before them, leading the way to Galilee?[3] They all repudiated the possibility of such an abandonment of their Lord, and Peter, touched

[1] Luke xxii. 39.
[2] Matt. xxvi. 31—35; Mark xiv. 27—31.
[3] Zech. xiii. 7; Matt. xxvi. 32, προάξω ὑμᾶς.

already by this apparent distrust of His stability, haunted perhaps by some dread lest Jesus felt any doubt of *him*, was loudest and most emphatic in his denial. Even if all should be offended, yet never would he be offended. Was it a secret misgiving in his own heart which made his asseveration so prominent and so strong? Not even the repetition of the former warning, that, ere the cock should crow, he would thrice have denied his Lord, could shake him from his positive assertion that even the necessity of death itself should never drive him to such a sin. And Jesus only listened in mournful silence to vows which should so soon be scattered into air.

So they came to Gethsemane, which is about half a mile from the city walls. It was a garden or orchard[1] marked probably by some slight enclosure; and as it had been a place of frequent resort for Jesus and His followers, we may assume that it belonged to some friendly owner. The name Gethsemane means "the oil-press," and doubtless it was so called from a press to crush the olives yielded by the countless trees from which the hill derives its designation. Any one who has rested at noonday in the gardens of En-gannim or Nazareth in spring, and can recall the pleasant shade yielded by the interlaced branches of olive and pomegranate, and fig and myrtle, may easily imagine what kind of spot it was. The traditional site, venerable and beautiful as it is from the age and size of the grey gnarled olive-trees, of which one is still known as the Tree of the Agony, is perhaps, too public—being, as it always must have been, at the angle formed by the two paths which lead over the summit and shoulder of Olivet—to be regarded as the actual spot. It was more

[1] κῆπος (John xviii. 1); χωρίον (Matt. xxvi. 36).

probably one of the secluded hollows at no great distance from it which witnessed that scene of awful and pathetic mystery.[1] But although the exact spot cannot be determined with certainty, the general position of Gethsemane is clear, and then as now the chequering moonlight, the grey leaves, the dark brown trunks, the soft greensward, the ravine with Olivet towering over it to the eastward and Jerusalem to the west, must have been the main external features of a place which must be regarded with undying interest while Time shall be, as the place where the Saviour of mankind entered alone into the Valley of the Shadow.

Jesus knew that the awful hour of His deepest humiliation had arrived—that from this moment till the utterance of that great cry with which He expired, nothing remained for Him on earth but the torture of physical pain and the poignancy of mental anguish. All that the human frame can tolerate of suffering was to be heaped upon His shrinking body; every misery that cruel and crushing insult can inflict was to weigh heavy on His soul; and in this torment of body and agony of soul even the high and radiant serenity of His divine spirit was to suffer a short but terrible eclipse. Pain in its acutest sting, shame in its most overwhelming brutality, all the burden of the sin and mystery of man's

[1] I had the deep and memorable happiness of being able to see Gethsemane with two friends, unaccompanied by any guide, late at night and under the full glow of the Paschal moon, on the night of April 14th, 1870. It is usually argued that the eight old time-hallowed olive-trees cannot reach back to the time of Christ, because Titus cut down the trees all round the city. This argument is not decisive; but still it is more probable that these trees are only the successors and descendants of those which have always given its name to the sacred hill. It is quite certain that Gethsemane must have been *near* this spot, and the tradition which ffxes the site is very old.

existence in its apostacy and fall—this was what He must now face in all its most inexplicable accumulation. But one thing remained before the actual struggle, the veritable agony, began. He had to brace His body, to nerve His soul, to calm His spirit by prayer and solitude to meet that hour in which all that is evil in the Power of Evil should wreak its worst upon the Innocent and Holy. And He must face that hour alone: no human eye must witness, except through the twilight and shadow, the depth of His suffering. Yet He would have gladly shared their sympathy; it helped Him in this hour of darkness to feel that they were near, and that those were nearest who loved Him best. "Stay here," He said to the majority, "while I go there and pray." Leaving them to sleep on the damp grass, each wrapped in his outer garment, He took with Him Peter and James and John, and went about a stone's-throw farther. It was well that Peter should face all that was involved in allegiance to Christ: it was well that James and John should know what was that cup which they had desired pre-eminently to drink. But soon even the society of these chosen and trusted ones was more than He could bear. A grief beyond utterance, a struggle beyond endurance, a horror of great darkness, a giddiness and stupefaction of soul overmastered Him, as with the sinking swoon of an anticipated death.[1] It was a tumult of emotion which none must see. "My soul," He said, "is full of anguish, even unto death.

[1] Matt. xxvi. 37, ἤρξατο λυπεῖσθαι καὶ ἀδημονεῖν; Mark xiv. 33, ἐκθαμβεῖσθαι. Cf. Job xviii. 20 (Aqu., ἀδημονήσουσιν); Ps. cxvi. 11. See Pearson, *On the Creed*, Art. iv. *n.* The derivation may be from ἀ δημέω, "I am carried away from myself;" or, perhaps more probably, from ἀδῆσαι, "to loathe." It is remarkable that this verse (Matt. xxvi. 38), and John xii. 27, are the only passages where Jesus used the word ψυχὴ of Himself.

Stay here and keep watch." Reluctantly He tore Himself away from their sustaining tenderness and devotion,[1] and retired yet farther, perhaps out of the moonlight into the shadow. And there, until slumber overpowered them, they were conscious of how dreadful was that paroxysm of prayer and suffering through which He passed. They saw Him sometimes on His knees, sometimes outstretched in prostrate supplication upon the damp ground;[2] they heard snatches of the sounds of murmured anguish in which His humanity pleaded with the divine will of His Father. The actual words might vary, but the substance was the same throughout. "Abba, Father, all things are possible unto Thee; take away this cup from me; nevertheless, not what I will, but what Thou wilt."[3]

And that prayer in all its infinite reverence and awe was heard;[4] that strong crying and those tears were not rejected. We may not intrude too closely into this scene. It is shrouded in a halo and a mystery into which no footstep may penetrate. We, as we contemplate it, are like those disciples—our senses are confused, our perceptions are not clear. We can but enter into their amazement and sore distress. Half waking, half oppressed with an irresistible weight of troubled slumber, they only felt that they were dim witnesses of an unutterable agony, far deeper than anything which they could fathom, as it far transcended all that, even

[1] Luke xxii. 41, ἀπεσπάσθη ἀπ' αὐτῶν. Cf. Acts xxi. 1.

[2] Luke xxii. 41, θεὶς τὰ γόνατα. Matt. xxvi. 39, ἔπεσεν ἐπὶ πρόσωπον αὐτοῦ.

[3] Nothing, as Dean Alford remarks, could prove more decisively the insignificance of the letter in comparison with the spirit, than the fact that the three Evangelists vary in the actual expression of the prayer.

[4] Heb. v. 7, εἰσακουσθεὶς ἀπὸ τῆς εὐλαβείας

in our purest moments, we can pretend to understand. The place seems haunted by presences of good and evil, struggling in mighty but silent contest for the eternal victory. They see Him, before whom the demons had fled in howling terror, lying on His face upon the ground. They hear that voice wailing in murmurs of broken agony, which had commanded the wind and the sea, and they obeyed Him. The great drops of anguish which drop from Him in the deathful struggle, look to them like heavy gouts of blood. Under the dark shadows of the trees, amid the interrupted moonlight, it seems to them that there is an angel with Him, who supports His failing strength, who enables Him to rise victorious from those first prayers with nothing but the crimson traces of that bitter struggle upon His brow.[1]

And whence came all this agonised failing of heart, this fearful amazement, this horror of great darkness, this passion which almost brought Him down to the grave before a single pang had been inflicted upon Him—which forced from Him the rare and intense phenomenon of a blood-stained sweat—which almost prostrated body, and soul, and spirit with one final blow? Was it the mere dread of death—the mere effort and determination to face that which He foreknew in all its dreadfulness,

[1] The verses (Luke xxii. 43, 44) are omitted in some of the best MSS. (*e.g.*, even A, B, and the first corrector of ℵ), and were so at a very early age. Professor Westcott thinks that the varying evidence for their authenticity points to a recension of the Gospel by the Evangelist himself (*Introd.*, p. 306). Olshausen and Lange here understand the angel of "the accession of spiritual power"—"the angel of the hearing of prayer" (verse 43, ὤφθη δὲ αὐτῷ). It seems certain that an αἱματώδης ἱδρὼς under abnormal pathological circumstances is not unknown; and even if it were, all that the Evangelist *says* is ἐγένετο ὁ ἱδρὼς αὐτοῦ ὡσεὶ θρόμβοι αἵματος, κ.τ.λ. See Dr. Stroud, *On the Physical Cause of the Death of Christ*, p. 183; Bynaeus, *De Morte Christi*, ii. 33.

but from which, nevertheless, His soul recoiled? There have been those who have dared—I can scarcely write it without shame and sorrow—to speak very slightingly about Gethsemane; to regard that awful scene, from the summit of their ignorant presumption, with an almost contemptuous dislike—to speak as though Jesus had there shown a cowardly sensibility. Thus, at the very moment when we should most wonder and admire, they

"Not even from the Holy One of Heaven
Refrain their tongues blasphèmous."[1]

And yet, if no other motive influence them—if they merely regard Him as a Prophet preparing for a cruel death—if no sense of decency, no power of sympathy, restrain them from thus insulting even a Martyr's agony at the moment when its pang was most intense—does not common fairness, does not the most ordinary historic criticism, show them how cold and false, if nothing worse, must be the miserable insensibility which prevents them from seeing that it could have been no mere dread of pain, no mere shrinking from death, which thus agitated to its inmost centre the pure and innocent soul of the Son of Man?[2] Could not even a child see how inconsistent would be such an hypothesis with that heroic fortitude which fifteen hours of subsequent sleepless agony could not disturb—with the majestic silence before priest, and procurator, and king—with the endurance from which the extreme of torture could not

[1] Ps. xl. 13.

[2] So Celsus (ap. Orig. ii. 24), and Julian (Theod. Mops.; Munter, *Fragm. Patr.* i. 121). Vanini, when taken to the scaffold, boasted his superiority to Jesus, "Illi in extremis prae timore imbellis sudor; *ego imperturbatus morior*" (Grammond, *Hist. Gall.* iii. 211). The Jews made the same taunt (R. Isaak b. Abraham, *Chissuh Emunah,* in Wagenseil). The passages are all quoted by Hofmann, p. 439.

wring one cry—with the calm and infinite ascendancy which overawed the hardened and worldly Roman into involuntary respect—with the undisturbed supremacy of soul which opened the gates of Paradise to the repentant malefactor, and breathed compassionate forgiveness on the apostate priests? The Son of Man humiliated into prostration by the mere abject fear of death, which trembling old men, and feeble maidens, and timid boys —a Polycarp, a Blandina, an Attalus—have yet braved without a sigh or a shudder, solely through faith in His name! Strange that *He* should be thus insulted by impious tongues, who brought to light that life and immortality from whence came the

> "Ruendi
> In ferrum mens prona viris, animaeque capaces
> Mortis, et ignavum rediturae parcere vitae!"[1]

The meanest of idiots, the coarsest of criminals, have advanced to the scaffold without a tremor or a sob, and many a brainless and brutal murderer has mounted the ladder with a firm step, and looked round upon a yelling mob with an unflinching countenance. To adopt the commonplace of orators, "There is no passion in the mind of man so weak but it mates and masters the fear of death. Revenge triumphs over death; love slights it; honour aspireth to it; grief flieth to it; fear pre-occupateth it. A man would die, though he were neither valiant nor miserable, only upon a weariness to do the same thing so oft over and over. It is no less worthy to observe how little alteration in good spirits the approaches of death make: for they appear to be the same men till the last instant." It is as natural to die as to be born. The Christian hardly needs to be told that it

[1] Luc. *Phars.* i. 455.

was no such vulgar fear which forced from his Saviour that sweat of blood. No, it was something infinitely more than this: infinitely more than the highest stretch of our imagination can realise. It was something far deadlier than death. It was the burden and the mystery of the world's sin which lay heavy on His heart; it was the tasting, in the divine humanity of a sinless life, the bitter cup which sin had poisoned; it was the bowing of Godhead to endure a stroke to which man's apostacy had lent such frightful possibilities. It was the sense, too, of how virulent, how frightful, must have been the force of evil in the Universe of God which could render necessary so infinite a sacrifice. It was the endurance, by the perfectly guiltless, of the worst malice which human hatred could devise; it was to experience in the bosom of perfect innocence and perfect love, all that was detestable in human ingratitude, all that was pestilent in human hypocrisy, all that was cruel in human rage. It was to brave the last triumph of Satanic spite and fury, uniting against His lonely head all the flaming arrows of Jewish falsity and heathen corruption—the concentrated wrath of the rich and respectable, the yelling fury of the blind and brutal mob. It was to feel that His own, to whom He came, loved darkness rather than light—that the race of the chosen people could be wholly absorbed in one insane repulsion against infinite goodness and purity and love.

Through all this He passed in that hour which, with a recoil of sinless horror beyond our capacity to conceive, foretasted a worse bitterness than the worst bitterness of death. And after a time—victorious indeed, but weary almost to fainting, like His ancestor Jacob, with the struggle of those supplications—He came to seek one touch of human support and human sympathy from the chosen of the chosen—His three Apostles. Alas! He found them sleeping. It was an hour of fear and peril; yet no certainty of danger, no love for Jesus, no feeling for His unspeakable dejection, had sufficed to hold their eyes waking. Their grief, their weariness, their intense excitement, had sought relief in heavy slumber. Even Peter, after all his impetuous promises, lay in deep sleep, for his eyes were heavy. "Simon, sleepest thou?" was all He said. As the sad reproachful sentence fell on their ears, and startled them from their slumbers, "Were ye so unable," He asked, "to watch with me a single hour? Watch and pray that ye enter not into temptation." And then, not to palliate their failure, but rather to point out the peril of it, "The spirit," He added, "is willing, but the flesh is weak."

Once more He left them, and again, with deeper intensity, repeated the same prayer as before, and in a pause of His emotion came back to His disciples. But they had once more fallen asleep; nor, when He awoke them, could they, in their heaviness and confusion, find anything to say to Him. Well might He have said, in the words of David, "Thy rebuke hath broken my heart; I am full of heaviness; I looked for some to have pity on me, but there was no man, neither found I any to comfort me."[1]

For the third and last time—but now with a deeper calm, and a brighter serenity of that triumphant confidence which had breathed through the High-Priestly prayer—He withdrew to find His only consolation in communing with God. And there he found all that He needed. Before that hour was over He was prepared

[1] Ps. lxix. 20.

for the worst that Satan or man could do. He knew all that would befall Him; perhaps He had already caught sight of the irregular glimmering of lights as His pursuers descended from the Temple precincts. Yet there was no trace of agitation in His quiet words when, coming a third time and finding them once more sleeping, "Sleep on now," He said, "and take your rest. It is enough. The hour is come. Lo! the Son of Man is being betrayed into the hands of sinners." For all the aid that you can render, for all the comfort your sympathy can bestow, sleep on. But all is altered now. It is not I who now wish to break these your heavy slumbers. They will be very rudely and sternly broken by others. "Rise, then; let us be going. Lo! he that betrayeth me is at hand."[1]

Yes, it was more than time to rise, for while saints had slumbered sinners had plotted and toiled in exaggerated preparation. While they slept in their heavy anguish, the traitor had been very wakeful in his active malignity. More than two hours had passed since from the lighted chamber of their happy communion he had plunged into the night, and those hours had been very fully occupied. He had gone to the High Priests and Pharisees, agitating them and hurrying them on with his own passionate precipitancy; and partly perhaps out of genuine terror of Him with whom he had to deal, partly to enhance his own importance, had got the leading Jews to furnish him with a motley band composed of their own servants, of the Temple watch with

[1] It has been asked why St. John tells us nothing of the agony? We do not know; but it may very likely have been because the story had already been told as fully as it was known. *Certainly,* his silence did not spring from any notion that the agony was unworthy of Christ's grandeur (see xii. 27; xviii. 11).

their officers, and even with a part at least of the Roman garrison from the Tower of Antonia, under the command of their tribune.[1] They were going against One who was deserted and defenceless, yet the soldiers were armed with swords, and even the promiscuous throng had provided themselves with sticks. They were going to seize One who would make no attempt at flight or concealment, and the full moon shed its lustre on their unhallowed expedition; yet, lest He should escape them in some limestone grotto, or in the deep shade of the olives, they carried lanterns and torches in their hands. It is evident that they made their movements as noiseless and stealthy as possible; but at night a deep stillness hangs over an Oriental city, and so large a throng could not move unnoticed. Already, as Jesus was awaking His sleepy disciples, His ears had caught in the distance the clank of swords, the tread of hurrying footsteps, the ill-suppressed tumult of an advancing crowd. He knew all that awaited Him; He knew that the quiet garden which He had loved, and where He had so often held happy intercourse with His disciples, was familiar to the traitor. Those unwonted and hostile sounds, that red glare of lamps and torches athwart the moonlit interspaces of the olive-yards, were enough

[1] ἡ οὖν σπεῖρα καὶ ὁ χιλίαρχος (John xviii. 12; cf. 3); but clearly St. John does not mean that *all the* 600 soldiers of the garrison accompanied Judas. Of course the consent of Pilate must have been obtained with the express object of prejudicing him against Jesus as a dangerous person. The στρατηγοὶ τοῦ ἱεροῦ of Luke xxii. 52 are Levitical officers. Critics have tried, as in so many instances, to show that there is an error here because there was only one "captain of the Temple" (or *ish 'ar ha-bait*) whose office seems to date from the Captivity [Neh. ii. 8; vii. 2 (*sar ha-bîrah*); cf. 2 Macc. iii. 4]. But in 3 Esdr. i. 8, we find οἱ ἐπιστατάται τοῦ ἱερôυ, *three* in number; and as the captain had guards under him, to make the rounds, (Jos. *B. J.* vi. 5, § 3, οἱ τοῦ ἱεροῦ φύλακες ἤγγειλαν τῷ στρατηγῷ), the name might be applied generally to the whole body.

to show that Judas had betrayed the secret of His retirement, and was even now at hand.

And even as Jesus spoke the traitor himself appeared.[1] Overdoing his part—acting in the too-hurried impetuosity of a crime so hideous that he dared not pause to think—he pressed forward into the enclosure, and was in front of all the rest.[2] "Comrade," said Jesus to him as he hurried forward, "the crime for which thou art come——"[3] The sentence seems to have been cut short by the deep agitation of His spirit, nor did Judas return any answer, intent only on giving to his confederates his shameful preconcerted signal. "He whom I kiss," he had said to them, "the same is He. Seize

[1] Throughout the description of these scenes I have simply taken the four Gospel narratives as one whole, and regarded them as supplementing each other. It will be seen how easily, and without a single violent hypothesis, they fall into one harmonious, probable, and simple narrative. Lange here adopts what seems to me to be the best order of sequence. The fact that Judas gave the signal too early for his own purpose seems to follow from John xviii. 4—9 (ἐξῆλθεν). Alford thinks it "inconceivable" that Judas had given his traitor-kiss *before* this scene; but his own arrangement will surely strike every careful reader as much more inconceivable.

[2] Luke xxii. 47.

[3] Matt. xxvi. 50, ἐφ' ὃ πάρει—perhaps this is an exclamation for "What a crime!" I have taken it in the sense of an aposiopesis, "What thou art here for (do)." But perhaps ἐφ' ὃ; may = ἐπὶ τί; in Hellenistic Greek (Winer, III. xxiv. 4). It is not, however, likely that Jesus would have asked a question on the purpose of Judas's coming. Observe Ἑταῖρε (Matt. xxvi. 50), "Comrade," *not* "friend" (φίλε), as most versions wrongly translate it. Never, even in the ordinary conventionalities of life, would Christ use a term which was not strictly true. There is even something stern in the use of ἑταῖρε (cf. Matt. xx. 13; xxii. 12). Judas, in the strictest sense of the word, *had* been an ἑταῖρος; but as Ammonius says, ὁ ἑταῖρος οὐ πάντως φίλος. Hence the lines of Houdenius (*De Pass.*)—

"Si honoras, O dulcis Domine,
Inimicum amici nomine,
Quales erunt amoris carmine
Qui te canunt et modulamine?"

although exquisitely beautiful, are not strictly accurate.

Him at once, and lead Him away safely."[1] And so, advancing to Jesus with his usual cold title of address, he exclaimed, "Rabbi, Rabbi, hail!" and profaned the sacred cheek of his Master with a kiss of overacted salutation.[2] "Judas," said Jesus to him, with stern and sad reproach, "dost thou betray the Son of Man with a kiss?" These words were enough, for they simply revealed the man to himself, by stating his hideous act in all its simplicity; and the method of his treachery was so unparalleled in its heinousness, so needless and spontaneously wicked, that more words would have been superfluous. With feelings that the very devils might have pitied, the wretch slunk back to the door of the enclosure, towards which the rest of the crowd were now beginning to press.

"Lord, shall we smite with the sword?" was the eager question of St. Peter, and the only other disciple provided with a weapon; for, being within the garden, the Apostles were still unaware of the number of the captors.[3] Jesus did not at once answer the question;

[1] Mark xiv. 44, κρατήσατε . . . καὶ ἀπαγάγετε ἀσφαλῶς—one of the many slight undesigned traces of Judas's involuntary terror and misgiving. His words probably were *Schalôm alêka rabbi*, "*Peace* be to thee, Rabbi!" but there came no *alêka Shalôm* in reply: there *was* no peace for the errand on which Judas had come. Mr. Monro observes how characteristic are these snatches of dialogue like τὸ εἰ δύνασαι in Mark ix. 23 (*v.* p. 34), and the τὴν ἀρχὴν ὅτι καὶ λαλῶ ὑμῖν (John viii. 25; *v.* p. 75), and ἐᾶτε ἕως τούτου (Luke xxii. 51; *v. infr.*, p. 320). Surely the most inventive of inventors neither could nor would invent phrases like these!

[2] The κατεφίλησεν of Matt. xxvi. 49; Mark xiv. 45, as compared with the φιλήσω before, is clearly meant to imply a fervent kiss. Something of the same kind seems to be intended by the "Rabbi! Rabbi!" of Mark xiv. 45. Κύριε was the ordinary address of the Apostles to Christ; but the colder and feebler "Rabbi" seems to have been the title always used by Judas (Bengel). Cf. *supr.*, p. 288.

[3] All this is obvious from the context. The place which, since the days of St. Helena, has been pointed out as the garden of Gethsemane may or

for no sooner had He repelled the villainous falsity of Judas than He Himself stepped out of the enclosure to face His pursuers. Not flying, not attempting to hide Himself, He stood there before them in the full moonlight in His unarmed and lonely majesty, shaming by His calm presence their superfluous torches and superfluous arms.

"Whom are ye seeking?" He asked.

The question was not objectless. It was asked, as St. John points out,[1] to secure His Apostles from all molestation; and we may suppose also that it served to make all who were present the witnesses of His arrest, and so to prevent the possibility of any secret assassination or foul play.

"Jesus of Nazareth," they answered.

Their excitement and awe preferred this indirect answer, though if there could have been any doubt as to who the speaker was, Judas was there—the eye of the Evangelist noticed him, trying in vain to lurk amid the serried ranks of the crowd—to prevent any possible mistake which might have been caused by the failure of his premature and therefore disconcerted signal.

"I am He,"[2] said Jesus.

Those quiet words produced a sudden paroxysm of

may *not* be the authentic site; but there can be little doubt that the actual *κῆπος* or *χωοίον* had an enclosing wall.

[1] John xviii. 8. How absolutely does this narrative shatter to pieces the infamous calumny of the Jews, *κρυπτόμενος μὲν καὶ διαδιδράσκων ἐπονειδέστατα ἑάλω* (Orig. c. *Cels.* 2, 9, quoted by Keim, III. ii. 298). Keim, without ignoring Celsus's use of Jewish calumnies, thinks that this attack is founded on John x. 39, &c.

[2] John xviii. 5. One of those minute touches which so clearly mark the eye-witness—which are inexplicable on any other supposition, and which abound in the narrative of the beloved disciple. To give to the "I am He" any mystic significance (Isa. xliii. 10, LXX.; John viii. 28), as is done by Lange and others, seems unreasonable.

amazement and dread. That answer so gentle "had in it a strength greater than the eastern wind, or the voice of thunder, for God was in that 'still voice,' and it struck them down to the ground." Instances are not wanting in history in which the untroubled brow, the mere glance, the calm bearing of some defenceless man, has disarmed and paralysed his enemies. The savage and brutal Gauls could not lift their swords to strike the majestic senators of Rome. "I cannot slay Marius," exclaimed the barbarian slave, flinging down his sword and flying headlong from the prison into which he had been sent to murder the aged hero.[1] Is there, then, any ground for the scoffing scepticism with which many have received St. John's simple but striking narrative, that, at the words "*I am He,*" a movement of contagious terror took place among the crowd, and, starting back in confusion, some of them fell to the ground? Nothing surely was more natural. It must be remembered that Judas was among them; that *his* soul was undoubtedly in a state of terrible perturbation; that Orientals are specially liable to sudden panic; that fear is an emotion eminently sympathetic; that most of them must have

[1] Vell. Paterc. ii. 19. Other commentators adduce the further instances of M. Antonius (Val. Max. viii. 9, 2), Probus, Pertinax, Teligny, stepson to Admiral Coligny, Bishop Stanislaus, &c. No one, so far as I have seen, quotes the instance of Avidius Cassius, who, springing to the door of his tent in night-dress, quelled a mutinous army by his mere presence. In the Talmud, seventy of the strongest Egyptians fall to the earth in attempting to bind Simeon, the brother of Joseph. Jeremy Taylor beautifully says, "But there was a divinity upon Him that they could not seize Him at first; but as a wave climbing of a rock is beaten back and scattered into members, till falling down it creeps with gentle waftings, and kisses the feet of the stony mountain, and so encircles it: so the soldiers coming at first with a rude attempt, were twice repelled by the glory of His person, till they falling at His feet, were at last admitted to a seizure of His body." (*Life of Christ,* III. xv.)

heard of the mighty miracles of Jesus, and that all were at any rate aware that He claimed to be a Prophet; that the manner in which He met this large multitude, which the alarms of Judas had dictated as essential to His capture, suggested the likelihood of some appeal to supernatural powers; that they were engaged in one of those deeds of guilty violence and midnight darkness which paralyse the stoutest minds. When we bear this in mind, and when we remember too that on many occasions in His history the mere presence and word ot Christ had sufficed to quell the fury of the multitude, and to keep Him safe in the midst of them,[1] it hardly needs any recourse to miracle to account for the fact that these official marauders and their infamous guide recoiled from those simple words, "I am He," as though the lightning had suddenly been flashed into their faces.

While they stood cowering and struggling there, He again asked them, "Whom are ye seeking?" Again they replied, "Jesus of Nazareth." "I told you," He answered, "that I am He. If, then, ye are seeking me, let these go away." For He Himself had said in His prayer, "Of those whom Thou hast given me have I lost none."

The words were a signal to the Apostles that they could no longer render Him any service, and that they might now consult their own safety if they would. But when they saw that He meant to offer no resistance, that He was indeed about to surrender Himself to His enemies, some pulse of nobleness or of shame throbbed in the impetuous soul of Peter; and hopeless and useless as all resistance had now become, he yet drew his sword, and with a feeble and ill-aimed blow severed the ear of

[1] Luke iv. 30; John vii. 30; viii. 59; x. 39; Mark xi. 18 (see Vol. I., p. 228, &c.)

a man named Malchus, a servant of the High Priest. Instantly Jesus stopped the ill-timed and dangerous struggle. "Return that sword of thine into its place," He said to Peter, "for all they that take the sword shall perish with the sword;" and then He reproachfully asked His rash disciple whether he *really* supposed that He could not escape if He would? whether the mere breathing of a prayer would not secure for Him—had He not voluntarily intended to fulfil the Scriptures by drinking the cup which His Father had given Him—the aid, not of twelve timid Apostles, but of more than twelve legions of angels?"[1] And then, turning to the soldiers who were holding Him, He said, "Suffer ye thus far,"[2] and in one last act of miraculous mercy touched and healed the wound.

In the confusion of the night this whole incident seems to have passed unnoticed except by a very few. At any rate, it made no impression upon these hardened men. Their terror had quite vanished, and had been replaced by insolent confidence. The Great Prophet had voluntarily resigned Himself; He was their helpless captive. No thunder had rolled; no angel flashed down from heaven for His deliverance; no miraculous fire devoured amongst them. They saw before them nothing but a weary unarmed man, whom one of His own

[1] A legion during the Empire consisted of about 6,000 men. The fact that St. John alone mentions the names of St. Peter and Malchus may arise simply from his having been more accurately acquainted than the other Evangelists with the events of that heart-shaking scene; but there is nothing absurd or improbable in the current supposition, that the name of Peter may have been purposely kept in the background in the earliest cycle of Christian records.

[2] This may either mean, "Let me free for one moment only, while I heal this wounded man," as Alford not improbably understands it; or, "Excuse this single act of resistance."

most intimate followers had betrayed, and whose arrest was simply watched in helpless agony by a few terrified Galilæans. They had fast hold of Him, and already some chief priests, and elders, and leading officers of the Temple-guard had ventured to come out of the dark background from which they had securely seen His capture, and to throng about Him in insulting curiosity. To these especially[1] He turned, and said to them, "Have ye come out as against a robber with swords and staves? When I was daily with you in the Temple ye did not stretch out your hands against me. But this is your hour, and the power of darkness." Those fatal words quenched the last gleam of hope in the minds of His followers. "Then His disciples, all of them"[2]—even the fiery Peter, even the loving John—"forsook Him, and fled." At that supreme moment only one unknown youth—perhaps the owner of Gethsemane, perhaps St. Mark the Evangelist,[3] perhaps Lazarus the brother of

[1] Luke xxii. 52, εἶπε δὲ . . . πρὸς τοὺς προσγενομένους πρὸς αὐτὸν ἀρχιερεῖς, κ. τ. λ.

[2] Matt. xxvi. 56, οἱ μαθηταὶ πάντες. Many readers will thank me here for quoting the fine lines from Browning's *Death in the Desert* :—

"Forsake the Christ thou sawest transfigured, Him
Who trod the sea and brought the dead to life
What should wring this from thee? Ye laugh and ask
What wrung it? Even a torchlight and a noise,
The sudden Roman faces, violent hands,
And fear of what the Jews might do! Just that,
And it is written, 'I forsook and fled.'
There was my trial, and it ended thus."

[3] Mark xiv. 51, 52 only. As to the supposition that it was Lazarus—founded partly on the locality, partly on the probabilities of the case, partly on the fact that the σινδὼν was a garment that only a person of some wealth would possess—see a beautiful article on "Lazarus," by Professor Plumptre, in the *Dict. of the Bible.* Ewald's supposition, that it was St. Paul (!), seems to me amazing. The word עָרוֹם, γυμνὸς, though, like the Latin *nudus,* it constantly means "with only the *under* robe on" (1 Sam. xix. 24; John xxi. 7; Hes. Ἔργ., 391; Virg. *G.* i. 299), is here probably *literal.*

Martha and Mary—ventured, in his intense excitement, to hover on the outskirts of the hostile crowd. He had apparently been roused from sleep, for he had nothing to cover him except the *sindón*, or linen sheet, in which he had been sleeping. But the Jewish emissaries, either out of the mere wantonness of a crowd at seeing a person in an unwonted guise, or because they resented his too close intrusion, seized hold of the sheet which he had wrapped about him; whereupon he too was suddenly terrified, and fled away naked, leaving the linen garment in their hands.

Jesus was now absolutely alone in the power of His enemies. At the command of the tribune His hands were tied behind His back,[1] and forming a close array around Him, the Roman soldiers, followed and surrounded by the Jewish servants, led Him once more through the night, over the Kedron, and up the steep city slope beyond it, to the palace of the High Priest.

[1] John xviii. 12.

CHAPTER LVIII.

JESUS BEFORE THE PRIESTS AND THE SANHEDRIN.

הוו מתונים בדין, "Be slow in judgment."—*Pirke Abhôth*, i. 1.

ALTHOUGH sceptics have dwelt with disproportioned persistency upon a multitude of "discrepancies" in the fourfold narrative of Christ's trial, condemnation, death, and resurrection, yet these are not of a nature to cause the slightest anxiety to a Christian scholar; nor need they awaken the most momentary distrust in any one who—even if he have no deeper feelings in the matter—approaches the Gospels with no preconceived theory, whether of infallibility or of dishonesty, to support, and merely accepts them for that which, at the lowest, they claim to be—histories honest and faithful up to the full knowledge of the writers, but each, if taken alone, confessedly fragmentary and obviously incomplete. After repeated study, I declare, quite fearlessly, that though the slight variations are numerous—though the lesser particulars cannot in every instance be rigidly and minutely accurate—though no one of the narratives taken singly would give us an adequate impression—yet, so far from there being, in this part of the Gospel story, any irreconcilable contradiction, it is perfectly possible to discover how one Evangelist supplements the details furnished by another, and perfectly possible to understand the true sequence of the incidents by combining into one whole the separate indications which they furnish. It is easy to call such combinations arbitrary and baseless; but they are only arbitrary in so far as we cannot always be absolutely *certain* that the succession of facts was exactly such as we suppose; and so far are they from being baseless, that, to the careful reader of the Gospels, they carry with them a conviction little short of certainty. If we treat the Gospels as we should treat any other authentic documents recording all that the authors knew, or all that they felt themselves commissioned to record, of the crowded incidents in one terrible and tumultuous day and night, we shall, with care and study, see how all that they tell us falls accurately into its proper position in the general narrative, and shows us a sixfold trial, a quadruple derision, a triple acquittal, a twice-repeated condemnation of Christ our Lord.

Reading the Gospels side by side, we soon perceive that of the three successive trials which our Lord underwent at the hands of the Jews, the first only—that before Annas—is related to us by St. John; the second —that before Caiaphas—by St. Matthew and St. Mark; the third—that before the Sanhedrin—by St. Luke alone.[1] Nor is there anything strange in this, since the first was the practical, the second the potential, the third the actual and formal decision, that sentence of death

[1] But nevertheless, St. John distinctly alludes to the *second* trial (xviii. 24, where ἀπέστειλεν means "sent," not "had sent," as in the E. V.; and cf. xi. 46); and St. Matthew and St. Mark imply the *third* (Matt. xxvii. 1; Mark xv. 1). St. Luke, though he contents himself with the narration of the third only—which was the only legal one—yet also distinctly leaves room for the first and second (xxii. 54).

should be passed judicially upon Him. Each of the three trials might, from a different point of view, have been regarded as the most fatal and important of the three. That of Annas was the authoritative *praejudicium*, that of Caiaphas the real determination, that of the entire Sanhedrin at daybreak the final ratification.[1]

When the tribune, who commanded the detachment of Roman soldiers, had ordered Jesus to be bound, they led Him away without an attempt at opposition. Midnight was already passed as they hurried Him, from the moonlit shadows of green Gethsemane, through the hushed streets of the sleeping city, to the palace[2] of the High Priest. It seems to have been jointly occupied by the prime movers in this black iniquity, Annas and his son-in-law, Joseph Caiaphas. They led Him to Annas first. It is true that this Hanan, son of Seth, the Ananus of Josephus, and the Annas of the Evangelists, had only been the actual High Priest for seven years (A.D. 7—14), and that, more than twenty years before this period, he had been deposed by the Procurator Valerius Gratus. He had been succeeded first by Ismael Ben Phabi, then by his son Eleazar, then by his son-in-law, Joseph Caiaphas. But the priestly families would not be likely to attach more importance than they chose to a deposition which a strict observer of the Law would have regarded as invalid and sacrilegious;

[1] One might, perhaps, from a slightly different point of view, regard the questioning before Annas as mere conspiracy; that before Caiaphas as a sort of preliminary questioning, or ἀνάκρισις; and that before the Sanhedrin as the only real and legal trial.

[2] αὐλὴ means both the entire palace (Matt. xxvi. 58) and the open court within the πυλὼν or προαύλιον (*id.* 69). Probably the house was near the Temple (Neh. xiii. 4, seqq.). That Hanan and Caiaphas occupied one house seems probable from a comparison of John xviii. 13 with 15. John being known to *Caiaphas* is admitted to witness the trial before *Annas*.

nor would so astute a people as the Jews be likely to lack devices which would enable them to evade the Roman fiat, and to treat Annas, if they wished to do so, as their High Priest *de jure*, if not *de facto*. Since the days of Herod the Great, the High Priesthood had been degraded from a permanent religious office, to a temporary secular distinction; and, even had it been otherwise, the rude legionaries would probably care less than nothing to whom they led their victim. If the tribune condescended to ask a question about it, it would be easy for the Captain of the Temple—who may very probably have been at this time, as we know was the case subsequently, one of the sons of Annas himself—to represent Annas as the *Sagan*[1] or *Nasî*—

[1] The title *Sagan haccohanîm*, "deputy" or "chief" of the priests, is *said* to date from the day when the Seleucids neglected for seven years to appoint a successor to the wicked Alcimus, and a "deputy" had to supply his place. But accident must often have rendered a *sagan* necessary, and we find "the second priest" prominently mentioned in 2 Kings xxv. 18; Jer. lii. 24 (Buxtorf, *Lex. Talm.* s. v. סגן). Thus on one occasion, on the evening of the great Day of Atonement, Hareth, King of Arabia, was talking to Simeon Ben Kamhith, who, being High Priest, was rendered legally impure, and unable to officiate the next day, because some of the king's saliva happened to fall on his vestments. His brother then supplied his place. It is, however, doubtful whether the title of *Sagan* did not originate later, and whether any but the real High Priest *could*, under ordinary circumstances, be the *Nasî*. In fact, the name *Nasî* seems to be enveloped in obscurity. Perhaps it corresponds to the mysterious σάραμελ (= *Sar am El*, "Prince of the People of God). Ewald says that Hanan might have been *Ab Beth Dîn*, as the *second* in the Sanhedrin was called; and it is at any rate clear, among many obscurities, that short of being High Priest, he might have even exceeded him in influence (cf. Acts iv. 6; Maimon. *Sanhedr.* 2, 4). The High Priesthood at this time was confined to some half-dozen closely-connected families, especially the Boëthusians, and the family of Hanan, the Kamhiths, and the Kantheras; yet, since the days of Herod, the High Priests were so completely the puppets of the civil power that there were no less than twenty-eight in 107 years (Jos. *Antt.* xx. 10, § 1). Both Josephus (εἷς τῶν ἀρχιέρεων, *B. J.* ii. 20, § 4) and the Talmud (בני כהנים גדולים) quite bear out the language of the Gospels in attributing the pontifical power more to a caste than to any individual.

the "Deputy," or the President of the Sanhedrin—and so as the proper person to conduct the preliminary investigation.

i. Accordingly, it was before Hanan that Jesus stood first as a prisoner at the tribunal.[1] It is probable that he and his family had been originally summoned by Herod the Great from Alexandria, as supple supporters of a distasteful tyranny. The Jewish historian calls this Hanan the happiest man of his time, because he died at an advanced old age, and because both he and five of his sons in succession—not to mention his son-in-law—had enjoyed the shadow of the High Priesthood;[2] so that, in fact, for nearly half a century he had practically wielded the sacerdotal power. But to be admired by such a

The fact seems to be that even in these bad times the office demanded a certain amount of external dignity and self-denial which some men would only tolerate for a time; and their ambition was that as many members of their family as possible should have "passed the chair." Such is the inference drawn by Derenbourg from Jos. *Antt.* xx. 9, § 1; and still more from the letter of the High Priest Jonathan, son of Hanan, to Agrippa (*id.* xix. 6, § 4). Martha, daughter of Boethus, bought the priesthood for her husband, Jesus, son of Gamala, and had carpets spread from her house to the Temple when she went to see him sacrifice. This man had silk gloves made, that he might not dirty his hands while sacrificing! (See Renan, *L'Antechrist*, 49 seqq.)

[1] John xviii. 13, 19—24.

[2] Eleazar, A.D. 16; Jonathan, A.D. 36; Theophilus, A.D. 37; Matthias, A.D. 42—43; Annas the younger, A.D. 63. The Talmudic quotations about Annas and his family are given in Lightfoot. They were remarkable for boldness and cunning (Jos. *Antt.* xx. 9, § 1), and also for avarice and meanness (*Sifr.* Deuteron. § 105). (*Jer. Pea.* 1, 6, quoted by Derenbourg, who calls them "ces pontifes détestés" [*Hist. Pal.*, p. 468].)—An energetic malediction against all these families is found in *Pesachîm*, 57 *a*, in which occur the words, "Woe to the house of Hanan! woe to their serpent hissings!" (אוי לי מבית חנן אוי לי מלחישתן, Id. 232.)—The Boëthusians are reproached for their "bludgeons;" the Kantheras for their libels; the Phabis for their "fists" (Raphall, *Hist. of the Jews*, ii. 370). The passage is a little obscure, but the Talmud has many allusions to the worthlessness and worldliness of the priests of this period. (Renan, *L'Antechrist*, pp. 50, 51.)

renegade as Josephus is a questionable advantage. In spite of his prosperity he seems to have left behind him but an evil name, and we know enough of his character, even from the most unsuspected sources, to recognise in him nothing better than an astute, tyrannous, worldly Sadducee, unvenerable for all his seventy years, full of a serpentine malice and meanness which utterly belied the meaning of his name,[1] and engaged at this very moment in a dark, disorderly conspiracy, for which even a worse man would have had cause to blush. It was before this alien and intriguing hierarch that there began, at midnight, the first stage of that long and terrible trial.[2]

And there was good reason why St. John should have preserved for us *this* phase of the trial, and preserved it apparently for the express reason that it had been omitted by the other Evangelists. It is not till after a lapse of years that people can always see clearly the prime mover in events with which they have been contemporary. At the time, the ostensible agent is the one usually regarded as most responsible, though he may be in reality a mere link in the official machinery. But if there were one man who was more guilty than any other of the death of Jesus, that man was Hanan. His advanced age, his preponderant dignity, his worldly position and influence, as one who stood on the best terms with the Herods and the Procurators, gave an exceptional weight to his prerogative decision. The mere fact that he should have noticed Jesus at all showed that he attached to His teaching a *political* significance—showed that he was at last afraid lest Jesus should alienate the people

[1] חנן, "clement," or "merciful."

[2] John xviii. 19—24.

yet more entirely from the pontifical clique than had ever been done by Shemaia or Abtalion. It is most remarkable, and, so far as I know, has scarcely ever been noticed, that, although the Pharisees undoubtedly were actuated by a burning hatred against Jesus, and were even so eager for His death as to be willing to co-operate with the aristocratic and priestly Sadducees—from whom they were ordinarily separated by every kind of difference, political, social, and religious—yet, from the moment that the plot for His arrest and condemnation had been matured, the Pharisees took so little part in it that their name is not once directly mentioned in any event connected with the arrest, the trial, the derisions, and the crucifixion. The Pharisees, as such, disappear; the chief priests and elders take their place. It is, indeed, doubtful whether any of the more distinguished Pharisees were members of the degraded *simulacrum* of authority which in those bad days still arrogated to itself the title of a Sanhedrin. If we may believe not a few of the indications of the Talmud, that Sanhedrin was little better than a close, irreligious, unpatriotic confederacy of monopolising and time-serving priests —the Boëthusim, the Kamhits, the Phabis, the family of Hanan, mostly of non-Palestinian origin—who were supported by the government, but detested by the people, and of whom this bad conspirator was the very life and soul.

And, perhaps, we may see a further reason for the apparent withdrawal of the Pharisees from all active co-operation in the steps which accompanied the condemnation and execution of Jesus, not only in the superior mildness which is attributed to them, and in their comparative insignificance in the civil administration, but also in their total want of sympathy with those into whose too fatal toils they had delivered the Son of God. There seems, indeed, to be a hitherto unnoticed circumstance which, while it would kindle to the highest degree the fury of the Sadducees, would rather enlist in Christ's favour the sympathy of their rivals. What had roused the disdainful insouciance of these powerful aristocrats? Morally insignificant—the patrons and adherents of opinions which had so little hold upon the people that Jesus had never directed against them one tithe of the stern denunciation which He had levelled at the Pharisees—they had played but a very minor part in the opposition which had sprung up round the Messiah's steps. Nay, further than this, they would be wholly at one with Him in rejecting and discountenancing the minute and casuistical frivolities of the Oral Law; they might even have rejoiced that they had in Him a holy and irresistible ally in their opposition to all the *Hagadôth* and *Halachôth* which had germinated in a fungous growth over the whole body of the Mosaic institutions.[1] Whence, then, this sudden outburst of the very deadliest and most ruthless opposition? It is a conjecture that has not yet been made, but which the notices of the Talmud bring home to my mind with strong conviction, that the rage of these priests was mainly due to our Lord's words and acts concerning that House of God which they regarded as their exclusive domain, and, above all, to His second public cleansing of the Temple. They could not indeed *press* this point in their accusations, because the act was one of which, secretly at least, the Pharisees, in all probability, heartily approved; and had they urged it against Him they

[1] Jos. *Antt.* xiii. 10, § 6.

would have lost all chance of impressing upon Pilate a sense of their unanimity. The first cleansing might have been passed over as an isolated act of zeal, to which little importance need be attached, while the teaching of Jesus was mainly confined to despised and far-off Galilee; but the second had been more public, and more vehement, and had apparently kindled a more general indignation against the gross abuse which called it forth. Accordingly, in all three Evangelists we find that those who complained of the act are not distinctively Pharisees, but "*Chief Priests* and Scribes" (Matt. xxi. 15; Mark xi. 18; Luke xix. 47), who seem at once to have derived from it a fresh stimulus to seek His destruction.

But, again, it may be asked, Is there any reason beyond this bold infraction of their authority, this indignant repudiation of an arrangement which *they* had sanctioned, which would have stirred up the rage of these priestly families? Yes—for we may assume from the Talmud that it tended *to wound their avarice, to interfere with their illicit and greedy gains.* Avarice —the besetting sin of Judas—the besetting sin of the Jewish race—seems also to have been the besetting sin of the family of Hanan. It was they who had founded the *chanujôth*—the famous four shops under the twin cedars of Olivet—in which were sold things legally pure, and which they had manipulated with such commercial cunning as artificially to raise the price of doves to a gold coin apiece, until the people were delivered from this gross imposition by the indignant interference of a grandson of Hillel. There is every reason to believe that the shops which had intruded even under the Temple porticoes were not only sanctioned by their authority, but even managed for their profit. To interfere with these was to rob them of one important source of that wealth and worldly comfort to which they attached such extravagant importance. There was good reason why Hanan, the head representative of "the viper brood," as a Talmudic writer calls them, should strain to the utmost his cruel prerogative of power to crush a Prophet whose actions tended to make him and his powerful family at once wholly contemptible and comparatively poor.

Such then were the feelings of bitter contempt and hatred with which the ex-High Priest assumed the initiative in interrogating Jesus. The fact that he dared not avow them—nay, was forced to keep them wholly out of sight—would only add to the intensity of his bitterness. Even his method of procedure seems to have been as wholly illegal as was his assumption, in such a place and at such an hour, of any legal function whatever. Anxious, at all hazards, to trump up some available charge of secret sedition, or of unorthodox teaching, he questioned Jesus of His disciples and of His doctrine. The answer, for all its calmness, involved a deep reproof. "*I* have spoken openly to the world; *I* ever taught in the synagogue and in the Temple, where all the Jews come together, and in secret I said nothing. Why askest thou *me?* Ask those who have heard me what I said to them. Lo! these"—pointing, perhaps, to the bystanders[1]—"know what *I* said to them." The emphatic repetition of the "I," and its unusually significant position at the end of the sentence, show that a contrast was intended; as though He had said, "This midnight, this sedition, this secrecy, this indecent mockery of justice, are *yours*, not *mine*. There has never

[1] οὗτοι, not ἐκεῖνοι.

been anything esoteric in my doctrine; never anything to conceal in my actions; no hole-and-corner plots among my followers. But thou? and thine?" Even the minions of Annas felt the false position of their master under this calm rebuke; they felt that before the transparent innocence of this youthful Rabbi of Nazareth the hoary hypocrisy of the crafty Sadducee was abashed. "Answerest thou the High Priest so?" said one of them with a burst of illegal insolence; and then, unreproved by this priestly violator of justice, he profaned with the first infamous blow the sacred face of Christ. Then first that face which, as the poet-preacher says, "the angels stare upon with wonder as infants at a bright sunbeam," was smitten by a contemptible slave. The insult was borne with noble meekness. Even St. Paul, when similarly insulted, flaming into sudden anger at such a grossly illegal violence, had scathed the ruffian and his abettor with "God shall smite thee, thou whited wall:"[1] but He, the Son of God—He who was infinitely above all apostles and all angels—with no flash of anger, with no heightened tone of natural indignation, quietly reproved the impudent transgressor with the words, "If I spoke evil, bear witness concerning the evil; but if well, why smitest thou me?" It was clear that nothing more could be extorted from Him; that before such a

[1] Acts xxiii. 3. It is remarkable that in the Talmudic malediction of these priestly families (*Pesach.* 57; *Toseft. Menachôth,* 15) there is an express complaint that they monopolised all offices by making their sons treasurers, captains (of the Temple), &c., and that "*their servants* (עבדיהן) *strike the people with their rods.*" When Josephus talks of Hanan the son of Hanan as "a prodigious lover of liberty and admirer of democracy," the mere context is quite sufficient to show that this is a very careless, if not dishonest, judgment; as for his wonderful "virtue" and "justice," it is probable that Josephus hardly cared to reconcile his own statements with what he records of him in *Antt.* xx. 9, § 1.

tribunal He would brook no further question. Bound, in sign that He was to be condemned—though unheard and unsentenced—Annas sent Him across the court-yard to Joseph Caiaphas, his son-in-law, who, not by the grace of God, but by the grace of the Roman Procurator, was the titular High Priest.

ii. Caiaphas, like his father-in-law, was a Sadducee —equally astute and unscrupulous with Annas, but endowed with less force of character and will. In his house took place the second private and irregular stage of the trial.[1] There—for though the poor Apostles could not watch for one hour in sympathetic prayer, these nefarious plotters could watch all night in their deadly malice—a few of the most desperate enemies of Jesus among the Priests and Sadducees were met. To form a session of the Sanhedrin there must at least have been twenty-three members present. And we may perhaps be allowed to conjecture that this particular body before which Christ was now convened was mainly composed of Priests. There were in fact three Sanhedrins, or as we should rather call them, committees of the Sanhedrin, which ordinarily met at different places —in the *Lishcat Haggazzith*, or Paved Hall; in the *Beth Midrash* or Chamber by the Partition of the Temple; and near the Gate of the Temple Mount. Such being the case, it is no unreasonable supposition that these committees were composed of different elements, and that one of them may have been mainly sacerdotal in its constitution. If so, it would have been the most likely of them all, at the present crisis, to embrace the most violent measures against One whose teaching

[1] Matt. xxvi. 59—68; Mark xiv. 55—65. Irregular, for capital trials could only take place by daylight (*Sanhedr.* iv. 1).

now seemed to endanger the very existence of priestly rule.[1]

But, whatever may have been the nature of the tribunal over which Caiaphas was now presiding, it is clear that the Priests were forced to change their tactics. Instead of trying, as Hanan had done, to overawe and entangle Jesus with insidious questions, and so to involve Him in a charge of secret apostacy, they now tried to brand Him with the crime of public error. In point of fact their own bitter divisions and controversies made the task of convicting Him a very difficult one. If they dwelt on any supposed opposition to civil authority, *that* would rather enlist the sympathies of the Pharisees in His favour; if they dwelt on supposed Sabbath violations or neglect of traditional observances, that would accord with the views of the Sadducees. The Sadducees dared not complain of His cleansing of the Temple: the Pharisees, or those who represented them, found it useless to advert to His denunciations of tradition. But Jesus, infinitely nobler than His own noblest Apostle, would not foment these latent animosities, or evoke for His own deliverance a contest of these slumbering prejudices. He did not disturb the temporary compromise which united them in a common hatred against Himself. Since, therefore, they had nothing else to go upon, the Chief Priests and the entire San-

[1] Twenty-three would be about a third of the entire number (Maimonides, *Sanhedr.* 3). Unless there be some slight confusion between the second and third trials, the πάντες of Mark xiv. 53 cannot be taken *au pied de la lettre,* but must mean simply "all who were engaged in this conspiracy." Indeed, this seems to be distinctly implied in Mark xv. 1. Similarly in Matt. xxvi. 59, τὸ συνέδριον ὅλον must mean "that entire *committee* of the Sanhedrin," as may be seen by comparing it with xxvii. 1. That συνέδριον may be used simply for a small *Beth Dîn* is clear from Matt. v. 22. (Jost. i. 404.)

hedrin "*sought false witness*"—such is the terribly simple expression of the Evangelists—"*sought* false witness against Jesus to put Him to death." Many men, with a greedy, unnatural depravity, *seek* false witness—mostly of the petty, ignoble, malignant sort; and the powers of evil usually supply it to them. The Talmud seems to insinuate that the custom, which they pretend was the *general* one, had been followed in the case of Christ, and that two witnesses had been placed in concealment while a treacherous disciple—ostensibly Judas Iscariot—had obtained from His own lips an avowal of His claims. This, however, is no less false than the utterly absurd and unchronological assertion of the tract *Sanhedrin*, that Jesus had been excommunicated by Joshua Ben Perachiah, and that though for forty days a herald had proclaimed that He had brought magic from Egypt and seduced the people, no single witness came forward in His favour.[1] Setting aside these absurd inventions, we learn from the Gospels that though the agents of these priests were eager to lie, yet their testimony was *so* false, so shadowy, so self-contradictory, that it all melted to nothing, and even those unjust and bitter judges could not with any decency accept it. But at last two came forward, whose false witness looked more promising.[2] They had heard Him say something about destroying the Temple, and rebuilding it in three days. According to one version His expression had been, "*I can destroy* this Temple;" according to another, "*I will destroy* this Temple." The fact was that He had said

[1] *Sanhedr.*, 43 *a.* (Grätz, *Gesch. Jud.* iii. 242.)—See Excursus II., "Allusions to Christ and Christians in the Talmud."

[2] The brevity of the Evangelists prevents us from knowing whether the ordinary Jewish rules of evidence were observed. For Josephus's account of the trial of Zechariah the son of Baruch, see *Bell. Jud.* iv. 5, § 4.

neither, but "*Destroy* this Temple;" and the imperative had but been addressed, hypothetically, to them. *They* were to be the destroyers; He had but promised to rebuild. It was just one of those perjuries which was all the more perjured, because it bore some distant semblance to the truth; and by just giving a different *nuance* to His actual words they had, with the ingenuity of slander, reversed their meaning, and hoped to found upon them a charge of constructive blasphemy. But even this semblable perjury utterly broke down, and Jesus listened in silence while His disunited enemies hopelessly confuted each other's testimony. Guilt often breaks into excuses where perfect innocence is dumb. He simply suffered His false accusers and their false listeners to entangle themselves in the hideous coil of their own malignant lies, and the silence of the innocent Jesus atoned for the excuses of the guilty Adam.

But that majestic silence troubled, thwarted, confounded, maddened them. It weighed them down for the moment with an incubus of intolerable self-condemnation. They felt, before that silence, as if *they* were the culprits, He the judge. And as every poisoned arrow of their carefully-provided perjuries fell harmless at His feet, as though blunted on the diamond shield of His white innocence, they began to fear lest, after all, their thirst for His blood would go unslaked, and their whole plot fail. Were they thus to be conquered by the feebleness of their own weapons, without His stirring a finger, or uttering a word? Was this Prophet of Nazareth to prevail against *them*, merely for lack of a few consistent lies? Was His life charmed even against calumny confirmed by oaths? It was intolerable.

Then Caiaphas was overcome with a paroxysm of fear and anger. Starting up from his judgment-seat, and striding into the midst[1]—with what a voice, with what an attitude we may well imagine!—"Answerest Thou NOTHING?" he exclaimed. "What is it that these witness against Thee?" Had not Jesus been aware that these His judges were wilfully feeding on ashes and seeking lies, He might have answered; but now His awful silence remained unbroken.

Then, reduced to utter despair and fury, this false High Priest—with marvellous inconsistency, with disgraceful illegality—still standing as it were with a threatening attitude over his prisoner, exclaimed, "I adjure Thee by the living God to tell us"—what? whether Thou art a malefactor? whether Thou *hast* secretly taught sedition? whether Thou hast openly uttered blasphemy?—no, but (and surely the question showed the dread misgiving which lay under all their deadly conspiracy against Him)—"WHETHER THOU ART THE CHRIST, THE SON OF GOD?"

Strange question to a bound, defenceless, condemned criminal; and strange question from such a questioner—a High Priest of His people! Strange question from the judge who was hounding on his false witnesses against the prisoner! Yet so adjured, and to such a question, Jesus could not be silent; on such a point He could not leave Himself open to misinterpretation. In the days of His happier ministry, when they would have taken Him

[1] Mark xiv. 60, ἀναστὰς . . . εἰς μέσον. The Sanhedrin sat on opposite divans of a circular hall; the *Nasî*, or President, who was usually the High Priest, sat in the middle at the farther end, with the *Ab Beth Dîn*, or Father of the House of Judgment, on his right, and the *Chakam*, or Wise Man, on his left. The accused was placed opposite to him. (See Jos. *Bell. Jud.* iv. 5, § 4; Keim, III. ii. 328.)

by force to make Him a King—in the days when to claim the Messiahship in *their* sense would have been to meet all their passionate prejudices half way, and to place Himself upon the topmost pinnacle of their adoring homage—in *those* days He had kept His title of Messiah utterly in the background: but now, at this awful decisive moment, when death was near—when, humanly speaking, nothing could be gained, everything *must* be lost, by the avowal—there thrilled through all the ages—thrilled through that Eternity, which is the synchronism of all the future, and all the present, and all the past—the solemn answer, "I AM;[1] *and ye shall see the Son of Man sitting on the right hand of power, and coming with the clouds of heaven.*"[2] In that answer the thunder rolled—a thunder louder than at Sinai, though the ears of the cynic and the Sadducee heard it not then, nor hear it now. In overacted and ill-omened horror, the unjust judge who had thus supplemented the failure of the perjuries which he had vainly sought—the false High Priest rending his linen robes before the True[3]—demanded of the assembly His instant condemnation.

[1] In Matt. xxvi. 64, Σὺ εἶπας. Alford refers to John xii. 49.

[2] Dan. vii. 13: "I saw in the night visions, and, behold, one like the Son of Man came with the clouds of heaven, and came to the Ancient of Days, and they brought him near before him." Hence the hybrid term, Bar-νεφέλη, "Son of a cloud," applied to the Messiah in *Sanhedr*. 96, 6.

[3] This was forbidden to the High Priest in cases of mourning (Lev. x. 6; xxi. 10); but the Jewish *Halacha* considered it lawful in cases of blasphemy (גדוף, *gidduph*) (1 Macc. xi. 71; Jos. *B. J.* ii. 15, § 4). As to Joseph Caiaphas the Talmud is absolutely silent; but the general conception which it gives of the priests of this epoch agrees entirely with the Gospels. It tells how since the days of Valerius Gratus the office had constantly been bought and sold; how the widow Martha, daughter of Boethus, gave Agrippa II. two bushels of gold *denarii* to buy it for Joshua Ben Gamala, her betrothed; how it was disgraced by cringing meanness and supple sycophancy; how there were more than eighty of these High Priests of the second Temple

"Blasphemy!" he exclaimed; "what further need have we of witnesses? See, *now* ye *heard* his blasphemy! What is your decision?" And with the confused tumultuous cry, "He is *ish maveth*," "A man of death," "Guilty of death," the dark conclave was broken up, and the second stage of the trial of Jesus was over.[1]

(which they quoted in illustration of Prov. x. 27), whereas there were only eighteen of the first Temple (Frankl, *Monatsschrift*, Dec. 1852, p. 588; Raphall, *Hist. of Jews*, ii. 368); and many other disgraces and enormities.

[1] Cf. Numb. xxxv. 31.

CHAPTER LIX.

THE INTERVAL BETWEEN THE TRIALS.

"I gave my back to the smiters, and my cheeks to them that plucked off the hair: I hid not my face from shame and spitting."—ISA. l. 6.

AND this was how the Jews at last received their promised Messiah—longed for with passionate hopes during two thousand years; since then regretted in bitter agony for well-nigh two thousand more! From this moment He was regarded[1] by all the apparitors of the Jewish Court as a heretic, liable to death by stoning; and was only remanded into custody to be kept till break of day, because by daylight only, and in the *Lishcat Haggazzith*, or Hall of Judgment, and only by a full session of the entire Sanhedrin, could He be legally condemned. And since now they looked upon Him as a "fit person to be insulted with impunity, He was haled through the court-yard to the guard-room with blows and curses, in which it may be that not only the attendant menials, but even the cold but now infuriated Sadducees took their share. It was now long past midnight, and the spring air was then most chilly. In the centre of

[1] "Millionen gebrochener Herzen und Augen haben seinen Tod noch nicht abgebüsst" (Grätz, iii. 245). On the whole of this trial, see the powerful and noble remarks of Lange (iv. 309) and Keim (*ubi supra*).

the court the servants of the priests were warming themselves under the frosty starlight as they stood round a fire of coals. And as He was led past that fire He heard—what was to Him a more deadly bitterness than any which His brutal persecutors could pour into His cup of anguish—He heard His boldest Apostle denying Him with oaths.

For during these two sad hours of His commencing tragedy, as He stood in the Halls of Annas and of Caiaphas, another moral tragedy, which He had already prophesied, had been taking place in the outer court.

As far as we can infer from the various narratives,[1] the palace in Jerusalem, conjointly occupied by Annas the real, and Caiaphas the titular High Priest, seems to have been built round a square court, and entered by an arched passage or vestibule; and on the farther side of it, probably up a short flight of steps,[2] was the hall in which the committee of the Sanhedrin had met. Timidly, and at a distance, two only of the Apostles had so far recovered from their first panic as to follow far in the rear [3] of the melancholy procession. One of these —the beloved disciple—known perhaps to the High Priest's household as a young fisherman of the Lake of Galilee—had found ready admittance, with no attempt to conceal his sympathies or his identity. Not so the

[1] In this narrative again there are obvious *variations* in the quadruple accounts of the Evangelists; but the text will sufficiently show that there is no irreconcileable discrepancy if they are judged fairly and on common-sense principles. The conception of accuracy in ancient writers differed widely from our own, and a document is by no means necessarily inaccurate, because the brevity, or the special purpose, or the limited information of the writer, made it necessarily incomplete. "Qui plura dicit, pauciora complectitur; qui pauciora dicit, plura non negat."

[2] Mark xiv. 66, κάτω ἐν τῇ αὐλῇ.

[3] Luke xxii. 54, μακρόθεν.

other. Unknown, and a Galilæan, he had been stopped at the door by the youthful portress. Better, far better, had his exclusion been final. For it was a night of tumult, of terror, of suspicion; and Peter was weak, and his intense love was mixed with fear, and yet he was venturing into the very thick of his most dangerous enemies. But John, regretting that he should be debarred from entrance, and judging perhaps of his friend's firmness by his own, exerted his influence to obtain admission for him. With bold imprudence, and concealing the better motives which had brought him thither, Peter, warned though he had been, but warned in vain, walked into the court-yard, and sat down in the very middle of the servants[1] of the very men before whom at that moment his Lord was being arraigned on a charge of death. The portress, after the admission of those concerned in the capture, seems to have been relieved (as was only natural at that late hour) by another maid, and advancing to the group of her fellow-servants, she fixed a curious and earnest gaze[2] on the dubious stranger as he sat full in the red glare of the firelight, and then, with a flash of recognition, she exclaimed, "Why, *you*, as well as the other, were with Jesus of Galilee."[3] Peter was off his guard. At this period of life his easy impressionable nature was ever liable to be moulded by the influence of the moment, and he passed readily into passionate extremes. Long, long afterwards,

[1] Luke xxii. 55, μέσος αὐτῶν.

[2] Luke xxii. 56, ἀτενίσασα. For the other particulars in this clause compare John xviii. 17 with Matt. xxvi. 69; Mark xiv. 67. For female porters, see Mark xiii. 34; Acts xii. 13.

[3] It is most instructive to observe that no one of the Evangelists puts exactly the same words into her mouth (showing clearly the nature of their report), and yet each faithfully preserves the καὶ, which, in the maid's question, couples Peter with John.

we find a wholly unexpected confirmation of the probability of this sad episode of his life, in the readiness with which he lent himself to the views of the Apostle of the Gentiles, and the equal facility with which a false shame, and a fear of "them which were of the circumcision," made him swerve into the wrong and narrow proprieties of "certain which came from James." And thus it was that the mere curious question of an inquisitive young girl startled him by its very suddenness into a quick denial of his Lord. Doubtless, at the moment, it presented itself to him as a mere prudent evasion of needless danger. But did he hope to stop there? Alas, "once denied" is always "thrice denied;" and the sudden "manslaughter upon truth" always, and rapidly, develops into its utter and deliberate murder; and a lie is like a stone set rolling upon a mountain-side, which is instantly beyond its utterer's control.

For a moment, perhaps, his denial was accepted, for it had been very public, and very emphatic.[1] But it warned him of his danger. Guiltily he slinks away again from the glowing brazier to the arched entrance of the court, as the crowing of a cock smote, not quite unheeded, on his guilty ear.[2] His respite was very short.

[1] Matt. xxvi. 70, *ἔμπροσθεν πάντων*; Mark xiv. 68, *οὐκ οἶδα* (sc. *αὐτὸν*), *οὐδὲ ἐπίσταμαι σὺ τί λέγεις*.

[2] Matt. xxvi. 71, *εἰς τὸν πυλῶνα*; Mark xiv. 68, *εἰς τὸ προαύλιον*. There must be some trivial "inaccuracy," if any one cares to press the word, either here or in John xviii. 25 (*εἶπον οὖν αὐτῷ*), Luke xxii. 58 (*ἕτερος*). A wretched pseudo-criticism has fixed on the cock as "unhistorical," because the Jews are thought to have held cocks unclean, from their scratching in the dung. But not to mention that the bird may have belonged to some Roman in the Tower of Antonia, other Talmudical stories show that cocks *were* kept at Jerusalem: *e.g.*, the story of a cock that was stoned for killing an infant (*Berachôth*, 27, 1; see Buxtorf, *Lex. Talm.* 81, 2653). It is a condescension to notice such objections, particularly when they are supposed to rest on Talmudical authorities quoted from our imperfect know-

The portress—part of whose duty it was to draw attention to dubious strangers—had evidently gossiped about him to the servant who had relieved her in charge of the door. Some other idlers were standing about, and this second maid pointed him out to them as having certainly been with Jesus of Nazareth. A lie seemed more than ever necessary now, and to secure himself from all further molestation he even confirmed it with an oath. But now flight seemed impossible, for it would only confirm suspicion; so with desperate, gloomy resolution he once more—with feelings which can barely be imagined—joined the unfriendly and suspicious group who were standing round the fire.

A whole hour passed: for him it must have been a fearful hour, and one never to be forgotten. The temperament of Peter was far too nervous and vehement to suffer him to feel at ease under this new complication of ingratitude and falsehood. If he remain silent among these priestly servitors, he is betrayed by the restless self-consciousness of an evil secret which tries in vain to simulate indifference; if he brazen it out with careless talk, he is fatally betrayed by his Galilæan burr. It is evident that, in spite of denial and of oath, they wholly distrust and despise him; and at last one of the High Priest's servants—a kinsman of the wounded Malchus—once more strongly and confidently charged him with having been with Jesus in the garden, taunting him, in proof of it, with the misplaced gutturals of his provincial dialect. The others joined in the accusation.[1]

ledge of a literature which is inveterately unhistorical, and abounds in self-contradictions. See Excursus XII., "Notes on the Talmud."

[1] John xviii. 26 (συγγενὴς); Luke xxii. 59 (ἄλλος τις διϊσχυρίζετο); Matt. xxvi. 73 (οἱ ἑστῶτες); Mark xiv. 70 (οἱ παρεστῶτες).

Unless he persisted, all was lost which might seem to have been gained. Perhaps one more effort would set him quite free from these troublesome charges, and enable him to wait and see the end. Pressed closer and closer by the sneering, threatening band of idle servitors —sinking deeper and deeper into the mire of faithlessness and fear—" then began he to curse and to swear, saying, I know not the man." And at that fatal moment of guilt, which might well have been for him the moment of an apostacy as fatal and final as had been that of his brother apostle—at that fatal moment, while those shameless curses still quivered on the air—first the cock crew in the cold grey dusk, and at the same moment, catching the last accents of those perjured oaths, either through the open portal of the judgment-hall,[1] or as He was led past the group at the fireside through the open court, with rude pushing and ribald jeers, and blows and spitting—the Lord—the Lord in the agony of His humiliation, in the majesty of His silence—"*the Lord turned and looked upon Peter.*" Blessed are those on whom, when He looks in sorrow, the Lord looks also with love! It was enough. Like an arrow through his inmost soul, shot the mute eloquent anguish of that reproachful glance. As the sunbeam smites the last hold of snow upon the rock, ere it rushes in avalanche down the tormented hill, so the false self of the fallen Apostle slipped away. It was enough: " he saw no more enemies, he knew no more danger, he feared no more death." Flinging the fold of

[1] The room in which Jesus was being tried may have been one of the kind called *muck'ad* in the East, *i.e.*, a room with *an open front*, two or more arches, and a low railing, the floor of which is a paved *leewa'n.* (Lane, *Mod. Egyptians*, i. 22.)

his mantle over his head,[1] he too, like Judas, rushed forth into the night. Into the night, but not as Judas; into the unsunned outer darkness of miserable self-condemnation, but not into the midnight of remorse and of despair; into the night, but, as has been beautifully said, it was "to meet the morning dawn."[2] If the angel of Innocence had left him, the angel of Repentance took him gently by the hand. Sternly, yet tenderly, the spirit of grace led up this broken-hearted penitent before the tribunal of his own conscience, and there his old life, his old shame, his old weakness, his old self was doomed to that death of godly sorrow which was to issue in a new and a nobler birth.

And it was this crime, committed against Him by the man who had first proclaimed Him as the Christ—who had come to Him over the stormy water—who had drawn the sword for Him in Gethsemane—who had affirmed so indignantly that he would die with Him rather than deny Him—it was this denial, confirmed by curses, that Jesus heard immediately after He had been condemned to death, and at the very commencement of His first terrible derision. For, in the guard-room to which He was remanded to await the break of day, all the ignorant malice of religious hatred, all the narrow vulgarity of brutal spite, all the cold innate cruelty which lurks under the abjectness of Oriental servility, was let loose against Him. His very meekness, His very silence, His very majesty—the very stainlessness of His innocence, the very grandeur of His fame—every divine circumstance

[1] ἐπιβαλὼν (Mark xiv. 72). This seems a better meaning than (i.) "vehemently" (Matthew, Luke, πικρῶς), or (ii.) "when he thought thereon" (but cf. Marc. Aurel. *Comment.* x. 30), or (iii.) "hiding his face in his hands."

[2] Lange, vi. 319.

and quality which raised Him to a height so infinitely immeasurable above His persecutors—all these made Him an all the more welcome victim for their low and devilish ferocity. They spat in His face; they smote Him with rods; they struck Him with their closed fists and with their open palms.[1] In the fertility of their furious and hateful insolence, they invented against Him a sort of game. Blindfolding His eyes, they hit Him again and again, with the repeated question, "Prophesy to us, O Messiah, who it is that smote thee."[2] So they wiled away the dark cold hours till the morning, revenging themselves upon His impassive innocence for their own present vileness and previous terror; and there, in the midst of that savage and wanton varletry, the Son of God, bound and blindfold, stood in His long and silent agony, defenceless and alone. It was His first derision—His derision as the Christ, the Judge attainted, the Holy One a criminal, the Deliverer in bonds.

iii. At last the miserable lingering hours were over, and the grey dawn shuddered, and the morning blushed upon that memorable day. And with the earliest dawn —for so the Oral Law ordained,[3] and they who could trample on all justice and all mercy were yet scrupulous about all the infinitely little—Jesus was led into the *Lishcat Haggazzith*, or Paved Hall at the south-east of the Temple, or perhaps into the *Chanujôth*, or

[1] Matt. xxvi. 67, *ἐνέπτυσαν . . . ἐκολάφισαν* (slapped with open palm) . . . *ἐῤῥάπισαν* (struck, probably with sticks); Mark xiv. 65, *ῥαπίσμασιν . . ἔλαβον al. ἔβαλλον*; Luke xxii. 63, 64, *ἐνέπαιζον αὐτῷ δέροντες . . . τις ἐστιν ὁ παίσας σε;* There is a pathetic variety in these five forms of insult by blows [cf. Acts xxi. 32; xxiii. 2; Isa. l. 6; and the treatment of one of Annas's own sons (Jos. *B. J.* iv. 5, § 3)].

[2] Wetstein quotes from *Sanhedr*. f. 93 *b*, a similar tentative applied to the false Messiah, Bar-Cochebas.

[3] *Zohar*, 56. See Excursu V.

"Shops," which owed their very existence to Hanan and his family, where the Sanhedrin had been summoned, for His third actual, but His first formal and legal trial.[1] It was now probably about six o'clock in the morning, and a full session met. Well-nigh all—for there were the noble exceptions at least of Nicodemus and of Joseph of Arimathea, and we may hope also of Gamaliel, the grandson of Hillel—were inexorably bent upon His death. The Priests were there, whose greed and selfishness He had reproved; the Elders, whose hypocrisy He had branded; the Scribes, whose ignorance He had exposed;[2] and worse than all, the worldly, sceptical, would-be philosophic Sadducees, always the most cruel and dangerous of opponents,[3] whose empty sapience He

[1] Luke xxii. 66—71. It is only by courtesy that this body can be regarded as a Sanhedrin at all. Jost observes that there is in the Romish period no trace of any genuine legal Sanhedrin, apart from mere special incompetent gatherings. (See Jos. *Antt.* xx. 9, § 1; *B. J.* iv. 5, § 4.) But all the facts about the Sanhedrin of this period are utterly obscure. On Sabbaths and feast days they are said to have met in the *Beth Midrash*, or Temple Synagogue, which was built along the *Chêl*, or wall between the Outer Court and the Court of the Women. (Lightfoot, *Hor. Hebr.*; Keim, &c.) R. Ismael, son of R. Josè, the author of *Seder Olam*, is reported to have said that "forty years before the destruction of the Temple the Sanhedrin exiled itself (from the Paved Hall), and established itself in the *Chanujôth*" (*Aboda Zara*, 8 *b*); and this is the first of ten migrations of the Sanhedrin mentioned in *Rosh Hashana*, 31 *a*. These *Chanujôth*, four in number, are said to have been shops for the sale of doves, &c., under a cedar on the Mount of Olives, connected with the Temple by a bridge over the Kedron (*Taanith*, iv. 8). They seem to have been founded by the family of Annas, who made them very profitable, and they are called חנויות בני חני. They were destroyed by the mob when the goods of these detested priests were pillaged three years before the siege of Jerusalem. (Derenbourg, *Hist. de Pal.* 468; Buxtorf, *Lex. Talm.* s. v. דין, p. 514.)

[2] These are the Sopherîm, who may perhaps have ordinarily formed a separate committee of the Sanhedrin. See Excursus XIII., "The Sanhedrin."

[3] Though Josephus was a Pharisee, we may, from its probability, accept his testimony on this point—εἰσὶ περὶ τὰς κρίσεις ὠμοὶ παρὰ πάντας τοὺς Ἰουδαίους (*Antt.* xiii. 10, § 6; *B. J.* ii. 8, § 14). The philosophic insouciance of a man of the world, when once thoroughly irritated, knows no scruples.

had so grievously confuted. All these were bent upon His death; all filled with repulsion at that infinite goodness; all burning with hatred against a nobler nature than any which they could even conceive in their loftiest dreams. And yet their task in trying to achieve His destruction was not easy. The Jewish fables of His death in the Talmud, which are shamelessly false from beginning to end,[1] say that for forty days, though summoned daily by heraldic proclamation, not one person came forward, according to custom, to maintain His innocence, and that consequently He was first stoned as a seducer of the people (*mesíth*), and then hung on the accursed tree. The fact was that the Sanhedrists had not the power of inflicting death,[2] and even if the Pharisees would have ventured

Ordinarily the Sanhedrin was a mild tribunal. The members fasted a whole day when they had condemned any one to death, and many Rabbis declared themselves with strong abhorrence against capital punishments. Some of them—like R. Akiba—considered it a blot on a meeting of the Sanhedrin to condemn even one offender to death. (Salvador, *Institt. de Moïse*, ii.; *Vie de Jésus*, ii. 108.) Their savagery on this occasion was doubtless due to Sadducean influence. The *Megillath Taanith*, § 10, mentions a sort of traditional penal code of this party which seems to have been Draconian in its severity, and which the Pharisees got set aside. These Sadducean priests, like Simeon Ben Shetach before them, had "*hot hands*." (Derenbourg, p. 106.) See Excursus XIV., "Pharisees and Saducees."

[1] Any one who cares to look at the Talmudic falsehoods and confusion about Ben Sotada, Pandera, &c., may see them in Buxtorf, *Lex. Talm.* s. v סטד, p. 1458, seqq.; Derenbourg, *Hist. de Pal.* 468, seqq. In unexpurgated editions of the Talmud, the name of Jesus is said to occur twenty times. See Excursus II., "Allusions to Christ and Christians in the Talmud."

[2] This is distinctly stated by the Jews in John xviii. 31, and though contemporary notices seem to show that in any common case the Romans might *overlook* a judicial murder on religious grounds (John v. 18; vii. 25; Acts xxiii. 27), yet the Jews could not always act as they liked in such cases with impunity, as was proved by the reprimand and degradation of the younger Hanan for the part which he and the Sanhedrin took in the execution of James the brother of Jesus. Döllinger (*First Age of the Church*, E. Tr., p. 420) takes a different view, and thinks that all they

to usurp it in a tumultuary sedition, as they afterwards did in the case of Stephen, the less fanatic and more cosmopolitan Sadducees would be less likely to do so. Not content, therefore, with the *cherem*, or ban of greater excommunication, their only way to compass His death was to hand Him over to the secular arm.[1] At present they had only against Him a charge of constructive blasphemy, founded on an admission forced from Him by the High Priest, when even their own suborned witnesses had failed to perjure themselves to their satisfaction. There were many old accusations against Him, on which they could not rely. His violations of the Sabbath, as they called them, were all connected with miracles, and brought them, therefore, upon dangerous ground. His rejection of oral tradition involved a question on which Sadducees and Pharisees were at deadly feud. His authoritative cleansing of the Temple might be regarded with favour both by the Rabbis and the people. The charge of esoteric evil doctrines had been refuted by the utter publicity of His life. The charge of open heresies had broken down, from the total absence of supporting testimony. The problem before them was to convert the ecclesiastical charge of constructive blasphemy into a civil charge of constructive treason. But how could this be done? Not half the members of the Sanhedrin had been present at the hurried, nocturnal, and therefore illegal, session in the house of Caiaphas;[2] yet if they were all to condemn

meant was, that they could not crucify or put to death during a feast. But whatever may be the difficulties of the subject, the Talmud seems to confirm the distinct assertion of St. John. (*Berachôth*, f. 58, 1, and six or seven other places. See Buxtorf, *Lex. Talm.* p. 514.)

[1] Acts ii. 23, διὰ χειρῶν ἀνόμων προσπήξαντες.

[2] "Be tardy in judgment" (*Pirke Abhôth*; *Sanh.* i. f. 7). בת דינא בטל דינא (*Sanh.* 95, 1; Buxtorf, *Lex. Talm.*, p. 515).

Him by a formal sentence, they must all hear something on which to found their vote. In answer to the adjuration of Caiaphas, He had solemnly admitted that He was the Messiah and the Son of God. The latter declaration would have been meaningless as a charge against Him before the tribunal of the Romans; but if He would repeat the former, they might twist it into something politically seditious. But He would not repeat it, in spite of their insistence, because He knew that it was open to their wilful misinterpretation, and because they were evidently acting in flagrant violation of their own express rules and traditions, which demanded that every arraigned criminal. should be regarded and treated as innocent until his guilt was actually proved.

Perhaps, as they sat there with their King, bound and helpless before them, standing silent amid their clamorous voices, one or two of their most venerable members may have recalled the very different scene when Shemaia (Sameas) alone had broken the deep silence of their own cowardly terror upon their being convened to pass judgment on Herod for his murders. On that occasion, as Sameas had pointed out, Herod had stood before them, not " in a submissive manner, with his hair dishevelled, and in a black and mourning garment," but " clothed in purple, and with the hair of his head finely trimmed, and with his armed men about him." And since no one dared, for very fear, even to mention the charges against him, Shemaia had prophesied that the day of vengeance should come, and that the very Herod before whom they and their prince Hyrcanus were trembling, would one day be the minister of God's anger against both him and them.[1] What a contrast was the

[1] Jos. *Antt.* xiv. 9, § 4; *Bab. Sanhedrin,* f. 19, *a, b.* It is on this

present scene with that former one of half a century before! Now *they* were clamorous, their King was silent; they were powerful, their King defenceless; they guilty, their King divinely innocent; they the ministers of earthly wrath, their King the arbiter of Divine retribution.

But at last, to end a scene at once miserable and disgraceful, Jesus spoke. "If I tell you," He said, "ye will not believe; and if I ask you a question, you will not answer me." Still, lest they should have any excuse for failing to understand who He was, He added in tones of solemn warning, "But henceforth shall the Son of Man sit on the right hand of the power of God." "Art thou, then," they all exclaimed, "the Son of God?"[1] "Ye say that I am,"[2] He answered, in a formula with which they were familiar, and of which they understood the full significance. And then they too cried out, as Caiaphas had done before, "What further need have we of witness? for we ourselves heard from His own mouth." And so in this third condemnation by Jewish authority—a condemnation which they thought that Pilate would simply ratify, and so appease their burning hate—ended the third stage of the trial of our Lord. And this sentence also seems to have been followed by a *second* derision[3] resembling the first, but even more full

memorable occasion that we first meet with the name of Sanhedrin. Here Hyrcanus is, with the usual Jewish carelessness, called Jannæus, and Shemaia is called Simeon Ben Shetach. There seems, however, to be inextricable confusion between the names Hillel, Pollio, Abtalion, and Sameas, Shammai, Shemaia, and Simeon.

[1] Cf. Dan. vii. 13; Ps. viii. 4; cx. 1.

[2] On this formula (*antt' amarta*, Keim), which is found in the Talmud, see Schöttgen, *Hor. Hebr.*, p. 225, and the remarks of De Quincey, *Works*, iii. 304. It is clearly more than a mere affirmation.

[3] Unless Luke xxii. 63—65 (which seems as though it refers to

of insult, and worse to bear than the former, inasmuch as the derision of Priests, and Elders, and Sadducees is even more repulsively odious than that of menials and knaves.

Terribly soon did the Nemesis fall on the main actor in the lower stages of this iniquity. Doubtless through all those hours Judas had been a secure spectator of all that had occurred, and when the morning dawned upon that chilly night, and he knew the decision of the Priests and of the Sanhedrin, and saw that Jesus was now given over for crucifixion to the Roman Governor, then he began fully to realise all that he had done. There is in a great crime an awfully illuminating power.[1] It lights up the theatre of the conscience with an unnatural glare, and, expelling the twilight glamour of self-interest, shows the actions and motives in their full and true aspect. In Judas, as in so many thousands before and since, this opening of the eyes which follows the consummation of an awful sin to which many other sins have led, drove him from remorse to despair, from despair to madness, from madness to suicide. Had he, even then, but gone to his Lord and Saviour, and prostrated himself at His feet to implore forgiveness, all might have been well. But, alas! he went instead to the patrons and associates and tempters of his crime. From them he met with no pity, no counsel. He was a despised and broken instrument, and now he was tossed aside. They met his maddening remorse with chilly indifference and callous contempt. "I have sinned,"

verse 71) describes the issue of one of the trials which he has not narrated; but, literally taken, we might infer from Matt. xxvi. 67, that those who insulted Christ after the second trial were not *only* the servants.

[1] Tac. *Ann.* xiv. 10, "Perfecto demum scelere magnitudo ejus intellecta est" (cf. Juv. *Sat.* xiii. 238). I have tried to develop this strange law of the moral world in my *Silence and Voices of God*, p. 43.

he shrieked to them, "in that I have betrayed innocent blood." Did he expect them to console his remorseful agony, to share the blame of his guilt, to excuse and console him with their lofty dignity? "*What is that to us? See thou to that,*"[1] was the sole and heartless reply they deigned to the poor traitor whom they had encouraged, welcomed, incited to his deed of infamy. He felt that he was of no importance any longer; that in guilt there is no possibility for mutual respect, no basis for any feeling but mutual abhorrence. His paltry thirty pieces of silver were all that he would get. For these he had sold his soul; and these he should no more enjoy than Achan enjoyed the gold he buried, or Ahab the garden he had seized. Flinging them wildly down upon the pavement into the holy place where the priests sat, and into which he might not enter, he hurried into the despairing solitude from which he would never emerge alive. In that solitude, we may never know what "unclean wings" were flapping about his head. Accounts differed as to the wretch's death. The probability is that the details were never accurately made public. According to one account, he hung himself, and tradition still points in Jerusalem to a ragged, ghastly, wind-swept tree, which is called the "tree of Judas." According to another version—not irreconcilable with the first, if we suppose that a rope or a branch broke under his weight—he fell headlong, burst asunder in the midst, and all his bowels gushed out.[2] According to a third[3]—

[1] Matt. xxvii. 4, Σὺ ὄψῃ. The same words were given back to *them* by Pilate (ver. 24).

[2] Acts i. 18.

[3] Said to be derived from Papias (see Hofmann, 333; Cramer, *Cat. in Acts Ap.*, p. 12). In the Book of Jubilees the death of Cain is similarly described. (Ewald, *Gesch. Christ.*, p. 535.)

current among the early Christians—his body swelled to a huge size, under some hideous attack of elephantiasis, and he was crushed by a passing wagon. The arch-conspirators, in their sanctimonious scrupulosity, would not put the blood-money which he had returned into the "Corban," or sacred treasury, but, after taking counsel, bought with it the potter's field to bury strangers in—a plot of ground which perhaps Judas had intended to purchase, and in which he met his end. That field was long known and shuddered at as the Aceldama, or "field of blood," a place foul, haunted, and horrible.[1]

[1] St. Matthew, ever alive to Old Testament analogies, connects this circumstance with passages (apparently) of Jeremiah (xviii. 1, 2; xxxii. 6—12) and Zechariah (xi. 12, 13). It is curious that St. Matthew never *names* Zechariah, though he three times quotes him (xxi. 5; xxvi. 31; xxvii. 9); but it was a Jewish proverb that Zechariah had the spirit of Jeremiah, and it is possible (*vide* Wordsworth *ad loc.*) that this passage originally belonged to Jeremiah. The right translation seems to be, "cast it into the treasury." The notion that two fields were called Aceldama is probably a mistake of the Harmonists. Different sites for Aceldama have been pointed out at different times. Since Jeremiah's day pilgrims have been shown a field with a charnel-house in it, opposite the Pool of Siloam. Papias says that, as though the very ground were cursed, no one could pass it, ἐὰν μὴ τὰς ῥῖνας ταῖς χερσὶν ἐπιφράξῃ,

CHAPTER LX.

JESUS BEFORE PILATE.

"Per procuratorem Pontium Pilatum supplicio affectus erat."—TAC. *Ann.* xv. 44.

"SUFFERED under Pontius Pilate"—so, in every creed of Christendom, is the unhappy name of the Roman Procurator handed down to eternal execration. Yet the object of introducing that name was not to point a moral, but to fix an epoch; and, in point of fact, of all the civil and ecclesiastical rulers before whom Jesus was brought to judgment, Pilate was the least guilty of malice and hatred, the most anxious, if not to spare His agony, at least to save His life.

What manner of man was this in whose hands were placed, by power from above, the final destinies of the Saviour's life? Of his origin, and of his antecedents before A.D. 26, when he became the sixth Procurator of Judæa, but little is known. In rank he belonged to the *ordo equester*, and he owed his appointment to the influence of Sejanus. His name "Pontius" seems to point to a Samnite extraction; his cognomen "Pilatus" to a warlike ancestry. His *praenomen*, if he had one, has not been preserved. In Judæa he had acted with all the haughty violence and insolent cruelty of a typical

Roman governor. Scarcely had he been well installed as Procurator, when, allowing his soldiers to bring with them by night the silver eagles and other insignia of the legions from Cæsarea to the Holy City, he excited a furious outburst of Jewish feeling against an act which they regarded as idolatrous profanation. For five days and nights—often lying prostrate on the bare ground—they surrounded and almost stormed his residence at Cæsarea with tumultuous and threatening entreaties, and could not be made to desist on the sixth, even by the peril of immediate and indiscriminate massacre at the hands of the soldiers whom he sent to surround them. He had then sullenly given way, and this foretaste of the undaunted and fanatical resolution of the people with whom he had to deal, went far to embitter his whole administration with a sense of overpowering disgust.[1]

The outbreak of the Jews on a second occasion was perhaps less justifiable, but it might easily have been avoided, if Pilate would have studied their character a little more considerately, and paid more respect to their dominant superstition. Jerusalem seems to have always suffered, as it does very grievously to this day, from a bad and deficient supply of water. To remedy this inconvenience, Pilate undertook to build an aqueduct, by which water could be brought from the "Pools of Solomon." Regarding this as a matter of public benefit, he applied to the purpose some of the money from the "Corban," or sacred treasury, and the people rose in furious myriads to resent this secular appropriation of their sacred fund. Stung by their insults and reproaches, Pilate disguised a number of his soldiers in Jewish costume, and sent them among the mob, with

[1] Jos. *Antt.* xviii. 3, § 1; *B. J.* ii. 9, §§ 2, 3.

staves and daggers concealed under their garments, to punish the ringleaders. Upon the refusal of the Jews to separate quietly, a signal was given, and the soldiers carried out their instructions with such hearty good-will, that they wounded and beat to death not a few both of the guilty and the innocent, and created so violent a tumult that many perished by being trodden to death under the feet of the terrified and surging mob.[1] Thus, in a nation which produced the *sicarii*, Pilate had given a fatal precedent of sicarian conduct; the Assassins had received from their Procurator an example of the use of political assassination.

A third seditious tumult must still more have embittered the disgust of the Roman Governor for his subjects, by showing him how impossible it was to live among such a people—even in a conciliatory spirit—without outraging some of their sensitive prejudices. In the Herodian palace at Jerusalem, which he occupied during the festivals, he had hung some gilt shields dedicated to Tiberius. In the speech of Agrippa before the Emperor Caius, as narrated by Philo, this act is attributed to wanton malice; but since, by the king's own admission, the shields were perfectly plain, and were merely decorated with a votive inscription, it is fair to suppose that the Jews had taken offence at what Pilate simply intended for a harmless private ornament; and one which, moreover, he could hardly

[1] These two instances are twice related by Josephus, *Antt.* xviii. 3, §§ 1, 2; *B. J.* ii. 9, §§ 2, 3, 4. Ewald has precariously conjectured that the "tower of Siloam" which fell and crushed eighteen people may have been connected with these works, and so may have furnished ground to those who desired to interpret that accident as a Divine judgment (*Gesch.* v. 40; Luke xiii. 4). It has been suggested with some probability that the *real* disgust of the Jews against the plan for building an aqueduct was due to a belief that its construction would render the city less easy of defence.

remove without some danger of offending the gloomy and suspicious Emperor to whose honour they were dedicated. Since he would not give way, the chief men of the nation wrote a letter of complaint to Tiberius himself. It was a part of Tiberius's policy to keep the provinces contented, and his masculine intellect despised the obstinacy which would risk an insurrection rather than sacrifice a whim. He therefore reprimanded Pilate, and ordered the obnoxious shields to be transferred from Jerusalem to the Temple of Augustus at Cæsarea.

The latter incident is related by Philo only;[1] and besides these three outbreaks, we hear in the Gospels of some wild tumult in which Pilate had mingled the blood of the Galilæans with their sacrifices. He was finally expelled from his Procuratorship in consequence of an accusation preferred against him by the Samaritans, who complained to Lucius Vitellius, the Legate of Syria, that he had wantonly attacked, slain, and executed a number of them who had assembled on Mount Gerizim by the invitation of an impostor—possibly Simon Magus—who promised to show them the Ark and sacred vessels of the Temple, which, he said, had been concealed there by Moses.[2] The conduct of Pilate seems on this occasion to have been needlessly prompt and violent; and although, when he arrived at Rome, he found that Tiberius was dead, yet even Gaius refused to reinstate him in his government, thinking it no doubt a bad sign that he should thus have become unpleasantly involved with the people of every single district in his narrow government. Sejanus had shown

[1] *Legat. ad Caium*, § 38. Philo calls him βαρύμηνις, and τὴν φύσιν ἀκαμπὴς καὶ μετὰ τοῦ αὐθάδους ἀμείλικτος.

[2] Jos. *Antt.* xviii. 4, § 1. This was a Messianic expectation (Ewald, *Gesch. Isr.* v. 171, E. Tr.).

the most utter dislike against the Jews, and Pilate probably reflected his patron's antipathies.[1]

Such was Pontius Pilate, whom the pomps and perils of the great yearly festival had summoned from his usual residence at Cæsarea Philippi to the capital of the nation which he detested, and the head-quarters of a fanaticism which he despised. At Jerusalem he occupied one of the two gorgeous palaces which had been erected there by the lavish architectural extravagance of the first Herod. It was situated in the Upper City to the south-west of the Temple Hill, and like the similar building at Cæsarea, having passed from the use of the provincial king to that of the Roman governor, was called Herod's Praetorium.[2] It was one of those luxurious abodes, "surpassing all description," which were in accordance with the tendencies of the age, and on which Josephus dwells with ecstasies of admiration.[3] Between its colossal wings of white marble—called respectively Cæsareum and Agrippeum, in the usual spirit of Herodian flattery to the Imperial house—was an open space commanding a noble view of Jerusalem, adorned with sculptured porticos and columns of many-coloured marble, paved with rich mosaics, varied with fountains and reservoirs, and green promenades which furnished a delightful asylum to flocks of doves.[4] Externally

[1] See Salvador, *Dominion Romaine*, i. 428.

[2] Acts xxiii. 35. Verres occupied an old palace of Hiero at Syracuse (Cic. *Verr.* ii. 5, 12).

[3] Jos. *B. J.* v. 4, § 4: παντὸς λόγου κρείσσων; *id.*, οὐθ' ἑρμηνεῦσαι δυνατὸν ἀξίως τὰ βασίλεια.

[4] See Jos. *B. J.* ii. 14, § 8; 15, § 5, from which it appears that Florus usually occupied this palace. For the Caesareum and the Agrippeum, see *id.* i. 21, § 1, δύο τοὺς μεγίστους καὶ περικαλλεστάτους οἴκους οἷς οὐδὲ ναὸς πῄ συνεκρίνετο; *id.* v. 4, § 4, ἀδιήγητος ἡ ποικιλία τῶν λίθων ἦν.—Keim [Eine stolze Residenz für einen römischen Ritter] has partly reproduced the description of Josephus, III. ii. 2, 361.

it was a mass of lofty walls, and towers, and gleaming roofs, mingled in exquisite varieties of splendour; within, its superb rooms, large enough to accommodate a hundred guests, were adorned with gorgeous furniture and vessels of gold and silver. A magnificent abode for a mere Roman knight! and yet the furious fanaticism of the populace at Jerusalem made it a house so little desirable, that neither Pilate nor his predecessors seem to have cared to enjoy its luxuries for more than a few weeks in the whole year. They were forced to be present in the Jewish capital during those crowded festivals which were always liable to be disturbed by some outburst of inflammable patriotism, and they soon discovered that even a gorgeous palace can furnish but a repulsive residence if it be built on the heaving lava of a volcano.

In that kingly palace—such as in His days of freedom He had never trod—began, in three distinct acts, the fourth stage of that agitating scene which preceded the final agonies of Christ. It was unlike the idle inquisition of Annas—the extorted confession of Caiaphas—the illegal decision of the Sanhedrin; for here His judge was in His favour, and with all the strength of a feeble pride, and all the daring of a guilty cowardice, and all the pity of which a blood-stained nature was capable, did strive to deliver Him. This last trial is full of passion and movement: it involves a threefold change of scene, a threefold accusation, a threefold acquittal by the Romans, a threefold rejection by the Jews, a threefold warning to Pilate, and a threefold effort on his part, made with ever-increasing energy and ever-deepening agitation, to baffle the accusers and to set the victim free.[1]

[1] German criticism has, without any sufficient grounds, set aside as unhistorical much of St. John's narrative of this trial; but although it is

1. It was probably about seven in the morning that, thinking to overawe the Procurator by their numbers and their dignity, the imposing procession of the Sanhedrists and Priests, headed, no doubt, by Caiaphas himself, conducted Jesus, with a cord round His neck,[1] from their Hall of Meeting over the lofty bridge which spanned the Valley of the Tyropœon, in presence of all the city, with the bound hands of a sentenced criminal, a spectacle to angels and to men.

Disturbed at this early hour, and probably prepared for some Paschal disturbance more serious than usual, Pilate entered the Hall of Judgment, whither Jesus had been led, in company (as seems clear) with a certain number of His accusers and of those most deeply interested in His case.[2] But the great Jewish hierarchs, shrinking from ceremonial pollution, though not from moral guilt—afraid of leaven, though not afraid of innocent blood—refused to enter the Gentile's hall, lest they should be polluted, and should consequently be unable that night to eat the Passover. In no good humour, but in haughty and half-necessary condescension to what he would regard as the despicable superstitions of an inferior race, Pilate goes out to them

not mentioned either by Josephus or by Philo, it agrees in the very minutest particulars with everything which we could expect from the accounts which they give us, both of Pilate's own character and antecedents, and of the relations in which he stood to the Emperor and to the Jews.

[1] δήσαντες (Matt. xxvii. 2; Mark xv. 1). In sign of condemnation: such at least is the early tradition, and St. Basil derives from this circumstance the use of the *stole* (Jer. Taylor, III. xv.).

[2] Being only a procurator, Pilate had no *quaestor*, and therefore was obliged to try all causes himself. In this instance, he very properly refused to assume the responsibility of the execution without sharing in the trial. He did not choose to degraee himself into a mere tool of Jewish superstition.

under the burning early sunlight of an Eastern spring. One haughty glance takes in the pompous assemblage of priestly notables, and the turbulent mob of this singular people, equally distasteful to him as a Roman and as a ruler; and observing in that one glance the fierce passions of the accusers, as he had already noted the meek ineffable grandeur of their victim, his question is sternly brief: "What accusation bring ye against this man?" The question took them by surprise, and showed them that they must be prepared for an unconcealed antagonism to all their purposes. Pilate evidently intended a judicial inquiry; *they* had expected only a licence to kill, and to kill, not by a Jewish method of execution, but by one which they regarded as more horrible and accursed.[1] "If He were not a malefactor," is their indefinite and surly answer, "we would not have delivered Him up unto thee." But Pilate's Roman knowledge of law, his Roman instinct of justice, his Roman contempt for their murderous fanaticism, made him not choose to act upon a charge so entirely vague, nor give the sanction of his tribunal to their dark disorderly decrees. He would not deign to be an executioner where he had not been a judge. "Very well," he answered, with a superb contempt, "take ye Him and judge Him according to your law." But now they are forced to the humiliating confession that, having been deprived of the *jus gladii*, they cannot inflict the death

[1] Deut. xxi. 22, 23. Hence the name of hatred התלוי, "*the Hung*," applied to Christ in the Talmud; and Christians are called "servants of the Hung" (עובדי התלוי). Their reasons for desiring His crucifixion may have been manifold, besides the obvious motives of hatred and revenge. (1.) It would involve the name and memory of Jesus in deeper discredit. (2.) It would render the Roman authorities accomplices in the responsibility of the murder. (3.) It would greatly diminish any possible chance of a popular *émeute*.

which alone will satisfy them; for indeed it stood written in the eternal councils that Christ was to die, not by Jewish stoning or strangulation, but by that Roman form of execution which inspired the Jews with a nameless horror, even by crucifixion;[1] that He was to reign from His cross—to die by that most fearfully significant and typical of deaths—public, slow, conscious, accursed, agonising—worse even than burning—the worst type of all possible deaths, and the worst result of that curse which He was to remove for ever. Dropping, therefore, for the present the charge of blasphemy, which did not suit their purpose,[2] they burst into a storm of invectives against Him, in which are discernible the triple accusations, that He perverted the nation, that He forbade to give tribute, that He called himself a king. All three charges were flagrantly false, and the third all the more so because it included a grain of truth. But since they had not confronted Jesus with any proofs or witnesses, Pilate—in whose whole bearing and language is manifest the disgust embittered by fear with which the Jews inspired him—deigns to notice the third charge alone, and proceeds to discover whether the confession of the prisoner—always held desirable by Roman insti-

[1] Deut. xxi. 23; Numb. xxv. 4; 2 Sam. xxi. 6; Jos. *B. J.* vii. 6, § 4, *οὐκ ἀνασχετὸν εἶναι τὸ πάθος λέγοντες.* Some obscurity hangs over the question as to when and how the Jews had lost the power of inflicting capital punishment (John xviii. 31). The Talmud seems to imply (Lightfoot, *Hor. Hebr. in loc.*) that they had lost it by voluntarily abandoning the use of the *Lishcat haggazzith,* on account of the number of murderers whom they were forced to condemn. But this, in the usual loose Jewish way, is fixed "forty years before the destruction of the Temple" (*Aboda Zara,* f. 8, 2; Buxtorf, *Lex. Talm.*, p. 513). Others suppose that it was still permitted to them—or at any rate its use connived at—in ecclesiastical (Acts vii. 57; Jos. *Antt.* xx. 9, § 1) but not in civil cases. They had, legally, only the *cognitio caussae.*

[2] Cf. Acts xviii. 14.

tutions—would enable him to take any cognisance of it. Leaving the impatient Sanhedrin and the raging crowd, he retired into the Judgment Hall. St. John alone preserves for us the memorable scene. Jesus, though not "in soft clothing," though not a denizen of kings' houses, had been led up the noble flight of stairs, over the floors of agate and lazuli, under the gilded roofs, ceiled with cedar and painted with vermilion, which adorned but one abandoned palace of a great king of the Jews. There, amid those voluptuous splendours, Pilate —already interested, already feeling in this prisoner before him some nobleness which touched his Roman nature—asked Him in pitying wonder, "Art *thou* the King of the Jews?"—thou poor, worn, tear-stained outcast in this hour of thy bitter need[1]—oh, pale, lonely, friendless, wasted man, in thy poor peasant garments, with thy tied hands, and the foul traces of the insults of thine enemies on thy face, and on thy robes—thou, so unlike the fierce magnificent Herod, whom this multitude which thirsts for thy blood acknowledged as their sovereign—art *thou* the King of the Jews? There is a royalty which Pilate, and men like Pilate, cannot understand—a royalty of holiness, a supremacy of self-sacrifice. To say "No" would have been to belie the truth; to say "Yes" would have been to mislead the questioner. "Sayest thou this of thyself?" He answered with gentle dignity, "or did others tell it thee of me?"[2] "Am I a *Jew?*" is the disdainful answer. "Thy own nation and the chief priests delivered thee unto me.

[1] See J. Baldwin Brown, *Misread Passages of Scripture*, p. 2.

[2] This shows that Jesus, who seems to have been led immediately inside the walls of the Prætorium, had not heard the charges laid against Him before the Procurator.

What hast thou *done?*" Done?—works of wonder, and mercy, and power, and innocence, and these alone. But Jesus reverts to the first question, now that He has prepared Pilate to understand the answer: "Yes, He is a king; but not of this world; not from hence; not one for whom His servants would fight." "Thou *art* a king, then?" said Pilate to Him in astonishment. Yes! but a king not in this region of falsities and shadows, but one born to bear witness unto the truth, and one whom all who were of the truth should hear. "Truth," said Pilate impatiently, "what is *truth?*" What had he—a busy, practical Roman governor—to do with such dim abstractions? what bearing had they on the question of life and death? what unpractical hallucination, what fairyland of dreaming phantasy was this? Yet, though he contemptuously put the discussion aside, he was touched and moved. A judicial mind, a forensic training, familiarity with human nature which had given him some insight into the characters of men, showed him that Jesus was not only wholly innocent, but infinitely nobler and better than His raving sanctimonious accusers. He wholly set aside the floating idea of an unearthly royalty; he saw in the prisoner before his tribunal an innocent and high-souled dreamer, nothing more. And so, leaving Jesus there, he went out again to the Jews, and pronounced his first emphatic and unhesitating acquittal: "I FIND IN HIM NO FAULT AT ALL."

2. But this public decided acquittal only kindled the fury of His enemies into yet fiercer flame. After all that they had hazarded, after all that they had inflicted, after the sleepless night of their plots, adjurations, insults, was their purpose to be foiled after all by the

intervention of the very Gentiles on whom they had relied for its bitter consummation? Should this victim whom they had thus clutched in their deadly grasp, be rescued from High Priests and rulers by the contempt or the pity of an insolent heathen? It was too intolerable! Their voices rose in wilder tumult. "He was a *mesîth*;[1] He had upset the people with His teaching through the length and breadth of the land, beginning from Galilee, even as far as here."

Amid these confused and passionate exclamations the practised ear of Pilate caught the name of "Galilee," and he understood that Galilee had been the chief scene of the ministry of Jesus.[2] Eager for a chance of dismissing a business of which he was best pleased to be free, he proposed, by a master-stroke of astute policy, to get rid of an embarrassing prisoner, to save himself from a disagreeable decision, and to do an unexpected complaisance to the unfriendly Galilæan tetrarch, who, as usual, had come to Jerusalem—nominally to keep the Passover, really to please his subjects, and to enjoy the sensations and festivities offered at that season by the densely-crowded capital. Accordingly, Pilate secretly glad to wash his hands of a detestable responsibility, sent Jesus to[3] Herod Antipas, who was probably occu-

[1] In *Masseketh Sanhedrin* vii. 10 a *mesîth* is defined as an unauthorised person (ἰδιωτης) who leads others astray. (המסית זה הדיוט המסית את ההדיוט.)

[2] Luke xxiii. 6.

[3] Luke xxiii. 7, ἀνέπεμψεν, "*remisit;*" "propriam Romani juris vocem usurpavit" (Grotius): cf. Acts xxv. 21. Mutual jealousies, and tendencies to interfere with each other's authority, are quite sufficient to account for the previous ill-will of Pilate and Herod. Moreover, in all disputes it had been the obvious policy of Antipas to side with the Jews. Renan aptly compares the relations of the Herods to the Procurator with that of the Hindoo Rajahs to the Viceroy of India under the English dominion.

pying the old Asmonæan palace, which had been the royal residence at Jerusalem until it had been surpassed by the more splendid one which the prodigal tyrant, his father, had built.[1] And so, through the thronged and narrow streets, amid the jeering, raging multitudes, the weary Sufferer was dragged once more.

We have caught glimpses of this Herod Antipas before, and I do not know that all History, in its gallery of portraits, contains a much more despicable figure than this wretched, dissolute Idumæan Sadducee—this petty princeling drowned in debauchery and blood. To him was addressed the sole purely contemptuous expression that Jesus is ever recorded to have used.[2] Superstition and incredulity usually go together; avowed atheists have yet believed in augury, and men who do not believe in God will believe in ghosts.[3] Antipas was rejoiced beyond all things to see Jesus. He had long been wanting to see Him because of the rumours he had heard; and this murderer of the prophets hoped that Jesus would, in compliment to royalty, amuse by some miracle his gaping curiosity. He harangued and questioned Him in many words, but gained not so much as one syllable in reply. Our Lord confronted all his ribald questions with the majesty of

[1] We find the old Asmonæan palace occupied long afterwards by Agrippa II. (Jos. *B. J.* ii. 16, § 3; *Antt.* xx. 8, § 11). Sepp, in his fanciful way, points out that Jesus had thus been thrown into connection with a palace of David (at Bethlehem) of the Asmonæans, and of Herod.

[2] Luke xiii. 32, "This fox," τῇ ἀλώπεκι ταύτῃ (*v. supr.*, p. 95).

[3] Philippe d'Orleans (Egalité), a professed atheist, when in prison, tried to divine his fate by the grounds in a coffee-cup! This atheistic age *swarmed* with Chaldaei, mathematici, magicians, sorcerers, charlatans, impostors of every class. "Le monde était affolé de miracles, jamais on ne fut si occupé de présages. Le Dieu Père paraissait avoir voilé sa face; des larves impurs, des monstres sortis d'un limon mystérieux, semblaient errer dans l'air" (Renan, *L'Antechr.*, p. 323).

silence. To such a man, who even changed scorn into a virtue, speech would clearly have been a profanation. Then all the savage vulgarity of the man came out through the thin veneer of a superficial cultivation. For the second time Jesus is derided—derided this time as Priest and Prophet. Herod and his corrupt hybrid myrmidons "set Him at nought"—treated Him with the insolence of a studied contempt. Mocking His innocence and His misery in a festal and shining robe,[1] the empty and wicked prince sent Him back to the Procurator, to whom he now became half-reconciled after a long-standing enmity. But he contented himself with these cruel insults. He resigned to the *forum apprehensionis* all further responsibility as to the issue of the trial. Though the Chief Priests and Scribes stood about his throne unanimously instigating him to a fresh and more heinous act of murder by their intense accusations,[2] he practically showed that he thought their accusations frivolous, by treating them as a jest. It was the fifth trial of Jesus; it was His second public distinct acquittal.

3. And now, as He stood once more before the perplexed and wavering Governor, began the sixth, the last, the most agitating and agonising phase of this terrible inquisition. Now was the time for Pilate to have acted on a clear and right conviction, and saved himself for ever from the guilt of innocent blood. He came out once more, and seating himself on a stately *bema*—perhaps the golden throne of Archelaus, which

[1] Luke xxiii. 11, *ἐσθῆτα λαμπράν*, probably "white," as a festive colour; but the notion of his being a "*candidate*" for the kingdom, is quite alien from the passage.

[2] *εὐτόνως*. Cf. Acts xviii. 28.

was placed on the elevated pavement of many-coloured marble[1]—summoned the Priests, the Sanhedrists, and the people before him, and seriously told them that they had brought Jesus to his tribunal as a leader of sedition and turbulence; that after full and fair inquiry he, their Roman Governor, had found their prisoner absolutely guiltless of these charges; that he had then sent Him to Herod, their native king, and that *he* also had come to the conclusion that Jesus had committed no crime which deserved the punishment of death. And now came the golden opportunity for him to vindicate the grandeur of his country's imperial justice, and, as he had pronounced Him absolutely innocent, to set Him absolutely free. But exactly at that point he wavered and temporised. The dread of another insurrection haunted him like a nightmare. He was willing to go half way to please these dangerous sectaries. To justify them, as it were, in their accusation, he would chastise Jesus—scourge Him publicly, as though to render His pretensions ridiculous—disgrace and ruin Him—"make Him seem vile in their eyes"[2]—and *then* set Him free. And this notion of setting Him free suggested to him *another* resource of tortuous policy. Both he and the people almost simultaneously bethought themselves that it had always been a Paschal boon to liberate at the feast some condemned prisoner. He offered, therefore, to make the acquittal of Jesus an act not of imperious justice, but of artificial grace.

In making this suggestion—in thus flagrantly tam-

[1] John xix. 13, "Gabbatha." The Roman governors and generals attached great importance to these tessellated pavements on which their tribunals were placed (Suet. *Jul. Caes.* 46).

[2] Deut. xxv. 3. μάστιξιν αἰκίζεσθαι (Jos. *B. J.* vii. 6, § 4).

pering with his innate sense of right, and resigning against his will the best prerogative of his authority—he was already acting in spite of a warning which he had received. That first warning consisted in the deep misgiving, the powerful presentiment, which overcame him as he looked on his bowed and silent prisoner. But, as though to strengthen him in his resolve to prevent an absolute failure of *all* justice, he now received a *second* solemn warning—and one which to an ordinary Roman, and a Roman who remembered Cæsar's murder and Calpurnia's dream, might well have seemed divinely sinister. His own wife—Claudia Procula[1]—ventured to send him a public message, even as he sat there on his tribunal, that, in the morning hours, when dreams are true,[2] she had had a troubled and painful dream about that Just Man; and, bolder than her husband, she bade him beware how he molested Him.

Gladly, most gladly, would Pilate have yielded to his own presentiments—have gratified his pity and his justice—have obeyed the prohibition conveyed by this mysterious omen. Gladly even would he have yielded to the worse and baser instinct of asserting his power, and thwarting these envious and hated fanatics, whom he knew to be ravening for innocent blood. That they—to many of whom sedition was as the breath of life—should be sincere in charging Jesus with sedition was,

[1] Her name is given in the Gospel of Nicodemus, which says she was a proselyte. On the possibility of a wife's presence in her husband's province, in spite of the old Leges Oppiae, see Tac. *Ann.* iii. 33, 34; iv. 20. For similar instances of dreams, see Otho, *Lex. Rabb.*, p. 316; Winer, *Realwört.*, s. v. "Träume."

[2] Matt. xxvii. 19, σήμερον. "Post mediam noctem visus quum somnia vera" (Hor. *Sat.* i. 10, 31). "Sub auroram—tempore quo cerni somnia vera solent" (Ov. *Her.* xix. 195). Perhaps she had been awakened that morning by the noise of the crowd.

as he well knew, absurd. Their utterly transparent hypocrisy in this matter only added to his undisguised contempt. If he could have dared to show his real instincts, he would have driven them from his tribunal with all the haughty insouciance of a Gallio. But Pilate was guilty, and guilt is cowardice, and cowardice is weakness. His own past cruelties, recoiling in kind on his own head, forced him now to crush the impulse of pity, and to add to his many cruelties another more heinous still.[1] He knew that serious complaints hung over his head. Those Samaritans whom he had insulted and oppressed—those Jews whom he had stabbed promiscuously in the crowd by the hands of his disguised and secret emissaries—those Galilæans whose blood he had mingled with their sacrifices—was not their blood crying for vengeance? Was not an embassy of complaint against him imminent even now? Would it not be dangerously precipitated if, in so dubious a matter as a charge of claiming a kingdom, he raised a tumult among a people in whose case it was the best interest of the Romans that they should hug their chains? Dare he stand the chance of stirring up a new and apparently terrible rebellion rather than condescend to a simple concession, which was rapidly assuming the aspect of a politic, and even necessary, compromise?

His tortuous policy recoiled on his own head, and rendered impossible his own wishes. The Nemesis of

[1] We see the same notions very strikingly at work in his former dispute with the Jews about the shields—"He was afraid that, if they should send an embassy, they might discuss the many mal-administrations of his government, his extortions, his unjust decrees, his inhuman punishments. This reduced him to the utmost perplexity." (Philo, *Leg. ad Caium*, p. 38.) (*τὰς ὕβρεις, τὰς ἁρπαγὰς, τὰς αἰκίας, τὰς ἐπηρείας, τοὺς ἀκρίτους καὶ ἐπαλλήλους φόνους, τὴν ἀνήνυτον καὶ ἀργαλεωτάτην ὠμότητα.*)

his past wrong-doing was that he could no longer do right. Hounded on[1] by the Priests and Sanhedrists, the people impetuously claimed the Paschal boon of which he had reminded them; but in doing so they unmasked still more decidedly the sinister nature of their hatred against their Redeemer. For while they were professing to rage against the asserted seditiousness of One who was wholly obedient and peaceful, they shouted for the liberation of a man whose notorious sedition had been also stained by brigandage and murder. Loathing the innocent, they loved the guilty, and claimed the Procurator's grace on behalf, not of Jesus of Nazareth, but of a man who, in the fearful irony of circumstance, was also called Jesus—Jesus Bar-Abbas[2]—who not only *was* what they falsely said of Christ, a leader of sedition, but also a robber and a murderer. It was fitting that *they*, who had preferred an abject Sadducee to their true priest, and an incestuous Idumæan to their Lord and King, should deliberately prefer a murderer to their Messiah.

It may be that Bar-Abbas had been brought forth, and that thus Jesus the scowling murderer and Jesus the innocent Redeemer stood together on that high

[1] Mark xv. 11, ἀνέσεισαν τὸν λαόν. History, down to this day, has given us numberless instances of the utter fickleness of crowds; but it is clear that throughout these scenes the fury and obstinacy of the people are not spontaneous.

[2] Bar-Abbas, son of a (distinguished) father; perhaps Bar-Rabban, son of a Rabbi. The reading Jesus Bar-Abbas is as old as Origen, and is far from improbable, although Matt. xxvii. 20 tells a little against it. If, however, Origen (as seems to be the case) only found this reading in verse 17, the probability of its genuineness is weakened. The ingenious combinations of Ewald, that the *Sanhedrists* desired his release, as belonging by family to their order, and the *people* because he had been imprisoned in the Corban riot (Jos. *Antt.*, *ubi supr.*), are highly uncertain.

tribunal side by side.[1] The people, persuaded by their priests, clamoured for the liberation of the rebel and the robber. To him every hand was pointed; for him every voice was raised. For the Holy, the Harmless, the Undefiled—for Him whom a thousand Hosannas had greeted but five days before—no word of pity or of pleading found an utterance. "He was despised and rejected of men."

Deliberately putting the question to them, Pilate heard with scornful indignation their deliberate choice; and then, venting his bitter disdain and anger in taunts, which did but irritate them more, without serving any good purpose, "What then," he scornfully asked them, "do ye wish me to do with the King of the Jews?" Then first broke out the mad scream, "Crucify! crucify Him!" In vain, again and again, in the pauses of the tumult, Pilate insisted, obstinately indeed, but with more and more feebleness of purpose—for none but a man more innocent than Pilate, even if he were a Roman governor, could have listened without quailing to the frantic ravings of an Oriental mob[2]—"Why, what evil hath He done?" "I found *no* cause of death in Him." "I will chastise Him and let Him go." Such half-willed opposition was wholly unavailing. It only betrayed to the Jews the inward fears of their Procurator,[3] and practically made them masters of the

[1] Matt. xxvii. 21.

[2] See Isa. v. 7. These Jewish mobs could, as we see from Josephus, be very abusive. "They came about his (Pilate's) tribunal, and made a clamour at it" (*B. J.* ii. 9, § 4). "Many myriads of the people got together, and made a clamour against him, and insisted that he should leave off that design. *Some of them also used reproaches, and abused the man* (Pilate), *as crowds of such people usually do.* . . . So he bade the Jews go away, *but they, boldly casting reproaches upon him,*" &c. (*Antt.* xviii. 3, § 2).

[3] Thus, in the affair of the gilt votive shields, the Jewish leaders were

situation. Again and again, with wilder and wilder vehemence, they rent the air with those hideous yells —"*Αἶρε τοῦτον. Ἀπόλυσον ἡμῖν Βαραββᾶν. Σταύρωσον, σταύρωσον*—"Away with this man." "Loose unto us Bar-Abbas." "Crucify! crucify!"

For a moment Pilate seemed utterly to yield to the storm. He let Bar-Abbas free; he delivered Jesus over to be scourged. The word used for the scourging (*φραγελλώσας*[1]) implies that it was done, not with rods (*virgae*), for Pilate had no lictors, but with what Horace calls the "horribile flagellum," of which the Russian knout is the only modern representative. This scourging was the ordinary preliminary to crucifixion and other forms of capital punishment.[2] It was a punishment so truly horrible, that the mind revolts at it; and it has long been abolished by that compassion of mankind which has been so greatly intensified, and in some degree even created, by the gradual comprehension of Christian truth. The unhappy sufferer was publicly stripped, was tied by the hands in a bent position to a pillar, and then, on the tense quivering nerves of the naked back, the blows were inflicted with leathern

confirmed in their purpose, by perceiving that Pilate's mind was wavering (Philo, *ubi supr.*) This, no doubt, is the kind of ἀνανδρία with which he is charged in *App. Constt.* v. 14.

[1] Matt. xxvii. 26. St. Luke, with a deep touch of pathos, merely says that Pilate "gave up Jesus to their will," and then, as though he wished to drop a veil on all that followed, he does not even tell us that they led Him away, but adds, "And as they led Him away" (Luke xxiii. 25, 26).

[2] Matt. xxvii. 26. *Lora* (μάστιξ) not the ῥαβδοί (2 Cor. xi. 24, 25). It was illegal for Roman citizens, though sometimes inflicted, especially in the provinces (Acts xxii. 26; cf. Tac. *Hist.* iv. 27; Cic. *Verr.* v. 6, 62; Jos. *B. J.* ii. 14, §9). We are not told the number of the blows usually inflicted; they depended on the greater or less brutality of the presiding authority. The forty mentioned in the *Acts of Pilate* are clearly a reminiscence of *Jewish* customs. In John xix. 1, the word is ἐμαστίγωσεν —"ego in *flagella* paratus sum" (Vulg. Psa. xxxvii. 18); Isa. l. 6.

thongs, weighted with jagged edges of bone and lead; sometimes even the blows fell by accident—sometimes, with terrible barbarity, were purposely struck—on the face and eyes.[1] It was a punishment so hideous that, under its lacerating agony, the victim generally fainted, often died; still more frequently a man was sent away to perish under the mortification and nervous exhaustion which ensued. And this awful cruelty, on which we dare not dwell—this cruelty which makes the heart shudder and grow cold—was followed immediately by the third and bitterest derision—the derision of Christ as King.

In civilised nations all is done that can be done to spare every needless suffering to a man condemned to death; but among the Romans insult and derision were the customary preliminaries to the last agony. The "*et pereuntibus addita ludibria*" of Tacitus[2] might stand for their general practice. Such a custom furnished a specimen of that worst and lowest form of human wickedness which delights to inflict pain, which feels an inhuman pleasure in gloating over the agonies of another, even when he has done no wrong. The mere spectacle of agony is agreeable to the degraded soul. The low vile soldiery of the Prætorium—not Romans, who might have had more sense of the inborn dignity of the silent sufferer, but mostly the mere mercenary scum and dregs of the provinces—led Him into their barrack-room, and there mocked, in their savage hatred, the King whom they had tortured. It

[1] See Cicero, *Verr.* v. 54; Hor. *Sat.* i. 3; *μάστιξ ἀστραγαλωτὴ* (Athen. 153, A; Luc. *Asin.* 38); "flagrum pecuinis ossibus catenatum" (Apul. *Met.* 8), "I, lictor, *colliga manus*" (Liv. i. 26); "ad palum delegatus, lacerato virgis tergo" (id. xxvii. 13); "verberati crucibus affixi" (id. xxxiii. 36).

[2] *Ann.* xv. 44.

added keenness to their enjoyment to have in their power One who was of Jewish birth, of innocent life, of noblest bearing.[1] The opportunity broke so agreeably the coarse monotony of their life, that they summoned all of the cohort who were disengaged to witness their brutal sport. In sight of these hardened ruffians they went through the whole heartless ceremony of a mock coronation, a mock investiture, a mock homage. Around the brows of Jesus, in wanton mimicry of the Emperor's laurel, they twisted a green wreath of thorny leaves;[2] in His tied and trembling hands they placed a reed for sceptre; from His torn and bleeding shoulders they stripped the white robe with which Herod had mocked Him—which must now have been all soaked with blood—and flung on Him an old scarlet paludament—some cast-off war cloak, with its purple laticlave, from the Praetorian wardrobe.[3] This, with feigned solemnity, they buckled

[1] Josephus gives us several instances of the insane wantonness with which the soldiers delighted to insult the detested race among whom they were stationed (*B. J.* ii. 12, § 1; v. 11, § 1; *Antt.* xix. 9, § 1).

[2] It cannot be known of what plant this acanthine crown was formed. The *nubk* (*zizyphus lotus*) struck me, as it has struck all travellers in Palestine, as being most suitable both for mockery and pain, since its leaves are bright and its thorns singularly strong; but though the *nubk* is very common on the shores of Galilee, I saw none of it near Jerusalem. There may, however, have been some of it in the garden of Herod's palace, and the soldiers would give themselves no sort of trouble, but merely take the first plant that came to hand.

[3] Such presents were sent to allied kings (Liv. xxx. 17; Tac. *Ann.* xii. 56). (Keim.) Cf. 1 Macc. xiv. 44.—St. Matthew calls it "scarlet," St. Mark "purple." The ancients discriminated colours very loosely; or rather, very differently from what we do. Our nomenclature dwells chiefly on differences of *hue*, and their implicit analysis was of another kind. (See some excellent remarks in Mr. Gladstone's *Juventus Mundi*, p. 540; Ruskin, *Modern Painters*, iii. 225.)—For instance of similar mockery see Philo, *in Flacc.* 980, where Herod Agrippa II. is insulted in the person of an idiot, at Alexandria. Shakespeare's pathetic scene of the insults heaped upon Richard II. will recur to every English reader.

over His right shoulder, with its glittering fibula; and then—each with his derisive homage of bended knee—each with his infamous spitting—each with the blow over the head from the reed-sceptre, which His bound hands could not hold—they kept passing before Him with their mock salutation of "Hail, King of the Jews!"[1]

Even now, even yet, Pilate wished, hoped, even strove to save Him. He might represent this frightful scourging, not as the preliminary to crucifixion, but as an inquiry by torture, which had failed to elicit any further confession. And as Jesus came forth—as He stood beside him with that martyr-form on the beautiful mosaic of the tribunal—the spots of blood upon His green wreath of torture, the mark of blows and spitting on His countenance, the weariness of His deathful agony upon the sleepless eyes, the *sagum* of faded scarlet, darkened by the weals of His lacerated back, and dropping, it may be, its stains of crimson upon the tesselated floor—even then, even so, in that hour of His extremest humiliation—yet, as He stood in the grandeur of His holy calm on that lofty tribunal above the yelling crowd, there shone all over Him so Godlike a pre-eminence, so divine a nobleness, that Pilate broke forth with that involuntary exclamation which has thrilled with emotion so many million hearts—

"BEHOLD THE MAN!"

But his appeal only woke a fierce outbreak of the scream, "Crucify! crucify!" The mere sight of Him, even in this His unspeakable shame and sorrow, seemed to add fresh fuel to their hate. In vain the heathen soldier appeals for humanity to the Jewish priest; no

[1] John xix. 3.

heart throbbed with responsive pity; no voice of compassion broke that monotonous yell of "Crucify!"—the howling refrain of their wild "liturgy of death." The Roman who had shed blood like water, on the field of battle, in open massacre, in secret assassination, might well be supposed to have an icy and a stony heart; but yet icier and stonier was the heart of those scrupulous hypocrites and worldly priests. "Take ye Him, and crucify Him," said Pilate, in utter disgust, "for I find no fault in Him." What an admission from a Roman judge! "So far as I can see, He is wholly innocent; yet if you *must* crucify Him, take Him and crucify. I cannot approve of, but I will readily connive at, your violation of the law." But even this wretched guilty subterfuge is not permitted him. Satan will have from his servants the full tale of their crimes, and the sign-manual of their own willing assent at last. What the Jews want—what the Jews *will have*—is *not* tacit connivance, but absolute sanction. They see their power. They see that this blood-stained Governor dares not hold out against them; they know that the Roman statecraft is tolerant of concessions to local superstition. Boldly, therefore, they fling to the winds all question of a political offence, and with all their hypocritical pretences calcined by the heat of their passion, they shout, "We have a law, and by our law He ought to die, because He made Himself a Son of God."[1]

[1] "It is not Tiberius's pleasure that any of our laws should be violated." (Philo, *ubi suprà*, and *Leg. ad Caium*, 1014; and Tac. *Ann.* i. 9, and the boast of the Monumentum Ancyranum, "modestiam apud socios.") The inscription on the *Chêl* forbidding any Gentile on pain of death to pass beyond it, has recently been discovered built into the wall of a mosque at Jerusalem, and is a relic of the deepest interest.

A Son of God! The notion was far less strange and repulsive to a heathen than to a Jew; and this word, unheard before, startled Pilate with the third omen which made him tremble at the crime into which he was being dragged by guilt and fear. Once more, leaving the yelling multitude without, he takes Jesus with him into the quiet Judgment Hall, and—"*jam pro suá conscientiá Christianus,*" as Tertullian so finely observes[1]—asks Him in awe-struck accents, "Whence art thou?" Alas! it was too late to answer now. Pilate was too deeply committed to his gross cruelty and injustice; for *him* Jesus had spoken enough already; for the wild beasts who raged without, He had no more to say. He did not answer. Then, almost angrily, Pilate broke out with the exclamation, "Dost thou not speak even *to me?*[2] Dost Thou not know that I have power to set thee free, and have power to crucify Thee?" Power—how so? Was justice nothing, then? truth nothing? innocence nothing? conscience nothing? In the reality of things Pilate had *no* such power; even in the arbitrary sense of the tyrant it was an idle boast, for at this very moment he was letting "I dare not" wait upon "I would." And Jesus pitied the hopeless bewilderment of this man, whom guilt had changed from a ruler into a slave. Not taunting, not confuting him—nay, even extenuating rather than aggravating his sin—Jesus gently answered, "Thou hast no power against Me whatever, had it not been given thee from above; therefore he that betrayed me to thee hath the greater sin." Thou art indeed committing a great crime—but Judas, Annas, Caiaphas, these priests and Jews, are more to

[1] Tert. *Apol.* 21.

[2] The position of the ἐμοὶ is emphatic (John xix. 10, 11).

blame than thou. Thus, with infinite dignity, and yet with infinite tenderness, did Jesus judge His judge. In the very depths of his inmost soul Pilate felt the truth of the words—silently acknowledged the superiority of his bound and lacerated victim. All that remained in him of human and of noble—

> "Felt how awful Goodness is, and Virtue,
> In her shape how lovely; felt and mourned
> His fall."

All of his soul that was not eaten away by pride and cruelty thrilled back an unwonted echo to these few calm words of the Son of God. Jesus had condemned his sin, and so far from being offended, the judgment only deepened his awe of this mysterious Being, whose utter impotence seemed grander and more awful than the loftiest power. From that time Pilate was even yet more anxious to save Him. With all his conscience in a tumult, for the third and last time he mounted his tribunal, and made one more desperate effort. He led Jesus forth, and looking at Him, as He stood silent and in agony, but calm, on that shining Gabbatha, above the brutal agitations of the multitude, he said to those frantic rioters, as with a flash of genuine conviction, "BEHOLD YOUR KING!" But to the Jews it sounded like shameful scorn to call that beaten insulted Sufferer their King. A darker stream mingled with the passions of the raging, swaying crowd. Among the shouts of "Crucify," ominous threatenings began for the first time to be mingled. It was now nine o'clock, and for nearly three hours[1] had they been raging and waiting

[1] As to the hour there is a well-known discrepancy between John xix. 14, "And it was . . . . about the *sixth* hour; and he saith unto the Jews, Behold your king;" and Mark xv. 25, "And it was the *third* hour, and they crucified Him. . ." There are various suggestions for removing this

there. The name of Cæsar began to be heard in wrathful murmurs. "Shall I crucify your King?" he had asked, venting the rage and soreness of his heart in taunts on *them*. "*We have no king but Cæsar,*" answered the Sadducees and Priests, flinging to the winds every national impulse and every Messianic hope.[1] "If thou let this man go," shouted the mob again and again, "thou art not *Cæsar's* friend. Every one who tries to make himself a king speaketh against *Cæsar.*"[2] And at that dark terrible name of Cæsar, Pilate trembled. It was a name to conjure with. It mastered him. He thought of that terrible implement of tyranny, the accusation of *laesa majestas*,[3] into

difficulty, but the only ones worth mentioning are: (α.) *That in the word "crucified" St. Mark practically includes all the preparations for the crucifixion*, and therefore much of the trial: this is untenable, because he uses the aorist, ἐσταύρωσαν, not the imperfect. (β.) *That one of the Evangelists is less accurate than the other.* If no other solution of the difficulty were simple and natural, I should feel no difficulty in admitting this; but as the general, and even the minute, accuracy of the Evangelists seems to me demonstrable in innumerable cases, it is contrary to the commonest principles of fairness to insist that there *must* be an inaccuracy when another explanation is possible. (γ.) *That St. John adopts the Roman civil reckoning of hours.* But (i.), the Romans had no such reckoning (see Vol. I., pp. 146, 206; John iv. 6, 52; xi. 9); and (ii.), this will make Pilate's exclamation to have been uttered at six in the morning, in which case the trial could hardly have begun at daylight, as no time is left for the intermediate incidents. (δ.) That the Γ′ (third) in John xix. 14, has by a very early error been altered into ϛ′ (sixth). This is the reading of a few MSS. and versions, and the *Chron. Alex.* actually appeals for its genuineness not only to τὰ ἀκριβῆ ἀντίγραφα, but even to αὐτὸ τὸ ἰδιόχειρον τοῦ Εὐαγγελιστοῦ. Unless great latitude be allowed to the word ὡς, this appears to me a possible solution; it is, however, perfectly true that the ancients, as a rule, were much looser than we are in their notes of time.

[1] "The formal equivalent of Emperor is, of course, αὐτοκράτωρ, ... but the provincials freely spoke of even the Julian Cæsars as βασιλεὺς." (Freeman, *Essays*, II. 316.)

[2] Agrippa I. inscribed his coins with the title φιλοκαίσαρ. (Akerman, p. 30.)

[3] Tac. *Ann.* iii. 38 (and *passim*). "Majestatis crimen. omnium accusa-

which all other charges merged, which had made confiscation and torture so common, and had caused blood to flow like water in the streets of Rome. He thought of Tiberius, the aged gloomy Emperor, then hiding at Capreæ his ulcerous features, his poisonous suspicions, his sick infamies, his desperate revenge. At this very time he had been maddened into a yet more sanguinary and misanthropic ferocity by the detected falsity and treason of his only friend and minister, Sejanus, and it was to Sejanus himself that Pilate is said to have owed his position. There might be secret delators in that very mob. Panic-stricken, the unjust judge, in obedience to his own terrors, consciously betrayed the innocent victim to thc anguish of death. He who had so often prostituted justice, was now unable to achieve the one act of justice which he desired. He who had so often murdered pity, was now forbidden to taste the sweetness of a pity for which he longed. He who had so often abused authority, was now rendered impotent to exercise it, for once, on the side of right. Truly for him, sin had become its own Erinnys, and his pleasant vices had been converted into the instrument of his punishment! Did the solemn and noble words of the Law of the Twelve Tables [1]—"Vanae voces populi non sunt audiendae, quando aut noxium crimine absolvi, aut innocentem condemnari desiderant" —come across his memory with accents of reproach as

tionum complementum erat." "He knew very well," says Agrippa (ap Philon. *ubi supr.*), "the inflexible severity of Tiberius;" and this was some years earlier—before the gloom of the Emperor's mind had become so deep and savage as was now the case. An Apocryphal book (*Revenges of the Saviour*), with scarcely an exaggeration, says that Tiberius was "full of ulcers and fevers, and had nine sorts of leprosy." (See Tac. *Ann.* iv. 57; Suet. *Tib.* 68; Julian, *Caes.*, p. 309, &c.)

[1] Lex. xii. *De poenis.*

he delivered Bar-Abbas and condemned Jesus? It may have been so. At any rate his conscience did not leave him at ease. At this, or some early period of the trial, he went through the solemn farce of trying to absolve his conscience from the guilt. He sent for water; he washed his hands before the multitude! he said, "I am innocent of the blood of this just person; see ye to it." Did he think thus to wash away his guilt? He could wash his hands; could he wash his heart? Might he not far more truly have said with the murderous king in the splendid tragedy—

> "Can all old Ocean's waters wash this blood
> Clean from my hand? Nay, rather would this hand
> The multitudinous seas incarnadine,
> Making the green—one red!"

It may be that, as he thus murdered his conscience, such a thought flashed for one moment across his miserable mind, in the words of his native poet—

> "Ah nimium faciles qui tristia crimina caedis
> Fluminéâ tolli posse putatis aquâ!"[1]

But if so, the thought was instantly drowned in a yell, the most awful, the most hideous, the most memorable that History records. "*His blood be on us and on our children.*" Then Pilate finally gave way. The fatal "*Ibis ad crucem*" was uttered with reluctant wrath. He delivered Him unto them, *that He might be crucified.*

And now mark, for one moment, the revenges of History. Has not His blood been on them, and on their children? Has it not fallen most of all on those

[1] Ov. *Fast.* ii. 45. The custom, though Jewish (Deut. xxi. 6, 7, "all the elders . . . shall wash their hands . . . and say, Our hands have not shed this blood, neither have our eyes seen it"), was also Greek and Roman.

most nearly concerned in that deep tragedy? Before the dread sacrifice was consummated, Judas died in the horrors of a loathsome suicide. Caiaphas was deposed the year following. Herod died in infamy and exile. Stripped of his Procuratorship very shortly afterwards, on the very charges he had tried by a wicked concession to avoid, Pilate, wearied out with misfortunes, died in suicide and banishment, leaving behind him an execrated name.[1] The house of Annas was destroyed a generation later by an infuriated mob, and his son was dragged through the streets, and scourged and beaten to his place of murder. Some of those who shared in and witnessed the scenes of that day—and thousands of their children—also shared in and witnessed the long horrors of that siege of Jerusalem which stands unparalleled in history for its unutterable fearfulness. "It seems," says Renan, "as though the whole race had appointed a rendezvous for extermination." They had shouted, "We have no king but

[1] Euseb. *Chron.* p. 78, ποικίλαις περιπεσὼν συμφοραῖς. His banishment to Vienna Allobrogum, his tomb, his connection with Mount Pilate, &c., are all uncertain traditions. The *Paradosis Pilati, Mors Pilati,* &c., are as spurious as his "martyrdom," which is observed by the Abyssinian Church on June 25. But Evang. Nicod. i. 13, which speaks of Pilate as "circumcised in heart," shows that the early Christians were not insensible of his efforts to save Jesus. "Upon all murderers," says Bishop Jeremy Taylor, "God hath not thrown a thunderbolt, nor broken all sacrilegious persons upon the wheel of an inconstant and ebbing estate, nor spoken to every oppressor from heaven in a voice of thunder, nor cut off all rebels in the first attempts of insurrection; but because He hath done so to some, we are to look upon those judgments as divine accents and voices of God, threatening all the same crimes with the like events, and with the ruins of eternity." (*Life of Christ,* III. xv.)—How much more true and reverent is this than the despairing cynicism which says, "Gardons-nous d'une expression si naïvement impie. Il n'y a pas plus de vengeance dans l'histoire que dans la nature; les revolutions ne sont pas plus justes que le volcan qui éclate ou l'avalanche qui roule." (Renan.)

Cæsar!" and they *had* no king but Cæsar; and leaving only for a time the fantastic shadow of a local and contemptible royalty, Cæsar after Cæsar outraged, and tyrannised, and pillaged, and oppressed them, till at last they rose in wild revolt against the Cæsar whom they had claimed, and a Cæsar slaked in the blood of its best defenders the red ashes of their burnt and desecrated Temple. They had forced the Romans to crucify their Christ, and though they regarded this punishment with especial horror,[1] they and their children were themselves crucified in myriads by the Romans outside their own walls, till room was wanting and wood failed, and the soldiers had to ransack a fertile inventiveness of cruelty for fresh methods of inflicting this insulting form of death.[2] They had given thirty pieces of silver for their Saviour's blood, and they were themselves sold in thousands for yet smaller sums. They had chosen Bar-Abbas in preference to their Messiah, and for them there has been no Messiah more, while a murderer's dagger swayed the last counsels of their dying nationality. They had accepted the guilt of blood, and the last pages of their history were glued together with the rivers of their blood, and that blood continued to be shed in

[1] See Jos. *B. J.* vii. 6, § 4.

[2] Jos. *B. J.* v. 11, § 1, *προσήλουν οἱ στρατιῶται ἄλλον ἄλλῳ σχήματι πρὸς χλεύην, καὶ διὰ τὸ πλῆθος χώρα τε ἐνελείπετο τοῖς σταυροῖς καὶ σταυροὶ τοῖς σώμασιν.* "So that they who had nothing but 'crucify' in their mouths were therewith paid home in their own bodies" (Sir T. Browne, *Vulg. Err.* v. 21). The common notion, that having bought Christ for thirty pieces of silver, they were sold by thirties for one piece of silver, seems to be solely derived from a mediæval forgery called *The Revenging of the Saviour.* Still it is true that "the blood of Jesus shed for the salvation of the world became to them a curse. . . . So manna turns to worms, and the wine of angels to vinegar and lees, when it is received into impure vessels or tasted by wanton palates, and the sun himself produces rats and serpents when it reflects upon the slime of Nilus." (Jer. Taylor, III. xv.)

wanton cruelties from age to age. They who will, may see in incidents like these the mere unmeaning *chances* of History; but there is in History nothing unmeaning to one who regards it as the Voice of God speaking among the destinies of men; and whether a man sees any significance or not in events like these, he must be blind indeed who does not see that when the murder of Christ was consummated, the axe was laid at the root of the barren tree of Jewish nationality. Since that day Jerusalem and its environs, with their "ever-extending miles of grave-stones and ever-lengthening pavement of tombs and sepulchres," have become little more than one vast cemetery—an Aceldama, a field of blood, a potter's field to bury strangers in. Like the mark of Cain upon the forehead of their race, the guilt of that blood has seemed to cling to them—as it ever must until that same blood effaceth it. For, by God's mercy, that blood was shed for them also who made it flow; the voice which they strove to quench in death was uplifted in its last prayer for pity on His murderers. May that blood be efficacious! may that prayer be heard![1]

[1] It is in the deepest sincerity that I add these last words. Any one who traces a spirit of vindictiveness in the last paragraph wholly misjudges the spirit in which it is written. This book may perhaps fall into the hands of Jewish readers. They, of all others, if true to the deepest lessons of the faith in which they have been trained, will acknowledge the hand of God in History. And the events spoken of here are not imaginative; they are indisputable facts. The Jew at least will believe that in external consequences God visits the sins of the fathers upon the children. Often and often in History have the crimes of the guilty *seemed* to be visited even on their *innocent* posterity. The apparent injustice of this is but on the surface. There is a fire that purifies, no less than a fire that scathes; and who shall say that the very afflictions of Israel—afflictions, alas! so largely caused by the sin of Christendom—may not have been meant for a refining of the pure gold? God's judgments—it may be the very sternest and most irremediable of them—come, many a time, in the guise, not of affliction, but of immense earthly prosperity and ease.

CHAPTER LXI.

THE CRUCIFIXION.

"Dum crucis inimicos
Vocabis, et amicos,
O Jesu, Fili Dei,
Sis, oro, memor mei."

THOMAS OF CELANO, *De Cruce Domini.*

"I, MILES, EXPEDI CRUCEM" ("Go, soldier, get ready the cross"). In some such formula of terrible import Pilate must have given his final order.[1] It was now probably about nine o'clock, and the execution followed immediately upon the judgment. The time required for the necessary preparation would not be very long, and during this brief pause the soldiers, whose duty it was to see that the sentence was carried out, stripped Jesus of the scarlet war-cloak, now dyed with the yet deeper stains of blood, and clad Him again in His own garments.[2]

[1] That Pilate sent some official account of the trial and crucifixion to Tiberius would be *à priori* probable, and seems to be all but certain (Just. Mart. *Apol.* i. 76; Tert. *Apol.* 21; Euseb. *Hist. Eccl.* ii. 2; Lardner, vi. 606); but it is equally certain that the existing *Acta, Paradosis, Mors* and *Epistolae Pilati* are spurious. Tischendorf (*De Evang. Apocr., Orig.*, p. 67) thinks that, though interpolated, they may contain old materials, but I can find nothing of any interest or value in them.

[2] Some have supposed that a second scourging took place, the first being the question by torture, the second the προαικισμὸς. It seems clear, however, that Pilate had *meant* the scourging to be this preliminary to crucifixion, though, at the last moment, it suited him to let it pass as inquisitorial. Further, it is inconceivable that Jesus could have been capable of physically enduring *two* such fearful inflictions, either of which

When the cross had been prepared they laid it—or possibly only one of the beams of it—upon His shoulders, and led Him to the place of punishment. The nearness of the great feast, the myriads who were present in Jerusalem, made it desirable to seize the opportunity for striking terror into all Jewish malefactors. Two were therefore selected for execution at the same time with Jesus—two brigands and rebels of the lowest stamp. Their crosses were laid upon them, a maniple of soldiers in full armour were marshalled under the command of their centurion, and, amid thousands of spectators, coldly inquisitive or furiously hostile, the procession started on its way.

The cross was not, and could not have been, the massive and lofty structure with which such myriads of pictures have made us familiar. Crucifixion was among the Romans a very common punishment, and it is clear that they would not waste any trouble in constructing the instrument of shame and torture.[1] It would undoubtedly be made of the very commonest wood that

was often sufficient to cause convulsions and death. It is better to regard the φραγελλώσας of Matt. xxvii. 26 as retrospective.

[1] Of the various kinds of cross—the *crux decussata* (X), the *crux ansata*, &c., it is certain that the cross on which Jesus was crucified was either the *crux commissa* (T, St. Anthony's cross), or the *crux immissa*, the ordinary Roman cross (†). The fact that the former was in the shape of the Greek capital *tau* has given ample room for the allegorising propensities of the Fathers. (Cf. Lucian, *Jud. Vocal.* 12; Gesenius s. v. תָּו, Ezek. ix. 4.) See abundant O. T. instances of this in Just. Mart. *Dial.* 89; Tert. *Adv. Jud.* 10, 11; Barnab. *Ep.* ix.; Clem. Alex. *Strom.* vi. See too Theophyl. on Matt. v. 18; Sepp, *Leben Christi*, vi. 115; *Mysterium des Kreuzes.*—I have not alluded to the so-called "invention of the cross," for the story is intrinsically absurd, and the Jews generally burnt their crosses (Otho, *Lex. Rabb.* s. v. "Supplicia"). What seems decisive in favour of the shape preserved by the traditions of art for nearly 1,500 years is the expression of Matt. xxvii. 37, that the title was put ἐπάνω τῆς κεφαλῆς αὐτοῦ. I have collected all that seemed archæologically interesting on this subject in the articles "Cross" and "Crucifixion" in Smith's *Dict. of the Bible.*

came to hand, perhaps olive or sycamore, and knocked together in the very rudest fashion. Still, to support the body of a man, a cross would require to be of a certain size and weight; and to one enfeebled by the horrible severity of the previous scourging, the carrying of such a burden would be an additional misery.[1] But Jesus was enfeebled not only by this cruelty, but by previous days of violent struggle and agitation, by an evening of deep and overwhelming emotion, by a night of sleepless anxiety and suffering, by the mental agony of the garden, by three trials and three sentences of death before the Jews, by the long and exhausting scenes in the Prætorium, by the examination before Herod, and by the brutal and painful derisions which He had undergone, first at the hands of the Sanhedrin and their servants, then from Herod's body-guard, and lastly from the Roman cohort. All these, superadded to the sickening lacerations of the scourging, had utterly broken down His physical strength. His tottering footsteps, if not His actual falls under that fearful load, made it evident that He lacked the physical strength to carry it from the Prætorium to Golgotha. Even if they did not pity His feebleness, the Roman soldiers would naturally object to the consequent hindrance and delay. But they found an easy method to solve the difficulty. They had not proceeded farther than the city gate,[2] when they

[1] Cf. Gen. xxii. 6 (Isa. ix. 6). It is not certain whether the condemned carried their *entire* cross or only a part of it—the *patibulum*, or transom, as distinguished from the *crux* (cf. Plaut. *fr. ap.* Non. 3, 183, "*Patibulum* ferat per urbem deinde affigatur *cruci*"). If the entire cross was carried, it is probable that the two beams were not (as in pictures) nailed to each other, but simply fastened together by a rope, and carried like a V (*furca*). If, as tradition says (*Acts of Pilate*, B. 10), the hands were tied, the difficulties of supporting the burden would be further enhanced.

[2] *Act. Pilat.* x. ἦλθε μεχρὶ τῆς πύλης.

met a man coming from the country, who was known to the early Christians as "Simon of Cyrene, the father of Alexander and Rufus;" and perhaps, on some hint from the accompanying Jews that Simon sympathised with the teaching of the Sufferer, they impressed him without the least scruple into their odious service.[1]

The miserable procession resumed its course, and though the apocryphal traditions of the Romish Church narrate many incidents of the *Via Dolorosa,* only one such incident is recorded in the Gospel history.[2] St. Luke tells us that among the vast multitude of people who followed Jesus were many women. From the *men* in that moving crowd He does not appear to have received one word of pity or of sympathy. *Some* there must surely have been who had seen His miracles, who had heard His words; some of those who had been almost, if not utterly, convinced of His Messiahship, as they

[1] ἠγγάρευσαν. It seems to have been a common thing for Roman soldiers to impress people to carry burdens for them (Epict. *Dissert.* iv. 1). The Cyrenians had a synagogue at Jerusalem (Acts ii. 10; vi. 9). The names Alexander and Rufus are too common to enable us to feel any certainty as to their identification with those of the same name mentioned in Acts xix. 33; 1 Tim. i. 20; Rom. xvi. 13. The belief of the Cerinthians, Basilidians, Carpocratians, and other Gnostics, that Simon was crucified for Jesus by mistake (!), is not worth notice here (Iren. *Adv. Haeres.* i. 23). One of these wild distortions was that Judas was crucified for Him; and another that it was a certain Titian, or a phantom created by God in the semblance of Jesus. It is a curious trace of the dissemination of Gnostic and Apocryphal legends in Arabia that Mahomet treats the actual crucifixion of Jesus as an unworthy calumny. (Koran, *Surat.* 3, 4; Sale's *Koran,* i. 64, 124, "They slew Him not, neither crucified Him, but He was represented by one in His likeness.")

[2] These form the subjects of the stations which are to be seen in all Romish churches, and are mainly derived from apocryphal sources. They originated among the Franciscans. The so-called Via Dolorosa does not seem to be mentioned earlier than the fourteenth century. That Jesus, before being eased of His burden, was scourged and goaded onward is but too sadly probable (Plaut. *Most.* I. i. 53, "Ita te forabunt patibulatum per viam stimulis"). (Cf. Jer. Taylor, *Life of Christ,* III. xv. 2.)

hung upon His lips while He had uttered His great discourses in the Temple; some of the eager crowd who had accompanied Him from Bethlehem five days before with shouted hosannas and waving palms. Yet if so, a faithless timidity or a deep misgiving—perhaps even a boundless sorrow—kept them dumb. But these women, more quick to pity, less susceptible to controlling influences, could not and would not conceal the grief and amazement with which this spectacle filled them. They beat upon their breasts and rent the air with their lamentations, till Jesus Himself hushed their shrill cries with words of solemn warning. Turning to them—which He could not have done had He still been staggering under the burden of His cross—He said to them, "Daughters of Jerusalem, weep not for me; but for yourselves weep, and for your children. For lo! days are coming in which they shall say, Blessed are the barren, and the wombs which bare not, and the breasts which gave not suck. Then shall they begin to say to the mountains, Fall on us, and to the hills, Cover us; for if they do these things in the green tree, what shall be done in the dry?" Theirs was but an emotional outburst of womanly tenderness, which they could not repress as they saw the great Prophet of mankind in His hour of shame and weakness, with the herald proclaiming before Him the crimes with which He was charged, and the Roman soldiers carrying the title of derision,[1] and Simon bending under the weight of the wood to which He was to be nailed. But He warned them that, if this were *all* which they saw in the passing spectacle, far bitterer

[1] Suet. *Calig.* 32, "Praecedente titulo qui caussam poenae indicaret." This was sometimes hung round the neck.

causes of woe awaited them, and their children, and their race. Many of them, and the majority of their children, would live to see such rivers of bloodshed, such complications of agony, as the world had never known before—days which would seem to overpass the capacities of human suffering, and would make men seek to hide themselves, if it might be, under the very roots of the hill on which their city stood.[1] The fig-tree of their nation's life was still green: if such deeds of darkness were possible *now*, what should be done when that tree was withered and blasted, and ready for the burning?[2]—if in the days of hope and decency they could execrate their blameless Deliverer, what would happen in the days of blasphemy and madness and despair? If, under the full light of day, Priests and Scribes could crucify the Innocent, what would be done in the midnight orgies and blood-stained bacchanalia of zealots and murderers? This was a day of crime; that would be a day when Crime had become her own avenging fury.—The solemn warning, the last sermon of Christ

[1] Hos. ix. 12—16; x. 8; Isa. ii. 10; Rev. vi. 16. These words of Christ met with a painfully literal illustration when hundreds of the unhappy Jews at the siege of Jerusalem hid themselves in the darkest and vilest subterranean recesses, and when, besides those who were hunted out, no less than 2,000 were killed by being buried under the ruins of their hiding-places (Jos. *B. J.* vi. 9, § 4).

[2] The *exact* meaning of this proverbial expression is not certain. It is often explained to mean, "If, in the fulfilment of God's purposes, I the Holy and the Innocent must suffer thus—if the green tree be thus blasted—how shall the dry tree of a wicked life, with its abominable branches, be consumed in the uttermost burning?" (Cf. Prov. xi. 31; Ezek. xx. 47; xxi. 4; and especially 1 Peter iv. 17.) (See Schenkel, *Charakterbild*, p. 30, E. Tr.) The difficulty of understanding the words was early felt, and we find an absurd allusion to them in the *Revenging of the Saviour*, where Titus exclaims, "They hung our Lord on a green tree . . . let us hang them on a dry tree."

on earth, was meant primarily for those who heard it; but, like all the words of Christ, it has deeper and wider meaning for all mankind. Those words warn every child of man that the day of careless pleasure and blasphemous disbelief will be followed by the crack of doom; they warn each human being who lives in pleasure on the earth, and eats, and drinks, and is drunken, that though the patience of God waits, and His silence is unbroken, yet the days shall come when He shall speak in thunder, and His wrath shall burn like fire.

And so with this sole sad episode, they came to the fatal place, called Golgotha, or, in its Latin form, Calvary—that is, "a skull." Why it was so called is not known. It may conceivably have been a well-known place of execution; or possibly the name may imply a bare, rounded, scalp-like elevation. It is constantly called the "*hill* of Golgotha," or of Calvary; but the Gospels merely call it "a place," and not a hill.[1] Respecting its site volumes have been written, but nothing is known. The data for anything approaching to certainty are wholly wanting; and, in all probability, the actual spot lies buried and obliterated under the mountainous rubbish-heaps of the ten-times-taken city. The rugged and precipitous mountain represented in sacred pictures is as purely imaginary as the skull of Adam, which is often painted lying at the foot of the

[1] Matt. xxvii. 33; Mark xv. 22. Calvary is used by the E. V. as a rendering of *κράνιον*, "scull," only in Luke xxiii. 33. It is called "monticulus" in the old *Itiner. Burdig. Hieros.* vii. Renan compares the French word "Chaumont" (*Vie de Jésus*, 416). Ewald identifies it with the hill Gareb (Jer. xxxi. 39). It is hardly worth while to enter into elaborate arguments about the site, which may any day be overthrown by a discovery of the course of the second wall.

cross,[1] or as any other of the myriads of legends, which have gathered round this most stupendous and moving scene in the world's history. All that we know of Golgotha, all that we shall ever know, all that God willed to be known, is that it was without the city gate. The religion of Christ is spiritual; it needs no relic; it is independent of Holy Places; it says to each of its children, not "Lo, here!" and "lo, there!" but "The kingdom of God is within you."

Utterly brutal and revolting as was the punishment of crucifixion, which has now for fifteen hundred years been abolished by the common pity and abhorrence of mankind,[2] there was one custom in Judæa, and one occasionally practised by the Romans, which reveal some touch of passing humanity. The latter consisted

[1] "Ibi erectus est medicus ubi jacebat aegrotus" (Aug.). Origen compares 1 Cor. xv. 22. There was a legend that three drops of Christ's blood fell on Adam's skull, and caused his resurrection, fulfilling the ancient prophecy quoted in Eph. v. 14, where Jerome had heard a preacher adopt the reading, "Awake, Adam that sleepest . . . and Christ shall touch thee" (ἐπιψαύσει). (Jer. in Matt. xxvii. 33; Reland, *Palest.* 860, for the true reading ἐπιφαύσει.) The words in the original are rhythmical, and as they do not occur in Scripture, they are now usually considered to be a fragment of some early Christian hymn.

[2] It was abolished by Constantine (Aur. Vict. *Const.* 41). The infamy of crucifixion is still preserved in the reproachful name *Talui* (תלוי) in which the Talmud speaks of Jesus, and עובדי תלוי, "worshippers of the Hung," which they apply to Christians, though, according to *their* fable, He was first stoned, *then* hung on the tree. "Servile," "infame," "crudelissimum," "taeterrimum," "summum," "extremum," "supplicium," are the names given to it by the Romans. (Cic. *Verr.* v. 66 and *passim.* See Phil. ii. 8; Cic. *Pro Rab.* 5, "Nomen ipsum crucis absit non modo a corpore civium Romanorum, sed etiam a cogitatione, oculis, auribus.") Maecenas, in one of the few interesting fragments of his verses, speaks of it as the extreme of horror, and the ultimate agony.

"Vita dum superest bene est
Hanc mihi *vel acutâ*
Si sedeam cruce, sustine." (Sen. *Ep.* 101.)

in giving to the sufferer a blow under the arm-pit, which, without causing death, yet hastened its approach.[1] Of this I need not speak, because, for whatever reason, it was not practised on this occasion. The former, which seems to have been due to the milder nature of Judaism, and which was derived from a happy piece of Rabbinic exegesis on Prov. xxxi. 6, consisted in giving to the condemned, immediately before his execution, a draught of wine medicated with some powerful opiate.[2] It had been the custom of wealthy ladies in Jerusalem to provide this stupefying potion at their own expense, and they did so quite irrespectively of their sympathy for any individual criminal. It was probably taken freely by the two malefactors, but when they offered it to Jesus He would not take it. The refusal was an act of sublimest heroism. The effect of the draught was to dull the nerves, to cloud the intellect, to provide an anæsthetic against some part, at least, of the lingering agonies of that dreadful death. But He, whom some modern sceptics have been base enough to accuse of feminine feebleness and cowardly despair, preferred rather "to look Death in the face"—to meet the king of terrors without striving to deaden the force of one agonising anticipation, or to still the throbbing of one lacerated nerve.

The three crosses were laid on the ground—that of Jesus, which was doubtless taller than the other two,

[1] So Sen. *Ep.* 101; Orig. *in Matth.* 140 (Keim). Sometimes men were killed before crucifixion (Suet. *Jul. Cæs.* i. 74).

[2] St. Mark calls it ἐσμυρνισμένον οἶνον, "myrrh-mingled wine;" it is not likely that the exact ingredients would be known. St. Matthew mentally refers it to Ps. lxix. 21, ὄξος (or *possibly* οἶνον, which Tischendorf admits from א, B, D, K, L, &c.) μετὰ χολῆς. The Romans called these medicated cups "sopores" (Plin. xx. 18; Sen. *Ep.* 83. &c.).

being placed in bitter scorn in the midst. Perhaps the cross-beam was now nailed to the upright, and certainly the title, which had either been borne by Jesus fastened round His neck, or carried by one of the soldiers in front of Him, was now nailed to the summit of His cross. Then He was stripped naked of all His clothes,[1] and then followed the most awful moment of all. He was laid down upon the implement of torture. His arms were stretched along the cross-beams; and at the centre of the open palms, the point of a huge iron nail was placed, which, by the blow of a mallet, was driven home into the wood.[2] Then through either foot separately, or possibly through both together as they were placed one over the other, another huge nail tore its way through the quivering flesh.[3] Whether the sufferer was *also* bound to the cross we do not know; but, to prevent the hands and feet being torn away by the weight of the body, which could not "rest upon nothing but four great wounds," there was, about the centre of the cross, a wooden projection strong enough to support, at least in part, a human body which soon became a weight of agony.

[1] We can but hope that the περιέζωσαν αὐτὸν λέντιον of the *Acts of Pilate* (ch. 10), is true; if so, it was exceptional, and the evidence of later martyrdoms—even of women—points the other way, as does also the Jewish custom.

[2] I write thus because the familiarity of oft-repeated words prevents us from realising what crucifixion really was, and because it seems well that we *should* realise this. The hideous custom was probably copied by the Romans from the Phœnicians. The Egyptians simply *bound* the hands and feet, leaving the sufferer to die mainly of starvation.

[3] This was the earlier tradition, hence Greg. Naz. (*De Christ. Patient.*) calls the cross ξύλον τρίσηλον, and Nonnus calls the feet ὁμοπλοκέες. But Cyprian, who had witnessed crucifixions, speaks of four nails (*De Pass.*).

[4] πῆγμα. Hence the expressions ἐποχεῖσθαι ἐπὶ σταυροῦ. "Sedere in cruce, sedilis excessus," &c. (Jer. Taylor, *Life of Christ*, III. xv. 2). On the

It was probably at this moment of inconceivable horror that the voice of the Son of Man was heard uplifted, not in a scream of natural agony at that fearful torture, but calmly praying in Divine compassion for His brutal and pitiless murderers—aye, and for all who in their sinful ignorance crucify Him afresh for ever[1]—"FATHER, FORGIVE THEM, FOR THEY KNOW NOT WHAT THEY DO."

And then the accursed tree[2]—with its living human burden hanging upon it in helpless agony, and suffering fresh tortures as every movement irritated the fresh rents in hands and feet—was slowly heaved up by strong arms, and the end of it fixed firmly in a hole dug deep in the ground for that purpose.[3] The feet were but a little raised above the earth. The victim was in full

other hand, there was no *suppedaneum*, or "foot-rest:" though it is still repeated in modern pictures. The illustrations by G. Durrant in the popular edition of Renan's *Vie de Jésus*, though evidently meant to serve a purpose, are, in general, extremely true to Oriental life; but those of the Crucifixion seem to me to be incorrect in many particulars. The hands were *probably* bound as well as nailed (Luc. vi. 543—"*laqueum nodosque nocentes* ore suo rupit; pendentia corpora carpsit Abrasitque cruces . . . Insertum manibus chalybem . . . . sustulit").

[1] The thought is more than once expressed by Mr. Browning (*A Death in the Desert*):—

"Is not His love, at issue still with sin,
Closed with, and cast, and conquered, crucified
Visibly when a wrong is done on earth?"

[2] Infelix lignum (Liv. i. 26; Sen. *Ep.* 101, &c.). Now that this "tree of cursing and shame sits upon the sceptres, and is engraved and signed on the foreheads of kings" (Jer. Taylor), we can hardly imagine the disgust and horror with which it was once regarded when it had no associations but those "of pain, of guilt, and of ignominy" (Gibbon, ii. 153).

[3] Compare the old prophecy alluded to by Barnabas, *Ep.* 12, ὅταν ξύλον ϵλιθῇ καὶ ἀναστῇ. Sometimes the sufferer was lifted and nailed after the cross had been erected (ἀνῆγον ἦγον ἦγον εἰς ἄκρον τέλος, Greg. Naz., "Crucisalus;" Plaut. *Bacch.* ii. 3, 128).

reach of every hand that might choose to strike, in close proximity to every gesture of insult and hatred. He might hang for hours to be abused, outraged, even tortured by the ever-moving multitude who, with that desire to see what is horrible which always characterises the coarsest hearts, had thronged to gaze upon a sight which should rather have made them weep tears of blood.

And there, in tortures which grew ever more insupportable, ever more maddening as time flowed on, the unhappy victims might linger in a living death so cruelly intolerable, that often they were driven to entreat and implore the spectators, or the executioners, for dear pity's sake, to put an end to anguish too awful for man to bear—conscious to the last, and often, with tears of abject misery, beseeching from their enemies the priceless boon of death.[1]

For indeed a death by crucifixion seems to include all that pain and death *can* have of horrible and ghastly —dizziness, cramp, thirst, starvation, sleeplessness, traumatic fever, tetanus, publicity of shame, long continuance of torment, horror of anticipation, mortification of untended wounds—all intensified just up to the point at which they can be endured at all, but all stopping just short of the point which would give to the sufferer the relief of unconsciousness. The unnatural position made every movement painful; the lacerated veins and crushed tendons throbbed with incessant anguish; the wounds, inflamed by exposure, gradually gangrened; the

[1] And hence there are many ancient instances of men having been first strangled, or *nearly* killed, and *then* crucified; and of men who bought by large bribes this mournful but merciful privilege (Cic. *Verr.* 2, 45).

arteries—especially of the head and stomach—became swollen and oppressed with surcharged blood; and while each variety of misery went on gradually increasing, there was added to them the intolerable pang of a burning and raging thirst; and all these physical complications caused an internal excitement and anxiety, which made the prospect of death itself—of death, the awful unknown enemy, at whose approach man usually shudders most—bear the aspect of a delicious and exquisite release.[1]

Such was the death to which Christ was doomed; and though for Him it was happily shortened by all that He had previously endured, yet He hung from soon after noon until nearly sunset, before "He gave up His soul to death."

When the cross was uplifted, the leading Jews, for the first time, prominently noticed the deadly insult in which Pilate had vented his indignation. Before, in their blind rage, they had imagined that the manner of His crucifixion was an insult aimed at *Jesus;* but now that they saw Him hanging between the two robbers, on a cross yet loftier, it suddenly flashed upon them that it was a public scorn inflicted upon *them.* For on the white wooden tablet smeared with gypsum,[2] which was to be seen so conspicuously over the head of Jesus on the cross, ran, in black letters, an inscription in the three civilised languages of the ancient world—the three languages of which *one* at least was certain to be known by every single man in that assembled multitude—in the official Latin, in the current Greek, in the

[1] See the epitome of Richter (a German physician) in Jahn's *Archaeol. Bibl.*, p. 261.

[2] Called σανὶς, τίτλος, λεύκωμα, πίναξ.

vernacular Aramaic—informing all that this Man who was thus enduring a shameful, servile death—this Man thus crucified between two *sicarii* in the sight of the world,[1] was

"THE KING OF THE JEWS."[2]

To Him who was crucified the poor malice seemed to have in it nothing of derision. Even on His cross He reigned; even there He seemed divinely elevated above the priests who had brought about His death, and the coarse, idle, vulgar multitude who had flocked to feed their greedy eyes upon His sufferings. The malice was quite impotent against One whose spiritual and moral nobleness struck awe into dying malefactors and heathen executioners, even in the lowest abyss of His physical degradation. With the passionate ill-humour of the Roman governor there probably blended a vein of seriousness. While he was delighted to revenge himself on his detested subjects by an act of public insolence, he probably meant, or half meant, to imply that this *was*, in one sense, the King of the Jews—the greatest, the noblest, the truest of His race, whom

[1] Mark xv. 28 (Isa. liii. 12) is probably spurious, not being found in א, A, B, C, D, &c. St. Mark, writing for the Romans, never once quotes from the Old Testament.

[2] We cannot tell which of the Evangelists gives the *exact* title: it is, however, possible that the *longest* one is accurately given by St. John (xix. 19), and that it was the one in Aramaic, which would require least room. It is, at least, a probable conjecture that they ran as follows in the order mentioned by St. Matthew:—

ישו הנצרי מלך היהודים
Ὁ βασιλεὺς τῶν Ἰουδαίων.
Rex Judaeorum hic est. (Luke xxiii. 38.)

Professor Westcott remarks that, as given by St. Luke, it "seems like the scornful turn of the Latin title" (*Introd.*, p. 307). The true reading in St. Luke is Ὁ βασιλεὺς τῶν Ἰουδαίων οὗτος (א). There is a monograph by S. Reyherus, *De Crucifixi Jesu Titulis*, 1694. (See Hofmann, *Leb. Jes.* 375.)

therefore His race had crucified. The King was not unworthy of His kingdom, but the kingdom of the King. There was something loftier even than royalty in the glazing eyes which never ceased to look with sorrow on the City of Righteousness, which had now become a city of murderers. The Jews felt the intensity of the scorn with which Pilate had treated them. It so completely poisoned their hour of triumph, that they sent their chief priests in deputation, begging the Governor to alter the obnoxious title. "Write not," they said, "'The King of the Jews,' but that 'He *said*, I am the King of the Jews.'" But Pilate's courage, which had oozed away so rapidly at the name of Cæsar, had now revived. He was glad in any and every way to browbeat and thwart the men whose seditious clamour had forced him in the morning to act against his will. Few men had the power of giving expression to a sovereign contempt more effectually than the Romans. Without deigning any justification of what he had done, Pilate summarily dismissed these solemn hierarchs with the curt and contemptuous reply, "What I have written, I have written."[1]

In order to prevent the possibility of any rescue, even at the last moment—since instances had been known of men taken from the cross and restored to life[2]—a quaternion of soldiers with their centurion were

[1] Such conduct on the part of Pilate would probably have been called "mythical," &c., if we did not find Philo attributing to him just the same "malicious intention to vex the people" (*Leg. ad Caium*, p. 38).

[2] At the request of Josephus, who prostrated himself at the feet of Titus, three men who had been crucified were taken down alive, and every possible effort made to save them; but in spite of θεράπεια ἐπιμελεστάτη, two of the three died (*Vit.* 75). A similar instance is narrated of Sandôkes (Herod. vii. 194), and of the Convulsionnaires in the reign of Louis XV.

left on the ground to guard the cross. The clothes of the victims always fell as perquisites to the men who had to perform so weary and disagreeable an office. Little dreaming how exactly they were fulfilling the mystic intimations of olden Jewish prophecy, they proceeded, therefore, to divide between them the garments of Jesus. The *tallîth* they tore into four parts, probably ripping it down the seams;[1] but the *cetóneth*, or under-garment, was formed of one continuous woven texture, and to tear would have been to spoil it; they therefore contented themselves with letting it become the property of any one of the four to whom it should fall by lot. When this had been decided, they sat down and watched Him till the end, beguiling the weary lingering hours by eating and drinking, and gibing, and playing dice.

It was a scene of tumult. The great body of the people seem to have stood silently at gaze;[2] but some few of them as they passed by the cross—perhaps some of the many false witnesses and other conspirators of the previous night—mocked at Jesus with insulting noises[3] and furious taunts, especially bidding Him come down from the cross and save Himself, since He could destroy the Temple and build it in three days. And the chief priests, and scribes, and elders, less awe-struck, less compassionate than the mass of the people, were not ashamed to disgrace their grey-haired dignity and lofty reputation by adding their heartless reproaches to those of the evil few. Unrestrained by the noble patience of

[1] Deut. xxii. 12. Some have imagined in this *cetôneth* a priestly garment; but it was more probably the ordinary dress of the poor in Galilee—*ἧπερ οἱ πτωχοὶ κέχρηνται τῶν Γα˙ ιλαίων* (Isid.).

[2] Luke xxiii. 35, *εἱστήκει ὁ λαὸς θεωρῶν*. This seems to be clearly contrasted with *οἱ ἄρχοντες* and *οἱ στρατιῶται*.

[3] Mark xv. 29, Οὐὰ.

the Sufferer, unsated by the accomplishment of their wicked vengeance, unmoved by the sight of helpless anguish and the look of eyes that began to glaze in death, they congratulated one another[1] under His cross with scornful insolence—"He saved others, Himself He cannot save." "Let this Christ, this King of Israel, descend now from the cross, that we may see and believe." No wonder then that the ignorant soldiers took their share of mockery with these shameless and unvenerable hierarchs: no wonder that, at their midday meal, they pledged in mock hilarity the Dying Man, cruelly holding up towards His burning lips their cups of sour wine, and echoing the Jewish taunts against the weakness of the King whose throne was a cross, whose crown was thorns. Nay, even the poor wretches who were crucified with Him caught the hideous infection; comrades, perhaps, of the respited Bar-Abbas—heirs of the rebellious fury of a Judas the Gaulonite—trained to recognise no Messiah but a Messiah of the sword, they reproachfully bade Him, if His claims were true, to save Himself and them.[2] So *all* the voices about Him rang with blasphemy and spite, and in that long slow agony His dying ear caught no accent of gratitude, of pity, or of love. Baseness, falsehood, savagery, stupidity—such were the characteristics of the world which thrust itself into hideous prominence before the Saviour's last

[1] Mark xv. 31, ἐμπαίζοντες πρὸς ἀλλήλους . . . . ἔλεγον.

[2] In this, as in many other places, I have contented myself with silently showing that the supposed contradictions between the narratives of the Gospels do not necessarily exist. There is no contradiction in the text, yet I have only translated correctly the ὠνείδιζον (Matt. xxvii. 44), the *reproach* in which the robbers at first joined, and the ἐβλασφήμει (Luke xxiii. 39), the *furious reviling* of which only the unrepentant one was guilty. (See Lange, v. 398.)

consciousness—such the muddy and miserable stream that rolled under the cross before His dying eyes.[1]

But amid this chorus of infamy Jesus spoke not. He *could* have spoken. The pains of crucifixion did not confuse the intellect, or paralyse the powers of speech. We read of crucified men who, for hours together upon the cross, vented their sorrow, their rage, or their despair in the manner that best accorded with their character; of some who raved and cursed, and spat at their enemies; of others who protested to the last against the iniquity of their sentence; of others who implored compassion with abject entreaties; of one even who, from the cross, as from a tribunal, harangued the multitude of his countrymen, and upbraided them with their wickedness and vice.[2] But, except to bless and to encourage, and to add to the happiness and hope of others, Jesus spoke not. So far as the malice of the passers-by, and of priests and Sanhedrists, and soldiers, and of these poor robbers who suffered with Him, was concerned—as before during the trial so now upon the cross—He maintained unbroken His kingly silence.

But that silence, joined to His patient majesty and the divine holiness and innocence which radiated from

[1] A friend supplies me with a sad and striking passage from the martyrdom of a true servant of Jesus—Savonarola. "Hic quoque non praeteribo silentio fuisse illum pendentem in ligno a puerorum multitudine saxis impetitum: a quibus antea solitus erat in templo ante praedicationis initium hymnis et laudibus excipi." (Pietro Delfrini [an eye-witness], *Epist.* v. 73.)

[2] Such instances are given in Keim, III. ii. 431—*e.g.*, Gavius, who to the last kept shouting "Civis Romanus sum" (Cic. *Verr.* v. 62); Eleazar (Jos. *B. J.* vii. 6, § 4); Niger of Peræa, who showed his wounds, and entreated that he might be buried (*Id. ib.* iv. 6, § 1); Bomilcar, the Carthaginian, who harangued "de summâ cruce velut de tribunali in Poenorum scelera" (Justin. xxii. 7). "Crederem, nisi quidam de patibulo spectatores conspuerent" (Sen. *De Vit. Beat.* 19).

Him like a halo, was more eloquent than any words. It told earliest on one of the crucified robbers. At first this "bonus latro" of the Apocryphal Gospels seems to have faintly joined in the reproaches uttered by his fellow-sinner; but when those reproaches merged into deeper blasphemy, he spoke out his inmost thought. It is probable that he had met Jesus before, and heard Him, and perhaps been one of those thousands who had seen His miracles. There is indeed no authority for the legend which assigns to him the name of Dysmas, or for the beautiful story of his having saved the life of the Virgin and her Child during their flight into Egypt.[1] But on the plains of Gennesareth, perhaps from some robber's cave in the wild ravines of the Valley of the Doves, he may well have approached His presence—he may well have been one of those publicans and sinners who drew near to Him for to hear Him. And the words of Jesus had found some room in the good ground of his heart; they had not all fallen upon stony places. Even at this hour of shame and death, when he was suffering the just consequence of his past evil deeds, faith triumphed. As a flame sometimes leaps up among dying embers, so amid the white ashes of a sinful life which lay so thick upon his heart, the flame of love towards his God and his Saviour was not quite quenched. Under the hellish outcries which had broken loose around the cross of Jesus, there had lain a deep misgiving. Half of them seem to have been instigated by doubt and fear. Even in the self-congratulations of the priests we catch an undertone of dread. Suppose that even now some imposing miracle should be wrought? Suppose

[1] Arab. Evang. Infant. xxiii. See the beautiful poem on this subject in Professor Plumptre's *Lazarus, and other Poems.*

that even now that martyr-form should burst indeed into Messianic splendour, and the King, who seemed to be in the slow misery of death, should suddenly with a great voice summon His legions of angels, and springing from His cross upon the rolling clouds of heaven, come in flaming fire to take vengeance upon His enemies? And the air seemed to be full of signs. There was a gloom of gathering darkness in the sky, a thrill and tremor in the solid earth, a haunting presence as of ghostly visitants who chilled the heart and hovered in awful witness above that scene. The dying robber had joined at first in the half-taunting, half-despairing appeal to a defeat and weakness which contradicted all that he had hoped; but now this defeat seemed to be greater than victory, and this weakness more irresistible than strength. As he looked, the faith in his heart dawned more and more into the perfect day. He had long ceased to utter any reproachful words; he now rebuked his comrade's blasphemies. Ought not the suffering innocence of Him who hung between them, to shame into silence their just punishment and flagrant guilt? And so, turning his head to Jesus, he uttered the intense appeal, "O Jesus, remember me when Thou comest in Thy kingdom."[1] Then He, who had been mute amid invectives, spake at once in surpassing answer to that humble prayer, "VERILY, I SAY TO THEE, TO-DAY SHALT THOU BE WITH ME IN PARADISE."

Though none spoke to comfort Jesus—though deep grief, and terror, and amazement kept them dumb—yet there were hearts amid the crowd that beat in sympathy with the awful Sufferer. At a distance stood a number

[1] Tischendorf reads 'Ιησοῦ with ℵ, B, C, L, &c. The E. V. wrongly renders "*into* Thy kingdom."

of women looking on, and perhaps, even at that dread hour, expecting His immediate deliverance. Many of these were women who had ministered to Him in Galilee, and had come from thence in the great band of Galilæan pilgrims. Conspicuous among this heart-stricken group were His mother Mary, Mary of Magdala, Mary the wife of Clopas, mother of James and Joses, and Salome the wife of Zebedee. Some of them, as the hours advanced, stole nearer and nearer to the cross, and at length the filming eye of the Saviour fell on His own mother Mary, as, with the sword piercing through and through her heart, she stood with the disciple whom He loved.[1] His mother does not seem to have been much with Him during His ministry. It may be that the duties and cares of a humble home rendered it impossible. At any rate, the only occasions on which we hear of her are occasions when she is with His brethren, and is joined with them in endeavouring to influence, apart from His own purposes and authority, His Messianic course. But although at the very beginning of His ministry He had gently shown her that the earthly and filial relation was now to be transcended by one far more lofty and divine, and though this end of all her high hopes must have tried her faith with an overwhelming and unspeakable sorrow, yet she was true to Him in this supreme hour of His humiliation, and would have done for Him all that a mother's sympathy and love can do. Nor had He for a moment forgotten her who had bent over His

[1] Although it seems to me (even apart from the authority of the Peschito) that four women are mentioned in John xix. 25; and although it is far from impossible that "His mother's sister" *may* mean, as Meyer conjectures, Salome herself (in which case James and John were His cousins), yet any certain decision of the point is from the nature of the case impossible.

infant slumbers, and with whom He had shared those thirty years in the cottage at Nazareth. Tenderly and sadly He thought of the future that awaited her during the remaining years of her life on earth, troubled as they must be by the tumults and persecutions of a struggling and nascent faith. After His resurrection her lot was wholly cast among His Apostles, and the Apostle whom He loved the most, the Apostle who was nearest to Him in heart and life, seemed the fittest to take care of her. To him, therefore—to John whom He had loved more than His brethren—to John whose head had leaned upon His breast at the Last Supper, He consigned her as a sacred charge. "WOMAN," He said to her, in fewest words, but in words which breathed the uttermost spirit of tenderness, "BEHOLD THY SON;" and then to St. John, "BEHOLD THY MOTHER." He could make no gesture with those pierced hands, but He could bend His head. They listened in speechless emotion, but from that hour—perhaps from that very moment—leading her away from a spectacle which did but torture her soul with unavailing agony, that disciple took her to his own home.[1]

It was now noon, and at the Holy City the sunshine should have been burning over that scene of horror with a power such as it has in the full depth of an English summer-time. But instead of this, the face of the heavens was black, and the noonday sun was "turned into darkness," on "this great and terrible day of the Lord." It could have been no darkness of any natural eclipse, for the Paschal moon was at the full; but it was

[1] John xix. 27, εἰς τὰ ἴδια. Perhaps this furnishes us with a fresh proof that St. John was more closely connected with Jerusalem than the other Apostles, which would account for his fuller knowledge and record of the Judæan ministry.

one of those "signs from heaven" for which, during the ministry of Jesus, the Pharisees had so often clamoured in vain. The early Fathers appealed to Pagan authorities—the historian Phallus, the chronicler Phlegon—for such a darkness; but we have no means of testing the accuracy of these references, and it is quite possible that the darkness was a local gloom which hung densely over the guilty city and its immediate neighbourhood. But whatever it was, it clearly filled the minds of all who beheld it with yet deeper misgiving. The taunts and jeers of the Jewish priests and the heathen soldiers were evidently confined to the earlier hours of the crucifixion. Its later stages seem to have thrilled alike the guilty and the innocent with emotions of dread and horror. Of the incidents of those last three hours we are told nothing,[1] and that awful obscuration of the noonday sun may well have overawed every heart into an inaction respecting which there was nothing to relate. What Jesus suffered *then* for us men and our salvation we cannot know, for during those three hours He hung upon His cross in silence and darkness; or, if He spoke, there were none there to record His words. But towards the close of that time His anguish culminated, and—emptied to the very uttermost of that glory which He had since the world began—drinking to the very deepest dregs the cup of humiliation and bitterness—enduring, not only to have taken upon Him the form of a servant, but also to suffer the last infamy which human hatred could impose on servile helplessness—He uttered that mysterious cry, of which the full significance will never be fathomed by man—

[1] On the obvious discrepancy between the existing texts of St. John and of the Synoptists as to this reckoning of hours, see *supra*, p. 385.

"ELI, ELI, LAMA SABACHTHANI?"[1] ("My God, my God, why hast thou forsaken me?")

In those words, quoting the Psalm in which the early Fathers rightly saw a far-off prophecy of the whole passion of Christ,[2] He borrowed from David's utter agony the expression of His own. In that hour He was alone. Sinking from depth to depth of unfathomable suffering, until, at the close approach of a death which—because He was God, and yet had been made man—was more awful to Him than it could ever be to any of the sons of men, it seemed as if even His Divine Humanity could endure no more.

Doubtless the voice of the Sufferer—though uttered loudly in that paroxysm of an emotion which, in another, would almost have touched the verge of despair—was yet rendered more uncertain and indistinct from the condition of exhaustion in which He hung; and so, amid the darkness, and confused noise, and dull footsteps of the moving multitude, there were some who did not hear what He had said. They had caught only the first syllable, and said to one another that He had called on the name of Elijah.[3] The readiness with

[1] This utterance on the cross is the only one recorded by the two first Evangelists, and is recorded *by them alone*. שבקתני is for אֲזַבְתָּנִי. St. Mark preserves the more purely Aramaic form *Eloi*. The fact that thus in His last moments Jesus speaks in Aramaic, would seem to prove that this had been the ordinary language of His life.

[2] Tert. *Adv. Marc.* iii. 19, "Si adhuc, quaeris dominicae crucis praedicationem, satis tibi potest facere vicesimus primus psalmus, *totam Christi continens passionem*. (Keim.)

[3] It has been urged that it would be impossible to confuse *Eloi* with *Elijahu*, and that every Jew would have known what *Eloi* meant. But the first assertion is by no means self-evident under the circumstances; and as for the second, there might be many in this motley multitude—the Paschal gathering of pilgrims from all nations—to whom Aramaic was by no means familiar.

which they seized this false impression is another proof of the wild state of excitement and terror—the involuntary dread of something great, and unforeseen, and terrible—to which they had been reduced from their former savage insolence. For Elijah, the great prophet of the Old Covenant, was inextricably mingled with all the Jewish expectations of a Messiah, and these expectations were full of wrath. The coming of Elijah would be the coming of a day of fire, in which the sun should be turned into blackness and the moon into blood, and the powers of heaven should be shaken. Already the noonday sun was shrouded in unnatural eclipse: might not some awful form at any moment rend the heavens and come down, touch the mountains and they should smoke? The vague anticipation of conscious guilt was unfulfilled. Not such as yet was to be the method of God's workings. His messages to man for many ages more were not to be in the thunder and earthquake, not in rushing wind or roaring flame, but in the "still small voice" speaking always amid the apparent silences of Time in whispers intelligible to man's heart, but in which there is neither speech nor language, though the voice is heard.

But now the end was very rapidly approaching, and Jesus, who had been hanging for nearly six hours upon the cross, was suffering from that torment of thirst which is most difficult of all for the human frame to bear—perhaps the most unmitigated of the many separate sources of anguish which were combined in this worst form of death. No doubt this burning thirst was aggravated by seeing the Roman soldiers drinking so near the cross; and happily for mankind, Jesus had never sanctioned the unnatural affectation of stoic impassibility.

And so He uttered the one sole word of physical suffering which had been wrung from Him by all the hours in which He had endured the extreme of all that man can inflict. He cried aloud, "I THIRST."[1] Probably a few hours before, the cry would have only provoked a roar of frantic mockery; but now the lookers-on were reduced by awe to a readier humanity. Near the cross there lay on the ground the large earthen vessel containing the *posca*, which was the ordinary drink of the Roman soldiers. The mouth of it was filled with a piece of sponge, which served as a cork. Instantly some one —we know not whether he was friend or enemy, or merely one who was there out of idle curiosity—took out the sponge and dipped it in the *posca*[2] to give it to Jesus. But low as was the elevation of the cross, the head of the Sufferer, as it rested on the horizontal beam of the accursed tree, was just beyond the man's reach; and therefore he put the sponge at the end of a stalk of hyssop—about a foot long—and held it up to the parched and dying lips.[3] Even this simple act of pity, which Jesus did not refuse, seemed to jar upon the condition of nervous excitement with which some of the multitude were looking on. "Let be," they said to the man, "let us see whether Elias is coming to save Him." The man did not desist from his act of mercy, but when it was done he too seems to have echoed those uneasy

[1] Διψῶ. As-Sujûti, an Arabic writer, describing the crucifixion of a young Turk in 1247, says that he complained of intense thirst on the first day, and his sufferings were increased by seeing constantly before him the waters of the Baradâ, on the banks of which he was crucified. (Dr. Nicholson, in Kitto, i. 595.)

[2] Mark xv. 36, *γεμίσας σπόγγον ὄξους.* The hyssop is either a species of marjoram, or the caper-plant (*Capparis spinosa*), of which the stem is woody (Royle, *Journ. Sacr. Lit.*, Oct. 1849).

[3] The *καλάμῳ* of Matt. xxvii. 48 = *ὑσσώπῳ* (John xix. 29).

words.[1] But Elias came not, nor human comforter, nor angel deliverer. It was the will of God, it was the will of the Son of God, that He should be "perfected through sufferings;"[2] that—for the eternal example of all His children as long as the world should last—He should "endure unto the end."

And now the end was come. Once more, in the words of the sweet Psalmist of Israel,[3] but adding to them that title of trustful love which, through Him, is permitted to the use of all mankind, "FATHER," He said, "INTO THY HANDS I COMMEND MY SPIRIT." Then with one more great effort He uttered the last cry—the one victorious word Τετέλεσται, "IT IS FINISHED." It may be that that great cry ruptured some of the vessels of His heart; for no sooner had it been uttered than He bowed His head upon His breast, and yielded His life, "a ransom for many"—a willing sacrifice to His Heavenly Father.[4] "Finished was His holy life; with His life His struggle, with His struggle His work, with His work the redemption, with the redemption the foundation of the new world."[5] At that moment the

[1] Mark xv. 36.

[2] Heb. v. 7, 8; ii. 10; Phil. ii. 8, 9.

[3] Ps. xxxi. 5. Cf. Acts vii. 59; 1 Pet. ii. 23.

[4] There may be something intentional in the fact that in *describing* the death of Christ the Evangelists do not use the neuter verb ἔθανεν, but the phrases, ἐξέπνευσεν (Mark xv. 37; Luke xxiii. 46); ἀφῆκεν τὸ πνεῦμα (Matt. xxvii. 50); παρέδωκεν τὸ πνεῦμα (John xix. 30); as though they imply with St. Augustine that He gave up His life, "*quia voluit, quando voluit, quomodo voluit.*" "Oblatus est quia ipse voluit," Isa. liii. 7 (Vulg.). (Bunsen, *Bibelwerk*, ix. 455.)—I have not here touched on any questions as to the suffering of Jesus in His humanity, but not in His divinity, &c. (Pearson *On the Creed*, Art. iv.). All these theological questions about the αντίδοσις, ἀντιμετάστασις, περιχώρησις, *communicatio idiomatum*, &c., seem to me far to transcend our powers of reasoning. But Christ's perfectly voluntary resignation of His own life is distinctly asserted in John x. 18.

[5] Lange, v. 420.

vail of the Temple was rent in twain from the top to the bottom.[1] An earthquake shook the earth and split the rocks, and as it rolled away from their places the great stones which closed and covered the cavern sepulchres of the Jews, so it seemed to the imaginations of many to have disimprisoned the spirits of the dead, and to have filled the air with ghostly visitants, who after Christ had risen appeared to linger in the Holy City.[2] These circumstances of amazement, joined to all they had observed in the bearing of the Crucified, cowed even the cruel and gay indifference of the Roman soldiers. On the centurion, who was in command of them, the whole scene had exercised a yet deeper influence. As he stood opposite to the cross and saw the Saviour die, he glorified God, and exclaimed, "This Man was in truth righteous"—nay, more, "This Man was a Son of God." Even the multitude, utterly sobered from their furious excitement and frantic rage, began to be weighed down with a guilty consciousness that the scene which they had witnessed had in it something more awful than they could have conceived, and as they returned to Jerusalem they wailed, and beat upon their breasts. Well might they do so! This was the last

[1] Heb. vi. 19; ix. 3; x. 19, 20. The vail intended must be the *parocheth*, or inner vail. The Gospel to the Hebrews said that at the same moment a vast beam over the Temple lintel was shattered (Jer. *ad Matt.* xxvii. 51). It is far from improbable that the Jewish legends of strange portents which happened "forty years" (as they say in their usual loose and vague manner) before the destruction of the Temple, are in reality the echoes and reminiscences of those which in fact took place at the death of Christ. Tertullian says to the Jews with unanswerable force, "Non potuisse cessare legem antiquam et prophetas, nisi venisset is, qui per eandem legem et per eosdem prophetas venturus adnuntiabatur" (*Adv. Jud.* 6).

[2] Only in some such way as this can I account for the singular and wholly isolated allusion of Matt. xxvii. 52, 53.

drop in a full cup of wickedness: this was the beginning of the end of their city, and name, and race.

And in truth that scene was more awful than they, or even we, can know. The secular historian, be he ever so sceptical, cannot fail to see in it the central point of the world's history. Whether he be a believer in Christ or not, he cannot refuse to admit that this new religion grew from the smallest of all seeds to be a mighty tree, so that the birds of the air took refuge in its branches; that it was the little stone cut without hands which dashed into pieces the colossal image of heathen greatness, and grew till it became a great mountain and filled the earth. Alike to the infidel and to the believer the crucifixion is the boundary instant between ancient and modern days. Morally and physically, no less than spiritually, the Faith of Christ was the Palingenesia of the world. It came like the dawn of a new spring to nations "effete with the drunkenness of crime." The struggle was long and hard, but from the hour when Christ died began the death-knell to every Satanic tyranny and every tolerated abomination. From that hour Holiness became the universal ideal of all who name the name of Christ as their Lord, and the attainment of that ideal the common heritage of souls in which His Spirit dwells.

The effects, then, of the work of Christ are even to the unbeliever indisputable and historical. It expelled cruelty; it curbed passion; it branded suicide; it punished and repressed an execrable infanticide; it drove the shameless impurities of heathendom into a congenial darkness. There was hardly a class whose wrongs it did not remedy. It rescued the gladiator; it freed the slave; it protected the captive; it nursed the sick; it sheltered the orphan; it elevated the woman; it shrouded as with a halo of sacred innocence the tender years of the child. In every region of life its ameliorating influence was felt. It changed pity from a vice into a virtue.[1] It elevated poverty from a curse into a beatitude.[2] It ennobled labour from a vulgarity into a dignity and a duty. It sanctified marriage from little more than a burdensome convention into little less than a blessed sacrament. It revealed for the first time the angelic beauty of a Purity of which men had despaired and of a Meekness at which they had utterly scoffed. It created the very conception of charity, and broadened the limits of its obligation from the narrow circle of a neighbourhood to the widest horizons of the race. And while it thus evolved the idea of Humanity as a common brotherhood, even where its tidings were *not* believed—all over the world, wherever its tidings *were* believed, it cleansed the life, and elevated the soul of each individual man. And in all lands where it has moulded the characters of its true believers, it has created hearts so pure, and lives so peaceful, and homes so sweet, that it might seem as though those angels who had heralded its advent had also whispered to every depressed and despairing sufferer among the sons of men, "Though ye have lien among the pots, yet shall ye be as the wings of a dove, that is covered with silver wings, and her feathers like gold."

Others, if they *can* and *will*, may see in such a work as this no Divine Providence; they may think it philosophical enlightenment to hold that Christianity and Christendom are adequately accounted for by the idle

[1] "Misericordia animi vitium est" (Sen. *De Clem.*). "Nec ille Aut doluit miserans inopem" (Verg.).

[2] "Ingens vitium magnum opprobrium pauperies' (Sen.). "Blessed are the poor in spirit" (Matt. v. 3).

dreams of a noble self-deceiver, and the passionate hallucinations of a recovered demoniac. We persecute them not, we denounce them not, we judge them not; but we say that, unless all life be a hollow, there could have been no such miserable origin to the sole religion of the world, which holds the perfect balance between philosophy and popularity, between religion and morals, between meek submissiveness and the pride of freedom, between the ideal and the real, between the inward and the outward, between modest stillness and heroic energy, nay, between the tenderest conservatism and the boldest plans of world-wide reformation.[1] The witness of History to Christ is a witness which has been given with irresistible cogency; and it has been so given to none but Him.

But while even the unbeliever must see what the life and death of Jesus have effected in the world, to the believer that life and death are something deeper still; to him they are nothing less than a resurrection from the dead. He sees in the cross of Christ something which far transcends its historical significance. He sees in it the fulfilment of all prophecy as well as the consummation of all history; he sees in it the explanation of the mystery of birth, and the conquest over the mystery of the grave. In that life he finds a perfect example; in that death an infinite redemption. As He contemplates the Incarnation and the Crucifixion, he no longer feels that God is far away, and that this earth is but a disregarded speck in the infinite azure, and he himself but an insignificant atom chance-thrown amid the thousand million living souls of an innumerable race, but he exclaims in faith and hope and love, "Behold, the tabernacle of God is with men; yea, He will be their God, and they shall be His people." "Ye

[1] Keim, p. 370 (abridged edition).

are the temple of the living God; as God hath said, I will dwell in them, and walk in them."[1]

The sun was westering as the darkness rolled away from the completed sacrifice. They who had not thought it a pollution to inaugurate their feast by the murder of their Messiah, were seriously alarmed lest the sanctity of the following day—which began at sunset—should be compromised by the hanging of the corpses on the cross. And horrible to relate, the crucified often lived for many hours—nay, even for two days—in their torture. The Jews therefore begged Pilate that their legs might be broken, and their bodies taken down. This *crurifragium,* as it was called, consisted in striking the legs of the sufferers with a heavy mallet, a violence which seemed always to have hastened, if it did not instantly cause their death. Nor would the Jews be the only persons who would be anxious to hasten the end, by giving the deadly blow. Until life was extinct, the soldiers appointed to guard the execution dared not leave the ground. The wish, therefore, was readily granted. The soldiers broke the legs of the two malefactors first,[2] and then, coming to Jesus, found that the great cry had been indeed His last, and that He was dead already. They did not, therefore, break His legs, and thus unwittingly preserved the symbolism of that Paschal lamb, of which He was the antitype, and of which it had been commanded that "a bone of it shall not be broken."[3] And yet, as He might be only in a

[1] Ezek. xxxvii. 26; 2 Cor. vi. 16.

[2] If we must look for any reason, we may suppose that two soldiers broke the legs of a malefactor on either side first; or possibly that the cross of Jesus being a little loftier may have rendered it less easy to give the blow at once.

[3] Exod. xii. 46 (St. John also refers to Zech. xii. 10); Rev. i. 7. It is a striking circumstance that the body of the Paschal lamb was literally crucified on two transverse spits. I witnessed the Samaritan Passover

syncope—as instances had been known in which men apparently dead had been taken down from the cross and resuscitated—and as the lives of the soldiers would have had to answer for any irregularity, one of them, in order to make death certain, drove the broad head of his *hasta* into His side. The wound, as it was meant to do, pierced the region of the heart, and "forthwith," says St. John, with an emphatic appeal to the truthfulness of his eye-witness (an appeal which would be singularly and impossibly blasphemous if the narrative were the forgery which so much elaborate modern criticism has wholly failed to prove that it is), "forthwith came there out blood and water." Whether the water was due to some abnormal pathological conditions caused by the dreadful complication of the Saviour's sufferings—or whether it rather means that the pericardium had been rent by the spear-point, and that those who took down the body observed some drops of its serum mingled with the blood—in either case that lance-thrust was sufficient to hush all the heretical assertions that Jesus had only *seemed* to die;[1] and as it assured the soldiers, so should it assure all who have doubted, that He, who on the third day rose again, had in truth been crucified, dead, and buried, and that His soul had passed into the unseen world.

on the summit of Mount Gerizim in 1870, and the bodies of the seven lambs as they were prepared for roasting looked exactly as though they were laid on seven crosses.

[1] The early Fathers all appeal to this fact in refutation of the Docetae. As the effusion of lymph and blood after a *post-mortem* incision, though rare, is asserted by some physicians not to be unknown, there seems to be no need to regard the fact as miraculous. Opinions are divided as to whether the water was merely the lymph of the pericardium, or the decomposed *crassamentum* and *serum* of extravasated blood. That the circumstance is not impossible, especially if our Lord died of a ruptured heart (Ps. xxii. 14; lxix. 20) [or from a state of pleurisy?], may be regarded as proved by the letters of Sir J. Simpson and other eminent physicians to Dr. Hanna (*Last Day of Our Lord's Passion*, pp. 333—343), as well as by the book of Dr. Stroud, *On the Physical Cause of the Death of Christ.*

CHAPTER LXII.

THE RESURRECTION.

"Necesse est pauca dicamus de Christo ut Deo."—TERT. *Apolog.* 21.

AT the moment when Christ died, nothing could have seemed more abjectly weak, more pitifully hopeless, more absolutely doomed to scorn, and extinction, and despair, than the Church which He had founded. It numbered but a handful of weak followers, of which the boldest had denied his Lord with blasphemy, and the most devoted had forsaken Him and fled. They were poor, they were ignorant, they were hopeless. They could not claim a single synagogue or a single sword. If they spoke their own language, it bewrayed them by its mongrel dialect; if they spoke the current Greek, it was despised as a miserable *patois.* So feeble were they and insignificant, that it would have looked like foolish partiality to prophesy for them the limited existence of a Galilæan sect. How was it that these dull and ignorant men, with their cross of wood, triumphed over the deadly fascinations of sensual mythologies, conquered kings and their armies, and overcame the world?

What was it that thus caused strength to be made perfect out of abject weakness? There is one, and one only *possible* answer—the resurrection from the dead. All this vast revolution was due to the power of Christ's resurrection. "If we measure what seemed to be the hopeless ignominy of the catastrophe by which His work was ended, and the Divine prerogatives which are claimed for Him, not *in spite of*, but *in consequence of* that suffering and shame, we shall feel the utter hopelessness of reconciling the fact, and that triumphant deduction from it, without some intervening fact as certain as Christ's passion, and glorious enough to transfigure its sorrow."[1]

The sun was now on the edge of the horizon, and the Sabbath day was near. And "that Sabbath day was a high day," a Sabbath of peculiar splendour and solemnity, because it was at once a Sabbath and a Passover.[2] The Jews had taken every precaution to prevent the ceremonial pollution of a day so sacred, and were anxious that immediately after the death of the victims had been secured, their bodies should be taken from the cross. About the sepulture they did not trouble themselves, leaving it to the chance good offices of friends and relatives to huddle the malefactors into their nameless graves. The dead body of Jesus was left hanging till the last, because a person who could not easily be slighted had gone to obtain leave from Pilate to dispose of it as he wished.

This was Joseph of Arimathæa,[3] a rich man, of high

[1] Westcott, *Gospel of the Resurrection,* p. 111. He adds: "If Christ did not rise, we have not only to explain how the belief in His resurrection came to be received without any previous hopes which could lead to its reception, but also how it came to be received with that intensity of personal conviction which could invest the life and person of Christ with attributes never before assigned to any one, and that by Jews who had been reared in the strictest monotheism" (p. 112).

[2] John xix. 31; Deut. xxi. 22, 23; Lev. xxiii. 7.

[3] Arimathæa, or Rama, is a place of uncertain site; it may be Rama in

character and blameless life, and a distinguished member of the Sanhedrin. Although timidity of disposition, or weakness of faith, had hitherto prevented him from openly declaring his belief in Jesus, yet he had abstained from sharing in the vote of the Sanhedrin, or countenancing their crime. And now sorrow and indignation inspired him with courage. Since it was too late to declare his sympathy for Jesus as a living Prophet, he would at least give a sign of his devotion to Him as the martyred victim of a wicked conspiracy. Flinging secrecy and caution to the winds, he no sooner saw that the cross on Golgotha now bore a lifeless burden, than he went to Pilate on the very evening of the crucifixion, and begged that the dead body might be given him. Although the Romans left their crucified slaves to be devoured by dogs and ravens, Pilate had no difficulty in sanctioning the more humane and reverent custom of the Jews, which required, even in extreme cases, the burial of the dead.[1] He was, however, amazed at the speediness with which death had supervened, and sending for the centurion, asked whether it had taken place sufficiently long to distinguish it from a faint or swoon.[2] On ascertaining that such was

Benjamin (Matt. ii. 18), or Ramathaim in Ephraim (1 Sam. i. 1), but certainly is not Ramleh in Dan.

[1] For the Greek and Roman custom, see Herod. iii. 12; Cic. *Tusc. Q.* i. 43; Plaut. *Mil. Glor.* ii. 4, 19; Hor. *Ep.* i. 16, 48, &c.; Suet. *Ner.* 49; Juv. *Sat.* xiv. 77. For the Jewish, Deut. xxi. 23; Josh. viii. 29; Jos. *Antt.* iv. 8, § 24; Mark vi. 29; Acts viii. 2. The request of Joseph was not, however, without danger, and in later martyrdoms such a request cost men their lives, as was the case with the martyr Porphyrios. Pilate might, perhaps, have exacted a bribe (cf. Acts xxiv. 26; Plut. *Galb.* 28), but apparently did not do so, because the care of the Jews for burial was well known, and any violation of this usage would have been resented (Jos. *B. J.* iv. 5, § 2).

[2] Such seems to be the significance of εἰ πάλαι ἀπέθανεν in Mark xv. 44.

the fact, he at once assigned the body, doubtless with some real satisfaction, to the care of this "honourable councillor." Without wasting a moment, Joseph purchased a long piece of fine linen,[1] and took the body from its cross. Meanwhile the force of his example had helped to waken a kindred feeling in the soul of the candid but fearful Nicodemus. If, as seems extremely probable, he be identical with the Nakdimon Ben Gorion of the Talmud, he was a man of enormous wealth;[2] and however much he had held back during the life of Jesus, now, on the evening of His death, his heart was filled with a gush of compassion and remorse, and he hurried to His cross and burial with an offering of truly royal munificence. The faith which had once required the curtain of darkness, can now venture at least into the light of sunset, and brightened finally into noonday confidence. Thanks to this glow of kindling sorrow and compassion in the hearts of these two noble and wealthy disciples, He who died as a malefactor, was buried as a king. "He made His grave with the wicked, and with the rich in His death." The fine linen (*sindôn*)

The Martyrologies tell us that Victorinus, crucified head-downwards, lived for three days, and Paulinus and Macra for nine; but we cannot be sure of these facts. The average time of survival in the case of a healthy man seems to have been thirty-six hours; without cold, exposure, &c., the ordinary course of the mortification (which caused death) would require forty-eight hours.

[1] Another clear indication, even in the Synoptists, that this Friday was not the Passover. The *sindôn* was probably of white linen, such as that in which Gamaliel II. ordered himself to be buried, in order to discourage the extravagant burial garments of the Jews. The three words used of the cerements of Jesus are *σινδών* (Mark xv. 46); *ὀθόνια* (John xix. 40); *σουδάριον* (xx. 7); *κειρίαι* is used of Lazarus (xi. 44).

[2] He and his house are said to have perished at the fall of Jerusalem; and I have already (Vol. I., p. 197) mentioned the dreadful story that his daughter, who had received as her dower a million denarii of gold, was seen picking the grains of corn out of the horses' dung. May not this fable point to Jewish hatred against one who in heart at least was a Christian?

which Joseph had purchased was richly spread with the hundred *litras* of myrrh and perfumed aloe-wood which Nicodemus had brought,[1] and the lacerated body—whose divinely-human spirit was now in the calm of its sabbath rest in the Paradise of God—was thus carried to its loved and peaceful grave.

Close by the place of crucifixion—if not an actual part of it[2]—was a garden belonging to Joseph of Arimathæa, and in its enclosure he had caused a new tomb to be hewn for himself out of the solid rock, that he might be buried in the near precincts of the Holy City.[3] The tomb had never been used, but, in spite of the awful sacredness which the Jews attached to their rock-hewn sepulchres, and the sensitive scrupulosity with which they shrank from all contact with a corpse, Joseph never hesitated to give up for the body of Jesus the last home which he had designed for his own use. But the preparations had to be hurried, because when the sun had set the Sabbath would have begun. All that they could do, therefore, was to wash the corpse, to lay it amid the spices, to wrap the head in a white napkin, to roll the fine linen round and round the wounded limbs, and to lay the body reverently in the rocky niche. Then, with the united toil of several men, they rolled a *gôlal,* or great stone, to the horizontal aperture; and scarcely had they accomplished this when, as the sun sank behind the hills of Jerusalem, the new Sabbath dawned.[4]

[1] Even at the burial of Gamaliel II. only eighty pounds of spices were burnt by Onkelos. At Herod's funeral there had been 500 spice-bearers (Jos. *Antt.* xvii. 8, § 3).

[2] ἦν δὲ ἐν τῷ τόπῳ, ὅπου ἐσταυρώθη, κῆπος (John xix. 41).

[3] The circuit of Jerusalem is one great graveyard, and such tombs may be seen in Judæa by hundreds.

[4] Luke xxiii. 54. It was not unusual among the Jews to regard the *sunset* of Friday as the *dawn* of their Sabbath, and to give it the name of אור.

Mary of Magdala, and Mary the mother of James and Joses, had seated themselves in the garden to mark well the place of sepulture, and other Galilæan women had also noticed the spot, and had hurried home to prepare fresh spices and ointments before the Sabbath began, that they might hasten back early on the morning of Sunday, and complete that embalming of the body, which Joseph and Nicodemus had only hastily begun. They spent in quiet that miserable Sabbath, which, for the broken hearts of all who loved Jesus, was a Sabbath of anguish and despair.

But the enemies of Christ were not so inactive. The awful misgiving of guilty consciences was not removed even by His death upon the cross. They recalled, with dreadful reminiscence, the rumoured prophecies of His resurrection—the sign of the prophet Jonah, which He had said would alone be given them[1]—the great utterance about the destroyed Temple, which He would in three days raise up; and these intimations, which were but dim to a crushed and wavering faith, were read, like fiery letters upon the wall, by the illuminating glare of an uneasy guilt. Pretending, therefore, to be afraid lest His body should be stolen by His disciples for purposes of imposture, they begged that, until the third day, the tomb might be securely guarded. Pilate gave them a brief and haughty permission to do anything they liked;[2] for—apparently in the evening, when the great Paschal Sabbath was over — they

[1] Matt. xii. 39.

[2] ἔχετε κουστωδίαν can hardly be an imperative. It has usually been referred to some soldiers who may possibly have been lent to the Jews to act as a sort of police during the great Paschal gathering. The context seems to preclude the notion of the "guard" being composed of the Temple watchmen.

sent their guard to seal the *gôlal*, and to watch the sepulchre.

Night passed, and before the faint streak of dawn began to silver the darkness of that first great Easter-day,[1] the passionate love of those women, who had lingered latest by the cross, made them also the earliest at the tomb. Carrying with them their precious spices, but knowing nothing of the watch or seal, they anxiously inquired among themselves, as they groped their way with sad and timid steps through the glimmering darkness, "Who should roll away for them the great stone which closed the sepulchre?" The two Marys were foremost of this little devoted band, and after them came Salome and Joanna.[2] They found their difficulty solved for them. It became known then, or afterwards, that some dazzling angelic vision in white robes had terrified the keepers of the tomb, and had rolled the stone from the tomb amid the shocks of earthquake. And as they came to the tomb, there they too saw angels in white apparel, who bade them hasten back to the Apostles, and tell them—and especially Peter—that Christ, according to His own word, had risen from

[1] Those who think it right or fair to find and to press "discrepancies" between writers who simply say the truth to the best of their power in the ordinary language of common life, may find such a discrepancy between the *σκοτίας ἔτι οὔσης* of John xx. 1, and the *ἀνατείλαντος τοῦ ἡλίου* of Mark xvi. 2. But such criticism scarcely deserves serious notice. I have endeavoured throughout the narrative silently to show the perfect *possible* coherence and truthful simplicity of the fragmentary Gospel accounts. More than this is neither possible nor necessary. I do not hold the mechanical view of inspiration advocated in Gaussen's *Theopneustia;* but he at least shows how simply these supposed "discrepancies" are accounted for, and how perfectly harmless are the assaults on Christian faith which take them as a basis (*Theopn.* 218—229, E. Tr.).

[2] Mark xvi. 1—7, compared (throughout the paragraph) with John xx. 1; Luke xxiv. 1—10; Matt. xxviii. 1—7.

the dead, and would go before them, like a shepherd, into their own beloved and native Galilee. They hurried back in a tumult of rapture and alarm, telling no one except the disciples; and even to the disciples their words sounded like an idle tale. But Mary of Magdala, who seems to have received a separate and special intimation, hastened at once to Peter and John.[1] No sooner

[1] Any one who will attentively read side by side the narratives of these appearances on the first day of the resurrection, will see that they have only been preserved for us in general, interblended and scattered notices (see Matt. xxviii. 16; Luke xxiv. 34; Acts i. 3), which, in strict exactness, render it impossible, without many arbitrary suppositions, to produce from them a *certain* narrative of the order of events. The *lacunae*, the compressions, the variations, the actual differences, the subjectivity of the narrators as affected by spiritual revelations, render all harmonies at the best uncertain. Our belief in the Resurrection, as an historic fact, as absolutely well attested to us by subsequent and contemporary circumstances as any other event in history, rests on grounds far deeper, wider, more spiritual, more eternal, than can be shaken by divergences of which we can only say that they are not necessarily contradictions, but of which the true solution is no longer attainable. Hence the "ten discrepancies" which have been dwelt on since the days of Celsus, have never for one hour shaken the faith of Christendom. The phenomena presented by the narratives are exactly such as we should expect, derived as they are from different witnesses, preserved at first in oral tradition only, and written 1,800 years ago at a period when *minute circumstantial accuracy*, as distinguished from perfect truthfulness, was little regarded. St. Paul, surely no imbecile or credulous enthusiast, vouches, both for the reality of the appearances, and also for the fact that the vision by which he was himself converted came, at a long interval after the rest, to him as "to the abortive-born" of the Apostolic family (1 Cor. xv. 4—8). If the narratives of Christ's appearance to His disciples were *inventions*, how came they to possess the severe and simple character which shows no tinge of religious excitement? If those appearances were purely *subjective*, how can we account for their sudden, rapid, and total cessation? As Lange finely says, the great fugue of the first Easter tidings has not come to us as a "monotonous chorale," and mere boyish verbal criticism cannot understand the common feeling and harmony which inspire the individual vibrations of those enthusiastic and multitudinous voices (v. 61). Professor Westcott, with his usual profundity and insight, points out the differences of purpose in the narrative of the four Evangelists. St. Matthew dwells chiefly on the majesty and glory of the Resurrection; St. Mark, both in the original part and in the addition

had they received this startling news than they rose to see with their own eyes what had happened. John outstripped in speed his elder companion, and arriving first, stooped down, and gazed in silent wonder into that open grave. The grave was empty, and the linen cerements were lying neatly folded each in its proper place. Then Peter came up, and with his usual impetuosity, heedless of ceremonial pollution, and of every consideration but his love and his astonishment, plunged into the sepulchre. John followed him, and saw, and believed; and the two Apostles took back the undoubted certainty to their wondering brethren.[1] In spite of fear, and anxiety, and that dull intelligence which, by their own confession, was so slow to realise the truths they had been taught, there dawned upon them, even then, the trembling hope, which was so rapidly to become the absolute conviction, that Christ had risen indeed. That on that morning the grave of Christ was untenanted—that His body had not been removed by His enemies—that its absence caused to His disciples the profoundest amazement, not unmingled, in the breasts of some of them, with sorrow and alarm[2]—that they subsequently became convinced, by repeated proofs, that He had indeed risen from the dead—that for the truth of this

(Mark xvi. 9—20), insists upon it as *a fact;* St. Luke, as a *spiritual necessity;* St. John, as a *touchstone of character* (*Introd.* 310—315).

[1] Compare the exactly similar feature in the character of the two Apostles, in John xxi. 7.

[2] And that (as the Evangelists honestly admit), in spite of such repeated forewarnings that it should be so, as we find in John ii. 18—22; vi. 61—64; x. 17, 18; xiii. 31; Matt. xii. 38—42; xvi. 13—27; xvii. 1—9; xxvi. 63, 64; Mark ix. 30—32; x. 32—34; Luke ix. 43—45. It is, of course, true that they themselves may not have heard all of these predictions, but they had heard enough to cause our Lord's exclamation ὦ ἀνοητοὶ καὶ βραδεῖς τῇ καρδίᾳ τοῦ πιστεύειν (Luke xxiv. 25).

belief they were ready at all times themselves to die—that the belief effected a profound and total change in their character, making the timid courageous, and the weak irresistible—that they were incapable of a conscious falsehood, and that, even if it had not been so, a conscious falsehood could never have had power to convince the disbelief and regenerate the morality of the world—that on this belief of the resurrection were built the still-universal observance of the first day of the week, and the entire foundations of the Christian Church—these, at any rate, are facts which even scepticism itself, if it desires to be candid, can hardly fail, however reluctantly and slowly, to admit.

But as yet no eye had seen Him; and to Mary of Magdala—to her who loved most because she had been forgiven most, and out of whose soul, now ardent as flame and clear as crystal, He had cast seven devils—was this glorious honour first vouchsafed.[1] Even the vision of angels had not soothed the passion of agitation and alarm which she experienced when, returning once more to the tomb, she found that it was no longer possible for her to pay the last offices of devotion and tenderness to the crucified body of her Lord. From her impassioned soul not even the white-robed visions and angel voices could expel the anguish which she experienced in the one haunting thought, "They have taken away my Lord out of the sepulchre, and I know not where

[1] John xx. 11—18. [Mark xvi. 9—20 is canonical, but almost certainly unauthentic. It is omitted in ℵ, B, and in the Armenian Version. In L it is greatly altered, and in some MSS. it is marked with asterisks. Eusebius and Jerome testify to its general absence from the Greek MSS. If this external evidence be insufficient against the authority of A, C, D, Irenæus and Hippolytus, yet the internal evidence seems to be decisive—take, for instance, the fact, that in this short section πορεύομαι occurs three times, θεάομαι twice, and ὁ Κύριος twice, though not found elsewhere in St. Mark.]

they have laid Him." With her whole heart absorbed in this thought she turned away—and lo! Jesus Himself standing before her. It was Jesus, but not as she had known Him. There was something spiritual, something not of earth, in that risen and glorified body. Some accident of dress, or appearance, made her fancy that it was the keeper of the garden, and in the eager hope that he can explain to her the secret of that empty and angel-haunted grave, she exclaims to Him in an agony of appeal—turning her head aside as she addressed Him, perhaps that she might hide her streaming tears —"Oh, sir, if you took Him away, tell me where you put Him, and I will take Him."

Jesus saith to her, "Mary!"

That one word, in those awful yet tender tones of voice, at once penetrated to her heart. Turning towards Him, trying apparently to clasp His feet or the hem of His garment, she cried to Him in her native Aramaic, "Rabboni!" "Oh, my Master!" and then remained speechless with her transport. Jesus Himself gently checked the passion of her enthusiasm. "Cling not to Me,"[1] He exclaimed, "for not yet have I ascended to the Father; but go to My brethren, and say to them, I am ascending

[1] John xx. 17, Μή μου ἅπτου. Although ἅψασθαι is used of the woman who touched the hem of Christ's garment (Mark vi. 56), yet the "*Noli me tangere*," "Touch me not," conveys quite a false impression. It meant that the day for personal, physical presence, for merely human affection, for the grasp of human tenderness, was over now. Henceforth, He was to be with His people more nearly, more intimately, because *in spirit*. "Prohibitum tangere Dominum; non eum corporali tactu Dominum, sed *fide* tangimus" (Ambr.). The "for" is one of St. John's difficult causal connections, which seem to be dictated far more by the syllogism of emotion than by formal grammar. Perhaps it implies, "Be not clinging to me, for this *is but a brief interval between* my former close physical society with you, and my future spiritual union." For the τὸν πατέρα μου καὶ πατέρα ὑμῶν, κ. τ. λ., see Pearson *On the Creed*, p. 42.

to My Father and your Father, and My God and your God." Awe-struck, she hastened to obey. She repeated to them that solemn message—and through all future ages has thrilled that first utterance, which made on the minds of those who heard it so indelible an impression—"I HAVE SEEN THE LORD!"

2. Nor was her testimony unsupported. Jesus met the other women also, and said to them, "All hail!" Terror mingled with their emotion, as they clasped His feet. "Fear not," He said to them; "go, bid My brethren that they depart into Galilee, and there shall they see Me."[1]

It was useless for the guards to stay beside an empty grave. With fear for the consequences, and horror at all that they had seen, they fled to the members of the Sanhedrin who had given them their secret commission. To these hardened hearts belief and investigation were alike out of the question. Their only refuge seemed to be in lies. They instantly tried to hush up the whole matter. They suggested to the soldiers that they must have slept, and that while they did so the disciples had stolen the body of Jesus.[2] But such a tale was too infamous for credence, and too ridiculous for publicity. If it became known, nothing could have saved these soldiers, supposing them to have been Romans, from disgrace and execution. The Sadducees therefore bribed the men to consult their

[1] Matt. xxviii. 9, 10. Matthew alone mentions this adoration. The προσκυνήσαντες αὐτῷ of Luke xxiv. 52 are omitted in some good MSS.

[2] Matt. xxviii. 11—15. Those who are shocked at this suggested possibility of deceit on the part of a few hard, worldly, and infatuated Sanhedrists, do not shrink from insinuating that the faith of Christendom was founded on most facile and reprehensible credulity, almost amounting to conscious deception, by men who died for the truth of what they asserted, and who have taught the spirit of truthfulness as a primary duty of the religion which they preached.

common interests by burying the whole matter in secrecy and silence. It was only gradually and later, and to the initiated, that the base calumny was spread. Within six weeks of the resurrection, that great event was the unshaken faith of every Christian; within a few years of the event the palpable historic proofs of it and the numerous testimonies of its reality—strengthened by a memorable vision vouchsafed to himself—had won assent from the acute and noble intellect of a young Pharisaic zealot and persecutor whose name was Saul.[1] But it was only in posthumous and subterranean whispers that the dark falsehood was disseminated which was intended to counteract this overwhelming evidence. St. Matthew says that when he wrote his Gospel it was still commonly bruited among the Jews. It continued to be received among them for centuries, and is one of the blasphem-ing follies which was repeated and amplified twelve cen-turies afterwards in the *Toldôth Jeshu*.[2]

3. The third appearance of Jesus was to Peter. The details of it are wholly unknown to us.[3] They may have been of a nature too personal to have been revealed. The fact rests on the express testimony of St. Luke and of St. Paul.

4. On the same day the Lord's fourth appearance was accompanied with circumstances of the deepest interest. Two of the disciples were on their way to a village named Emmaus,[4] of uncertain site, but about

[1] Rom. vi. 4; Eph. i. 20; Gal. i. 1; 1 Cor. xv. 4—8, &c. The latter is the earliest *written* allusion to the resurrection (A.D. 54).

[2] Eisenmenger, *Entdecktes Judenthum*, i. 189.

[3] Luke xxiv. 34; 1 Cor. xv. 5.

[4] Emmaus can hardly be Amwâs (Nicopolis), which is 160 stades (about twenty-two miles) from Jerusalem, even if, with a few bad MSS., we read ἕκατον ἑξήκοντα in Luke xxiv. 13. The name means "warm springs."

eight miles from Jerusalem, and were discoursing with sad and anxious hearts on the awful incidents of the last two days, when a Stranger joined them, and asked them the cause of their clouded looks and anxious words. They stopped, and looked at this unknown traveller with a dubious and unfriendly glance;[1] and when one of the two, whose name was Cleopas,[2] spoke in reply, there is a touch of surprise and suspicion in the answer which he ventured to give. "Dost thou live alone as a stranger in Jerusalem, and dost thou not know what things happened there in these last days?" "What things?" He asked them. Then they told Him how all their yearning hopes that Jesus had been the great Prophet who should redeem His people had been dashed to the earth, and how all His mighty deeds before God and the people had ended two days back on the shameful cross. They described the feeling of amazement with which, on this the third day, they had heard the women's rumours of angel visions, and the certain testimony of some of their brethren that the tomb was empty now. "But," added the speaker with a sigh of incredulity and sorrow—"but Him they saw not."

Then reproaching them with the dulness of their intelligence and their affections, the Stranger showed them

Culonieh (see Jos. *B. J.* vii. 6, § 6) seems to be a more likely site, but nothing whatever depends on the identification of a locality so incidentally alluded to.

[1] Luke xxiv. 13—35, verse 17, *καὶ ἐστάθησαν σκυθρωποὶ* (א, A, B, L, and various versions, &c.). This, as well as the somewhat emphatic answer of Cleopas, shows that they were not quite at their ease at the Stranger's intervention. After the recent events such caution was very natural.

[2] If, as Keim, &c., suppose, the story is mythic, &c., why was so obscure a name as Cleopas chosen to authenticate it? and why was the other disciple left nameless? Would it not have been just as easy to select two of the most prominent Apostles? It is a mere assumption that Cleopas (or Cleopater) was the same as Clopas, or Alphæus.

how through all the Old Testament from Moses onwards there was one long prophecy of the sufferings no less than of the glory of Christ. In such high converse they drew near to Emmaus, and the stranger seemed to be going onwards, but they pressed Him to stay, and as they sat down to their simple meal, and He blessed and brake the bread, suddenly their eyes were opened, and in spite of the altered form,[1] they recognised that He who was with them was the Lord. But even as they recognised Him, He was with them no longer. "Did not our heart burn within us," they exclaimed to each other, "while He was speaking with us in the way, while He was opening to us the Scriptures?" Rising instantly, they returned to Jerusalem with the strange and joyous tidings. They found no dubious listeners now. They, too, were received with the rapturous affirmation, "The Lord is risen indeed, and hath appeared unto Simon!"

5. Once more, for the fifth time on that eternally memorable Easter day, Jesus manifested Himself to His disciples. Ten of them were sitting together, with doors closed for fear of the Jews. As they exchanged and discussed their happy intelligence, Jesus Himself stood in the midst of them, with the words, "Peace be with you." The unwonted aspect of that glorified body—the awful significance of the fact that He had risen from the dead—scared and frightened them.[2] The presence of their Lord was indeed corporeal, but it was changed.

[1] Mark xvi. 12, *ἐφανερώθη ἐν ἑτερᾳ̂ μορφῃ̂.* It must be remembered that the Appendix to this Gospel (xvi. 9—20), though not genuine, has every claim to our respect. Mr. Burgon's elaborate vindication of these verses (Lond., 1871) is quite unconvincing (see Mr. Hort's remarks in the *Academy*, Nov. 15, 1871).

[2] Ignatius (*ad Smyrn.*). Jesus uses the words, *οὔκ ειμι δαιμόνιον*

They thought that it was a spirit which was standing before them. "Why are ye troubled?" He asked, "and why do anxious doubts rise in your hearts? See my hands and my feet, that it is I; handle me, and see; for a spirit hath not flesh and bones as ye see me have." Even while He spoke He showed them His hands and His side. And then, while joy, amazement, incredulity, were all struggling in their hearts, He asked them if they had there anything to eat; and yet further to assure them, ate a piece of broiled fish in their presence.[1] Then once more He said, "Peace be unto you. As my Father hath sent me, even so send I you." Breathing on them, He said, "Receive ye the Holy Ghost. Whose-soever sins ye remit, they are remitted to them: whose-soever sins ye retain, they are retained."[2]

6. One only of the Apostles had been absent—Thomas the Twin. His character, as we have seen already, was affectionate, but melancholy. To him the news seemed too good to be true. In vain did the other disciples assure him, "We have seen the Lord." Happily for us, though less happily for him, he declared with strong asseveration that nothing would convince him, short of actually putting his own finger into the print of the nails, and his hands into His side. A week

ἀσώματον. Some, from the mention of σάρκα καὶ ὀστέα (Luke xxiv. 39) without αἷμα (which was the sign of the ψυχὴ, or "animal life"), have perhaps too rashly and literally inferred that the resurrection-body was bloodless. In a very curious translated fragment of Clemens Alexandrinus on John i. 1, a tradition is mentioned that St. John, touching the body, found no substance there; his hand passed through it (quoted by Keim, III. ii. 568).

[1] The words καὶ ἀπὸ μελισσίου κηρίου (omitted in א, A, B, D, &c.) are of dubious authenticity.

[2] The perfects ἀφέωνται, κεκράτηνται, imply permanence of result. On this commission, see *supra*, Vol. II., pp. 13—16.

passed, and the faithfully-recorded doubts of the anxious Apostle remained unsatisfied. On the eighth, or, as *we* should say, on the seventh day afterwards[1]—for already the resurrection had made the first day of the week sacred to the hearts of the Apostles—the eleven were again assembled within closed doors. Once more Jesus appeared to them, and after His usual gentle and solemn blessing, called Thomas, and bade him stretch forth his finger, and put it in the print of the nails, and to thrust his hand into the spear-wound of His side, and to be "not faithless, but believing." "My Lord and my God!" exclaimed the incredulous Apostle, with a burst of conviction. "Because thou hast seen Me," said Jesus, "thou hast believed; blessed are they who saw not and yet believed."

7. The next appearance of the risen Saviour was to seven of the Apostles by the Sea of Galilee—Simon, Thomas, Nathanael, the sons of Zebedee, and two others—not improbably Philip and Andrew—who are not named.[2] A pause had occurred in the visits of Jesus, and before they returned to Jerusalem at Pentecost to receive the promised outpouring of the Spirit, Simon said that he should resume for the day his old trade of a fisherman. There was no longer a common purse, and as their means of subsistence were gone, this seemed to be the only obvious way of obtaining an honest maintenance. The others proposed to join him, and they set sail in the evening because night is the best time

[1] Why did they not go to Galilee immediately on receiving our Lord's message? The circumstance is unexplained, for the identification of Galilee with the peak of the Mount of Olives—now called Viri Galilæi, from Acts i. 11—is wholly absurd. Perhaps the *entire* message of Jesus to them is not recorded; perhaps they awaited the end of the feast.

[2] John xxi. 1—24.

for fishing. All night they toiled in vain. At early dawn, in the misty twilight, there stood on the shore the figure of One whom they did not recognise. A voice asked them if they had caught anything. "No," was the despondent answer. "Fling your net to the right side of the vessel, and ye shall find." They made the cast, and instantly were scarcely able to draw the net from the multitude of fishes. The incident awoke, with overwhelming force, the memory of earlier days. "It is the Lord," whispered John to Peter; and instantly the warm-hearted enthusiast, tightening his fisher's tunic[1] round his loins, leaped into the sea, to swim across the hundred yards which separated him from Jesus, and cast himself, all wet from the waves, before His feet. More slowly the others followed, dragging the strained but unbroken net, with its 153 fishes. A wood fire was burning on the strand, some bread lay beside it, and some fish were being broiled on the glowing embers. It is a sight which may often be seen to this day by the shores of Galilee. And He who stood beside it bade them bring more fish of those which they had caught. Instantly Simon started up, and helped with his strong arm to drag the net ashore. And He whom they all knew to be the Lord, but whose voice and aspect made their hearts so still with awful reverence that they dared not question Him, bade them "Come and breakfast," and distributed to them the bread and fish.

The happy meal ended in silence, and then Jesus said to His weak but fond Apostle, "Simon"—(it was no time as yet to restore to him the name of Peter)—

[1] Perhaps the ἐπενδύτης is only a subligaculum (λινοῦν τι ὀθόνιον Theophyl.). It is very common in the East to work naked, or with nothing but a cloth round the waist.

"Simon, son of Jonas, honourest thou Me more than these?"

"Yea, Lord, Thou knowest that I love Thee."

"Feed My little lambs."

Simon had felt in his inmost heart what was meant by that kind rebuke—"more than these." It called back to his penitent soul those boastful words, uttered so confidently among his brethren, "Although all shall be offended, yet will not I." Failure had taught him humility, and therefore he will neither claim a pre-eminence in affection, nor adopt the word of the Saviour's question (ἀγαπᾷς), which involved deep honour and devotion and esteem; but will substitute for it that weaker word, which yet best expressed the warm human affection of his heart. And the next time the question reminded him less painfully of his old self-confidence, for Jesus said to him only—

"Simon, son of Jonas, honourest thou Me?"

Again the Apostle humbly answered in the same words as before—

"Yea, Lord, Thou knowest that I love Thee."

"Tend my sheep."[1]

But Simon had thrice denied, and therefore it was fitting that he should thrice confess. Again, after a brief pause, came the question—and this time with the weaker but warmer word which the Apostle himself had chosen—

"Simon, son of Jonas, *lovest* thou Me?"

And Simon, deeply humbled and distressed, exclaimed, "Lord, Thou knowest all things; Thou seest that I love Thee."[2]

[1] John xxi. 15. The verb is *ποίμαινε*, not *βόσκε*.

[2] Verse 17, *οἶδας* . . *γιγνώσκεις*.

"Feed My beloved sheep."[1] Then very solemnly He added, "Verily, verily, I say unto thee, When thou wast younger thou didst gird thyself, and walk where thou wouldest; but when thou art old thou shalt stretch out thy hands, and another shall gird thee, and shall lead thee where thou willest not."

The Apostle understood Him; he knew that this implied the years of his future service, the pangs of his future martyrdom; but now he was no longer "Simon," but "Peter"—the heart of rock was in him; he was ready, even to the death, to obey the voice which said to him, "Follow Me." While the conversation had been taking place he had been walking by the side of Jesus, a few steps in front of his comrades. Looking back he saw John, his only favourite companion, and the disciple whom Jesus loved, slowly following them. Pointing to him, he asked, "Lord, and what shall he do?" The answer checked the spirit of idle curiosity—"If I will that he tarry till I come, what is that to thee? Follow *thou* Me." Peter dared ask no more, and the answer—which was intentionally vague—led to the wide misapprehension prevalent in the early Church, that John was not to die until Jesus came. The Apostle quietly corrects the error by quoting the exact words of the risen Christ. The manner of his death we do not know, but we know that he outlived all his brother disciples, and that he survived that terrible overthrow of his nation which, since it rendered impossible a strict obedience to the institutions of the Old Covenant, and opened throughout the world an unimpeded path for the establishment of the New Commandment and the Kingdom not of earth, was—in a sense more true than

[1] John xxi. 17, προβάτια (A, B, C).

any other event in human history—a second coming of the Lord.

8. It may have been on this occasion that Jesus told His disciples of the mountain in Galilee, where He would meet all who knew and loved Him for the last time. Whether it was Tabor, or the Mountain of Beatitudes, we do not know, but more than five hundred of His disciples collected at the given time with the eleven, and received from Jesus His last commands, to teach and baptise throughout all nations; and the last promise, that He would be with them always, even to the end of the world.[1] Writing more than twenty years after this time, St. Paul gives us the remarkable testimony, that the greater number of these eye-witnesses of the resurrection were yet alive, and that some only were "fallen asleep."

9. A ninth appearance of Jesus is unrecorded in the Gospels, and is known to us from a single allusion in St. Paul alone. "I delivered unto you," he writes to the Corinthians,[2] "that which also I received, how that Christ died for our sins, according to the Scriptures; and that He was buried, and that He rose again the third day, according to the Scriptures: and that He was seen of Cephas, then of the Twelve: after that, he was seen of above five hundred brethren at once: . . . . *after that, He*

The *οἱ δὲ ἐδίστασαν* of Matt. xxviii. 17 can only mean "but some doubted"—not, as Wetstein and others take it, whether they should worship or not, but respecting the whole scene. All may not have stood near to Him, and even if they did, we have seen in four previous instances (Matt. xxviii. 17; Luke xxiv. 16; *id.* 37; John xxi. 4) that there was something unusual and not instantly recognisable in His resurrection body. At any rate, here we have another inestimable proof of the candour of the Evangelists, for there is nothing to be said in favour of the conjectural emendation, *οὐδέ*. "Dubitatum est ab illis," says St. Leo, "ne dubitaretur a nobis" (*Serm.* lxxi., ap. Wordsw. *in loc.*).

[2] 1 Cor. xv. 3—8.

was seen of James; then of all the Apostles. And last of all He appeared to me also, as to the abortive-born (of the Apostolic family)." Respecting this appearance to James we know nothing further, unless there be any basis of true tradition in the story preserved to us in the Gospel of the Hebrews. We are there told that James, the first Bishop of Jerusalem, and the Lord's brother,[1] had, after the Last Supper, taken a solemn vow that he would neither eat nor drink until he had seen Jesus risen from the dead. Early, therefore, after His resurrection, Jesus, after He had given the *sindôn* to the servant of the priest, had a table with bread brought out, blessed the bread, and gave it to James, with the words, "Eat thy bread now, my brother, since the Son of Man has risen from the dead."[2]

10. Forty days had now elapsed since the Crucifixion. During those forty days nine times had He been visibly present to human eyes, and had been touched by human hands. But His body had not been merely the human body, nor liable to merely human laws, nor had He lived during those days the life of men. The time had now come when His earthly presence should be taken away from them for ever, until He returned in glory to judge the world. He met them in Jerusalem, and as He led them with Him towards Bethany,[3] He bade them wait in the Holy City until they had received the promise of the Spirit. He checked their eager inquiry about the times and the seasons, and bade them be His witnesses in all the world. These last farewells must have been

[1] Or it may possibly have been James the son of Zebedee.

[2] Jer. *De Viris Illustr.* ii. The allusion to the *sindôn* is curious. See Excursus XV., "Traditional Sayings of Christ."

[3] Luke xxiv. 50. The best reading seems to be ἕως πρὸς Βηθανίαν (א, B, C, L, &c.).

uttered in some of the wild secluded upland country that surrounds the little village;[1] and when they were over, He lifted up His hands and blessed them, and, even as He blessed them, was parted from them, and as He passed from before their yearning eyes "a cloud received Him out of their sight."

Between us and His visible presence—between us and that glorified Redeemer who now sitteth at the right hand of God—that cloud still rolls. But the eye of Faith can pierce it; the incense of true prayer can rise above it; through it the dew of blessing can descend. And if He is gone away, yet He has given us in His Holy Spirit a nearer sense of His presence, a closer infolding in the arms of His tenderness, than we could have enjoyed even if we had lived with Him of old in the home of Nazareth, or sailed with Him in the little boat over the crystal waters of Gennesareth. We may be as near to Him at all times—and more than all when we kneel down to pray—as the beloved disciple was when he laid his head upon His breast. The word of God is very nigh us, even in our mouths and in our hearts. To ears that have been closed His voice may seem indeed to sound no longer. The loud noises of War may shake the world; the eager calls of Avarice and of Pleasure may drown the gentle utterance which bids us "Follow Me;" after two thousand years of Christianity the incredulous murmurs of an impatient scepticism may make it scarcely possible for Faith to repeat, without insult, the creed which has been the regeneration of the

[1] "It was solitude and retirement in which Jesus kept His vigils: the desert places heard Him pray; in a privacy He was born; in the wilderness He fed His thousands; upon a mountain apart He was transfigured; upon a mountain He died; and from a mountain He ascended to His Father" (Petr. Cell. iv. 12, quoted by Jer. Taylor, *Life of Christ,* I. viii.).

world. Ay, and sadder even than this, every now and then may be heard, even in Christian England, the insolence of some blaspheming tongue which still scoffs at the Son of God as He lies in the agony of the garden, or breathes His last sigh upon the bitter tree. But the secret of the Lord is with them that fear Him, and He will show them His covenant. To all who will listen He still speaks. He promised to be with us always, even to the end of the world, and we have not found His promise fail. It was but for thirty-three short years of a short lifetime that He lived on earth; it was but for three broken and troubled years that He preached the Gospel of the Kingdom; but for ever, even until all the Æons have been closed, and the earth itself, with the heavens that now are, have passed away, shall every one of His true and faithful children find peace and hope and forgiveness in His name, and that name shall be called Emmanuel, which is, being interpreted,

"God with us."

APPENDIX.

EXCURSUS I. (Vol. I., pp. 74, 104.)

The Date of Christ's Birth.

Although the date of Christ's birth cannot be established with absolute certainty, there is yet a large amount of evidence to render it at least probable that He was born four years before our present era. It is universally admitted that our received chronology, which is not older than Dionysius Exiguus in the sixth century, is wrong. I ought to say here that I have not pretended to discuss the new theories of chronology proposed by Keim; not only because I am not well fitted for elaborate chronological inquiries, but because (i.) they would have required inordinate space, and (ii.) they depend on views of the Gospels altogether remote from my own.

1. Our one most certain datum is obtained from the fact that Christ was born before the death of Herod the Great. The date of that event is known with absolute certainty, for (i.) Josephus tells us that he died thirty-seven years after he had been declared king by the Romans. Now it is known that he was declared king A.U.C. 714; and therefore, since Josephus always reckons his years from Nisan to Nisan, and counts the initial and terminal fractions of Nisan as complete years, Herod must have died between Nisan A.U.C. 750, and Nisan A.U.C. 751—*i.e.*, between B.C. 4 and B.C. 3 of our era. (ii.) Josephus says that on the night in which Herod ordered Judas, Matthias, and their abettors to be burnt, there was an eclipse of the moon.[2] Now this eclipse took place on the night of March 12, B.C. 4; and Herod was dead at least seven days before the Passover,[3]

[1] *Antt.* xvii. 8, § 1.

[2] Id. xvii. 6, § 4. Ideler, *Handb. Chron.* ii. 391.

[3] Id. xvii. 3, § 4.

which, if we accept the Jewish reckoning, fell in that year on April 12. But, according to the clear indication of the Gospels, Jesus must have been born at least forty days before Herod's death. It is clear, therefore, that under no circumstances can the Nativity have taken place *later* than February, B.C. 4.

2. The only other *certain* datum which we have is furnished by St. Luke, who fixes the beginning of St. John the Baptist's preaching in the 15th year of Tiberius, and says that when Jesus began His ministry, he was about thirty years old (Luke iii. 23).[1]

Now if the 15th year of Tiberius be dated from the death of Augustus (Aug. 19, A.U.C. 767), then Jesus was baptised A.U.C. 782; but since, as we have seen, he *could* not have been born later than February, A.U.C. 750, this would make him at least thirty-two, an age inconsistent with the natural meaning of St. Luke's expression. There is therefore good ground to believe that St. Luke dates the year of the reign of Tiberius from his association with Augustus as joint Emperor in A.U.C. 765,[2] a method of computation which certainly existed, and would be especially likely to prevail in the Provinces. Jesus would then have begun His public teaching A.U.C. 780, a date which exactly agrees with the only secure datum about the year of His birth.

All attempts to discover the month and day of the Nativity are useless. No data whatever exist to enable us to determine them with even approximate accuracy.

The census of Quirinius, the order of the courses of priests, the cycle of lessons in the Jewish Calendar, the consulships, &c., mentioned by Tertullian, the arrival of the Magi, and the astrological conjunction which is supposed to have caused their journey, the third closing by Augustus of the Temple of Janus, and other indications which have been pressed into the service of chronology, are all too vague to be of any use, and are only likely to lead to highly uncertain or entirely erroneous results.

A *general* confirmation of the conclusion at which we have arrived may be deduced from John ii. 20, "Forty and six years was this Temple in building." Herod's reconstruction of the Temple began in the eighteenth year of his reign, probably in Cisleu, A.U.C. 734. This will bring the forty-sixth year of its continuance to A.U.C. 780, which we have already seen reason to regard as the first year of

[1] The rendering of the English Version, "began to be about thirty years old, for ἦν . . . ὡσεὶ ἐτῶν τριάκοντα ἀρχόμενος, is wholly untenable.

[2] Tac. *Ann.* 1, 3; Suet. *Aug.* 97; Vell. Paterc. 103.

Christ's ministry, and the thirtieth of His age. There is, however, an element of doubt in this computation, owing to St. John's use of the aorist ᾠκοδομήθη, unless it be regarded as a less accurate expression for οἰκοδομεῖται (cf. Ezra v. 16).

The only difficulties in the data mentioned by Luke iii. 1, 2, are the mention of Annas as High Priest, and of Lysanias tetrarch of Abilene.

1. As regards Annas, it is true that some MSS. read ἐπὶ ἀρχιερέων, but there is so complete a consensus of *all* the best MSS. (א, A, B, C, D, E, &c.) in favour of ἐπὶ ἀρχιερέως, that there can be no doubt of its being the true reading. The same expression occurs in Acts iv. 6. It will then be asked, how is it that St. Luke calls *Annas* High Priest, when the office was really held by Caiaphas? The question is sufficiently answered *infra*, Vol. II., p. 328; but we may here observe, (i.) that Annas, having been merely superseded by the will of Valerius Gratus,[1] would, by all serious-minded Jews, be still regarded as High Priest *de jure*, according to the Mosaic Law (Numb. xxxv. 25). (ii.) That whether he held the office of *Sagan* or of *Nasî*, or not, there is sufficient evidence to show that he was at this time the most influential and powerful leader of the aristocratic, sacerdotal, and Sadducæan party at Jerusalem. (iii.) That this leading position of Annas is clearly recognised by Josephus (*Antt.* xx. 9, § 1), who, like the Evangelists, speaks vaguely about the mere puppets of civil power who at this period became titular High Priests in rapid succession.[2]

2. It used to be assumed that St. Luke had made some mistake about Lysanias. The facts, however, seem to be, (i.) that there was a Lysanias, King of Chalcis under Mount Lebanon, and therefore, in all probability, also tetrarch of Abilene, in the time of Antony and Cleopatra, *sixty years before* the date mentioned by St. Luke (Jos. *B. J.* i. 13, § 1); and *another* in the reigns of Caligula and Claudius, *twenty years after* St. Luke's date (Jos. *Antt.* xv. 4, § 1). We know nothing certain of any intermediate Lysanias, but there is nothing whatever to *prove* that there may not have been one; or even that this Lysanias may not be the second whom we have mentioned. Even Renan admits that, after reading the inscription of Zenodorus at Baalbek, he sees less reason to suppose that the Evangelist is in error. ("Une étude de l'inscription . . . m'a mené à croire que

[1] Annas was High Priest A.D. 7—14, and there had been three intermediate High Priests—one of whom, Eleazar, was his son—before his son-in-law, Joseph Caiaphas (Jos. *Antt.* xviii. 2, § 2) had been appointed in A.D. 24.

[2] *Vit.* 38; *B. J.* iv. 3, § 9.

l'évangéliste pouvait n'avoir pas aussi gravement tort que d'habiles critiques le pensent," *Vie de Jésus*, p. xiii.) The tetrarchate of Lysanias might well serve to mark a date, because, for a time, Abilene had been actually a part of Jewish territory, having been assigned in A.D. 36 by Caligula to his favourite Herod Agrippa I.

For a full commentary on these chronological data of St. Luke see Wieseler, *Chron. Synops.*, E. Tr., pp. 157—175. But enough has been said to show that, so far from the Evangelist having fallen into a demonstrable error, there is every reason to believe that he has independently preserved an obscure historical fact. Unless he had been perfectly well acquainted with the actual circumstances, it is inconceivable that he should have introduced so minute, and apparently superfluous an allusion, at the risk of falling into a needless blunder.

EXCURSUS II. (Vol. I., p. 76.)

Christ and the Christians in the Talmud.

The name of Jesus occurs some twenty times only in unexpurgated editions of the Talmud, the last of which appeared at Amsterdam in 1645.[1]

The allusions to Him are characterised by intense hatred, disguised by intense fear. They are also marked by all the gross and reckless carelessness of these utterly uncritical and unhistorical writers.

The Christians are usually called—partly, no doubt, to conceal the allusions to them—pupils of Balaam, Minîm (heretics), Gentiles, Nazarenes.

In *Sanhedr.* 43 *a* Jesus is said to have had five disciples:—Matthaeus; Thaddaeus; נצר (which clearly means "Nazarene"); Booni—apparently meant for Nikdimon Ben Gorion (Nikodemus), or Banus; and Niki—perhaps some confusion of Nikolaitan.[2]

Our Blessed Lord is called—

"That man" (cf. Acts v. 28 and פלוני, "So and so," ὁ δεῖνα).

"He whom we may not name."

"Ha-Notzrî," *i.e.*, "The Nazarene."

"The fool."

[1] Jost, *Gesch. d. Judenth.* i. 405, 414.

[2] Grätz, iii. 243. *Taanith*, f. 19, 2. See Ewald, *Gesch. Christ.*, p. 397.

"The Hung" (תָּלוּי). Thus Abn Ezra (on Gen. xxvii. 39) says that Constantine put on his labarum, "a figure of the hung;" and in Ps. xxx. 14, R. Bechai says that in the word מִיָּעַר the letter ע is suspended, to indicate that it is the "worshippers of the Hung"—*i.e.*, the Christians—who devastate the vineyard of Israel.

"Absalom."

"Ben Stada."

"Ben Pandera."

Putting into Hebrew letters the Grecised form of His name (ישו), they made each letter the first of a Hebrew word, so as to mean "May his memory (ז) be destroyed (י), and his name (ש) be blotted out (ו)."

Little is said about Jesus in the Talmud, except that He was a scholar of Joshua Ben Perachiah (who lived a century before!), accompanied him into Egypt, there learned magic, was a seducer (*mesîth*) of the people, and was first stoned, then hung as a blasphemer after forty days, during which no one had come forward to speak in His favour.[1]

The *Toldôth Jeshu* is a late and detestable compilation, put together out of fragmentary Talmudic legends, and regarded as utterly contemptible, even by the Jews themselves.[2] It is printed with a Latin translation by Wagenseil, in his *Tela Ignea Satanae;* but its blasphemies are too gross and grotesque to need further notice.

Some account of the wretched follies blasphemously indicated by the name Ben Stada, Ben Pandera, &c., may be seen in Buxtorf, *Lex. Talm.*, p. 1458, seq.

EXCURSUS III. (Vol. I., p. 89.)

Jesus and Hillel.

The conjectural dates of Hillel's life are that he was born B.C. 75; came to Jerusalem B.C. 36; became Nasî B.C. 30; and died about B.C. 10. Geiger, a learned Rabbi of Frankfort, author of *Das Judenthum und seine Geschichte*, and *Urschrift*, says, "Jesus was a Pharisee (!) who walked in the paths of Hillel; that He uttered no

[1] Lightfoot *ad Matt.* xii. 24; *Bab. Sanhedr.* 67 *a*; *Shabbath*, 104 *b*; Grätz, iii. 242.

[2] "Ein elendes Machwerk." (Grätz, iii. 243.)

new thought. Hillel, on the contrary, presents us with the picture of a genuine Reformer." This Hillel, he continues, with an undercurrent of contrast, is a really historical personage;[1] others have a halo of legend and miracle about them which merely tends to obscure and conceal their actual personality. Renan improves upon the hint, and, while he acknowledges the superiority of Jesus, says that Hillel was His real master.[2] The Messiah, it seems, was but the pupil and the plagiarist of a Rabbi, who, with less faults than others of his countrymen, is said to have declared "that no such Messiah would ever come."

Now I would premise at once that these questions about "originality" seem to me supremely idle and irrelevant in all cases, but most of all when they are irreverently applied to the teaching of our Lord. The originality of Jesus, even to those who regard Him as a mere human teacher, consists in this—that His words have touched the hearts of all men in all ages, and have regenerated the moral life of the world. Who but a pedant in art would impugn the originality of Michael Angelo because his Pietà is said to have resembled a statue of Signorelli; or of Raphael, because his earlier works betray the influence of Perugino? Who but an ignoramus would detract from the greatness of Milton because his *Paradise Lost* offers some points of similarity to the *Adam* of Battista Andreini? But if there

[1] Does M. Geiger consider it *quite historical* that Hillel knew the language of mountains, hills, valleys, trees, vegetables, wild and tame beasts, and demons (*Sofrîm*, xvi. 9); that the *Bath kôl* decided in his favour as against Shammai (*Bab. Erubhîn*, 13 *b*); that thirty of his scholars were worthy of being overclouded by the Shechina like Moses, and thirty more to make the sun stand still like Joshua (*Babha Bathra*, 134 *a*); and that such was the fiery zeal of his most eminent pupil, Jonathan Ben Uzziel, that, when he was studying the Law, birds who flew over his head were consumed (*B. Succa*, 28 *a*)? (See Otho, *Lex. Rab.* 242; Buxtorf, *Lex. Talm.*, p. 617; Gfrörer, *Jahrh. d. Heils*, i. 37.)

[2] "Par sa pauvreté humblement supportée, par la douceur de son caractère, par l'opposition qu'il faisait aux hypocrites et aux prêtres, Hillel fut *le maître de Jésus*, s'il est permis de parler de maître quand il s'agit d'une si haute originalité" (*Vie de Jésus*, p. 38). Farther on he says, very truly, "Hillel cependant ne passera jamais pour le vrai fondateur du christianisme. Dans la morale, comme dans l'art, dire n'est rien, faire est tout . . . La vérité ne prend quelque valeur que si elle passe à l'état de sentiment, et elle n'atteint tout son prix que quand elle se réalise dans le monde à l'état de fait" (*id.*, p. 96). Geiger's remark, baseless as it is, has, however, found great currency (Grätz, *Gesch. d. Juden*, iii.). "Jesu Sanftmuth und Demuth erinnern an Hillel, den er sich überhaupt zum Muster genommen zu haben scheint." Yet it is not too much to say that there is hardly one page in any one of the Gospels which does not suffice to show its baselessness.

are any who cannot rise above this narrow ground, it is well that they should remember that, according to the Jewish writers themselves, we can never distinguish between the maxims which Hillel originated and those which merely belonged to his school. Since they were not committed to writing till long after the death of Christ, they may easily have been due to Christian teaching, which certainly would not have been without influence on Hillel's grandson, the Rabban Gamaliel.

It needs, however, but little knowledge of the real facts to see how utterly imaginary are these Jewish conjectures. The position of Jesus towards the Rabbinism of His nation and all that occupied it—its *Hagadôth*, or legendary matter, its *Halachôth*, or traditional customs, its puerile minutiæ, its benumbing ritual, its inflated emptiness, its irreligious arrogance, its servile second-handness, its to-and-fro balancing of conflicting opinions—is one not of submissive reverence, but of uncompromising hostility. Hillel was a "sweet and noble" Rabbi; he is the loftiest figure which Rabbinism has produced; he seems to have been really learned, humble, peaceful, and enlightened; but the distance between him and Jesus is a distance absolutely immeasurable, and the resemblance of his teaching to that of Jesus is the resemblance of a glowworm to the sun. Their whole scope and method are utterly different. Hillel rested on precedent, Jesus spoke with authority. Hillel spoke in the schools to students and separatists; Jesus in the streets and by the roadsides to publicans and sinners. Hillel confined his teaching to Jerusalem; Jesus traversed the length and breadth of Palestine. Hillel mainly occupied himself with the Levitical law, and modified its regulations to render them more easy and more palatable; Jesus taught only the moral law, and extended its application from external actions to the very thoughts of the heart. Would Christ have ever uttered a sentiment so deeply dyed in Pharisaism as this?—"No uneducated man easily avoids sin; no common person (*am ha-arets*) is pious."[1] Is not this the very echo of the haughty exclusive insolence which said, "Have any of the rulers believed on Him, or of the Pharisees? But this mob that knoweth not the Law are cursed?" Is it not the very spirit which Christ's

[1] I have already given instances (*supra*, Vol. I., p. 86) of the contempt poured on the poor *am ha-ratsîm*, and may add others. Their testimony was not received; they are not admitted into society; no one is to take the trouble to restore to them their lost property; the terms "beasts" and "vermin" are applied to them, their wives, and their daughters; and finally, leave is given "to rend an *am ha-arets* like a fish" (עם הארץ מותר לירעו כדג). See McCaul, *Old Paths*, pp. 6, 458, &c.

whole life and practice combated, and which His whole teaching most utterly condemned?

I. Three main anecdotes are told of Hillel. One is that, though descended from David, he came at the age of forty-one (about B.C. 36) to Jerusalem, where he worked as a common porter, earning a *victoriatus* (about 3d.) a day, and giving half of it to the porter of the School of Shemaia and Abtalion, to admit him to their lectures. One day, at dawn in the month Tebeth—about the end of December—said Shemaia to Abtalion, "Brother, why is the school so dark? it seems to be a cloudy day." They looked up, and, darkening the window, was some semblance of a human figure lying under a mass of snow. In spite of the Sabbath they uncovered him, rubbed him with oil, and placed him near the fire. It was Hillel, who, having earned nothing the day before, and having been churlishly excluded by the porter, had climbed in the twilight into the window of the Beth Midrash, and there got buried and benumbed under a fall of snow.[1] To restore him to life by rubbing, warming, bathing him, Shemaia and Abtalion not only broke the Sabbath, but declared that he was well worthy of having the usual sabbatical rules superseded in his favour.

2. A pagan once came to Shammai, and said, "Make me a proselyte, but you must teach me the whole Law while I stand on one leg!" Shammai drove the man from his presence with blows. He went to Hillel, who replied with perfect suavity, "What is unpleasing to thee do not to thy neighbour. This is the whole Law; all the rest is commentary. Go and learn *that*."[2]

3. "Now or never," said a man to his friend; "400 zouzim[3] to the man who can make Hillel angry." "Done!" exclaimed the other. It was a Friday afternoon, and Hillel was washing and combing his hair for the Sabbath. "Is Hillel there?" rudely and bluntly asked the man, as he knocked at the door. "My son,"

[1] *Joma*, 35 *b*.

[2] *Shabbath*, 31 *a*.—I have had repeated occasion to observe how idle is the question of "originality" in teaching of this kind; but we find the same thing long before, not only in the Pentateuch, but even in the Book of Tobit iv. 15: "Do that to no man which thou hatest." The probable date of the Book of Tobit is two centuries before Hillel. For yet earlier and even heathen parallels to the saying, see Ewald, *Gesch. Isr.* iv. 270. It is also found to all intents and purposes in Confucius (*Doctrine of the Mean*, xx., and *Analects*, xv. 23, where he tells Tsze Kung that the one word "reciprocity" [*i.e.*, altruism] will serve him as a rule of practice for all his life) and Buddha (see Barth. St. Hilaire, *Le Buddha et sa Religion*, p. 92); see, too, Hesiod, *Opp. et Dies*, i. 284, 312, 330.

[3] A coin apparently worth a denarius, with a head of Zeus on it.

he exclaimed, hastily putting on his mantle, "what dost thou want?"

"I have a question to ask."

"Ask on, my son."

"Why have the Babylonians such round heads?"

"An important question, my son," said Hillel, laughing; "it is because they have skilful midwives."

The man turned his back on him, went off, and returned in an hour. The same rude interruption was repeated, and this time the man asked—

"Why have the 'Thermudians'[1] [Palmyrenes] such narrow eye-slits?"

"An important question, my son. It is because they live in the middle of a sandy desert."

A third time the man returned as before, and impudently asked—

"Why have the Africans such broad soles to their feet?"

Hillel calmly replied that it was because they live on such loose soil.

"I should have had plenty more questions to ask you were I not afraid that you would get into a passion."

Hillel only drew his mantle more closely round him, and quietly replied—

"Ask on, whatever thou hast to ask."

"So," said the man, thoroughly disarmed, "you are the Hillel whom they call the *Nasî* of Israel?"

"Yes."

"Well, then, I hope there are not many like you."

"Why, my son?"

"Because through you I have lost 400 zouzim."

"Calm thyself, my son: better that thou shouldst lose for Hillel's sake 400, ay, and 400 more, than that Hillel should lose patience."[2]

No doubt these are beautiful anecdotes, as is also the story that once for a rich man who had lost his property he hired a horse and an attendant, and, when the latter was not forthcoming, went himself three miles as his attendant.[3] Sometimes, however, we see, even in the few records of him, facts and tendencies which, however well meant, cannot be praised. Thus, in opposition to Shammai, he

[1] This is a wrong reading for the people of *Tadmor* or Palmyra. (Buxtorf, *Lex.* s. v.; Ewald, *Jahrbüch*, x. 69.)

[2] *Shabbath*, 30, 31.

[3] Other striking anecdotes are mentioned by Ewald, *Gesch. Christ.* 31—33.

directed that in the bridal song the beauty of a bride should be praised, however ugly she were; and on one occasion, to avoid any question or dispute with the school of Shammai, he passed off an ox, which was going to be sacrificed for him, as a cow.[1] The Rabbis praise these proceedings, yet we feel instinctively what a shock they would have given us, how injurious they would have been to the world's morality, had they occurred in the life of Christ. He alone, of all who have ever lived in the world, could say, "Which of you convinceth me of sin?" Little as we know by comparison of a Socrates, of a Confucius, of a Sakya Mouni, of a Hillel, of a Mahomet, and *much* as we know of Jesus, yet in the scanty records of *their* lives we find much to disapprove; but there is nothing which is not divine and sinless in the fourfold record of the life of Christ.

II. Turning from Hillel's life to his teaching, we see how the notion of his being in any way a master of Christ crumbles into dust. Even his noblest answer, already recorded, is gravely defective. It may do for a summary of the *second* table of the Law, but, unlike the infinitely deeper wisdom of Jesus, it omits all reference to the first table, on which the second is alone founded, and with reference to which it is alone possible. Why did Hillel, in his famous answer, forget the Shema (Deut. vi. 4, 5), and remember only Lev. xix. 18? So did not Jesus (Matt. vii. 12; Luke vi. 31).

It is said, indeed, that Jesus sometimes applies one or other of the seven famous *middôth* (מִדּוֹת) laid down by Hillel for the interpretation of Scripture. But in point of fact these *middôth* are a mere summary of existing and perfectly obvious processes (Inference from major to minor or *vice versâ*, Matt. vii. 11, x. 29; analogy, connection, &c., Matt. xii. 5); and, in the next place, these were only contrivances to support the credit and authority of that Oral Law which Jesus utterly rejected and—it is hardly too much to say—despised. The instances in which the decisions of Christ coincide with those of Shammai are at least as numerous, and refer to subjects of greater importance (*e.g.* Matt. v. 32; xix. 9; xviii. 17); yet who has ever thought of saying that He was a disciple of Shammai?

For instance, one of Hillel's most celebrated and elaborate decisions was on a trumpery series of questions as to whether one might or might not eat an egg which a hen had laid on a feast-day, when the feast-day came in connection with a sabbath. This precious

[1] *Kethubôth*, 67 *b*, 16 *b*. Jost, *Gesch. d. Judenthums*, i. 267. Delitzsch, *Jes. und Hillel*, 35: "Er bewegte wedelnd den Schweif des Thieres, um dessen Geschlecht zu verbergen."

inquiry gives its name, *Bîtsa* (egg), to an entire Talmudical treatise. Is it possible to imagine that Jesus would have treated it otherwise than with the finest yet tenderest irony? Yet in his decision on this point Hillel was more strict and more Shammaitic than Shammai himself.[1]

In some points, too, Hillel's teaching was, to say the least, very dubious. He ruled, for instance—owing to a vague expression in Deut. xxiv. 1—that a man might put away his wife "even if she cooked his dinner badly" (*Gjt.* 90). It is true that Jost (*Gesch. d. Judenthums*, i. 264) and later writers interpret this to mean "bringing discredit on his home;" but the "even if" (אפילו) evidently points to a *minimum*. His manner, too, of evading the Mosaic rules about the sabbatical year (mentioned in Excursus IX.) can only be regarded as a disingenuous shuffle. Better specimens of Hillel's teaching are—

"Separate not thyself from the congregation, and have no confidence in thyself till the day of thy death."

"If I do not care for my soul, who will do it for me? If I care only for my own soul, what am I? If not now, when then?" (*Abhôth* i. 14.)

"Judge not thy neighbour till thou art in his situation."

"Say not, I will repent when I have leisure, lest that leisure should never be thine."

"The passionate man will never be a teacher."

"In the place where there is not a man be thou a man."

"Be of the disciples of Aaron, who loved peace."

"Whoever is ambitious of aggrandising his name will destroy it."[2]

Hillel was undoubtedly a great and good man, and he deserved the wail uttered over his grave—"Ah, the gentle, the holy, the scholar

[1] All ceremonialising and particularising religions are liable to be evaporated into idle cases of casuistry. Some few years ago the Mohammedans at the Cape were agitated by such a dispute. The Sultan had sent some one to look after their spiritual condition. This person found that they were in the habit of eating cray-fish of a particular species, which in an evil hour he pronounced to be unclean. Objecting to this decision, they said that there was nothing about crayfish in the Koran. However, he looked up a prohibition to eat spiders, and declared that for all ceremonial purposes a cray-fish *was* practically a spider. Referring the question to the curator of the Cape Museum, they were (naturally) informed that a crayfish was *not* a species of spider. The more scrupulous, however, objected to the decision, and as far as my informant knows, the dispute may be as lively as ever to this day.

[2] Some of these (*e.g.*, the last) are obscure in the original, and admit a widely different interpretation. (Ewald, *ubi sup.*) These and others are in the *Pirke Abhôth* (Etheridge, *Hebr. Lit.*, p. 36). But it must not be forgotten that even this treatise is not older than the second century after Christ.

of Ezra!"—but to compare his teaching with that of the Saviour is absurd. It was legal, casuistic, and narrow, while that of Jesus was religious, moral, and human. If Jesus uttered nothing original, as modern Jewish Rabbis are so fond of saying, how is it that, whereas the very name of Hillel is unknown except to scholars, the words of Jesus wrought the mightiest revolution that has ever been witnessed in the world? Had Humanity nothing better to live on than the words of Hillel, it would be dwarfed and starved indeed. The shortest and slightest of our Saviour's parables is worth all that he ever said.[1] Nay, even the least of the Old Testament prophets is transcendently greater than this "greatest and best of the Pharisees." He and his school, and Shammai and *his* school, spent a century of unprofitable and groundless jangling on the exegesis of two short words of the Law (*ervath dabhar*, Deut. xxiv. 1), without approaching a single sound principle, which would have rendered their quarrel needless: but Jesus furnished that principle, and solved the question for ever the moment that it was brought before Him (Matt. xix. 3—9). Let any candid reader consult the translation of the Talmudic treatise *Berachôth*, by M. Schwab, and see (pp. 264, 266, 314, 375, 404, &c.) the *kind* of miserably minute questions of infinitely little matters of formalism which occupied the mind and life of Hillel,[2] and calmly consider the mixture of scorn and pity with which Jesus would have treated the notion that there was in such questions any intrinsic importance. He will then be able to judge for himself of the folly and untenability of the statement that Hillel was the true master of Jesus!

[1] See further the admirable *brochure* of *Jesus und Hillel* by F. Delitzsch (Erlangen, 1867); Ewald, *Gesch. Christ.*, pp. 12—48; Budaeus, *Philos. Hebr.* 108, seqq.; Geiger, *De Hillel et Shammai;* Ugolini, xxi.; Grätz, *Gesch. d. Judenth.* iii. 172—179; Jost, *Gesch. d. Jud.* 254, seqq.; Herzfeld, *Gesch. d. Volkes Isr.* i. 257—261.

[2] *Ex. gr.*, Whether, when you are carrying perfumed oil and myrtles, you ought to bless first the myrtles and then the oil; whether you ought to take off your phylacteries or not in certain places of daily resort; whether you ought or ought not to be in a particular position at particular times of studying the Law; whether you ought first to wash your hands and then fill the glasses, or *vice versâ;* whether you ought to lay the napkin on the table or on the seat, &c. &c. The mere enumeration of one tithe of such points in serious dispute between the schools of Hillel and Shammai is wearisomely repulsive; yet it is of such deadening and frivolous matters—only very often unspeakably more nauseous—that the Talmud is full. One cannot blame Hillel for not being before his age; but to compare Rabbinism with Christianity, and Hillel with Christ, requires either a consummate effrontery, or a total paralysis of the critical faculty.

EXCURSUS IV. (Vol. I., p. 91.)

Greek Learning.

There is a story, several times repeated in the Talmud, that during the siege of Jerusalem in the civil war between Hyrcanus II. and Aristobulus, a box was daily let down the wall by the adherents of the latter, full of money, in return for which it was re-filled with the victims necessary for the daily sacrifice. But an "ancient" who knew "Greek wisdom" (*chôchmath Javanîth*) made the besiegers understand that the Temple would never be yielded so long as they supplied the means for continuing the daily sacrifice. Consequently, the next day, *a pig* was put in the box, which, when half-way up the wall, clung to the wall with its feet. An earthquake ensued. On this occasion the Doctors pronounced a curse on all who bred pigs, and on all who taught their children Greek wisdom. (*Sota* 19 *b*; *Menachôth* 64 *b*.)[1]

But, as Grätz (iii. 502) and Derenbourg (*Hist. Pal.* 114) point out, by "Greek wisdom" elsewhere is probably intended a sort of magic; and, in this instance, the art of secretly communicating with an enemy—as the traitorous ancient had done—by means of arrows with letters attached to them. The "ancient" is conjectured to have been Antipater.

It remains, however, true that, although the Rabbis on this, as on most other matters, contradict themselves, many of them wholly despised and discouraged Greek learning. Josephus, at the end of the *Antiquities*, distinctly tells us that they thought it slavish to be a good linguist, and, necessary as the Greek language was for commercial purposes, very few had attained it with accuracy.

Origen gives us the same testimony, saying that the Jews cared little either for the Greek language or literature.[2]

Rabbi Akiba says that no Israelite would be a partaker of eternal life who read the books of the Gentiles.[3] Gamaliel was the only eminent Rabbi who permitted his pupils to read them—a circumstance to which we may possibly owe the classical quotations of St. Paul from Aratus, Menander, and Epimenides (Acts xvii. 28; 1 Cor. xv. 33; Titus i. 12).

[1] See Gfrörer, *Jahrh. d. Heils*, i. 114, and *Philo und die Alex. Theo.* ii. 350.

[2] *C. Cels.* ii. 34.

[3] *Bab. Sanhedr.* 90 *a*.

EXCURSUS V. (Vol. I., page 267.)

The Talmud and the Oral Law.

The Jews believe that the Law falls under two divisions—the Written Law (*Torah shebeketeb*), and the Oral, or that "upon the lip" (*Torah shebeal pî*), of which the latter, or "tradition," is equally authoritative with the former, or even more so.

The Talmud proper consists of the Mishna and the Gemara.

The Oral Law remained absolutely unwritten *at least* down to the time of the later Tanaîm (about A.D. 30—80), who, indeed, thought it wrong to commit it to writing. The older *Megillath Taanîth*—a collection of *Hagadôth* ("legends or narrations") and *Halachôth* ("rules") on times and solemnities—is supposed to have been drawn up by Hanania Ben Hiskia in the time of our Lord. But the first who reduced the Mishna to writing was the famous Rabbi Jehuda Hakkôdesh, who died A.D. 190. His reason for doing so was the apparent danger of national extinction after the fearful massacre which ensued on the defeat of Bar-Cochebas and the capture of Bethyr; but although the reduction of the Oral Law to writing was discouraged, secret rolls (*megillôth setharîm*) of it are said to have existed before. In point of fact, laws are often, by a sort of fiction, supposed to be "unwritten" for centuries after they may be read in print.

The word Mishna means "repetition," and is usually rendered in Greek by δευτέρωσις. Maimonides divides the Oral Law into five classes—viz., (i.) *Perushîm*, explanations believed to date from Moses. (ii.) *Dinerîm*, or "constitutions," which are "modes of conduct" (*halachôth*) believed to have been delivered by Moses. (iii.) Generally received customs. (iv.) Decisions of the wise men, regarded as a "hedge about the Law" (סיג לתורה). (v.) Experimental suggestions.

Jehuda divided his immense materials into six *sedarîm*, or "orders," containing sixty-three *massiktôth*, or "tracts," and 525 *perakîm*, or "chapters"—viz.:

1. *Seder Zeraîm*, or "Seeds," containing the *Berachôth*, on worship; *Peah* ("corner"), on the rights of the soil; *Terumôth*, "oblations," &c.

2. *Seder Moed*, "Festival;" containing *Shabbath*, *Erubhîn*, or "mixtures" (*v. infr.*, Exc. IX.); *Pesachîm*, "the Passover;" *Yoma*, "Day ot Atonement;" *Sukka*, "Feast of Tabernacles;" *Bîtsa*, "an egg;" *Rosh Hashshanah*, "the new year;" *Taanîth*, "fasts;" *Chagiga*, "thank-offering," &c.

3. *Seder Nashîm*, on women; containing *Gittîn*, "divorce;" *Kethubhôth*, "wedding contracts," &c.

4. *Seder Nezikin*, on "Injuries;" containing *Babha Kama*, "the first;" *Metzia*, "the middle," and *Bathra*, "the last gate;" *Sanhedrin; Abhôda Zara*, "strange services;" *Abhôth*, "the Fathers," &c.

5. *Seder Kadashîm*, on "Consecrations."

6. *Seder Taharôth*, "Purifications," containing *Yadaîm*, or the purification of the hands, &c.[1]

The commentary on the Mishna, which is boundlessly voluminous, is called the *Gemara*, "complement," and the Mishna and Gemara together form the Talmud, or "that which should be learnt." The Jerusalem Talmud dates from about A.D. 390, and the Babylonian from about A.D. 420.

Appendices to the Mishna are called *Toseftôth;* exegetical additions to the Gemara are called *Tosafôth*. Supplements to the Mishna, consisting of commentaries (*e.g.*, *Sifra*, a Midrash or "comment" on Leviticus, *Sifri* on Numbers and Deuteronomy, and *Mechiltha* on Exodus), are called *Baraithas*.

The language of the Talmud is uncouth, corrupt, and often unintelligible. It contains some beautiful and noble things, but far fewer than any other such enormous mass of human writings; and nothing can be conceived more tedious and unprofitable than its "desultory and confused wrangle," teeming with contradictions and mistakes. A sufficient number of Talmudic treatises have been translated to enable any reader to judge of this for himself. Lightfoot, than whom no scholar had a better right to speak, says that "the almost unconquerable difficulty of the style, the frightful roughness of the language, and the amazing emptiness and sophistry of the matters handled, do torture, vex, and tire him that reads them."

For a continuation of this subject see Excursus XII., "Notes on the Talmud."

[1] The principal edition and translation of the Mishna is that by Surenhusius, Amsterd. 1668—1703. It has been translated into German by Rabe (1763), and Jost (1833); and eighteen treatises have been translated into English by Rabbis De Sola and Raphall (second edition, London, 1845); Gfrörer, *Jahr. d. Heils*, i. 10. I have abridged the above account from Etheridge's *Hebr. Literat.*, pp. 117 seqq. See, too, Dr. Davidson *s. v.* "Talmud" in Kitto's *Bibl. Cycl*

EXCURSUS VI. (Vol. I., pp. 150, 312.)

TRADITIONAL DESCRIPTION OF THE APPEARANCE OF OUR LORD.

THE earliest actual descriptions of Jesus are very late, yet it is possible that they may have caught some faint accent of tradition handed down from the days of Irenæus, Papias, and St. John. Nicephorus, quoting from a description given by John of Damascus, in the eighth century, says that He resembled the Virgin Mary; that He was beautiful and strikingly tall, with fair and slightly curling locks, on which no hand but His mother's had ever passed, with dark eyebrows, an oval countenance, a pale and olive complexion, bright eyes, an attitude slightly stooping, and a look expressive of patience, nobility, and wisdom.[1] The famous letter which professes to have been addressed by "Lentulus, president of the people of Jerusalem, to the Roman Senate,"[2] though not older than the twelfth century, is yet so interesting for the history of Christian art, and so clearly derived from long-current traditions, that we may here quote it entire.

"There has appeared in our times," it says, "a man of great virtue, named Christ Jesus. . . . . He is a man of lofty stature, beautiful, having a noble countenance, so that they who look on Him may both love and fear. He has wavy hair, rather crisp, of the colour of wine, and glittering as it flows down from His shoulders, with a parting in the middle of the head after the manner of the Nazarenes.[3] His forehead is pure and even, and His face without any spot or wrinkle, but glowing with a delicate flush. His nose and mouth are of faultless beauty; He has a beard abundant and of the same hazel-colour as His hair, not long, but forked. His eyes are blue and very bright.[4] He is terrible in rebuke, calm and loving in

[1] See Winer, *Realw.*, s. v. "Jesus;" Nicephorus, *Hist. Eccl.* i. 40. This description, with that of the pseudo-Lentulus and John of Damascus, were edited by J. G. Carpzov, of Helmstadt, in 1777. The fullest treatment of the subject is in Dr. Lewis Glückselig, *Studien über Jes. Christ und sein wahres Ebenbild.* Prag., 1863. (See *Quart. Rev.* 1867.) The *earliest* pictures of Christ, in the Catacombs, are purely symbolic (the Lamb, the Fish, Orpheus, &c.).

[2] No such office existed, nor did any one of that name fill any analogous position.

[3] He evidently meant Nazarites.

[4] More than one of these touches recalls the description of the youthful David (1 Sam. xvi. 12). "He was ruddy, and withal of a beautiful countenance (Heb. 'fair of eyes'), and goodly to look to." Cf. xvii. 42, and Cant. v. 10, "My

admonition, cheerful but preserving gravity. He has never been seen to laugh, but oftentimes to weep. His stature is erect, and His hands and limbs are beautiful to look upon. In speech He is grave, reserved, and modest; and He is fair among the children of men."[1]

EXCURSUS VII. (Vol. I., p. 341).

Jewish Angelology and Demonology.

It is the characteristic of the Oriental, and especially of the Semitic mind, to see in every event, even the most trivial, a direct supernatural interference, wrought by the innumerable unseen ministers—both good and evil—of the Divine Will. The definite form in which the belief clothed itself was, by the admission of the Jews themselves, derived from Babylon.[2]

Even the most ordinary forces and phenomena of Nature, and passions of the mind, were by them regarded as angels. Thus, in the Jer. Targum on Deut. ix. 19, it is said that, to punish the Israelites for worshipping the golden calf, God sent five angels—Indignation, Anger, Fury, Ruin, Wrath. And they would have interpreted quite literally the verse—"He maketh the winds his angels, and fiery flames his ministers" (Ps. civ. 4).

beloved is white and ruddy, and chiefest (Heb. 'a standard-bearer') among ten thousand. . . . . His locks are bushy (Heb. 'curled'), and black as a raven. His eyes are as the eyes of doves," &c.

[1] B. H. Cowper, *The Apocr. Gospels*, p. 221; Hofmann, pp. 291—294; Hase, p. 80.—Pictures and statues of Christ are said to have originated on the gems, &c., of the Gnostics—*e.g.*, Basilidians, Carpocratians, &c.; but symbolic representations were common in the Catacombs (Iren. *c. Haer.* i. 24; Hippol., *Philosoph.* vii. 32). A statue of Christ is said to have found its way into the private *lararium* of the Emperor Alexander Severus (Lamprid., *Vit. Alex. Sever.* c. 29). The one which has acquired most fame is the supposed representation at Cæsarea Philippi (Paneas) of the healing of the woman with the issue of blood, as related in the apocryphal story of Veronica (Cowper, p. 233; Hofmann, 293 354, 357), which Eusebius saw, but despised (*Hist. Ecc.* vii. 18), and which Julian is said to have destroyed (Sozomen, *H. E.* v. 20; Philostorg., *H. E.* vii. 3). I need merely allude to the miraculous impression on the napkin of Veronica the shroud given by Nicodemus, &c.

[2] *Rosh Hashshanah*, 56; Gfrörer, *Jahrh. d. Heils*, i. 124.—The facts in this Excursus are derived mainly from Gfrörer and Frankl, *Jews in the East*. Göthe's demonology in *Faust* is mainly Talmudic, and is borrowed from Eisenmenger.

The number of the angels—the *Tsebha hashamaîm*—was immense. R. Eliezer said that at Sinai 600,000 descended, according to the number of the 600,000 Israelites;[1] and in *Bab. Berachôth* (32 *b*) we find the following story:—"According to R. Rish Lakish, Isa. xlix. 14 is to be understood as follows. The Church of Israel complains to God: Lord of the World, even when a man takes a second wife he thinks of the first; but thou hast utterly forgotten me.' But God answered, 'Daughter, I have 12 *mazalôth* (signs of the zodiac), and to each *massal* 30 *chêl* (commanders), and to each *chêl* 30 legions (generals), and to each legion 30 *rabatôn* (officers), and to each *rabatôn* 30 *kartôn* (captains), and to each *kartôn* 30 *kistra* (camps), and to each *kistron* I have assigned 3,650,000,000 stars. All these have I created for thy sake, and yet thou sayest I have forgotten thee.'"

This, it will be seen, makes the number of the *Tsebaoth* (or Hosts of Heaven) 12 × 30 × 30 × 30 × 30 × 30 × 3,650,000, which makes 1,064,340,000,000,000, *i.e.*, on the old English plan of notation, one trillion, sixty-four billion, three hundred and forty thousand million; or according to the newer English plan and the French plan (recommended, says M. Littré, by Locke), one *quintillion*, &c. The factors are evidently a muddle of days, months, &c., the same factors being occasionally repeated to make sure of not being under the mark! The military terms (*castra*, &c.) have an interesting bearing on the Λεγεὼν of Mark v. 9; for the devils were supposed to be under similar military organisation. Wier, *De Praestigiis Daemonum* calculates that there are 7,405,926 devils.

These angels were all divided into ranks and classes,

"Thrones, dominations, virtues, princedoms, powers,

to which there seems to be an allusion in Eph. i. 21.

The evil spirits—offspring, according to various Rabbinic legends, of Adam and Lilith, or of Sammael and Eve, or of "the sons of God and daughters of men"—were equally numerous. To them were attributed many results which we should undoubtedly assign to purely natural causes, especially the phenomena of epilepsy, as is very clearly described in the Book of Enoch (xv. 8).

Their home was supposed to be the region of the middle air (John xii. 31; xiv. 30; 2 Cor. iv. 4; and especially Eph. ii. 2; vi. 12), and they were regarded as lords of the existing state of things. An exaggeration of this view led to certain Ebionite heresies, and even

[1] *Pirke Eliezer*, 41.

in the Book *Zohar* Satan is called "the second God" (*El achêr;* cf. 2 Cor. iv. 4). R. Joshua Ben Levi says that he has seven names—Lust, Impurity, the Hater, &c., and "the Man of Midnight" (Joel ii. 20, *Heb.*).

In *Bab. Berachôth* (6 *a*) we are told that if we could but see the devils no one could stand the shock. Every man has 10,000 at his right hand, and 1,000 at his left. They are remarkably powerful at night; hence no one should greet a person by night, for fear of saluting a devil (*Sanhedr.* 44 *a*). They live chiefly in ruins, and deserts and sepulchres, and under trees (especially the service-tree), and foul places.

Headache was caused by a demon named *Kardaikoos.* On the sabbath-night all hide themselves except one Asiman, who causes the birth of epileptic children.

The belief in these *Schedîm*, or evil spirits, has continued unabated to this day. "There are houses in Jerusalem in which men and women cannot dwell together; the *Schedîm* will not allow it; and thus they are occupied by women alone." The celebrated cabalist, Jehuda Bivas of Corfu, explained that they have no power in the West. The *chalebi,* the old traditional head-dress of the Jewish women, seems to have been invented for the express purpose of keeping off the *Schedîm*, who sit on the hair of women whose heads are uncovered (see 1 Cor. xi. 10). "Its ugliness is only equalled by the difficulty of describing it:" it seems to be a sort of chignon, except that it is made entirely of linen, and conceals the hair of all who wear it.[1]

EXCURSUS VIII. (Vol. I. p. 368.)

The Unnamed Feast of John v. 1, and the Length of the Ministry.

"After this" (the healing of the nobleman's son), says St. John, "there was a feast of the Jews, and Jesus went up to Jerusalem."

What this feast was, is in all probability a question which, though interesting and important in settling the length of our Lord's ministry, will never receive a final answer. Whole volumes have been written on it, and to enter upon all the discussions which they open would be idle, and endless, and, after all, unconvincing. In spite

[1] See Frankl, *Jews in the East*, E. Tr., ii. 160, seqq.; i. 227, &c.

of the patient thought and consummate learning which have been devoted to the consideration, the data are clearly insufficient to decide convincingly how long Christ publicly taught on earth, nor shall we ever be able to attain any *certainty* on that deeply interesting question. The few remarks which I shall make on the subject shall be as brief and clear as possible.

1. St. John groups his entire narrative round the Jewish festivals,[1] and mentions—

i. "The Passover of the Jews" (ii. 13), τὸ πάσχα τῶν Ἰουδαίων.

ii. "A" or "the" Feast of the Jews (v. 1), ἑορτὴ or ἡ ἑορτὴ τῶν Ἰουδαίων.[2]

iii. The Passover, the Feast of the Jews (vi. 4), τὸ πάσχα ἡ ἑορτὴ τῶν Ἰουδαίων.

iv. "The Tabernacles, the Feast of the Jews" (vii. 2), ἡ ἑορτὴ τῶν Ἰουδαίων ἡ σκηνοπηγία.

v. "The Dedication" (x. 22), τὰ ἐγκαίνια.

vi. "The Passover of the Jews" (xi. 55), τὸ πάσχα τῶν Ἰουδαίων.

2. The feasts of the Jews occurred in the following order, and if we take a particular year, we can (though this cannot be regarded as *certain* or beyond dispute) fix the very day of the month and week on which they occurred. *Ex. gr.*, taking the year 28 A.D., we have—

NISAN	1.	Tues.	MARCH	16.	Jewish New Year's Day.
,,	14.	Mon.	,,	29.	Passover; the days of unleavened bread lasting seven days.
SIVAN	6.	Wed.	MAY	19.	Pentecost.
TISRI	10.	Sat.	SEPT.	18.	Day of Atonement.
,,	15—21.		,,	23—29.	Tabernacles.
KISLEU	25.	Wed.	DEC.	1.	Dedication.
VEADAR	14.	Sat.	MARCH	19.	Purim.[3]

This last feast would thus be nearly a month before the Passover of the *ensuing* year, A.D. 29, in which year the Passover fell on *April 17th.*

3. Now the feast here mentioned could hardly be the Passover or the Feast of Tabernacles, because, as we have seen, St. John, when

[1] See Browne, *Ordo Saeclorum*, p. 91.

[2] The reading is profoundly uncertain. The Alexandrine and Vatican Manuscripts and the Codex Bezae have not the article; on the other hand, the Codex Ephraemi and the Sinaiticus have it. Yet it is much more likely to have been *inserted* than to have been *omitted*, and if we could be sure that it did not exist in the original text, this would seem to be nearly decisive against its being the Passover or Feast of Tabernacles.

[3] Wieseler, *Chron. Sun.* E. Tr. p. 434.

he mentions those feasts, mentions them by name; in fact, both those feasts had Greek names (πάσχα and σκηνοπηγία) familiarly known to Greek readers; and there seems to be no reason whatever why the name of either should be omitted here. It is impossible to suppose that the omission of the name is purely arbitrary or accidental. But there are still weightier reasons against the supposition that it was either of these two great feasts. For (α) if this were the Passover, St. John would omit a *whole year* of our Lord's ministry (vi. 4) without a word; and it cannot have been (β) the Feast of Tabernacles immediately succeeding the first Passover mentioned by St. John, because six months is too short a period for all the events which had intervened since the journey through Samaria (John ii. 13); nor (γ) can it have been the Feast of Tabernacles in the subsequent year, for then a year and a half would have elapsed without a single visit to Jerusalem. In short, if we assume, as we have done, that after His first Passover our Lord spent some time in Judea, and then, possibly *four months before harvest* (John iv. 35), passed through Samaria on His journey to Galilee; and if again we infer, as we seem entitled to do, that the Passover mentioned in John vi. 4 is the *second* which He attended, we must then look for this unnamed feast some time between the close of winter and the harvest—*i.e.*, between Kisleu or December and Nisan 16, on which day the first wheat-sheaf was offered, and harvest legally began.

If these reasons are not absolutely conclusive, they are at least very weighty, and if admitted they at once exclude the *greater* Jewish festivals.

4. Looking, therefore, at minor feasts, there is only one for which we can see a *reason* why the name should have been omitted—viz., the Feast of Purim. The mere fact of its being a minor feast would not alone be a sufficient reason for excluding the name, since, as we have seen, St. John mentions by name the comparatively unimportant and humanly appointed Feast of the Dedication. But the name of this feast was represented by a familiar Greek word (*Encaenia*), and explained itself; whereas the Feast of Purim was intensely Jewish, and the introduction of the name without an explanation would have been unintelligible. Purim means "lots," and if St. John had merely translated the name into Greek, it might have led to very mistaken impressions. The only Greek equivalents for it were Φρουραὶ or ἡ Μορδοχαϊκὴ ἡμέρα, neither of which was generally known or understood in the Gentile world.[1] Moreover, the fact that it was the

[1] Purim is corrupted from the Persian word *bahre*, "lots" (cf. *pars*), which

most unimportant, non-religious, and questionably-observed of the Jewish feasts, would be an additional reason for leaving the name unnoticed.

Mr. Browne, in his very learned and elaborate, but unconvincing *Ordo Saeclorum*, uses a powerful series of arguments to show that our Lord's ministry only lasted for a single year and a few weeks (pp. 342—391). He relies much on various astronomical arguments, which depend on dubious data, and on traditions which are not only conflicting, but can be easily accounted for.

Origen (*De Principiis*, iv. 5) says ἐνιαυτὸν καί που καὶ ὀλίγους μῆνας ἐδίδαξεν, and argues for our Lord's Divinity from the fact that His brief year of teaching was found adequate—so "full of grace were His lips"—to renovate the world.[1] Such seems to have been the most ancient opinion, and yet, as Mr. Browne candidly points out, Melito, Irenæus, and others take a very different view; and Irenaeus speaks of it as a certain fact, derived by tradition from St. John, that our Lord, at the time of His death, was between forty and fifty years old (*c. Haeres.* ii. 22, 5).

The tradition as to the duration of the ministry for a single year is sufficiently accounted for by Luke iv. 19, to which expression indeed St. Clement of Alexandria directly appeals in confirmation of this view (καὶ ὅτι ἐνιαυτὸν μόνον ἔδει αὐτὸν κηρῦξαι καὶ τοῦτο γέγραπται οὕτως, ἐνιαυτὸν δεκτὸν κυρίου κηρῦξαι ἀπέστειλέν με, *Strom.* i. xxi. § 145). The tradition as to our Lord's age is derived from the surprised remark of the Jews in John viii. 57.[2] We have already seen that neither of these passages support the inferences which have been drawn from them. This was early observed, and even Hippolytus, the scholar of Irenæus, says that our Lord died at the age of thirty-three;[3] and Eusebius (*H. E.* i. 10), Theodoret (*in Dan.* ix. 27), Jerome (*id.*), and others agree with him.

Mr. Browne proceeds ingeniously to show that if a year's ministry be supposed, and *if* τὸ πάσχα *be eliminated from* John vi. 4, St. John

the LXX. and Josephus corrupted into φρουραὶ and φρουραῖοι. Ewald long ago pointed out (*Morgenland. Zeitschr.* iii. 415) that it was regarded as "*a preliminary celebration of the Passover.*"

[1] Even Origen does not seem to be quite consistent with himself. See *c. Cels.* ii., p. 397, and *in Matt.* xxiv. 15. (Gieseler, *Ch. Hist.* i. 55, E. Tr.)

[2] The reading τεσσάρακοντα adopted by Chrysostom, Euthymius, &c., is probably a mere correction, and has no good MS. authority. The Jews only mentioned fifty as a round number, expressing complete manhood.

[3] *In Dan.* iv. Wordsw. *ad loc.*

may then be supposed to give the feasts of a year in regular chronological order, viz. :—

1. The Passover (ii. 13) . March.
2. The Pentecost (v. 1) . . . . . May.
3. The Feast of Tabernacles (vi. 4; vii. 2) . September.
4. The Dedication (x. 22) . . . . . December.
5. The Passover of the Crucifixion . . March.

But it is surely and finally fatal against this view that, whatever may be the case in the quotations or allusions of some of the Fathers, there is not *the very faintest MS. authority* for the omission of τὸ πάσχα in John vi. 4.[1] Such being the case, St. John certainly and definitely mentions *three* passovers. If, as on other grounds we have seen to be probable, there was one passover in our Lord's ministry which He did *not* attend, the length of ministry was, as most inquirers have now agreed to believe, three years and some weeks, or possibly months. This would account for the remarkable specification of "three years," and a reprieve for another year, as the time during which the unfruitful tree is spared in Luke xiii. 7, 8.

EXCURSUS IX. (Vol. I., p. 441.)

Hypocrisy of the Pharisees.

The very *raison d'être* of the Pharisees was to create "hedges" of oral tradition around the Law. Epiphanius, inventing a very forcible word to describe their character, says that they derived their name from their ἐθελοπερισσοθρησκεία,[2] voluntary, excessive, external service; and yet, in spite of these extravagant professions, they were perfectly ready to make devices to evade the law when it interfered with their own conveniences and plans.[3] Perhaps the most flagrant instance of

[1] Mr. Browne simply relies on the conjecture that it is an interpolation unknown to Irenæus, Origen, Clement, Tertullian, &c.

[2] *Haeres.* xvi. 34.

[3] "Une tendance importante des Pharisiens, *celle de transiger avec les* obligations de la Loi dans l'intérêt des nouveaux besoins" (Derenbourg, *Hist. Pal.* 144). "To make a hedge round the Law" was one of the lessons of Simon the Just (*Pirk. Abhôth*, i. 1; Jost, i. 95). For some further remarks see *infr.*, Excursus XIV.

this is the manner in which they managed to absolve themselves from the self-imposed obligation of not exceeding the 2,000 yards at which they fixed a Sabbath day's journey.[1]

It was the custom of the Pharisees to join in *syssitia,* or common daily banquets, which they subjected to the most stringent conditions, and which they assimilated in all respects to priestly meals. But as their houses were often more than 2,000 yards from the place of meeting, and as the bearing of burdens on the Sabbath was strictly forbidden (Neh. xiii. 15; Jer. xvii. 21; Exod. xvi. 29), they would, without a little ingenuity, have been prevented from dining in common on the very day on which they most desired it. A little management quite relieved them from their difficulty.

On the evening before the Sabbath, they deposited some food at a distance of 2,000 yards from their own house, thus creating a fictitious home: from this fictitious home they could then go 2,000 yards farther to the place of meeting, thus giving themselves double the real distance! This piece of transparent hypocrisy was euphemistically described as an ideal amalgamation of distances, or "connection of places," and was called *erûbh* ("mixture," ערוב), a name under which it exists to the present day.[2] In order to get over the second difficulty, a still more miserable subterfuge was adopted, by putting door-posts and lintels at the end of various streets, so that all the space between them might be regarded as one large house![3]

Could any words of burning denunciation be too strong to denounce such a playing at "fast and loose" with obligations which they professed to regard as infinitely and divinely sacred, and the violation of which they were ready to avenge by inflicting death on the transgressor? They must have thought that both their Deity and their conscience were easily cheated![4]

[1] This was founded on elaborate arguments drawn from Exod. xxi. 13; xvi. 29. In the latter passage, "beyond 2,000 cubits" is actually inserted by the Jer. Targum. See the excellent and thoroughly well-informed articles of Dr. Ginsburg on "Sabbath Day's Journey" and "Pharisees" in Kitto's *Bible Cyclopedia.*

[2] Among the Jews of Palestine (especially at Safed) there are many of these contemptible trickeries.

[3] These *Erubhîn,* or "combinations"—*i.e.,* the relations of places and limits, as affecting the observation of the Sabbath—fill ten chapters of the *Seder Moed.* The invention of these is attributed to Solomon. (*Shabb.* 14, 2; Reland, *Antt. Hebr.* 524.)

[4] Similarly it is found in Hindostan that *caste* is protected with the most minute and scrupulous fidelity, *except where it clashes with ordinary interests*—as, *e.g.,* in railway travelling.

The Sadducees got over the difficulty, too, in a manner more daring, but infinitely less despicable, by calmly asserting that their meals were a continuation of the Temple service, and therefore claiming the benefit of the maxim, that there was "no sabbatism in the Temple."

These instances might be indefinitely multiplied: *e.g.*, if a Jew's ox is dying, he may kill it on a *holy day*, provided he eats a piece of the meat as big as an olive, to make believe that it was killed for a necessary meal. If a Jew wants to buy anything which is sold by weight or measure on a holy day, he may do so, provided that he *pays* the next day, and *does not* mention the name, weight, or measure. If a Jew wants to buy cattle, fowls, &c., on a holy day, he may do so, only he must not mention money or the *number* required. He may buy from a butcher on a holy day, only he must not say, "Give me meat for so much money," but only "*Give me a portion, or half a portion,*" and he pays for it next day.[1] Can any stretch of charity, however tender, avoid calling this the legality of evasion designed to cheat God with the letter instead of the spirit. Is the word "hypocrites" too strong for those who thus reduced shiftiness to a sacred system?

Another instance of the same kind was the way in which they treated the sabbatical year. "Before and in the time of Christ they did away with the law of remitting debts, by regarding it as a meritorious act on the part of the debtor not to avail himself of the Mosaic enactment, but to pay his debts irrespective of the sabbatical year. But not glaringly to counteract the law, these doctors enacted that the creditor should say, 'In accordance with the sabbatical year I remit thee the debt:' whereunto the debtor had to reply, 'I nevertheless wish to pay it,' and then the creditor accepted the payment."[2] A very ingenious farce indeed! but intolerable in men who professed an intense zeal and illimitable devotion for "every sentence word—what say I?—every letter"—of the Mosaic legislation. Perhaps it may be said that these are simply legal fictions necessitated by a false position: but a far more shameful proof of organised hypocrisy is furnished in the advice given by Rabbi Ila to those who suffered from sensual temptations. It occurs in two separate passages

[1] See the original passages quoted in Dr. McCaul's *Old Paths*, pp. 108 ff.

[2] C. D. Ginsburg, "Sabbatic Year" in Kitto, iii. 722.—For the most favourable view that can be given of these legal fictions, see R. Astruc, *Studies on the Pentateuch;* and Judah Ben Halévy, *The Khosari*, iii. §§ 46, 47, quoted by Cohen, *Les Déicides*, xi. 3.

of the Talmud.[1] I cannot quote the passages, but the purport of them amounts to this, that the sin of fornication is permissible if it be effectually concealed. Another Rabbinic rule about divorce is just as thin a disguise, just as cynical a concession. "A man must not marry a woman *with the intention* of divorcing her; but if he previously inform her that he is going to marry her for a season, it is lawful.[2]

Again, in spite of their boundless professions of reverence for Scripture, many of their schemes of interpretation—*gematria, notarikon*, &c.—were used to get rid of facts and meanings which they disliked. Instances of this in the LXX. are very numerous, and they occur frequently in the Targums. For instance: disgusted with the notion that Moses should have married an Æthiopian woman (Numb. xii. 1), Jonathan renders *Koosith* (Cushite) by "of fair face," because the letters of *Koosith* = 736 and the words *Japhath mareh* give the same sum! This was to expand the interpretation of Scripture into the number of positive integral solutions of an indeterminate equation!

Shammai, the narrow-minded rival of Hillel, was so scrupulous, that he nearly starved his little son on the Day of Atonement, and made a sort of booth of his daughter-in-law's bed that his little grandson (just born!) might keep the Feast of Tabernacles (*Succah*, ii. 9). Yet we are told that he was a luxurious and selfish man. It is easier to tithe mint than to live a holy life. Those who venture to say that Jesus was too bitter and severe against the Pharisees, must remember the saying attributed to King Alexander Jannæus, that "a real Pharisee was one who wished to play the part of Cozbi, and to receive the reward of Phinehas."

EXCURSUS X. (Vol. II., p. 277.)

Was the Last Supper an Actual Passover?

It is certain, and is all but universally acknowledged, being expressly stated by *all* the Evangelists, that our Lord was crucified on Friday,[3]

[1] *Bab. Kiddushim*, 40 *a*; *Chagiga*, 16 *a*. See the forcible remarks of Gfrörer. "Heuchelei ist ein *Laster* zu dem die Menschen von Natur sehr geneigt sind, wird sie vollends durch geheiligte Autoritäten gebilligt, wie hier, so muss sie alle stande ergreifen." (*Jahrh. des Heils*, i. 167.)

[2] McCaul, *Old Paths*, p. 376.

[3] Matt. xxvii. 62; Mark xv. 42; Luke xxiii. 54; John xix. 31. See, however, Westcott's *Introduction*, p. 323.

and rose on Sunday, lying during the hours of the Jewish Sabbath in the tomb of Joseph of Arimathea. It is therefore certain that He ate His Last Supper, and instituted the sacrament of the Eucharist, on the evening of Thursday; but was this Last Supper the actual Paschal Feast, or an anticipation of it? was it eaten on Nisan 13, or Nisan 14—*i.e.*, in the year of the Crucifixion did the first day of the Passover begin on the evening of a Thursday or on the evening of a Friday?

The question would, of course, be settled—(1) If we knew with *certainty* the date of our Lord's crucifixion, and (2) could rely on the Jewish calendars with sufficient conviction to be sure on what day of the week in that year the Passover fell. But as neither of these data can be depended on, we must turn for the solution of the question to the Evangelists alone. Let us observe, in passing, that, as all the Evangelists are agreed as to the main order of the events, the question as to whether the Last Supper was or was not the Paschal Feast, though a question of deep interest for us, is not one which directly affects the object of the Evangelists in writing the life of Christ.

Now it must be admitted that the Synoptists are unanimous in the use of expressions which admit of no natural explanation except on the supposition that the Passover *did* begin on the evening of Thursday, and therefore that Thursday was Nisan 14, and that the Last Supper was in reality the ordinary Paschal Feast.

This appears from the following passages:—Matt. xxvi. 2—"Ye know that after two days is the *Passover;*" *id.* 17—"Now the first day of unleavened bread the disciples came to Jesus, saying unto Him, Where wilt thou that we prepare for thee *to eat the Passover?*" 18—"I *will keep the Passover* at thy house;" 19—"They made ready *the Passover*" [cf. Mark xiv. 14—16; Luke xxii. 11—13].

St. Luke is even more explicit, for he says (xxii. 7)—"Then came *the day of unleavened bread, when the Passover must be killed;*" *id.* 15—"With desire have I desired *to eat this Passover*[1] with you before I suffer."

[1] The Greek is τοῦτο τὸ πάσχα, and therefore cannot *of itself* be meant to imply "this meal as a sort of Passover," although such a meaning may have been, and probably was, involved in the actually Aramaic words spoken by Jesus. Prof. Westcott argues that though language like this, taken alone, would clearly point to the Paschal meal, yet this natural meaning of the words could not be intended by the Evangelists, since their clear identification of the day of crucifixion, as Nisan 14, excludes such a signification (*Introduction*, p. 321). We admit at once that our difficulties may arise from imperfect knowledge of ritual and other

And every other allusion to the day made by the Evangelists is equally plain; so that if they be correct in their statements, we must suppose that Peter and John procured from the Temple the Paschal Lamb between three and five in the afternoon, which was the *Jewish* (though not the *Samaritan*) interpretation of the expression "between the two evenings"—the time specified by the Law for the slaying of the lamb.

But now when we turn to the Gospel of St. John it seems equally indisputable on his authority that the Last Supper was *not* the Paschal Feast, and that the Passover really began on the Friday evening, and consequently that Thursday was the 13th, not the 14th, of Nisan.

For, passing over the disputed expression, "Before the Feast of the Passover," in John xiii. 1 (which is *capable*, though not naturally or probably, of another explanation),[1] we find that some of the disciples imagine that Jesus had sent out Judas to "buy those things that we have need of against the feast;"[2] and that the priests and Pharisees "went not into the judgment-hall lest they should be defiled;[3] but that they might eat the Passover." St. John also says in so many words that the Friday of the crucifixion was "the preparation of the Passover;"[4] and that the following Sabbath was "a high day"[5]—evidently because it was at once a Sabbath and the first day of the Paschal Feast.

customs which would be perfectly familiar to the Jews; but it still seems impossible to believe that the Synoptists used these expressions *knowing* that the meal eaten was not the Passover, when a word of explanation, or the slightest variation of language, would have removed all possibility of mistake.

[1] Some refer the words to ἀγαπήσας or εἰδώς; but, as Mr. Sanday remarks, we usually date *facts*, not feelings (*Fourth Gospel*, p. 202).

[2] If the Passover had actually been eaten at that time, the expression would be quite inappropriate; and it is further probable that during the feast all ordinary business was suspended.

[3] Joseph of Arimathea did indeed "go to Pilate" on this day before the evening (Mark xv. 43); but it cannot be inferred from this that he had eaten his Passover. It may be that he did not actually enter Pilate's house, or his notions of what constituted ceremonial defilement may have been less scrupulous than those of the Pharisees: for that *some* Jews must even have gone into the judgment-hall without noticing the "defilement" is clear.

[4] παρασκευή may indeed merely mean Friday, but it is perfectly incredible that St. John should have spoken of the day of the crucifixion as παρασκευὴ τοῦ πάσχα in the sense of "Friday in Paschal week," if Friday had been actually "the first day of unleavened bread."

[5] In John xix. 31, μεγάλη ἡμέρα seems to represent *yom tôbh*, *i.e.*, the first or last day of an octave feast; the *intermediate* days were called *moed katôn* (Sepp).

How is this apparent contradiction to be reconciled? It must, I think, be frankly confessed, that many of the solutions offered are eminently unsatisfactory, depending upon the assumption of Jewish customs and Jewish forms of speech which not only have no authority in their favour, but which even contravene such authority as we have. To go through and to sift them all would require a volume. Here I can only allude to some of the more important solutions, and then give the explanation which, after repeated and careful consideration of the question, appears to me the only satisfactory one.

1. That the day for keeping the Passover was fixed by astronomical considerations in which the possibility of error led to the observation of different days.

2. That "between the two evenings" *must* be interpreted to mean between the evening of the 13th and that of the 14th of Nisan, or between the evenings of the 14th and 15th, and therefore that the Passover might be eaten on either of those days.

3. That Jesus ate the Passover at the proper legal time, but the Jews, or some of them, in their zeal and hatred against Him, put off *their* Passover till the next evening.[1]

4. That "to eat the Passover" is an expression not confined to eating the Paschal lamb, but might be used also of eating the *chagiga*, and generally of keeping the entire feast, and that *this* explains the expressions used by St. John.[2]

5. That the supper spoken of by St. John is different from that described by the other Evangelists.

6. That when the 14th of Nisan fell on a Friday, the Paschal lamb was not killed till the 15th, in order to avoid the observance of two Sabbaths.[3]

7. That the Last Supper was a perfectly regular Paschal meal, but was eaten, *by anticipation*, a day earlier than the usual time.[4]

[1] It is surprising to find this theory adopted by Bishop Wordsworth on the authority of Eusebius.

[2] The *chagiga* was eaten at other festivals also (Deut. xvi. 16), and there was nothing specifically Paschal about it.

[3] This solution is adopted by Calvin (among others); but we have no reason for supposing that this custom was adopted till some centuries later.

[4] Other theories still more baseless may be found recorded in Andrews, *Life of our Lord*, pp. 369—397: *e.g.*, that of Rauch, that the Passover could be legally killed on the 15th as well as the 14th of Nisan; and that of Schneckenburger, that Jesus was crucified on Wednesday and lay four days in the grave. Professor Westcott's deservedly high authority gives indeed some sanction to the tenability of this latter opinion (*Introduction*, p. 322), but Luke xxiii. 54, 56 seems alone sufficient to set it aside. Matt. xii. 40 arises from the Jewish

Such hypotheses might be almost indefinitely multiplied, and some of them have been maintained with much learning; but none of them have commanded any general assent, either from failing to satisfy the natural probabilities of the case, or from being wholly unsupported by any adequate evidence. And even if we can *explain* how it came to happen that there could be this apparent discrepancy, it seems scarcely consistent with critical honesty to deny that the discrepancy really exists. If we construe the language of the Evangelists in its plain, straightforward, simple sense, and without reference to any preconceived theories, or supposed necessities for harmonising the different narratives, we should be led to conclude from the Synoptists that the Last Supper *was* the ordinary Paschal meal, and from St. John that it was not.

Assuming, then, for the moment, that our decision must be formed on *conflicting* testimonies, must we suppose that strict accuracy here rests with St. John or with the Synoptists?

We answer, that it must be regarded as all but certain that St. John's language is here the most strictly correct, and that the Last Supper was *not* the actual and legal and ordinary Paschal meal, which we should suppose it to have been if the Synoptists alone had come down to us. The grounds for this conviction are the following:—

1. The extreme improbability that St. John, whose accounts of the Last Supper are incomparably more full than those of the other Evangelists, and who was more immediately and completely identified with every act in those last tragic scenes than any one of the Apostles, should yet have gone out of his way to adopt an error on a point so remarkable. There were many reasons why the Last Supper should, in the course of a few years, have come to be identified, even in the memory of the Evangelists, with the Paschal meal; there could be no reason, except the real fact of the case, why it should have been carefully and expressly *distinguished from it*.[1] Thursday, the day on which a *leavened bread* was removed from the houses, would most naturally be confused with Friday, the first day of the *Passover*, especially at a time when little or no regard was paid to chronological niceties; but, on the other hand, it is perfectly incredible

custom of regarding "any fragment of a day, however short, as a νυχθημερον," just as, in reckoning the years of a reign, they counted the shortest fragment of a year as a whole year. [There is something analogous to this in English law. A person born on February 20 legally comes of age at midnight on February 18.]

[1] Unless, which on other grounds seems most improbable, the Quarto-deciman controversy has anything to do with it.

that St. John could have "invented," or got into circulation, a statement conflicting with the general stream of tradition.

2. The certainty that the Friday was spent, and spent apparently without any scruples, in a scene of work, turmoil, and excitement, such as would have been wholly unsuited to the first day of a pre-eminently sacred festival.[1] Yet, if the meal of the previous evening was the Passover, Friday must have been a Feast-Sabbath, and although Feast-Sabbaths were not observed so strictly as the weekly Sabbath, yet it appears, even on the testimony of late writers like Maimonides, that a certain amount of solemnity attached to them.

3. The fact that no single circumstance is alluded to which shows that there was any observation of the day whatever as a day of solemnity or of festivity. And yet, so strict were the notions of the Jews about these Feast-Sabbaths, that even Hillel decided that if a hen laid an egg on a Feast-Sabbath it ought not to be eaten.[2] But how, Neander asks, could the first day of the principal feast be treated as an ordinary Friday? All difficulties are removed by supposing that it *was* only a common Friday, and that the next day was at once the Sabbath and the first day of the Passover feast.

4. The fact that, before any apparent discrepancy in the Gospels had been noticed, *early* Christian tradition was predominant in the assertion that the Last Supper was different from the Passover.[3]

5. The sense of inherent and symbolical fitness in the dispensation

[1] Joseph buys the "linen cloth" (Mark xv. 46). The women prepare spices and ointments (Luke xxiii. 56); Simon the Cyrenian is coming home (ἀπ' ἀγροῦ) apparently from a day's husbandry (Mark xv. 21; Luke xxiii. 26). On the Feast-Sabbaths and mode of observing them, see Lev. xxiii. 7, 8. "Ye shall do no servile work therein," is an ordinance so important that it is twice emphatically repeated. We are told that in Galilee, at any rate, the first day of the Feast was *very strictly* observed, so that even if Jewish custom had sanctioned all this buying, selling, working, &c., at Jerusalem, we should not expect to find it among the *Apostles* (John xiii. 29).

[2] In *Beza*, f. 36, and Mishna, *Jom Tobh.* 5, 2, it is expressly said that criminal proceedings were inadmissible on feast days; cf. Philo, *in Flacc.*, p. 976.

[3] So Apollinaris, Clement of Alexandria, Jul. Africanus, Hippolytus, Tertullian ("die prima azymorum quo agnum ut occiderent ad vesperam a Moyse fuerat praeceptum," *Adv. Jud.* 8), &c. See Routh, *Rell. Sacr.* i. 168; Westcott, *Introduction*, p. 320. The *identification* of the Last Supper with the Passover appears to date mainly from the time of Chrysostom. Some, who refuse to see a real discrepancy, adopt one of the expedients suggested by Chrysostom, viz., either that by "Passover" St. John means the entire feast (John = Synoptists); or that Jesus ate the Passover before the proper time (Synoptists = John). (Keim, III. ii. 464; but compare 476, *n.* 4).

which ordained that Christ should be slain on the day and at the hour appointed for the sacrifice of the Paschal lamb.[1]

6. The fact that Jewish tradition, with no object whatever to gain by misleading us in this particular, fixes the death of Christ on the 14th Nisan,[2] the *erebh Pesach,* or evening before the Passover.

7. The fact that the language of St. Paul is most naturally interpreted on the supposition that the Last Supper was not the Passover, but another institution destined to supersede it (1 Cor. v. 7 ; xi. 23).

8. The fact that if Jesus had really partaken of the Passover on the very evening before His death, the Jews might fairly have argued that the observance of the Passover, and therefore of the entire Mosaic ritual, was for ever binding on the Christian, no less than on the Jewish Church.

If, then, we conclude that the view which we derive from St. John's Gospel is literally correct, we may further consider whether it is in any way borne out by *incidental* notices preserved in the Synoptists. We find that there *is* incidental confirmation of this kind which we cannot ignore; although the force of it is undoubtedly weakened by the conflicting Jewish testimonies as to what might and what might not be done on the days of these sacred festivals.

i. We find, for instance, that *the disciples* (John xiii. 22) suppose Judas to have left the room in order to buy what things they had need of against the feast.

ii. Not only does Judas leave the room, but he is afterwards followed by our Lord and His disciples—an action which may very possibly have become sanctioned by universal custom, but was not in accordance with the strict injunctions of the law (Exod. xii. 22).

iii. Judas hires a band composed, in part at least, of Levitical officers (Luke xxii. 52), and comes by night to arrest Jesus—an event which could hardly have been regarded as consonant with a night of peculiar solemnity.

iv. The Sanhedrin had already come to a distinct conclusion that it would be dangerous and impolitic to kill Jesus on the feast day

[1] The "ninth hour" (Matt. xxvii. 46, &c.), or three o'clock, would be the first legal moment at which the lamb could be slain according to the Jewish interpretation of "the two evenings."

[2] *Sanh.* vi. 2. (Similarly *Erebh yôm Kippur* means the evening before the Day of Atonement.) Salvador and the author of the *Sepher Jeshuah Hannotseri* actually argue that the Romans had far more to do with the crucifixion than the Jews, because the Jews could not have crucified on *the first day of the Passover* (Sepp); but Jewish traditions themselves here contradict the erroneous common impression.

(Mark xiv. 2); yet if the Last Supper was the Paschal meal, this was the very thing which they did. On the other hand, if the Last Supper was *not* the Passover, we see a reason for precipitating the arrest and hurrying on the execution.[1]

v. Herod Agrippa did indeed *arrest* Peter during "the days of unleavened bread," but he expressly avoided putting him to death till the feast was over. His execution was *to be delayed till after the Passover* (Acts xii. 4).

vi. The Synoptists, while they speak of bread and wine, give not the remotest hint which could show that *a lamb* formed the most remarkable portion of the feast.[2]

vii. The general incidents of the banquet as recorded by them bear no distinctive resemblance to the very peculiar ceremonies of the Paschal feast;[3] some of them, such as the washing of the feet, and the absence of all *hurry* in the banquet, are incongruous with its meaning and character.

viii. Several incidental expressions faithfully preserved by them seem to show that this Supper was eaten because the true Passover could *not* be eaten; such as "my time is at hand" (Matt. xxvi. 18) —as though this were a reason why He should *anticipate* the ordinary

[1] It is true that the hostile members of the Sanhedrin were quite capable of violating the sacredness of the day, or might have defended themselves by the supposed interests of religion (cf. the opinion of R. Akiba, *Sanhedr.* x. 4). But the two robbers at any rate had committed no *theological* offence.

[2] Had the lamb been there, then Peter, if not Jesus Himself, would, according to Jewish custom, have been compelled to slay the lamb with his own hands in the Temple precincts, drive through it a spit of pomegranate wood, and carry it away on his shoulders to be roasted whole. For the lambs were slain in a very solemn and formal manner. The people were admitted into the Temple only in groups, and the priests standing in two long lines from the entrance to the altar with cups of gold and silver, passed the blood of the lambs from hand to hand, and poured it into two openings by the side of the altar. Meanwhile there were alternate blasts of trumpets and chantings of the Hallel. It is impossible to suppose that the Priests would have sanctioned for any one—and least of all for this little band of Galilæans—an isolated departure from the universal custom.

[3] *Ex. gr.* we have not a word about the lamb, the *mazzôth* or unleavened bread the *merorîm* or bitter herbs, the sauce *charoseth*, the *hagada* or announcement, the *four* or *five* cups of wine. The "hymn," on the other hand, has been identified with the Hallel, and the "cup of blessing" in 1 Cor. x. 16 with the *côs habberâchâh;* but the first particular is inconclusive, the second expression metaphorical. The many modifications of the old memorial feast which have *now* been sanctioned for centuries by Jewish usage, have simply resulted from *necessity*. After the destruction of Jerusalem the Passover *could* not any longer be observed in accordance with the Mosaic regulations, and therefore it became a mere secondary question *to what extent* its observances could be relaxed and altered.

meal. Something, too, of the same kind seems to be involved in the expression of the earnest desire of Jesus to eat "this Passover with them before He suffered," particularly, if we attach any importance to the remarkable passage in Hippolytus, οὐκέτι φάγομαι τὸ πάσχα, "I shall never again eat the Passover," which, if it be a reminiscence of Luke xxii. 16, would be a prophecy that He was to be put to death before the actual Paschal feast.[1]

We conclude, then, that *the Last Supper was* NOT *the Paschal meal.* Such a meal could now have had no significance for Him, who, as the True Paschal Lamb, was now about to be offered; nor for the Apostles, who would henceforth recognise Him in that capacity.

But, on the other hand, nothing is easier than the supposition that, before the Synoptic Gospels assumed their final form, the Last Supper (to which the metaphorical name of πάσχα was often given) should have been identified with the ordinary Jewish Passover; and the more so if, as is most probable, Jesus had Himself spoken a few words to show that this sacrament which He thus ordained was to be *a new feast which should take the place of the ancient Passover;* and if the near approach of the actual Passover, perhaps even the observance of one or two Paschal customs, gave a certain Paschal tinge to the actual meal. In fact, although the *memorial* (πάσχα μνημονευτικὸν) as distinguished from the *sacrificial* Passover (π. θύσιμον) was unknown until after the destruction of Jerusalem, yet the supposition of Grotius, that the meal eaten by Christ bore a *sort of general relation* to the actual Paschal meal, is by no means improbable.

To sum up, then, it seems to me, from careful and repeated study of much that has been written on this subject by many of the best and most thoughtful writers, that Jesus ate His Last Supper with the disciples on the evening of Thursday, Nisan 13, *i.e.*, at the time when, according to Jewish reckoning, the 14th of Nisan began; that this supper was not, and was not intended to be, the actual Paschal meal, which neither was nor could be legally eaten till the *following* evening; but by a perfectly natural identification, and one which would have been regarded as unimportant, the Last Supper, *which was a quasi-Passover, a new and Christian Passover,* and one in which, as in its antitype, memories of joy and sorrow were strangely blended, got to be identified, even in the memory of the Synoptists,

[1] Hippolytus expressly says οὐκ ἔφαγε τὸ κατὰ νομον πάσχα. Hence the Eastern Church always uses *leavened* bread at the Eucharist; as did the Western Church also down to the ninth century.

with the Jewish Passover, and that St. John, silently but deliberately, corrected this erroneous impression, which, even in his time, had come to be generally prevalent.[1]

EXCURSUS XI. (Vol. II., p. 298.)

OLD TESTAMENT QUOTATIONS.

THE subject of the quotations from the Old Testament by the writers of the New is far too wide to be treated in the narrow limits of an excursus. All that I purpose here to do is to furnish the reader with a few facts in support of those principles at which I have glanced more than once in the body of the work, and which appear to me to be the only ones adequate to remove the difficulties by which the subject is encompassed.

The general phenomena of these quotations have recently been examined and tabulated with great care by Mr. D. C. Turpie, in his book, *The Old Testament in the New.* He establishes the following remarkable results :—That there are in the New Testament 275 passages which may be regarded—all but a very few of them quite indisputably —as quotations from the Old; and that of these, there are *only* 53 in which the Hebrew, the Septuagint, and the New Testament agree—*i.e.*, in which the Hebrew is correctly rendered by the LXX., and quoted from the LXX. by the Apostles and Evangelists. Besides these there are 10 passages where the incorrect version of the LXX. has been altered into accordance with the Hebrew; 76 where the version of the LXX. is correct, but has been varied by the New Testament writers into *less* agreement with the original; 37 where a faulty version of the LXX. has been accepted; and no fewer than 99 where the New Testament differs alike from the Hebrew and from the LXX. This result may be tabulated as follows :—

Passages in which the LXX. version is correctly accepted .	53
" " " " correctly altered .	10
" " " " incorrectly accepted	37
" " " " incorrectly altered .	76
Passages in which the Hebrew, the LXX., and the New Testament all differ	99

[1] I have said nothing about the obscure and meagre history of what is called "the Paschal controversy," or dispute between the Eastern and Western Churches

Of course, it will be understood that in the above tabulation, (i.) many of the differences are extremely minute, and (ii.) that the words "correct" and "incorrect" merely mean an accurate agreement or disagreement with the original Hebrew. To these must be added three passages (John vii. 38, 42, and Eph. v. 14) which can only be classed as doubtful allusions.

The important bearing of these results on the letter-worshipping theory of "inspired dictation" will be seen at once. It is hardly too much to say that while they leave untouched the doctrine of a Divine grace of inspiration and superintendence, they shatter to pieces the superstitious and anti-scriptural dogmatism which asserts that every "word and letter" of the Holy Book is *supernaturally* inspired. I dwell upon the subject—I have repeatedly referred to it—because I feel a deep conviction that to hold the theory of inspiration in this latter form is, in the first place, to deny the plain language of Scripture itself, the plain teaching of Christ, and the plain indications deducible from apostolic and prophetic usage ; and in the second place, to incur the guilt of setting up a colossal and perilous stumbling-block in the path of all rational godliness.

I have, in the plainest and most candid manner, stated what seem to me the sole truly orthodox and Scriptural views on the subject of Inspiration in some papers printed in Vol. I. of the *Bible Educator*. To those papers I must refer any theological critic who does not understand my point of view. It is impossible for me here to re-state the full arguments into which I there have entered ; but it may warn insufficiently educated readers from uncharitable attacks upon my references to this subject, to know that the views which I have supported are also those of not a few of those living as well as of former theologians whose names stand highest, and whose authority is the most deservedly respected, in the Church of England. Conspicuous among the latter are the names of Luther and Calvin. Any one who will read the comment of Luther on the 20th Psalm, and that of Calvin on Psalms viii., xl., and lxviii., will perhaps be surprised to see the freedom with which they have expressed on this subject the common sense and honest view which may startle the supporters of a mechanical theory of inspiration, but would not have startled on the one hand an Origen, a Jerome, an Augustine, a Gregory of Nyssa ; or on the other, the leading intellects among the great Reformers.

as to the proper time of keeping Easter, because it is now generally (though not universally) agreed that it has little or no bearing on the question before us. See Sanday, *Fourth Gospel*, p. 211 ; Westcott, *Introduction*, p. 320 ; and on the other side, Keim, III. 476—478.

EXCURSUS XII. (Vol. II., p. 348.)

Notes on the Talmud.

Anything more utterly unhistorical than the Talmud cannot be conceived. It is probable that no human writings ever confounded names, dates, and facts with a more absolute indifference. The genius of the Jews is the reverse of what in these days we should call historical. By the change of a ר into a ד Romans find themselves transmogrified into Idumeans; Vespasian is confounded with Titus, Titus with Trajan, Trajan with Hadrian, Herod with Jannæus. When we come to the names of the Rabbis we find an intolerable confusion of inextricable Hanans, Joshuas, and Simeons. As for events, they are, in the language of a profound and admiring student, "transformed for the edification, and even for the amusement of the audience. History is adorned and embellished by the invention of an imagination, poetic, but often extravagant; truth is not sufficiently attractive; everything is magnified and extended." Jerusalem, says a R. Samuel, included twenty-four cities; each city had twenty-four quarters; each quarter twenty-four roads, &c. &c. In Bethyr, one quarter of the city was engaged in song and dance, while, from another, torrents of blood were rolling four or forty miles to the sea.[1]

When to all these sources of doubt is added the immense uncertainty of the readings, the "lapidary brevity" of the style, the dim indirectness of the allusions, and the intentional or affected obscurity of many of the oracular utterances of the Rabbis, it may well be supposed that the Talmud must be used with caution. It is not only probable, but a well-known fact, that many of the apparently wild and absurd stories of the Talmud are only the veil adopted by timidity in the days of persecution. Jewish writers were driven to indicate obscurely and enigmatically the teaching and the notions which they dared not publicly propound. To this class of enigmas (φωνᾶντα συνετοῖσιν) belong the story about Absalom's eye, the bone of Goliath, &c.

[1] *Gittin*, 58 *a* (Derenbourg, *Hist. de la Pal. d'après les Thalmuds*, p. 11). It is, however, fair to add that these and similar passages are meant to be taken not *literally* (לפי הפשט), but *hyperbolically*, in ordinary Oriental fashion (לשון הבאי). See Reland, *Antt. Hebr.*, p. 140. "If you cannot find the kernel," says Maimonides, "let the shell alone, and learn to say, 'I cannot understand this.'" The Jews themselves utterly despise many of the *Hagadôth* or legends of which the Talmud is full.

It has been asked by some—as, for instance, by Mr. Deutsch—whether it is fair to judge of the Talmud by brief extracts, separated from the context. I answer, first, that any one may now examine for himself whole treatises of the Talmud, both Mishna and Gemara, in translations of unquestionable fidelity; and secondly, that my own views about the Talmud are drawn quite as much from Jewish writers, such as Maimonides, Grätz, Geiger, Jost, Munk, Derenbourg, Schwab, Cohen, Frankl, Raphall, Deutsch, Salvador, and others, as from writers like Lightfoot, Schöttgen, Otho, Surenhuys, Buxtorf, Reland, Wetstein, Gfrörer, Etheridge, Pieritz, and others. I have consulted all these writers, and the views which I derive from the professed admirers and adherents of Rabbinic literature is quite as unfavourable as that which I get even from Eisenmenger and Wagenseil.

Some excellent maxims—even some close parallels to the utterances of Christ—may be quoted, of course, from the Talmud, where they lie imbedded like pearls in "a sea" of obscurity and mud (the ים התלמוד)! It seems to me indisputable—and a matter which every one can now verify for himself—that these are amazingly few, considering the vast bulk of national literature from which they are drawn. And, after all, who shall prove to us that these sayings were always uttered by the Rabbis to whom they were attributed? Who will supply us with the faintest approach to a proof that (when not founded on the Old Testament) they were not directly or indirectly due to Christian influence or Christian thought? And how many of them are there which are independent of the Old Testament? Even Mr. Deutsch, one of the most ardent admirers of the Talmud, says, "These sayings were often tender, poetical, sublime; but they were not absolutely new; there was not one that was not substantially contained in the canonical and uncanonical writings of the Old Testament."[1]

Sayings of this kind, which have been brought into comparison with passages in the Gospels, are among others, the following:—

Matt. v. 9.—"*Love peace, and pursue it at any cost.*" Hillel (*Pirk. Abhôth*, i. 12); cf. Ps. cxxxiii. i.

[1] *Remains*, p. 138. R. Joshua Ben Levi proved (to his own satisfaction doubtless) that the Oral Law had been delivered to Moses on Sinai from Exod. xxiv. 12, because there the Tables = the Ten Commandments; the Law = Pentateuch; commandments = Mishna; "which I have written" = Prophets and Hagiographa; and "that thou mayst teach them" = Gemara (*Berachôth*, 5 *a*). (Schwab, *id.* p. 234.)

Matt. v. 10.—"*Remember that it is better to be persecuted than to persecute.*" (*Derech Erets Rab.* ii.)
Id. v. 22.—"*Be not prone to anger.*" (*P. Abhôth*, ii. 10; *Pesachîm*, 67.)
Id. v. 28.—A close parallel in *Massecheth Kalah.*
Id. v. 39.—"*If thy companion call thee an ass, put the saddle on thy back.*" (*Babha Kama*, 8, 7.) Cf. Ecclus. xxviii.; Prov. xx. 22; xxiv. 29.
Id. v. 42; vi. 1—4.—"*He who giveth alms in secret is greater than Moses himself.*" (*Chagiga*, i. &c. &c.) Cf. Ecclus. xxix. 15, 16; Prov. xix. 17, &c.
Id. vi. 7.—"*It is better to utter a short prayer with devotion, than a long one without fervour.*" (*Shabbath*, 10; *Menachôth*, 110.)
Id. vi. 31.—"*He who having but one piece of bread in his basket, says, 'What shall I eat to-morrow?' is a man of little faith.*" (*Sota*, 48.) Cf. Ps. xxxiv. 10; cxlvii. 9, &c.

These instances (and they might be multiplied from many sources) are chosen from a number more in Cohen's *Les Déicides*, E. T., 150, seq. This Jewish writer urges them as diminishing the "originality" of Jesus. Such an argument, common as it is, shows a total want of culture and insight. The "originality" of the Son of God, if such a word can be used at all, consisted in this, that He saved and regenerated a corrupt and dying world, on which the whole series of Jewish doctors—Sopherîm, Tanaîm, Amoraîm, Seboraîm, and Geonîm—produced no perceptible effect, and for which, from first to last, they and their "originality" have the smallest possible significance.[1]

It is, however, fair to bear in mind (1) the heterogeneous character of the Talmud, and (2) its character as being in great measure a *corpus juris.*

(1.) As regards the first point, I cannot do better than quote some of the remarks of Mr. Deutsch, whose premature death, before he had well begun the intended work of his life—a *History of the Talmud*—cannot be too deeply regretted. He says, "All those manifold assemblies wherein a people's mental, social, and religious life are considered and developed, are here represented—Parliament, Convocation, Law Courts, Academies, Colleges, the Temple, the Synagogue, even the Lobby and the Common Room, have left realistic traces upon it. The authors of this book, who may be *counted by hundreds*, were always the most prominent men of the people in

[1] For further remarks on this subject I may refer to my *Seekers after God*, pp. 181, 182, 320; and *Witness of History to Christ* (Hulsean Lectures), pp. 134, seqq.

their respective generations, and thus, undesignedly and designedly, show the fulness of this people's life and progress at every turn." Elsewhere he speaks of it as "those mazes of legal enactments, gorgeous day-dreams, masked history, ill-disguised rationalism, and the rest which form the Talmud and the Midrash."[1]

(2.) But it is chiefly as a *corpus juris* that the Talmud must be considered. "Speaking of it strictly as a book, the nearest approach to it is Hansard. Like Hansard, it is a law-book—a miscellaneous collection of parliamentary debates, of bills, motions, and resolutions; with this difference, that in Hansard these propositions &c., gradually grow into an Act, while in the Talmud the Act is the starting-point. . . . The Talmud in this wise contains—besides the social, criminal, international, human and divine law, along with abundant explanations of laws not perfectly comprehended, corollaries, and inferences from the law, which were handed down with more or less religious reverence—an account also of the education, the arts, the sciences, the history and religion of this people for about a thousand years."[2]

This view of the Talmud as a sort of statute-book makes an important difference in our estimate of it. The following remarks, with which I have been favoured by a friend, seem to me so original and so valuable—they seem, in fact, to place the whole controversy about the Talmud in such a completely new light—that I have asked his permission to incorporate them into this note:—

"The Talmud seems to be *a corpus juris in which the law has not yet been differentiated from morality and religion.* There is nothing exceptional in this non-differentiation: perhaps *we* are exceptional in having outgrown the stage in which it is normal. The strange thing is the prodigious quasi-scientific productiveness of Judaism within a certain area, combined with such pre-historic, not to say embryonic backwardness in the above respect. But even in this respect the contrast is less striking if Judaism be compared with the developments and documents of Hinduism and Islam.

"1. If we remember that the Talmud is a *corpus juris* one thing is explained immediately—namely, the rarity of moral or other truths of any value. The wonder is that there are any at all. The Statute Book is more bulky than the Talmud—at any rate the Reports are—and they contain no 'beautiful and noble things' at all, *unless perhaps in the obsolete parts.* We don't look for such things there. If English literature had been developed analogously

[1] Deutsch, *Literary Remains*, p. 194. [2] *Id. ib.*, p. 136.

to Jewish, we should have the great thoughts of Hooker and Bacon, not to say of Spenser and Shakespeare, imbedded in *Coke upon Littleton.* The arrangement would be objectionable ; but not on the ground that there was so little great thought in comparison to the amount of technicality.

"2. This first point is obvious on the most general view. But of the *fictions* of Rabbinism I cannot believe a right view is to be taken without looking at the fictions of other systems of law. Sir H. Maine has proved (*Ancient Law*, ch. ii., pp. 1—6) that legal fiction is the earliest, most imperfect, and most awkward means—but a perfectly normal means—of law reform. No example that you have adduced is more elaborate, more inconvenient, or more absurd than the devices which had by law to be employed in this country every time a man cut off an entail, from Edward IV. to 1833. Imaginary legal principles were too strong to allow us to do in a straightforward manner what the necessities of society insisted on having done in some way or other. In Judaism legal principles resisted still more stoutly, because they were more an affair of religion and morality than with us ; but the great point must have been the mischievous reaction of the fiction-system upon religion and morality themselves, which must thus have become steeped in hypocrisy. The *cause* of this would be the non-differentiation of law from morality and religion. The neglect of these considerations make the modern books suspicious in more than one respect. They seem to treat the traditional form which conservatism obliged a piece of law to assume, as if it was the essential thing; and they regard the social necessities which had to be provided for, as if they were rather superficially involved in the result, instead of *vice versâ.* And they seem to assume too readily that what the texts represent as *de jure* in force was operative *de facto.* These two things never go quite together, and they are peculiarly likely not to go together in a system which was more or less calculated with reference to an ideal polity, with a Jerusalem and a Temple supposed to be in existence to support it. And even the *unhistoricalness* of the Talmud (in which I suspect the writings of the Mohammedans beat it hollow for extravagance) has something answering to it at home. English law-books contain a number of historical statements, copied by one out of another, which have a very suspicious look to a reader of any sort of independence ; and in fact Rudolf Gneist says that there is a great deal of false history which, as in a manner part of the law itself, is even more directly important to the English law-student than the true.

"(3.) *Casuistry* is in a moral point of view the most disastrous, or at least the most obviously disastrous consequence of this anachronous extendedness of the province of jurisprudence; but also it is the least peculiar to Judaism. It is no great harm (besides that the thing is inevitable) if morality is a department of law, as long as things are in the early stage in which law itself is rather elastic. But when law is highly developed in precision and minuteness, morality cannot be stuffed into its pigeon-holes without becoming immoral, and in fact irrational. In obedience to logic, it is made immorally as well as irrationally strict; in order to stand in any real relation to the facts of life it is made irrationally as well as immorally lax. The necessity of this laxness will be seen by taking any of the Rabbinical examples at which you shudder most, and asking what the moralist is to do, *if he is to prescribe for the magistrate and policeman as well.* See the pleadings in 'Pascal *versus* Escobar and others,' *passim.* Pascal's position is untenable, unless it is recognised that morality is not a matter of rules at all. Here the danger of Gospel-interpreters—and it is a danger from which few of them altogether escape—is that of representing Christ as occupying the merely negative or revolutionary position of Pascal. Now, that the action of Jesus was not merely negative or revolutionary is sufficiently proved by the result. How expressive is His saying, that there is no place reserved for those whose law-abidingness does not transcend that of the men who are before all things zealous for the Law.

"4. The most obviously disastrous thing about Judaism, in an intellectual point of view, is not, I suppose, a *necessary* effect of its non-differentiation of law from religion and morality, though surely an easy and natural one. I mean the fact that its quasi-science is not founded even on the supposed necessities of an imaginary or obsolete state of things, but upon the interpretation of a written text. Within the 'four corners' (as our lawyers have it) of this narrow field it cuts itself off from all other intellectual culture. This distinguishes it from Hinduism and Islam in their more energetic days, and still more (thanks partly to the Greeks) from Rome. Mediæval scholasticism makes some approach to the like barrenness. One of the consequences was that folly of follies, the number-and-letter lore.

"It seems to me that the apparent eccentricities of the Talmud cannot be instructively set before the general reader without applying to them something like the above considerations, which in other applications are considered obvious enough."

This view of the Talmud is slightly touched upon by Ewald, though he makes no attempt to illustrate it by the comparative method. "When a supreme law of life," he says, "has been already given, and without troubling themselves about its ultimate foundations, men are only desirous to work it out into detail, and, if necessary, to bring it into actual life by means of a countless multitude of new regulations, . . . similar conditions everywhere produce similar results. The scholastic labours of the Middle Ages and those of the Papal jurists . . . are essentially the same."[1]

"Les meilleurs des hommes," says Renan,[2] "ont été des juifs; les plus malicieux des hommes ont aussi été des juifs. Race étrange, vraiment marquée du sceau de Dieu, qui a su produire parallèlement et comme deux bourgeons d'une même tige l'Église naissante et le fanatisme féroce des revolutionnaires de Jérusalem, Jésus, et Jean de Giscala, les apôtres et les zélotes sicaires, l'Évangile et le Talmud! Faut-il s'étonner si cette gestation mystérieuse fut accompagnée de déchirements, de délire, et d'une fièvre comme on n'en vit jamais?" The turn of expression is open to criticism, but the fact is striking.

EXCURSUS XIII. (Vol. II., p. 352.)

The Sanhedrin.

Orthodox Jews ascribe the origin of the Sanhedrin to Moses (Exod. xviii. 24—26, &c.), and identify it with the "elders of Israel" in Ezek. viii. 11, 12, and the "elders of the Jews" in the days of Darius (Ezra vi. 8.)[3] Some even saw a germ of the Sanhedrin in the tribunal established by Jehoshaphat (2 Chron. xix. 8—11).[4]

The Sanhedrin was the successor of the Great Synagogue, the last member of which died in the person of Simon the Just.

[1] Ewald, *Gesch. d. Volkes Isr.* (E. Tr., V. 196). I have already made a similar remark without knowing that I had been anticipated.

[2] *L'Antechrist*, p. 258. Elsewhere he says, "On peut dire de cette race le bien qu'on voudra et le mal qu'on voudra, sans cesser d'être dans le vrai; car . . . le bon juif est un être excellent, et le méchant juif est un être détestable. C'est ce qui explique la possibilité . . . que l'idylle évangélique et les horreurs racontées par Josephe aient été des réalités sur la même terre, chez le même peuple, vers le même temps." (p. 486.)

[3] Raphall, *Hist. of the Jews*, ii. 110.

[4] Munk, *Palestine*, 194. See Reland, *Antt. Hebr.* 243, seqq.

In 1 Macc. xiv. 28, the assembly of the Jews, which bestowed the supreme power on Simon, father of John Hyrcanus, is called "the great congregation of the priests and people, and rulers of the nation, and elders of the country," corresponding to the Hebrew names *Kenĕseth, Roshî Abhôth*, and *Zakain ha-Arets;* and it appears from coins that the Sanhedrin (the members of which are described much as in Mark xv. 1) are called the *Chebher*, or "Senate" of the Jews. In this were included both Pharisees and Sadducees. John became a Helleniser (Phil-hellene: Jos. *Antt.* xiii. 11, § 3), and a Sadducee, and was the first to adopt on his coins the Greek inscription and title of Ἰουδὰ βασιλεύς. At the end of a year he was succeeded by his brother Alexander Jannæus, who quarrelled furiously with the Pharisees, but on his deathbed recommended his wife Salome Alexandra to trust *true* Pharisees while she avoided the *painted* ones. Salome accordingly gave them such privileges during her reign of nine years that they ultimately ventured to summon her son Hyrcanus II. before their tribunal on the occasion alluded to on p. 355. It is on this occasion that we first find the *name* Sanhedrin (סנהדרין), which, although the Talmud talks of a Sanhedrin in the days of Moses (Buxtorf, *Lex.* s. v.), is certainly not præ-Asmonæan; indeed, until the Hellenising days of Jason, this Greek word would never have been adopted by the people in place of their own term *Beth Dîn*, "House of Judgment," or *Kenĕseth haggedôla*, "the great assembly."

In the Mishna mention is made of two kinds of Sanhedrin—the provincial, of five or seven members; and the Grand Sanhedrin of seventy-one, with their *Nasî* and *Ab Beth Dîn*. These two distinguished functionaries seem to have been regarded as representatives of the ancient *Zouggôth*, or "couples," who were in their turn representatives of the *Eshkolôth*, or "grape-clusters." The first *Nasî* under Hyrcanus II. is said to have been Joshua Ben Perachiah, and the first *Ab Beth Dîn* Nitai of Arbela.

It is said that in the Temple sat three Sanhedrins, or, as we should perhaps call two of them, "Committees of the Sanhedrin," of twenty-three members each; the Great Sanhedrin of seventy-one met in the *Lishcat Haggazîth;* another, or a committee of the same, in a chamber which abutted on the *Chêl* (חֵיל), or division between the Court of the Gentiles and of the women; and a third at the gate of the Har ha-Beit, or Temple mountain. Derenbourg conjectures, with some probability, that the Grand Sanhedrin was but the reunion of the three inferior ones of twenty-three ($23 \times 3 + 2$) with the two presiding officers, and that these three committees were composed, (i.) of priests, (ii.) of Levites, and (iii.) of "notables," *i.e.*, *Sopherîm*, *Tanaîm*, &c.[1] If this conjecture be admitted, we may, perhaps, suppose that the three trials of our Lord took place before these three divisions of the Sanhedrin; or, if the trial before Hanan be regarded as purely informal and extra-judicial, then the trial before Caiaphas may conceivably be the third of these bodies which met at the foot of the Temple-mountain. It gives some support to this conjecture that in Matt. xxvi. 57, "the Scribes and elders" (= the "notables," *i.e.*, the *Sopherîm* and *Zekênîm*) seem to be distinguished from "*all* the *chief priests* and elders"—*i.e.*, the Grand Sanhedrin (*id.* xxvii. 1).

But it must not be forgotten that the Sanhedrin which condemned our Lord was a dubious and hybrid kind of assembly. When the Sanhedrin had unanimously rejected the claim of Herod on the authority of Deut. xvii. 15, the Talmud (*Babha Bathra*, 3 *b*) says that he exterminated them all except Babha Ben Buta, whose eyes he put out; and that the rebuilding of the Temple was undertaken by the advice of the survivor in expiation of the atrocity.[2] Whatever the exact circumstances may have been, Herod, after the execution of Antigonus, seems to have inflicted on the Sanhedrin a frightful vengeance, from which it took them a long time to recover. It was soon after this that he thrust into the High Priesthood creatures of his own, of Egyptian and Babylonian origin, such as Simon and Joazar, the Boëthusians from Alexandria, and a certain obscure Hananel of Babylon (ἱερέα τῶν ἀσημοτέρων, Jos. *Antt.* xv. 2, § 4), who may possibly be identical with the Annas of the Gospels. For a time at least the real Sanhedrin seems to have been suspended, and its functions usurped by an assemblage of Herod's own adherents (Jos. *Antt.* xv. 7, § 4 (συναγαγὼν τοὺς οἰκειοτάτους αὐτῷ; xvii. 3, § 1, συνέδριον τῶν φίλων). The dignity of sacerdotalism might give to this spurious assemblage an appearance of dignity, but we have seen reason to believe that the Pharisees—here meaning by that title the leading doctors—took little, if any, part either in its deliberations or its proceedings. They left it to the obscure Benî Bethyra,[3] the Boëthusians, the Hananites, the Kantheras, the Kamhiths, the Phabis, and their adherents. The meetings of the Sanhedrin of which Josephus

[1] *Hist. Pal.*, ch. vi., the facts of which I have here summarised. See too Ewald, *Gesch. d. Volkes Isr.* (E. Tr., V. 168). He says that much which is told us about the Sanhedrin in Talmudic and later writings "flows from the increasing want of the historical spirit which characterised the Jews in the Middle Ages."

[2] Josephus mentions a massacre of Pharisees (*Antt.* xvii. 2, § 4).

[3] The well-known story of their dispute with Hillel is another indication of the hostile position held by the Doctors towards the priests.

speaks during this period were arbitrary, incompetent, and special gatherings. The Romans and Herod between them had abolished the old independent body.[1] It is true that Hillel, after overcoming the priestly pretensions of the Benî Bethyra, by quoting, as a last resource, the authority of Shemaia and Abtalion, is said to have been made *Nasî*; but Derenbourg is inclined to doubt the story altogether, and to distinguish between *Presidency of the Schools* and *Presidency of the Sanhedrin.*[2] At any rate, if Hillel really *was* a *Nasî* of the Sanhedrin, his political action must have been amazingly slight, considering that it is uncertain whether Josephus even recognises his existence[3] or not.

At the time of our Lord's trial it is certain that both Hillel and Shammai were dead. They had left no successors who attained immediate prominence. We hear indeed of a Simeon, son of Hillel, but the sole recorded trait respecting him is the aphorism that "nothing is superior to silence."

EXCURSUS XIV. (Vol. II., p. 353.)

Pharisees and Sadducees.

The origin of these names is buried in obscurity. All that is clear is that the Pharisees were politically descended from the *Chasidîm* (1 Macc. ii. 42; vii. 13), and were the heroic-national party; while the Sadducees were the priestly-aristocratic party, who allied themselves always with the ruling power, even when that power was anti-national in its aims.

Derenbourg, who subjects these titles to an elaborate examination, supposes that during the Graecomania which in the days of the Seleucid government began to spread more and more widely among the Jews—especially under the influence of "ungodly wretches" like Menelaus and Alcimus—the party which felt it necessary to defend the scrupulous observance of the Law by a closer "hedge," began to urge an extension of that ἀμιξία, or withdrawal from all intercourse

[1] "Von Synedrien ist in der ganzen Herodäer und Römer Zeit keine Spur." (Jost, i. 278.)

[2] *Nasî* was a title also given to the Chief of each tribe (Numb. iii. 24; xvi. 2, &c.) who in Numb. iii. 32 is called Nasî of Nasîm. (Munk, p. 195.)

[3] Josippon substitutes the names of Hillel and Shammai for the Pollio and Sameas of Josephus, *Antt.* xv. 1, § 1. (Munk, p. § 545.)

with the heathen, which was called in Hebrew *Perishût* (פרישות), a name which thus did not imply either political detachment or worldly separation (Jos. *Antt.* xiii. 8, § 3; 2 Macc. xiv. 3).

The Asmonæans, however, and their party did not follow the *Tanaîm*, or Doctors, in these views which they considered exaggerated, but contented themselves with that ordinary obedience to the written law which was not inconsistent with Phil-hellenic tendencies, and for which they retained the title of *Tsedakah*, or "righteousness" (צדקה, δικαιοσύνη: cf. Prov. xvi. 31), a name which more easily came into vogue, because the title of the last great and good Asmonæan, Simeon, had been *hatstsadîk*, "the Just."

But words which had originally described mere tendencies or aspirations, soon developed into the injurious party-titles of *Parouschîm* or Pharisees, and *Tsedûkîm* or Sadducees, to describe respectively the party of the Rabbis, whose tendencies were wholly patriotic[1] and popular, and that of the Priests, who were aristocratic and conservative[2] (Acts v. 17). Neither party willingly adopted names which had gradually acquired an insulting force. In our Lord's time, the names had gradually come to connote differences which were religious as well as political. The Sadducees may broadly be described as rationalists, the Pharisees as ritualists, names which, though not rigidly accurate, convey on the whole a true impression of their respective positions.

Geiger, who in his *Urschrift* and *Das Judenthum* was perhaps the first to put these parties in their true light, takes a different view of their origin. He derives the name of the Sadducees from Zadok, a descendant of Phinehas, who held the priesthood till the last unworthy representatives of Aaron's elder line were displaced by the sons of Mattathias, who belonged to the less distinguished priestly family of Joarib.[3] But the Sadducees continued to support the new power; while the Pharisees, inheriting the views of the separatists (*Nibdalîm*, who "separated themselves from the filthiness of the

[1] Φαρισαῖοι καλοῦνται βασιλεῦσι δυνάμενοι μάλιστα ἀντιπράσσειν (Jos. *Antt.* xvii. 2, § 4).

[2] Josephus distinctly says that connection with the priesthood is the one stamp of Jewish nobility.

[3] Geiger (*Urschr.*, p. 105) shows that the story of their origin from Zadok, a pupil of Antigonus of Socho, who carried too far his master's principle that men ought to serve God without desire for reward, is not mentioned in the Mishna or the Talmud, but is first found in the R. Nathan. If, as Epiphanius (*Haeres.* i. 4) supposes, the name is derived from צדק, "justice," the question occurs, why is it not *Tsaddikîm* instead of *Tseădûkîm*? Köster's strange and isolated notion, that it is a Hebrew transliteration of *Stoics*, is hardly worth refuting.

heathen," Ezra vi. 21), combated the pretensions, and usurped the influence of the privileged class. The difficulty in adopting this view rises from the silence of Josephus and the Books of Maccabees.

Common as is the name Pharisees in the Gospels, those who are so called seem always to have called themselves by other names in preference—such as *Sopherîm*, "scribes," *Thalmîdî chakamîm*, "pupils of the sages," and *Chabheerîm*, or "confraternities." In several passages of the Talmud they are called "plagues of Pharisees" (מכות פרושים, *J. Pea.* viii. 8; *J. Sota* iii. 4, &c.), and in one of these they are ranked as equally objectionable with "imbecile devotees, sly sinners, and bigoted women." But of course there were good and bad Pharisees, and while Jewish writers themselves admit that "the heavy charges which the Founder of the Christian faith brings against Pharisees are fully confirmed by the Talmud" (*Sota*, f. 22 *b*, &c.),[1] yet these were the hypocrites whom Alexander Jannæus called "dyed and varnished" Pharisees; and we may hope that Nicodemus and Gamaliel were not isolated specimens of a nobler class. The Sadducees are seldom mentioned, because with the cessation of the temporal power they practically ceased to exist as a party, although many of their distinctive views were revived by a certain Hanan, and are continued to this day by the Karaites.

The wealth, rank, connections, and offices of the Sadducees gave them much worldly influence and authority, but in all religious and ritual matters the people sided so absolutely with the Doctors or Pharisees, that the Sadducees, even against their real views, were often compelled to conform. This is the express statement of Josephus,[2] and is confirmed by the Talmud. "All your life you teach without practising," bitterly exclaimed a Boëthusian to the Priest, his father. The reply was a humiliating confession that they could not practise their real theories, but were obliged to conform to the teaching of the Doctors (חכמים). The Priest and his son in this story are believed to have been Hanan (the Annas of the Gospels), and his son Hanan the younger, who figures in Josephus in no very enviable colours, as the murderer of "James, the Lord's brother."[3]

A striking Rabbinic story (*Joma*, 71 *b*) illustrates their want of moral influence over the people. On the great Day of Atonement the High Priest, followed by the people, was leaving the Temple. Suddenly, however, the people caught sight of Shemaia and Abtalion —the "couple" of the day—walking undistinguished among the rest.

[1] Raphall, *Hist. of the Jews*, ii. 117. [2] *Antt.* xviii. 1, § 4.
[3] Jos. *Antt.* xx. 9, § 1; Jost, *Joma*, 1; Geiger, *Urschrift*, 112.

Instantly they abandoned the High Priest to form an escort to the Doctors. "All hail to the men of the people," said the High Priest bitterly to them, when they took leave of him. "All hail," they replied, "to the men of the people who do the work of Aaron, and no hail to the son of Aaron who does not act like Aaron." Josephus, though his account of these two sects (*Antt.* xviii. 1, §§3, 4; xiii. 5, §9; *B. J.* ii. 8, §14) is little to be relied on, and is probably borrowed in part from Nicolas of Damascus, is yet undoubtedly right in saying that in spite of the rank of the Sadducees they had no real reverence from the people. "They influence," he says, "the well-to-do" (τοὺς εὐπόρους), but have no popular following, while the Pharisees have the multitude as their allies."

I have several times spoken of the Sadducees as "worldly," and the epithet is justified by the ostentation which made them desire to be served in vessels of gold and silver, and to demand double dowry for every young girl married to a priest;[1] and by the greed which suffered them to grow rich at the expense of the people. Of the latter propensity two stories are told. One of them is a quarrel which they had with the Pharisees about the supply of victims for the daily sacrifice, which the Pharisees very properly said ought to be provided by the Temple treasury; whereas the Sadducees, regarding the Temple treasure as their own, wanted the victims to be paid for by separate subscriptions. Similarly the Sadducees claimed for the priests (*i.e.*, for themselves) the use of the meat-offerings, which the Pharisees said ought to be burnt on the altar. The Pharisees won the day, and appointed two festivals in honour of the double victory.[2] Thus both Pharisees and Sadducees were constantly driven into extremes by the repulsion of antagonistic errors.

Another story is that as they sold pigeons at the *chanujôth*, they multiplied to such an extent the cases in which the sacrifice of a pigeon was necessary, that the price of a single pigeon rose to a gold piece. Then R. Simeon Ben Gamaliel cried, "By the Temple I will not sleep till I have reduced their price to a denarius." Accordingly he pointed out such numerous reductions to the necessity of making this offering, that the price of a pigeon sank to the fourth of a denarius.[3] These shops are expressly called the shops of the sons of Hanan,

[1] *Abhôth de Rabbi Nathan*, v.; *Kethubhôth*, 1, 6. In the former passage we have a sort of deliberate theory of Epicureanism.

[2] *Megillath Taanîth*, §§ 1, 19. They also arranged that the Temple tribute should be received with great pomp (*Jer. Shekalîm*, 45 *d*; Grätz, iii. 460).

[3] *Keritôth*, i. 7.

and the Talmud distinctly alludes to the want of uprightness in the management of them.[1]

The one maxim of the political life of a Sadducee seems to have been quietism, even at the expense of patriotism. No wonder the priestly party were disliked and suspected, when ever since the days of Hyrcanus and Aristobulus the people had found cause to complain of them, that they were seeking to change the government of their nation in order to enslave them (Jos. *Antt.* xiv. 3, § 2).

Josephus, in describing the rupture between John Hyrcanus and the Pharisees (*Antt.* xiii. 10, §6), distinctly states that the main difference between the two sects consisted in the acceptance by the Pharisees and rejection by the Sadducees of the Oral Law or tradition of the elders; and although the assertion may be a little too sweeping, it is undoubtedly founded on a real fact.

Ewald, who, in his *History of the People of Israel*,[2] enters into a full account of the Pharisees and Sadducees, points out how the Pharisees were led to encourage and defend hypocrisy, and conventionalise all true piety, partly by the character of the Levitical dispensation, partly from motives of ambition, and partly out of strong antagonism to the Sadducees. Wishing to retain the advantages which they had received from the Asmonæan revival of national piety, "under the influence of ambition, and devoted more or less consciously to their own interests, *they made piety into a sort of art or trade in order permanently to secure their own power.*"

After observing that we only know the Sadducees from the reports of their avowed enemies, he says, "It was the school of freedom of life, of thought, and of action; but it was a freedom which sprang out of the Greek age, with its deep moral degradation, which corresponded with it, and was acceptable to it." But for this the Sadducees might have been of real use in counteracting the rigidity and one-sidedness of Pharisaic development. But in their opposition to this injurious scrupulosity they failed to note the deeper sores which at this time were eating into the Jewish and Gentile world.

He speaks slightingly of the notices of these sects in Josephus (*Antt.* xiii. 5, § 9; *Vit.* 2; *B. J.* i. 5, § 2; ii. 8, § 2) as abrupt, arbitrary, and devoid of deep knowledge, and says—too uncharitably—of Jost, Grätz, and Geiger, that their views are baseless, "because they are themselves Pharisees, and desire to be nothing else."

[1] *J. Pea.* i. 6.

[2] Vol. V., p. 366, seqq., E. Tr.

EXCURSUS XV. (Vol. II., p. 446.)

Traditional Sayings of Christ.

The apocryphal sayings (ἄγραφα δόγματα) of Christ—*i.e.*, the sayings attributed to Him by early writers, but unrecorded in the New Testament[1]—have been collected and arranged by Prof. Westcott (*Introd. to the Gosp.*, App. C.) with his usual care and learning. I here quote only the most remarkable, or those which are not mere variations of His actual words, referring all who are interested in the subject to Prof. Westcott (*l.c.*), or Hofmann (*Leben Jesu*, 317—329).

1. For the remarkable story appended in D to Luke vi. 5, *v. supra*, Vol. I., p. 438.

2. Cod. D also appends to Matt. xx. 28, "*But ye seek from little to increase, and that from the greater there be a less.*"

3. "*Show yourselves tried money-changers.*" (γίνεσθε τραπεζῖται δόκιμοι). (Epiphan. 44, 2.)

4. "*He that wonders shall reign, and he that reigns shall rest.*" "*Look with wonder at that which is before you.*" (Clem. Alex. *Strom.* ii. 9, 45.)

5. "*He who is near me is near the fire; he who is far from me is far from the Kingdom.*" (Orig. *Hom. in Jerem.*, iii., p. 778; Didymus in Ps. lxxxviii. 8.)

6. "*Keep the flesh pure and the seal unspotted.*" (Clem. Rom. *Ep.* ii. 8.)

7. "*For those that are sick I was sick, and for those that hunger I suffered hunger, and for those that thirst I suffered thirst.*" (Orig. *in Matt.*, I. xiii. 2.)

8. "*In whatsoever I may find you in this will I also judge you.*" (Just. Mart. *Dial.* 47.)

9. "*Never be joyful, except when ye shall look on your brother in love.*" (Jer. *in* Eph. v. 3.)

These are the most remarkable. One or two others have been quoted or alluded to in the body of the work (v. *supr.*, Vol. I., pp. 320, &c.), and of the remainder some are wholly unworthy of our Lord, or spring from a desire to claim His authority for false and exaggerated principles, or are mere amplifications and misquotations of His actual words.

One or two of the Mohammedan legends respecting Christ, preserved in the Koran or elsewhere, are striking—*e.g.*:

[1] *Ex. gr.* Acts xx. 35.

"Jesus, the Son of Mary, said, 'He who longs to be rich is like a man who drinks sea-water; the more he drinks the more thirsty he becomes, and never leaves off drinking till he perishes.'"

"Jesus once said, 'The world is like a deceitful woman, who, when asked how many husbands she had had, answered, so many that she could not count them.' And Jesus said, 'When they died, did they leave you behind?' 'On the contrary,' said she, 'I murdered and got rid of them.' 'Then,' said Jesus, 'It is strange that the rest had so little wisdom, that when they saw how you treated the others they still burned with such love for you, and did not take warning from their predecessors.'" See others in Hofmann, *ubi supr.*, p. 328. An interesting monograph might be written on the picture of Jesus as presented in the Mohammedan writings. In the Koran itself His name is frequently mentioned with those of various prophets; but the *special* references are not numerous.

INDEX.

Q.

R.

S.

T.

PASSAGES OF SCRIPTURE

(NEW TESTAMENT)

QUOTED OR REFERRED TO.

St. Mark (*continued*).

St. Luke.

St. Luke (*continued*).

St. Luke (*continued*).

Cassell, Petter & Galpin, Belle Sauvage Works, London, E.C.

www.ingramcontent.com/pod-product-compliance
Lightning Source LLC
LaVergne TN
LVHW021305110826
845150LV00003B/489

* 9 7 8 1 4 2 5 5 5 9 4 1 0 *